ht

THEM
AND US

THEM
AND US

THE AMERICAN INVASION
OF BRITISH HIGH SOCIETY

CHARLES JENNINGS

SUTTON PUBLISHING

First published in the United Kingdom in 2007 by
Sutton Publishing Limited · Phoenix Mill
Thrupp · Stroud · Gloucestershire · GL5 2BU

British Library Cataloguing in Publication Data
A catalogue record for this book is available from the British Library.

Hardback ISBN 978-0-7509-4356-7
Paperback ISBN 978-0-7509-4357-4

Typeset in Sabon.
Typesetting and origination by
Sutton Publishing Limited.
Printed and bound in England.

Contents

Acknowledgements

I would like to thank the staff of the Churchill Archives Centre, Churchill College, Cambridge, for their assistance during my researches into *Them and Us*. I would also like to thank Cambridgeshire Archives and Local Studies for their kind permission to quote from the Manchester Papers. Material from the Desborough Papers is reproduced with permission of Hertfordshire Archives and Local Studies. Material from the Paget Papers is reproduced by permission of the British Library.

I would also like to acknowledge the permissions of several publishers to quote from their works. Thanks are due to the Penguin Group for permission to quote from *A Passion for Friendship: Sibyl Colefax and Her Circle*, by Kirsty McLeod, originally published by Michael Joseph. I must also thank Weidenfeld & Nicolson for permission to quote from *Vita and Harold: The Letters of Vita Sackville-West and Harold Nicolson*, edited by Nigel Nicolson; and for permission to quote from *Chips: The Diaries of Sir Henry Channon*, edited by Robert Rhodes James. Little, Brown have granted permission to quote from *Letters from a Prince* by Rupert Godfrey. David Higham Associates have granted permission to quote material from *I Am My Brother*, by John Lehmann. I am grateful to Adam Nicolson for permission to quote material from Harold Nicolson's *Diaries and Letters*, 1930 through to 1962, edited by Nigel Nicolson. And I would like to thank Professor John Vincent for permission to quote from *The Journals of David Lindsay, Twenty-seventh Earl of Crawford*.

Thanks are also due to my wife, Susie, and my sons Alistair and Tim, for putting up with me while I wrote this book; and for putting up with me, generally.

Introduction

When the wealthy, American-born MP and socialite 'Chips' Channon had his dining room redecorated, he observed no half-measures. At the start of 1936, he and his wife Honor, daughter of the Earl of Iveagh, had moved to one of the stuccoed mansions which engirdle Belgrave Square: the house was heavy with the smell of fresh paint; the carpets and curtains had the bloom of newness on them; the gilt was dazzling; no surface had been left untouched. And, at the heart of it all, the gem in the jeweller's window, was Monsieur Stéphane Boudin's dining room.

Either a triumph of artisanal virtuosity or a coruscating piece of material overstatement, the dining room which M. Boudin had designed for the Channons was, above all, eye-catching. Its walls were painted blue and silver; pier-glasses rose to the ceiling; silver-gilt leaves and branches twisted up to the cornice; a massive crystal chandelier hung above the curlicued table, itself crowded with a busy grove of Meissen porcelain: the whole entity a homage, in fact, to the Amalienburg pavilion in the grounds of the Nymphenburg Palace in Munich. This latter masterpiece of rococo design had been a present from the Elector Karl Albrecht to his wife Amalia, and was built in the first half of the eighteenth century. Chips's dining room, on the other hand, was – what, exactly? A post-Depression gift to *his* wife? A monument to his own self-love? An advertisement of his prosperity? An expression of supersatisfied confidence in his position in English high society?

Perhaps the last. For who should be one of Chips's very first guests in the 'Amalienburg' dining room but His Royal Highness, King Edward VIII? 'The King had rung up', according to Chips's diaries, 'and said it was to be white ties.' A dinner had been arranged for 11 June 1936, and while the male guests wore black waistcoats and the women black dresses – in mourning, still, for

George V – there was an atmosphere of barely suppressed hysteria in the house. Why? Because this was a convocation of several excited members of the New Court – an agglomeration of personalities which had collected round the King and which, if the new courtiers believed all they told themselves, would soon be indispensable Establishment figures, distributing favours, punishing old enemies. Even now, they were as close to the King as it was possible to be, and were iridescent with reflected majesty.

Who were they? The King's brother, Prince George, Duke of Kent, was one; his wife, Princess Marina, was another. Lady Emerald Cunard was another. There was a baronet, in the form of the millionaire Philip Sassoon – a man whose exoticism, whose uncontainable Jewishness, had long made him an outsider, a figure mistrusted by society grandees. There were some Parliamentary figures – Leslie Hore-Belisha and Harold Balfour – and there was Barbie Wallace, an all-purpose social makeweight. There was also the well-known American divorcée, Mrs Wallis Simpson. Did it matter that society regarded these people, uniformly, as vacuities at best; at worst, as *demi-mondaine* seditionists? If so, it didn't bother Chips Channon: 'We processed into dinner and there was a pause as everyone's breath was quite taken away by the beauty of the dining room.' A moment's nervousness ensued as the party realised that Lady Cunard (who was to sit beside the King) hadn't turned up. Then she arrived, squeaking apologies. 'Dinner', fortunately, 'was perfect, we began with Blinis and caviare then Sole Muscat followed by Boeuf Provençal. It was served so speedily that we finished before eleven.' This meant a moment's unease as the party left the table before the musical entertainment – some pianists – had arrived. Nevertheless, the *gêne* was swiftly resolved, as conversational groups formed in the Channons' Regency drawing room, the pianists turned up along with some more after-party guests, and the King stayed to enjoy himself until 1.45 in the morning. He left, expressing pleasure and gratitude. Everyone else stood around, flushed with a numinous sense of power. 'The King of England', gasped Chips, 'dining with me!'

There was, of course, nothing innocent about this gathering. To the world beyond the walls of 5 Belgrave Square it was much more than a dinner party. It was the King Emperor himself, giving clear notice that his reign was to be tainted by association with nonentities, with Jews (Hore-Belisha, as well as Sassoon) and, worst of all, with Americans: Chips himself, American-born Lady Cunard and the loathed and feared Wallis Simpson. And it was this that really scandalised. It was this that confirmed the final, ghastly, term of a process which had begun some sixty years earlier. It meant that the Americans had at last taken over. Two generations earlier, the very idea of an American cabal at the centre of society would have been unthinkable. Now it was a pressing reality, a signal of the way the world had changed and an indication of how things were going to be from now on – the ineluctable shift from British power to American pre-eminence. Today, the American hegemony is a given – white noise in the background of everything we do. In 1936, it was altogether newer, altogether more frightening.

ONE

Young America

America in the last quarter of the nineteenth century was a conundrum. The dislocations of the Civil War – ending in 1865 – followed by a momentary lapse in economic growth after the Panic of 1873, did not obscure the dynamism of contemporary American realities or the fact that the new United States was the fastest-growing and most progressive nation in the world. Its land mass, its population and its economic status seemed to leapfrog one another as decade succeeded decade. Back in 1800, the nation occupied roughly one-third of the territory it held in 1880. In the intervening eighty years, it completed the Louisiana Purchase of 1803, which effectively doubled its territorial area. It also acquired Texas (following the 1846 war with Mexico), California and Florida. By 1825, it had built the Erie Canal, opening up the hinterland by connecting the Great Lakes to the Hudson River at New York City. The Union Pacific and the Central Pacific railroads came together at Promontory, Utah, in 1869, offering one eastbound and one westbound train a week and further annihilating the distinction between the civilised East and the unknowable West. The concept of 'Manifest Destiny' – the doctrine of the inevitable expansion of United States territory ever westwards towards the Pacific, first expressed in the middle of the century – was coming to pass.

Territorial gain was in itself an engine of population and economic growth. Having begun the 1800s with a population a quarter the size of Great Britain's, the United States now contained some 50 million people, compared with Britain's 30 million or so. In the last twenty years of the nineteenth century, it would welcome nine million immigrants, mostly from northern and western Europe, but increasingly, as the turn of the century approached, from southern and eastern Europe. And, provided they found paying work, these new Americans would enjoy a higher standard of living and produce a greater national output than any workers anywhere else in the world. Wages were on average one-third higher than those paid in western Europe. America's global share of manufacturing was doubling in size every couple of decades and would soon outstrip Britain's. Its energy consumption, its iron and steel production, its overall level of industrialisation were also at the precise point at which they would surpass those of the Old Country.

Much of the New World's wealth (despite its vast mutual trade with Britain in cotton and grain, capital and manufactures coming back to it across the Atlantic) derived from the exponential growth of its own internal markets. The processes of cultural and economic colonialism that characterise modern American relations with the rest of the world were only just beginning. America's was, in many ways, a hermetic triumph. But the power of this self-contained economic vitality was so great that the New Country already boasted a clique of super-rich business families, whose personal fortunes beggared almost anything the Old World had to offer: the Astors, Rockefellers, Stuyvesants, Vanderbilts, Goelets, Morgans, Fishes. Viewed materially, its problems were all to do with developing an infrastructure; financing new industries; arriving at a satisfactory national business strategy; ensuring the growth of the democratic franchise. Viewed more narrowly and emotionally, on the other hand, it had a problem of class.

To any reasonably cultured European – and to any similarly cultured American – late-nineteenth-century America was writhing with internal contradictions. It was a great country, a mighty, progressive continent, inhabited by an unpredictable mixture of the rapacious, the suave, the backward and the crashingly unsophisticated. It was a monumental achievement littered with starkly provincial townlets and backwaters. It was also as twitchy about the question of social status as any character in a Jane Austen novel. The Americans who were forging their New World had, inevitably, come from an Old World and helplessly carried with them a ragbag of Old World predispositions regarding status, culture, refinement. The United States may have been revolutionary in its origins; but it was in the nature of society, with all its evergreen social competitiveness, that its inhabitants couldn't help but care what people thought of them and what the rest of the world thought of their nation as a whole.

Where, after all, was the social and cultural hub of this New World? Once one had stepped off the boat at New York harbour, what was there to see beyond the steaming marshes south of Chesapeake Bay or the immense forests west of Albany? New Orleans, for instance, one of the noblest of American cities, dated all the way back to 1717: the era of Nouvelle Orléans. As such, it had a proud sense of its own society, and in the streets of the Garden District and the Vieux Carré offered a kind of civil space almost unknown in the rest of the States and indeed, in much of Europe. But after the Civil War, heavily indebted and dogged by municipal shortcomings, it lost its way. Having been the fourth greatest port in the world in 1840, replete with wealth, cultural diversity and architectural charm, it slumped into a shallow but irreversible decline. By the 1880s New Orleans had accrued a civic debt of over $24 million and was merely trying to stay in one piece, rather than reduce itself to a torrid, mossy, historical artefact. It did not offer a way forward for the socially ambitious.

At the other end of the scale, Chicago, the fastest-growing city in the world, having had its progress interrupted by a catastrophic fire in 1871, was coarse and remorseless. By 1880, it had a population of half a million, seventeen times greater than in 1850. It was the nation's lumber-distributing centre and the heart of all commodities trading. Wildly polyglot, blighted by poor sanitation, peopled by what Kipling had called 'savages', it was an experiment in the fiercest kind of capitalism and no more useful than New Orleans as a centre of social and cultural excellence. Washington DC was internationally significant, but, still concerned with realising Pierre-Charles L'Enfant's town plan and physically consolidating its place on the unlovely swamps of the Potomac river, the 'City of Magnificent Intentions' lacked charm and gravity. Philadelphia, the first city to be laid out on modern principles, the home of the Declaration of Independence, adequately provided with eighteenth-century houses, and a gateway to the new America, had none the less ceded place to New York as the nation's largest and most profitable port and, with it, its special pre-eminence, its social centrality. Rackety San Francisco was still marked by the hysteria generated by the Comstock Lode of 1859 and by its origins as a frontier boom town. Los Angeles, meanwhile, was barely beginning to exploit its lifelines to the East – the Southern Pacific and Santa Fe railroads – had no natural harbour, a population numbered in scant thousands, and insufficient drinking water.

Only New York, the nation's first capital and boasting a population of over one million inhabitants on Manhattan Island alone, could claim to be a truly global city. George Washington had been inaugurated first President there in 1789; by 1790 it was the largest city in the country. It had successfully quelled the riots of 1863 and was now the first great point of immigration for the hungry millions who were building the United States. It had transformed itself from the small aggregate of lanes and waterfront landings of a hundred years earlier to a modern latticework of roaring streets and avenues, studded with public buildings and gigantic offices.

Whereas upstate New York and, indeed, the northern end of Manhattan, still had a markedly bucolic feel, the nearer one got to the Battery, the more imposing and sophisticated was the city. The Metropolitan Museum of Art was founded in 1870 and moved to its new expansive Gothic Revival home in 1880. The Metropolitan Opera House was being built on Fifth Avenue, seven storeys high in a yellow-brick workaday adaptation of the Italianate, with the upper storeys pragmatically sold off as apartments. Central Park opened in 1876. Delmonico's new restaurant, banqueting hall and ballroom on Fifth Avenue and 26th Street, opened in 1876, was the most opulent in the country. Its ballroom was tricked out in red and gold; adjoining it were four private dining rooms, decorated in satins of different shades. Silver chandeliers hung in the restaurant, in the middle of which a fountain played. The building occupied the whole south side of 26th Street between Fifth Avenue and Broadway. It was, in itself, a declaration of intent. And in 1886, the Statue of Liberty arrived.

There was also the startling magnificence of the private buildings going up along Fifth Avenue or near Central Park to press the case. Architects such as Stanford White and Richard Hunt were interposing French châteaux and Italian palazzi among the brownstones of lower Manhattan, moving north from Washington

Square and Lafayette Place until even the farms and country estates of Harlem were starting to disappear under a ramshackle suburbanisation. The Vanderbilt mansion on Fifth Avenue towered over the sidewalks, a transplanted Loire Valley hunting lodge modelled by Hunt after the Château de Blois, while Panama railroad founder William H. Aspinwall's cod-Tudor castle towered over the Hudson river. A.T. Stewart, the world's most successful merchant, owned a huge white marble house on Fifth Avenue, where he sat in forlorn solitude, wondering why he had no social life to compare with that enjoyed by his more attractive neighbours.

Recognising that in other parts of the world these immense buildings would be surrounded by 700 acres of home park rather than by office blocks and traffic, some plutocrats moved further out. The Vanderbilt-Twomblys built a hundred-room Wren-influenced mansion in neighbouring New Jersey and called it Florham. New York merchant George Merritt commissioned a baronial Gothic Revival castle 25 miles north of Broadway and called it Lyndhurst. After their triumph with the Fifth Avenue mansion, the Vanderbilts rang the changes by erecting Rough Point, a beefy, sprawling, English-style manor house, on a bluff on Rhode Island. Skilled Italian stonemasons, carpenters and painters crossed the Atlantic in search of easy and lucrative employment and the Gilded Age came into being. In 1886 a writer called George Sheldon capitalised on the trend for superbly crafted gigantism by producing his *Artistic Country-Seats: Types of Recent American Villa and Cottage Architecture with Instances of Country-Club Houses*, lavishly presented and filled with photographs and drawings of buildings that resembled vast Scottish hunting lodges or Home Counties lunatic asylums.

Yet for all the prosperity and cultural energy flooding into New York in the last quarter of the nineteenth century, the moneyed social élite could not escape the sense that society was, as elsewhere in the States, at base provincial. Old society essentially meant Old Dutch – as expressed in the names Stuyvesant, Vanderbilt, Goelet, Schuyler; or German – the Astors, dating back to the eighteenth century; or sometimes British – the Paynes and the Whitneys. The very oldest names, naturally, dated back to the *Mayflower* voyage of 1620. But age, in so far as 250 years counted had. There was no *ton*. As the redoubtable Mrs Archer explains in Edith Wharton's *The Age of Innocence*, talk of a 'New York aristocracy' was misguided: 'Our grandfathers and great-grandfathers were just respectable English or Dutch merchants, who came to the colonies to make their fortune, and stayed here because they did so well . . . New York has always been a commercial community, and there are not more than three families in it who can claim an aristocratic origin in the real sense of the word.'[1]

Society was, at best, middle-class. The same novel's delicious Countess Olenska, by way of contrast, has lived in Europe just long enough to have been infected by its sense of caste; and to infect the little, parochial world of the New York upper classes on her return. Artlessly true American May Welland, with her outdoor pursuits and her uncertainties over Tennyson, is no match for Madame Olenska's murky sophistication. Indeed, the New York smart set as a whole is no match for a society of which it is permanently and resentfully conscious – being 'far too small, and too scant in its resources'. Madame Olenska herself expresses it as a poverty of ambition: 'It seems stupid to have discovered America only to make it into a copy of another country.'[2] Or, in Matthew Arnold's niggardly formulation, 'What really dissatisfies in American civilization, is the want of the *interesting*, a want due chiefly to the want of those two great elements of the interesting, which are elevation and beauty. And the want of these elements is increased and prolonged by the Americans being assured that they have them when they have them not.'[3]

Naturally, this nervousness affected only the wives and offspring of the rising indigenous *haute bourgeoisie*. Hoary pioneers such as John Jacob Astor and Cornelius Vanderbilt were either dead or untroubled by the social anxieties of their growing families. This meant that even if the sons and daughters of the new rich could be brought up to some kind of standard by means of imported continental governesses and a Harvard education, their plutocratic fathers were potential sources of embarrassment, their personalities rendered worn and graceless by the problems of business. The 5th Earl of Rosebery – an admirer of the New Country – none the less wrote on 5 October 1873, 'Coming out of church, I was shown

Mr. Astor, a hard dreary-looking old man and the richest in the world'[4] – a judgement equalled in its sharp reductiveness by that of the 5th Earl of Warwick, who once dined with the legendary nineteenth-century New York financier, William Whitney. 'I thought when we sat down to table he looked a tired, fagged man', wrote the Earl. 'Wall Street had left its mark on him . . . I don't suppose that Mr. Whitney himself realised how deeply his life labours controlled him. He could not throw off the coils.'[5] The drawing rooms of Manhattan and Long Island were rich in women and poor in men for the reason that most men, once they reached the age of business competence, were too busy to play any part in society. Fun-lovers such as John Jacob Astor III, Leonard Jerome and Oliver Belmont were exceptional because of their rarity, and frequently deplored because of their frank enjoyment of drink, women and racehorses. Society was, above all, serious: 'I suppose they never play games that are *just* games in America, do they?' the Earl of Desart once asked, wonderingly.[6] And the wealth that underpinned society was serious to the point of grimness. Elizabeth Drexel Lehr, member of a prominent New York banking family and ultimately the wife of the 5th Baron Decies, recalled how the Wall Street millionaires of her youth, at dinner, 'either talked of business or sat silent and apathetic through course after course, too nerve-racked by the strain of building a fortune to be able to relax'.[7] It was not only a thankless task searching for good breeding among the inhabitants of the wealthy East Coast; it was often excessively difficult to enjoy the company of those who did fill the bill.

One answer to the problem arrived, in true American fashion, in the form of a business model. This was supplied by a goateed dandy called Ward McAllister. Following a successful career as an attorney in Gold Rush California, Savannah-born McAllister toured Europe, gleaned the essence of European social smartness and rendered it down to one central notion: inaccessibility. Back in New York at the start of the 1870s, and by now, thanks to a judicious marriage, provided with a degree of independent wealth, he formed an alliance with Mrs Caroline Webster Schermerhorn Astor, wife to William Backhouse Astor Jr, himself heir to some $25 million of the family property fortune. Mrs Astor was a powerful enigma. By now in her forties, dumpy, dark-haired, plain of feature, in no sense especially brilliant or gifted, she was, crucially, bored by her husband and monumentally ambitious. Her dream was to assert an unbreakable hold over what then passed for New York society. The portrait of her by Carolus Duran which now hangs in the Metropolitan Museum of Art depicts a figure from sixteenth-century Spain or seventeenth-century Holland: strong-faced, dressed in black and gold, fiercely appraising some object or person beyond the picture's frame. The power of the Astor millions already made her one of New York's most prominent citizens. Ward McAllister imported a necessary sense of theatre (he once filled the field opposite his country house with rented sheep to improve the view for a party) and an impresario's vision, in order to translate her existing status into something larger. Between them, they would create fresh new social institutions over which they both could enjoy jurisdiction.

He began by organising 'Cotillion Dinners' at Delmonico's Restaurant, when it was still located on 5th and 14th Street. Then, in 1872, he launched 'The Patriarchs' – a group of twenty-five of 'the leading representative men of the city, who had the right to create and lead society'. Admission to this clique was controlled by an executive committee of three, 'who could make the best analysis of men; who knew their past as well as their present, and could foresee their future'.[8] This executive committee, in its turn, deferred to its organiser, Ward McAllister. Once the initial twenty-five members of the Patriarchs had been chosen – among them two Astors, a Rensselaer, a Hammersley and a Rutherfurd – they were each allowed to invite ten guests to the Patriarchs' Ball, ensuring a turnout of around 250 minutely inspected social figures. Lord Rosebery found himself taken to one of these in December 1873. Although his summary rings with indifference – 'I went to the Patriarchs' Ball at Delmonico's. It was largely attended, and the cotillion or German was like a public meeting'[9] – it at least points to the enthusiasm roused by McAllister's new project. The Patriarchs' Ball was instantly and permanently oversubscribed.

Fired by this success, McAllister invented the Junior Patriarchs, or Family Circle Dancing Classes, for younger members of the social élite. These too, were heavily oversubscribed and the source of much bitterness among Fifth Avenue families whose daughters failed to secure an invitation. In 1884, the tobacco baron, socialite and racehorse owner, Pierre Lorillard, invented the Tuxedo Club, which met at Delmonico's and whose main characteristic was likewise its extreme exclusivity. John Jacob Astor III, concerned that the hitherto-prestigious 35-year-old Union Club was being overrun by *arrivistes*, founded the far less approachable Knickerbocker Club. The Tuxedo and the Knickerbocker, in the manner of the Patriarchs' Ball and McAllister's Family Circle Dancing Classes, were immediate successes. Like Lawrence Lefferts – Edith Wharton's dogmatising fraud in *The Age of Innocence* ('If anybody can tell a fellow just when to wear a black tie with evening clothes and when not to, it's Larry Lefferts') – these self-elected arbiters took advantage of society's need for dynamic organisation, and, for a while, prospered. The high point for the Astor/McAllister co-operative undoubtedly came in the form of Mrs Astor's Ball, which she held at her house at 350 Fifth Avenue. An annual event, it took place on the first or second Monday in January, the length of its guest-list determined by the size of the ballroom in which it took place. This at least was Mrs Astor's rationale: since the ballroom only held 400 guests, there could only ever be 400 of the most superior people worth inviting. The envious phrase 'Mrs Astor's 400' grew up around this happy conceit and for several years the ball served as an earnest of her social importance.

McAllister's plan was necessary but not, in this case, sufficient. It only needed someone of equal means and equal determination to challenge Mrs Astor to expose the flaw at the heart of the McAllister/Astor programme and, indeed, at the heart of New York society. The radical in this case was Mrs Alva Vanderbilt, wife of William Kissam Vanderbilt, inheritor of some $60 million of the family fortune. Alva was an inordinately tough product of Mobile, Alabama. Her mother had been forced to flee Paris at the time of the Franco-Prussian War, return to New York and open a boarding house on West 23rd Street. Some twenty years younger than Mrs Astor, Alva too was dark-haired, robust and physically powerful. She also had a ferocity about her that grew from a compelling sense of disadvantage. The Astor family despised the Vanderbilts as parvenus whose wealth was the product of Cornelius Vanderbilt's dealings as a mid-century railroad robber baron. Mrs Astor especially scorned Mrs Vanderbilt, as being both a Vanderbilt and the daughter of a boarding-house proprietress. As with all provincial conflicts, it made no sense to the outside world. John Jacob Astor, who laid the foundations for the family's huge fortune at the end of the eighteenth century, had been a fur-trapper who spoke with the guttural German accent of his native town, Walldorf, in Baden-Württemberg. His son, William Backhouse Astor, doubled the family's wealth at the same time as he became a notorious slum landlord. The hard-living, foul-mouthed Cornelius Vanderbilt – the 'Commodore' – had started life as a Staten Island ferryman in the early 1800s, before getting into the railroad business and making even more money than the Astors. There was no obvious tradition of breeding or refinement in either family. Both were products of the same fiercely hectic mercantilism. Yet the Vanderbilts and Astors never met, exchanged cards, or coerced their children into playing together. Alva was, in Mrs Astor's worldview, simply the representative of an absurdly rich underclass.

The 9th Duke of Manchester, himself an Anglo-American, later puzzled over this bigotry:

> For some unaccountable cause, New York Society has a habit of forming unreasonable prejudices against certain people or families whom the impartial observer would consider perfectly eligible. Then, just as unaccountably as they were once barred, these people are admitted, and, like the Vanderbilts and the Goulds, quickly become leading figures in the circles that formerly refused to receive them.[10]

Alva had deep resources. She knew, as did the Duke of Manchester, that the East Coast social order was fundamentally protean and malleable. She conceived a masterplan: a costume ball of prodigious splendour to celebrate, on 26 March 1883, the completion of her new $3 million château at 660 Fifth Avenue: 1,200 guests were invited. Lanouette, the celebrated New York costumier, kept on a squad of 150 dressmakers to complete the outfits. Invitees planned to arrive as Queen Elizabeth I, Christopher Columbus, Joan of Arc, Marie-Antoinette, Daniel Boone and, in the case of Mrs Cornelius Vanderbilt II, dressed in a creation of white satin and diamonds, embodying 'Electric Light'.

Despite the lack of any formal family contact, Mrs Astor's daughter, Carrie, expected an invitation to this huge event, and devoted a good deal of her time to practising a star quadrille in readiness. But Alva Vanderbilt saw no reason to ask any Astor to her ball, reasonably observing that she had not met Carrie Astor, or indeed Mrs Astor. Such was the clamour generated by the event, however, that Mrs Astor realised that her position made it more difficult for her not to appear than to appear; and that she would have to propitiate Alva Vanderbilt, effectively begging for a ticket. She paid a visit to the Vanderbilt house for the first time in her life and left her card. Alva Vanderbilt at once replied with an invitation. The Astors had thus been forced to bow to the Vanderbilts, whose ball was a triumph and whose position was now openly established.

Two truths emerged from this encounter. The first was that such protocols as Mrs Astor and Ward McAllister maintained could only ever be provisional. The depth of society's obsession with rules turned out to be an index of how hard it tried to break them. The second was that Mrs Alva Vanderbilt was even more determined than anyone had previously realised.

TWO

The Old World

On the other side of the Atlantic there was, of course, a world whose caste values were much less open to such guerrilla attacks. The perfect aristocracy – the most substantial, the deepest-rooted and most highly structured – was at that time to be found in Britain.

The power and coherence of this aristocracy could be expressed statistically. In the late 1800s, some seven thousand families owned 80 per cent of all the land in the British Isles. Many of these were relatively small landowners, holding between 1,000 and 10,000 acres. Above them was a smaller, even more satisfying layer – comprising perhaps seven hundred and fifty families – with holdings larger than 10,000 acres but smaller than 30,000. And then, at the very top, were the handful of millionaires, the landowners with estates greater than 30,000 acres, with at least two great country estates plus a substantial London town house – and, in a perfect symmetry of wealth and nobility, frequently possessed of a great title. Territorial holdings and noble birth meant social influence; often political influence. The ruthlessness of male primogeniture promoted consolidation of wealth and power, while the pages of *Debrett* and *Burke's Peerage* detailed the structure of a system that was impenetrable yet unambiguous. The unrivalled position of the British monarchy legitimised it all. It was a creation which held sway in the material world and yet which, beyond the statistics, beyond the tangible evidence, attained to the level of art, with its pageantry, its magnificent country estates, its exquisite sense of hierarchy and its pointlessness.

While much of republican America, not least in the new Midwest, found this distasteful and even immoral, there were pockets of enthusiasm for British élitism, especially on the East Coast. The poet and Boston Brahmin Ralph Waldo Emerson responded unstintingly to England's entrenched sense of privilege.

The English nobles [he argued] are high-spirited, active, educated men, born to wealth and power, who have run through every country, and kept in every country the best company, have seen every secret of art and nature, and, when men of any ability or ambition, have been consulted in the conduct of every important action. You cannot wield great agencies without lending yourself to them, and, when it happens that the spirit of the earl meets his rank and duties, we have the best examples of behaviour. Power of any kind readily appears in the manners; and beneficent power, *le talent de bien faire*, gives a majesty which cannot be concealed or resisted.[1]

To the charge that the British aristocracy was good only for ornament rather than function, he replied,

The upper classes have only birth, say the people here, and not thoughts. Yes, but they have manners, and 'tis wonderful how much talent runs into manners: – nowhere and never so much as in England. They have the sense of superiority, the absence of all the ambitious effort which disgusts in the aspiring classes, a pure tone of thought and feeling, and the power to command, among their other luxuries, the presence of the most accomplished men in their festive meetings.[2]

This was a song of praise which many an English writer of the late nineteenth century would have found hard to top. But Emerson was not especially unusual. He was voicing a familiar weakness, a submission to form. 'You know what these English grandees are', says one of Edith Wharton's characters, helplessly, 'it's hopeless to expect people who are accustomed to the European courts to trouble themselves about our little republican distinctions. The Duke goes where he's amused.'[3] Empire and a royal family unflustered by revolution or fissiparous continental tendencies made it impossible to condescend to the British aristocracy.

More broadly, the informed American consensus of taste, although slowly shifting away from Europe in general and England in particular, was still sufficiently enthralled by the English model whenever snobbery made a difference. When the still-ascending

Vanderbilts commissioned Hunt to design their new Fifth Avenue mansion, they didn't care whether it was Italianate, Gothic or Loire château in style, as long as it was larger than A.T. Stewart's palace down the road. In contrast, it was important that George Merritt's Lyndhurst, subsequently bought by the mildly snobbish railroad magnate Jay Gould, should retain its mock-Tudor dignity, just as it became important to the newly accepted Vanderbilts that Rough Point at Newport should affect a kind of English understatement. Snobbish New York men-about-town dressed in London fashions and imitated the *faux*-cockney vocal mannerisms of the British urban aristocracy, complaining that they *cawn't dawnce, demmit*, and closing their sentences with a reflexive *y'know*. Charles Worth, the Parisian couturier, was the pole star of women's fashion; but London was the home of men's tailoring and bootmaking. Similarly, a Purdey shotgun from London was prized as highly as a Nicolson yacht built beside the Solent. In recognition of the essential self-pleasuring unemployability of the British grandee, some East Coast swells began referring to themselves as 'sportsmen', pointing up the chronic problem that Eastern society faced – not enough available men – by aping the conventions of British high society, in which men, not obliged not to work, were freely available.

Other, less visible citizens, such as the young Henry James, took to scrutinising the bestselling illustrated architectural history, Nash's *Mansions of England in the Olden Time*, developing a fixation with the shadowy nuances of European high society and dreaming of a time when he would be able to write home,

> I am sitting, in the livid light of a London November Sunday, before a copious fire, in my own particular sitting-room . . . I have been walking up Piccadilly this morning, and into Hyde Park, to get my land-legs on; I am duly swathed and smoked and chilled, and feel as if I had been here for ten years . . . It is the same old big black London, and seems, as always, half delicious, half dismal . . .[4]

Years later, a writer as conspicuously American as F. Scott Fitzgerald would still find himself paying lip-service to Britain's cultural centrality in *The Beautiful and Damned*, whose gadabout New York characters – Anthony Patch, Dick Caramel, Maury Noble – none the less season their pre-war banter with Englishisms such as *like the deuce*; and references to Shakespeare, Samuel Butler, H.G. Wells. And Van Wyck Brooks, East Coast aesthete and founder of the influential journal *Seven Arts*, would write this minatory note to a friend planning to move to the Midwest: 'All our will-to-live as writers comes to us, or rather stays with us, through our intercourse with Europe. Never believe people who talk to you about the west, Waldo; never forget that it is we New Yorkers and New Englanders who have the monopoly of whatever oxygen there is in the American continent.'[5]

At the same time, younger members of the British élite had been paying attention to the United States since well before the mid-1870s: visitors ranging from the brawling 8th Duke of Manchester and 9th Marquess of Queensberry; to the Prince of Wales; to James Bryce, an intensely respectable fellow at Oriel College, Oxford. It was a fashionable destination.

Bryce, later to become Viscount Bryce and British ambassador at Washington, was fascinated by the New World. 'The place, it is true, is in parts only half built', he wrote on his first visit to Chicago in 1870: 'Between the grand blocks there are often mean homes . . . sometimes open spaces; the river interrupts the traffic awkwardly and is not itself beautiful. But the scale and grandeur and newness of everything makes a strong impression. You feel that those who have built this city have felt it was becoming great, and have been inspired by this spirit to do their best.'[6]

Bryce might well have been moved by the meritocratic vigour of young Chicago. An establishment figure from a modest, indeed nonconformist, background, he was predisposed to think radically. Born the son of a Scottish mathematics teacher, he had risen through Glasgow University on to a First in History and Law at Trinity, Oxford, at last to his current position at Oriel, which he combined with a career at the Bar in Lincoln's Inn. Like Chicago itself, he was in the process of constructing something great from humble beginnings; and he found an echo of his own ambitions in the sense of liberation and possibility that infused the new city.

But other, more securely aristocratic, representatives of the Old World, conditioned to see themselves as the pinnacle of Western achievement, were also impressed. The Earl of Rosebery found himself sorrowfully returning to England after his three-month journey around the United States, greatly moved by what he had seen. His trip had taken him from New York to Wyoming, Cheyenne and Salt Lake City. Much of his time had been spent on the thriving East Coast, where the depredations of civil war had already been made good. Aboard the Cunarder *Russia*, he completed the final diary entry of his trip, noting on 28 December 1873,

> And so my dream is over. I suppose I have been there but can I be sure. At any rate I am back in England. Miserably smoky and narrow as ever. Is it a dream that I have been in a country where all are born equal before the law? Where every man has the means of obtaining the dearest object of the Anglosaxon's heart, a plot of land of his own on which to live and die? Where each son of the soil carries in his wallet not the staff of a field marshal, for field marshals are abhorrent to the spirit of the country, but a possible passport to the White House, to the Bench of the Supreme Court, to every eminent position without exception that the State can afford . . . It is easy to taunt and to deride, to point to a small vulgarism here and a petty venality there, and then to denounce the whole state as one stinking mass of corruption. The blotches exist indeed but they are the blemishes of the growing youth which are the virile promise of a coming beard and a splendid manhood.[7]

Rosebery was in no sense a revolutionary or closet republican. His patrician upbringing, his schooling at Eton and Christ Church, Oxford, his estate at Dalmeny House and his growing sense of Britain's imperial destiny, all marked him, at the age of 26, as a thoroughgoing representative of the High Victorian establishment. There was no reason, other than high spirits and a liberal temperament, for him to have regarded the United States as anything other than a mere novelty.

Yet, quite apart from his evident enthusiasm for what he saw, he was personally transformed – the new nation effacing 'the peculiar brand of shyness that puzzled many of his contemporaries', but which, in the States, 'did not affect his bearing either in the company of his intimate acquaintances or among strangers'.[8] And so, 'I slept capitally', he noted with relish, one Wednesday in October,

> and was up early to see a lovely morning and breakfast at Syracuse which was the first time I had seen Americans in the frenzy of eating. They appear not to eat for luxurious enjoyment but simply to make 'the 'tomach tiff' as the Hottentot says: and very stiff it must sometimes be. I soon fell into the way of it, and could finish my dinner in three minutes and enjoy the spare twenty two on the platform as well as anybody. I have not gained any agility with my knife, but intend practising in private.[9]

Later on, he even found room for a joke at the expense of the Englishman abroad: 'A gentleman with a red beard began hectoring and bullying the clerk and insisting on having my room. "At last, I said to myself, "I have found the insolent and domineering American so well known to the readers of English books on America." Alas! It was the English aide de camp, Mr. Clayden.'[10] His sympathies fully engaged with the American way of life, he could no longer be clear about whose prejudices he was confronting.

At the same time as Lord Rosebery was touring North America, Algernon Bertram Mitford, the 1st Baron Redesdale, was engaged on his own journey of exploration. Rosebery had already stumbled upon a crowd of Etonians at a hotel in New York. Then, on 11 October, he made a more extraordinary discovery as he 'dined at Cheyenne. Here I saw a figure that I felt sure I knew. It was Bertie Mitford. We parted at luncheon in the St James' Club nine or ten months ago, and we met at Cheyenne in the Territory of Wyoming in the Western States of America. He was bent homewards, and we only had a few minutes to talk as his train was going.'[11] For a moment it must have seemed as if America was studded like the night sky with bright pinpoints of light, each dot representing an entry in *Burke's Peerage*.

Redesdale similarly found much to admire in the States, but admired it with a distancing irony more typical of his class. He voiced his ambivalence by noting, among other things, that 'In America the word good is insufficient; you must say that everything

is for the best; less praise is an insult and an ignorant insult at that.'
(This mild criticism was mirrored in a letter from the Hon. Francis
Charles Lawley to Rosebery: 'On arriving there write down your
name in full, "the Earl of R. —— London, England", and do the
same wherever you go. Modesty and self abnegation are always
misinterpreted by Yankees.'[12]) Redesdale went on to illustrate his
point with a tale from St Louis, Missouri, in which

> Standing before a clean little white house with green shutters, and
> adorned at the entrance with some plaster of Paris statuary, our
> cicerone said, 'These are the residences of our rich townsmen.
> How do they compare with the mansions of your aristocracy in
> London?' I was foolish enough to say that they seemed to me a
> little small. He smiled a smile of pity at the insular jealousy of the
> Old World.[13]

This is the puzzled but essentially complacent humour of an older
civilisation condescending to a younger; an adult to a child. It
echoes the kind of self-deprecating levity seen in Rosebery's glimpse
of the New York press at work ('In the New York Herald of this
morning I see a long paragraph detailing an "interview" with me –
the able production of a man who came and talked to me in the hall
of the hotel. Thank Heavens, I did not answer many of his
questions, or I should have been put in a very ridiculous light'[14]); or
the cool appreciations of Sir Caspar Purdon Clarke on his appoint-
ment as head of the Metropolitan Museum in New York: 'The
arrangements at White House are very Royal at evening functions,
almost as good an imitation as a State dinner at the Guildhall in
London.'[15] It is a humour predicated on the storyteller's superior
social standing – and which, by its existence, draws attention to a
covert unease.

James Bryce wrestled more seriously with those problems of
cultural relativism which all thoughtful Victorian travellers to
America had to face. Excellence, he concluded, meant fundamentally
different things in America and England.

> An American who can, and in this frequently without much
> effort, get himself into the front rank, stays there, and devotes the

rest of his energy to money-making and having a good time; whereas in England, the same man having a higher point to reach to find himself among the first, struggles on, perfecting his powers, eventually makes more of himself and raises still the general standard.[16]

Thus the very best of men and things in America were more freely available, more widely spread, and therefore less excellent, than those in England. English excellence, by reason of its greater scarcity and the more protracted striving which brought it into being, was superior, and a finer example to the rest of society.

But even if Bryce could console himself with this rationalisation, the underlying truth remained: it was now quite seemly to compare American values with those of the English. And this from a country that was still almost all wilderness, and that had acheived independence but a couple of generations back.

The equivocation, felt on both sides – by Anglophile Americans and neophyte British enthusiasts for the States – was an inescapable part of the encounter. How could it have been otherwise? Every trip yielded some kind of conflict. Charles Dickens's visit in 1842 was greeted by the American public with something like adulation. Yet his own mood, pleased enough at first, later soured sufficiently for him to complain about the pigs rooting among the garbage outside the Astor House Hotel in New York; and then to write *Martin Chuzzlewit* on his return, reducing the United States to the sort of place where 'Fatal maladies, seeking whom they might infect, came forth at night in misty shapes'. The Prince of Wales's trip in 1860 evoked, according to the American diarist George Templeton Strong, a 'deep and almost universal feeling of respect and regard for Great Britain and for Her Britannic Majesty', a regard which – inevitably – came with a corrective, a hint of old enmities, in the reminder that 'The old anti-British patriotism of twenty years ago is nearly extinct.'[17] Caspar Purdon Clarke made the uncomfortable discovery that Americans 'are a most extraordinary people, possessing quite opposite qualities in each individual, generous and cruel, extravagant and mean, trusting no one yet taken in by pretentious impostors'.[18] And Oscar Wilde veered from acclaim to wounded discomfort in the space of a few months. At the start of his American tour in 1882, the aesthete, poet and essayist despatched a letter home from New York which sang of 'my success! The hall had an audience larger and more wonderful than even Dickens had', before going on to describe his several secretaries: 'One writes my autographs all day for my admirers, the other receives the flowers that are left really every ten minutes. A third whose hair resembles mine is obliged to send off locks of his own hair to the myriad maidens of the city, and so is rapidly becoming bald.'[19] But this was not to last. Soon, he was being pilloried by Harvard undergraduates; was forced to escape a group of aggressively unaesthetic Wall Street workers by climbing out of the back exit of an office building; and, at last, suffered a doomed encounter with Henry James. Wilde was an admirer of James's work, but James, the Anglophile neurotic, forever particularising the object of his affections, was unable to cope with the nomadic Anglo-Irishman, relishing the chance peculiarities of the New World. 'I am very nostalgic for London', said James; to which Wilde replied, 'Really? You care for places? The world is my home.' Things went from bad to worse after that, James finally announcing to a friend that 'Wilde is a fatuous fool, tenth-rate cad.'[20] Wilde returned, just slightly chastened, to London, admitting that the tour had been 'a failure'.

Even Lord Rosebery sometimes expressed a degree of uneasy ambivalence at the frictions between personal encounters and public consensus. In a letter to George Gore Higgins, he allowed an excess of sarcastic detestation to boil over:

> The curses of travelling here are the stove-heat of the carriages and the babies. Every carriage reeks with children of ages ranging from two days to three years. The first receive natural nourishment in a disagreeably public way, the second will seek food in any part of the carriage under your legs or in your hat. Moreover they howl abominably, which is I suppose why they all grow into practised public speakers.

As if embarrassed by his own bad manners, he was at once careful to remind Higgins that 'The people here are wonderfully kind and pleasant. My own private impression is that in their heart of hearts they like England very much.' Yet that, too, came with a proviso: 'But the public prints always select England for those comparisons which we know are odious.'[21] In fact it took an Englishman such as the young Winston Churchill to pronounce on the United States fearlessly but without any sense of vacillating meanness. 'Vulgarity is a sign of strength', he wrote to his brother, Jack, while visiting the States in 1895. 'A great crude, strong young people are the Americans – like a boisterous, healthy boy among enervated but well-bred ladies & gentlemen.'[22] In other words, it needed an Anglo-American aristocrat with his own highly American inner ambitions not to be affronted by the differences between the two nations.

An older generation, on the other hand, lacked all uncertainty and needed no special prompting to go on the attack. The 75-year-old Lord Ellenborough wrote, on the death of Richard Cobden, 'I think they [Cobden and Bright] were both unsuited to the present constitution of the country, and that they had a strange longing for something more on the American model. One would think that that depraved taste must now have passed from all reasonable beings.'[23] A view prefigured by that of the Prince of Wales, writing to his mother in the 1860s, after his trip to the United States. 'We have always been an aristocratic Country', he argued then, 'and I hope we shall always remain so, as they are the mainstay of this country, unless we become so Americanised that they are swept away, and then the state of things will be quite according to Mr. Bright's views, who wishes only for the Sovereign and the People, and no class in between.'[24] The 63-year-old 2nd Duke of Wellington so detested the idea of America that he once declined to let Mr J. Lothrop Motley, American Minister to the Court of St James, go in to dinner ahead of him. The fact that Mr Motley was staying with the Duke at his country seat at Stratfield Saye made no difference. 'I maintain that he ought to go in merely as an ordinary guest', Wellington complained to his friend, Lady Dorothy Nevill – daughter of the 3rd Earl of Orford, founder of the Primrose League and friend of the Countess of Warwick. She wisely answered that in that case the Duke must 'want war with America, for without doubt, Mr. Motley, as diplomatic representative of that great Republic, must be sent into dinner first of all, otherwise you will be offending, not only him, but his country as well'.

The Duke gave in, but not without much restiveness against 'brand-new countries and new-fangled nonsense'.[25] Indeed, it was this kind of impertinence that would eventually lead the American writer Price Collier to argue that

> Our enthusiastic and indiscriminating hospitality to foreigners, especially to Englishmen and Englishwomen, is simply looked upon by them as an acknowledgement of their superiority. Some day we shall realize this, and become more careful, but it is wonderful that an intelligent race like the Americans should take the cuffing and snubbing they get for their pains, whether at home or as Americans domiciled in England, not even now realizing that the Englishmen care nothing about them unless they come bearing gifts.[26]

Or, as the *New York Times* put it, the reason why the British so happily condescended to Americans was 'the obvious effort of many Americans to appear to their visitors to be something different from what they are, and to imitate English manners and ways. Another reason', it added, darkly, 'is the profuse attentions lavished on strangers, as if they were a higher order of beings.'[27]

The resentments were new, and doubly uncomfortable because of their newness. Detestation of the French – the Addisonian certainty that 'One Englishman could beat three Frenchmen' – was real, but familiar; predictable; even comfortable. Anglo-American relations, on the other hand, enjoyed no precedents. Unlike France, or even Germany, which were at least intelligible in terms of their size and ambitions, America was a young colossus whose potential not only unnerved the British but even appeared to unnerve some Americans. It didn't take much imagination to guess that this new nation would be capable of imposing a new destiny on the world, and that, soon enough, unfamiliar accommodations would have to be made.

It took time for Britain to see this potential problem as a problem. Mostly, when an Englishman went to America, he came back with the reasonable confidence that Britain was still superior in most of the ways that mattered. Lord Redesdale genuinely roughed it in the Midwest, living with buffalo hunters and dour, chaotic frontiersmen.

He found incompetence, gloom and resentment on a continental scale and came back satisfied. Rosebery was so relaxed about the United States that he went there three times, the last visit being in 1875. The following year he returned, and dined with Disraeli – recently ennobled as Lord Beaconsfield. Beaconsfield then wrote to Lady Bradford of how 'Rosebery came up to me and talked very well – just come from America – his third visit and full as an egg of quaint observations.' Rosebery's cheerfulness made perfect sense. He only had to call in on a party at one of the great aristocratic private palaces in London to find, as Lady Eastlake once wrote,

> Marble, gilding-mirrors, pictures and flowers; couches ranged round beds of geraniums and roses, every rare and sweet oddity lying about in saucers, bouquets without end, tiers of red and white camellias in gorgeous pyramids, two refreshment rooms spread with every delicacy in and out of season, music swelling from some masterly instrumental performers and the buzz of voices from the gay crowd, which were moving to and fro without any crush upon the smooth parquet[29]

– an opulence, in other words, as imposing as any that could be mustered anywhere in the world, emblematic proof of the nation's potency, its economic reach.

Yet, at the same time, the stateliness of Britain's world standing in the mid-1800s, the pomp of its aristocracy, even the material splendour hymned by Lady Eastlake, heralded a fatal decline – beginning in the 1880s, accelerating with the upheaval of the First World War and reaching its bitter end with the post-Second World War Attlee administration.

Much of the trouble was economic, centring on the fact that land – the territorial holdings, those broad acres that defined one's membership of the upper classes – was becoming less and less useful as time passed. The collapse of grain prices in the late 1800s – not least thanks to competition from the United States – was one part of the problem. Rents from tenant farmers followed a similar decline, only recovering patchily and impermanently. Harvests were apt to fail. The debts and mortgages that encumbered most estates were easy enough to service in the mid-1800s, when farming was straightforwardly profitable. But as incomes fell, the burden of overhanging debt became more marked. Taxation, especially in the form of death duties – Sir William Harcourt's ground-breaking 8 per cent tax of 1894, for instance – loomed horribly. Lord Monson complained to a friend as early as 1851, 'What an infernal bore is landed property. No certain income can be reckoned upon. I hope your future wife will have Consols or some such ballast. I think it is worth half as much again as what land is reckoned at.'[30] Worse still were the great houses at the centres of the great estates, all of which were remorseless drains on the unstable income from the surrounding fields, and which needed endless repair, refurbishment and, in some cases, more or less total reconstruction. Whether it was something out of *Mansions of England in the Olden Time* – a Knole or a Hardwick Hall – or a more up-to-date possession, such as a Chatsworth or a Blenheim Palace, a great house presented a mass of problems. Menaced by dry rot, leaking roofs and disintegrating stonework, it was the physical and spiritual heart of one's position in society, and it was sick.

New money from trade, industry, banking and insurance was there, all right, but it was too often kept distinct from the old. Britain's *arrivistes* – the Wills tobacco family; Sir Ernest Cassel, the King's personal financier; Lord Hambleden, of W.H. Smith's; Lord Armstrong, the munitions king – although nowhere nearly as wonderfully plutocratic as America's multimillionaires, were none the less both wealthy and able to enjoy their wealth, given that it was tied up in relatively manageable liquid forms: shares, gold, seams of coal. But, like their American equivalents, they cared less about sheer acreage than they did about comfortable grandeur. Their imperatives were not those of the landed gentry. Sir Ernest Cassel's overweening Brook House, in Park Lane, would not have been out of place on Park Avenue. William Armstrong's Cragside could have sat comfortably on the banks of the Hudson river. The Rothschilds' Waddesdon Manor was a Home Counties palace, but with a surrounding estate whose land could be counted out in hundreds of acres, rather than the thousands burdening, say, the Duke of Sutherland. In comparison with the established nobility, the Rothschilds were travelling light. The very richest traditional grandees – the Devonshires, the Westminsters – were, on the other hand, so rich, and had so many various forms of income, that they could still afford to keep their territorial spreads and remain passably sanguine about their prospects. But even they paused to think, from time to time: by 1880, the Duke of Devonshire was having to spend as much as 60 per cent of his disposable income on servicing his interest payments.

Almost everyone else was harassed by money worries, and by the knowledge that their ability to live a life of constant, pleasurable ritual left them unable to earn a living in the real world. Selling off the family possessions, as the 7th and 8th Dukes of Marlborough did, spectacularly, in 1875, 1881 and 1886, was one way to keep afloat. Selling off parcels of land – the Dukes of Newcastle, Leeds, Beaufort, Abercorn, all rushed to the market at the end of the nineteenth century – was another approach. Selling off the family land, of course – the destruction of a generations-old inheritance and the loss of the terrain which once nurtured you – was worse even than the panic selling of family diamonds, Van Dycks and first editions. Unlike the one-off dispersals of precious possessions, the sale of great tracts of land was also subject to trickier market forces. The more land became available, the more its value fell, to the point where, as the Duke of Leeds (and many others) found out at the end of the nineteenth century, it was effectively unsellable.

Title was no safeguard. Dukes suffered as much as baronets. 'Strath has a mad lust for destruction on the plea of death duties. Never is there another phrase in his mouth', wrote Millicent, Duchess of Sutherland, to Lord Esher, as she fulminated against her husband, the 4th Duke, and his failure to move with the times: 'I shall have to leave Stafford House and I can't afford to bring a single real bit of furniture. I can't live without lovely things around me, associated historically with the past. Strath lives in rooms with nouveau art furniture bought on the hire system. I feel as if my heart were breaking at this last blow . . . Strath is a monomaniac.' Drawing breath, she then concluded, 'If it weren't for Rosemary [their daughter] I'd separate tomorrow. You can't imagine what this destruction with no real power and no real friends means. S. [Strath] is a pitiable figure, mooning about like Scrooge and muttering about money.'[31] A similar gloom affected the feckless 9th Duke of Manchester as he ruefully picked over the financial mess left to him by his even more unreliable father. Writing about Kimbolton Castle, the exquisite Cambridgeshire family seat, designed by (among others) Vanbrugh, Hawksmoor and Adam, he observed how in the mid-1800s the Kimbolton property alone used to bring in an annual revenue of around £70,000, while the Irish possessions at Tandragee in County Armagh could be expected to generate a further £25,000. With a total annual income from the two estates rising to over £90,000, 'In those days of less taxation such a sum made a man passing wealthy.' But as a consequence of the agricultural depression, annual income from the Kimbolton estate was cut down to something between £10,000 and £11,000; while Tandragee found itself generating no more than £12,000 to £14,000 per year. Unluckily, 'Neither my father nor my mother seemed able to grasp the salient fact that to be economical in small things and liberal in large is not true economy.' The upshot for the 9th Duke? 'When it became my turn to succeed to the title, and a balance sheet was drawn up, it showed a debit balance of two thousand pounds a year instead of a substantial amount on the credit side.' Any remaining income got used up in paying for repairs and general outgoings on the estates. There was also a jointure of £8,000 per year plus interest on a clutch of mortgages, all of which had been raised by the Duke's fiscally incontinent ancestors. It now cost him £10,000 per year just to service his debts. Bankruptcy dogged the Duke like an illness throughout his life. 'I do not pretend to understand finance, or the intricacies of accountancy', he added, with valiant understatement.[32]

The son and heir of a ruined grandee such as the Duke of Manchester could look forward to inheriting nothing much more than a depreciating asset, a minimal source of income and a major financial burden. 'It is some time since I visited Tandragee', the 9th Duke confessed in his fifties, citing bottomless expenses and punitive taxation as the principal reasons why he couldn't keep the place open enough to make it worth visiting. The main rooms were shuttered and filled with druggets; the corridors had fallen silent. There were no more 'gay parties'. Occasionally the Duke's eldest son, burdened like his father with the certainty of loss, came down to keep an eye on the property, but the Duke himself was too stricken by the poignancy of his situation to go there. He was down, effectively, to Kimbolton: a grandee with only one home.[33]

Younger sons could expect only the slimmest of pickings: infrequent handouts and erratic subventions. And once those were exhausted, then funds had to be found wherever they could. Lord Randolph Churchill, younger son of the 7th Duke of Marlborough, was perpetually starved of cash. His robust, even combative, mental constitution couldn't stop him from worrying about money, as a letter sent to his wife in 1876 suggests. Writing about a recently negotiated sum of £500 borrowed from Coutt's Bank, he assured her that it 'will pay for little bills & keep us going till March. It will be a most excellent arrangement for us, only it is the last loan we can make on our present resources & we really must try to live in an economical manner.'[34] The Marlboroughs were, as much as anyone could be, asset-rich and cash-poor. The distress sales of 1875 had only gone a small way towards easing the burden of the Churchill family; and had done nothing at all to help Lord Randolph himself. His only possible comfort would have been that he was not alone and that his nervous injunctions were being repeated on a daily basis in hundreds of upper-class English families. As one commentator put it: 'There was no escape from the dilemma of wealth and status. Without land, they would no longer be a landed aristocracy. With land, only those whose estates were fortunate enough to benefit from industrial values were wealthy enough to remain dominant.'[35] The land that defined the landed upper classes was also slowly killing them.

What was to be done? Was this an apocalypse in the making, or merely a moment in the long history of Britain's ruling élite? At the very least, there seemed to be a growing rupture between Britain's position in the world and the personal circumstances of some members of its aristocracy. Back in 1813, when the crisis was all of Napoleon's army, rather than taxation and the New World economic dispensation, Jane Austen had had Colonel Fitzwilliam remark in *Pride and Prejudice*, 'Our habits of expence make us too dependant [sic], and there are not many in my rank of life who can afford to marry without some attention to money.' The problem, therefore, was scarcely new. But in 1813 Britain had been moving into its phase of greatest influence and prosperity. Sixty years later, it was starting its decline. Money had to be found somewhere, without an undue loss of dignity. And in America, meanwhile, the super-wealthy inhabitants of the East Coast, deeply conscious of their relationship with Britain – of its relationship with them – were busily wondering how they might gain some kind of social advantage over each other.

Marriage suddenly seemed an interesting possibility for both parties. Given the materials available, it would involve exchanging American wealth and American girls for English prestige. The mothers of the girls wanted it; as did many of the girls themselves. So did many among the British nobility. For all its apparent airtightness and perfection of internal structure, the British aristocracy was well known – given the right conditions – to be highly porous and receptive to new blood. That was an essential part of its strength. Dynastic marriages of wealth and power had been brokered for centuries, between families and nations. Back in 1791, for instance, Lord Sefton's financial adviser had come up with a useful scheme for clearing an overhanging debt of £40,000: Sefton's heir, Lord Molyneux, should marry into money. 'To marry a fine brought up lady with little or no fortune would be to hurt the Estate', he noted. Rather, Molyneux 'has a right to expect a large sum with a Lady, not to look at less than 60,000 . . . *many* a great and rich banker would be glad of the offer to give his daughter that fortune for her advancement and dignity (vide Messrs. Child), or many a rich heiress to a large estate and of good family would also be glad of the offer.'[36] And by 1836, the three Caton sisters (of Baltimore, Maryland) had helped inaugurate the concept of the American society bride by completing a remarkable triple union in which the three sisters married, variously, the Marquesses of Carmarthen and Wellesley, and Lord Stafford. This caused the society figure Thomas Raikes to observe that 'It is a singular instance of three sisters, foreigners, and of a nation hitherto little known in our aristocratic circles, allying themselves to such distinguished families in England.'[37] What's more, Americans were more suitable, in their way, than many local products – those mortifying offspring of recently ennobled tradesmen or bankers. Being from so far overseas, American girls' antecedents were exotic, hard to place, drawn from a wholly different cultural background, diffuse in outline. They would be that much easier to make allowances for.

The only flaw in the scheme was that the trade was patently unequal. The wealth – the dynamic force – was all American. The prestige – the inactive, effete, intangible force – was all British. Everything appeared to be flowing in one direction: from the stronger to the weaker. It was not, in the context of national fortunes – the Parliamentary Reform Acts, the Irish Question, the Turkish Problem – a huge realignment. But as an emblem of greater shifts and changes, it was fraught with significance.

THREE

The First Marriages

One of the first great Anglo-American marriages was all for love, rather than bleak financial gain. Lord Rosebery, with all his fondness for America, had been much touted as a possible groom for an American bride: his friend Francis Hawley wrote to George Higgins at the time of his first visit that 'It is evident that "the Hearl" is enjoying himself, but Heaven grant that the affection with which he is regarded by the American girls may not be reciprocated by him, for most of them are the most heartless worldly [bitches] that can be imagined.'[1] But Rosebery in the end married an English Rothschild; and it was against a more conventional aristocratic background of celebrity and menacing poverty that, in April 1874, Lord Randolph Churchill married the American Jennie Jerome at the British Embassy in Paris, following an intense and passionate courtship. Lord Randolph's father was not present, but his brother, the Marquess of Blandford, was. Francis Knollys, private secretary to the Prince of Wales, was best man. The bride wore white satin, before changing into a going-away outfit of a dark blue and white striped dress, accompanied by a feathered white hat. She left in an open carriage drawn by four grey horses, and with two postillions. Her sisters threw slippers at her and her mother 'collapsed weeping'. The marriage not only produced Winston Churchill, but evidence that such relationships could work on several complicated levels.

Randolph Churchill and Jennie Jerome were helped by the fact that neither was a conventional representative of his or her respective caste. Randolph, 25 years old, his exophthalmic Churchill eyes echoed in the baroque twirls of his moustache, was the younger son of the 7th Duke of Marlborough and, unusually for an English aristocrat, fiercely and critically clever. Later, he would help found the Primrose League and the Fourth Party; propound the notion of Tory democracy; as well as becoming Secretary for India, Chancellor of the Exchequer and Leader of the House of Commons. Jennie was the daughter of Leonard Jerome, a devil-may-care New York speculator who had been hit by stock market reverses in 1869 and 1873 (it is chastening to remember that the United States' runaway economic success was punctuated by shattering collapses) yet who insisted on living the life of a bohemian plutocrat, surrounded by music, racehorses and mistresses. Clara Jerome, her mother, was a steely raven-haired New York matriarch, believed to be part Iroquois Indian. Winston Churchill may have complained of his father that 'He was so self-centred no one else existed for him' – an assessment that almost anyone who knew him would have agreed with – but in the springtime of his life, he was besotted with Jennie.

His letters to her during the time of their courtship are not only extensive and incredibly frequent; they are filled with the language of helpless adoration, acquired from literature and the musty confines of the library, but applied with hectic intensity. The beauty of private correspondence in the late nineteenth century was that it could be intimate, passionate, spontaneous, freed from the bonds of social restraint. It provided a conduit for those emotions that decorum usually subdued. Randolph took full advantage of this. A letter from September 1873, written not long after their first meeting, started formally enough with a note about some partridges he wanted to send Jennie, but quickly devolved into an outpouring:

> Well it has been a great relief & comfort to me to write to you, tho I am afraid my letters have been very stupid. I shall be perfectly mad with disappointment & vexation & worry if I am not allowed to see you on Monday. I wish I knew the name of your hotel in London: it is somewhere in Albemarle Street I believe. You *must* let me know by telegraph or something; if you dont I shall think you have forgotten me, or changed your mind, & that you cld. never really have cared for me.

Tormented by 'cruel doubts' and the 'horrid melancholy thoughts [that] come into one's head', this most confident and assertive of men confessed that 'One gets at times almost mad. I shld have been quite happy if you had been allowed to write to me, but you have taken no notice of my almost despairing appeals to you for a line if only a short one at times – appeals I am sure that ought to have moved a flint.'[2] A week later, he was nearly beside himself at her tactless suggestion that he might be better off marrying one of his own kind. There was still something slightly shocking about the idea of a transatlantic relationship – an element of friction that she had chosen to exploit. 'How cld you so calmly write & recommend me to marry some English girl', he appealed. 'You have no idea how you pain me when I think you capable of imagining even for a moment that I shld ever look at or speak to again any other girl after you. I mean to marry you my darling & nobody else.'[3] A month after that, he was writing to her every other day – sometimes every day. A gloating, adolescent note crept in, when he declared, on 25 October, 'My dearest Jennie, your letters get more charming & more loving as they continue. The 2 I have received today gave me more pleasure than I can tell you. You certainly are the greatest little darling that ever breathed, & I get more conceited & stuck up every day at thinking that I have had the good fortune to win the love of one like you darling.'[4]

This was replaced a couple of days later, however, by the forensic chill of Lord Randolph Churchill with a grievance. 'For the first time, Jennie, since I knew you', he began, 'I am really rather cross with you (not that you will care much).' Why? Because – for three whole days – she had failed to write to him, leaving him abject – 'more low than a cat' – and stricken with imaginings. But worse was the apparent slovenliness with which she made reparation: 'Arriving in London I find a short line from you all about nothing & merely saying you did not find time to write oftener. Now I know very well how you pass your time, & also that you never have got any very heavy occupations on your hands and you wld be nearer the truth if you said you did not care to write.' He then went on in much the same vein, before ending with a terse 'Ever yrs. Randolph', instead of the more usual, 'Yours lovingly & ever devoted'. His P.S. added an extra chill: 'You have never sent the photographs that I have several times begged you to send, but please dont bother yourself about it as I know you have "*so much*" to do.'[5] But it is the end of this particular exchange that is so startling. No sooner had Jennie received Lord Randolph's complaint than she sent back a reply of such galvanic ferocity that Lord Randolph, the egoist, the snob, the intellectual bully, could only say in return, 'My dearest Jennie, I surrender without conditions & retreat from the battle field routed. I shall not indulge in epistolary combat with you again as I get the worst of it. I received four letters this morning the last one a crusher, & I apologize humbly & throw myself at your feet.'[6] This had nothing to do with mere rhetoric or utility. This was heartfelt.

Jennie Jerome was 19 when she met Randolph Churchill aboard the guardship *Ariadne* at Cowes. Much has been written of her panther-like good looks, her tumbling dark hair and her unwavering gaze. In point of fact, she was not enormously tall and, like her mother, enjoyed a distinctly stocky build. This, plus the essentially American firmness of her jaw, could combine with one of her trifle-with-me-if-you-dare facial expressions to produce an effect sometimes imperious, sometimes comically *farouche*. Her sisters, Leonie and Clara, were arguably prettier.

But Jennie was sexy. Time spent living with her family in Paris in the late 1860s, attending the court of Napoleon III and Empress Eugénie – with her *bals américains* – had taught her the art of being both provocative and mannerly. Her accomplishments were recognised: her piano playing, her excellent French, her horseriding, her talent for flirting. She was a sensual exotic, and Lord Randolph Churchill was besotted with her. Being by nature rude, intemperate and rashly opinionated, he was even more attracted to her whenever she cut up rough. Her fierce arrogance reminded him of himself, confirming the rightness of his choice; her sexuality made him greedy for more. And she was happy to pick a fight. She once furiously reproached him over some slight he had made against Leonard Jerome: 'I cannot tell you how deeply hurt I felt at the insinuation you gave me – as to yr having heard something against my father – I was unable to answer you or defend him – as you did not choose to confide in me – All I can say us that I love, admire, & respect my father more than any man living';[7] she made him vow not to 'indulge in epistolary combat with [her] again'; she fired off a letter which began, 'How could you write such a letter to Mama my darling *stupid* Randolph?'[8] And there were others in a similar vein. Despite his murmured disclaimer that 'I am normally very quiet, and hate bother and publicity', his ardour found a precise and validating response in her.

He was, naturally, terribly poor. As the Duke's second son, he was entitled to only those subventions that Marlborough felt able, periodically, to bestow on him. The 7th Duke's stuffy probity may have made him a favourite with Queen Victoria, but he had no capacity for acquiring wealth. Instead he had the constant burden of keeping up Blenheim Palace and its surrounding estates, as well as funding two sons and six daughters. In 1874, he was forced to sell off his estates at Winchendon and Waddesdon to Baron Rothschild. The following year, he sold the Marlborough gems in a single lot at Christie's, raising £10,000. He did his best to provide for Randolph at the time of his marriage, settling his debts and leasing a house in London, but without Leonard Jerome's active involvement the wedding could not have gone ahead. Yet Leonard Jerome was no Goelet, no Vanderbilt. Showing great forbearance, he made a settlement of £50,000 on the couple, despite his dwindling fortune and his nervousness concerning the absolute sovereignty an English husband enjoyed over his wife's money. 'It is quite wrong', he wrote to the Duke, 'to suppose that I entertain any distrust of Randolph. On the contrary, I firmly hope and believe there is no young man in the world safer, still I can but think your custom of making the wife so utterly dependent on the husband most unwise.'⁹ But there was never any suggestion that Randolph's marrying Jennie would set him up for life. She was hopeless with money and entirely profligate; it was part of her charm. Their settlement was barely enough to get by on. His income as Secretary for India, and as Chancellor of the Exchequer later on, was vital to them. But when his health and his career began to collapse, following his resignation in December 1886, the increasing ravages of illness saw to it that he rarely made any serious money again. What he did manage was – just – to hold on to Jennie, despite his selfishness and excruciating unpredictability; and despite the dismal oppressions of Blenheim, which they visited frequently and which beset her for years.

Whatever its formal brilliance as a monument and as a piece of architecture, Blenheim was rich in the drab compromises of day-to-day living. Sometimes it was the thick tumblers Jennie found set out on the dinner-table ('the kind that we use in bathrooms') that lowered her spirits. Sometimes it was something altogether larger – the rank atmosphere of English high society, trapping her in the great house, where, as she wrote to her mother, 'Tonight I suppose will be like last night. Some playing whist or billiards or working. You can't imagine what gossip & slander people talk, really to my discreet ears it seems quite incredible – everyone is pulled to pieces . . . it is usually the women who back bite – but the men I assure you are quite as bad.'[10] And again,

> The fact is I *loathe* living here. It is not on account of its dullness, *that* I don't mind, but it is gall & wormwood to me to accept anything or to be living on anyone I hate. It is no use disguising it, the Duchess hates me simply for what I am – perhaps a little prettier & more attractive than her daughters. Everything I do or say or wear is found fault with. We are always studiously polite to each other, but it is rather like a volcano, ready to burst out at any moment.[11]

When she stayed in Paris with Lord Randolph's brother, the Marquess of Blandford, she was encumbered by fresh disadvantages. Not only was Blandford, according to Lord Randolph, notorious for holding the floor interminably; he could not be trusted not to molest Jennie. 'What a bore Blandford must have been with his theological arguments', he wrote to her in March 1874:

> We have heard them so often at home over and over again, & I always change the conversation when he begins on that tack, or philosophy or politics. I know he is naturally clever, he is awfully badly read and talks the greatest nonsense on all three subjects, tho I have no doubt as it was new to you you were all vy. much impressed. Bye the Bye [he continued, sidling up to his main point], dont try and flirt with him as he is *un peu mauvais largué* & would be the first to come back to England and tell my family & everyone that he thought you rather fast & that you did not care for me etc.

Anxious candour then had to contest with fraternal loyalty: 'I am vy. fond of him, but I know him vy. well & *et je connais ses petits défauts*, so be careful dearest what you say to him or tell him.'[12] But even if she did escape from Blandford, she found herself caught up in other, more public embarrassments, such as Lord Randolph's refusal to let her attend the Prince of Wales's 'Pack of Cards' Ball in 1874, on account of the terrible expense of the costumes. Sometimes she was entangled in a family disaster, such as the one that compelled her to flee to America with Lord Randolph in 1876, followed by the banishment of her and the rest of the Marlborough household to Ireland as retribution for Randolph's behaviour in the Aylesford Scandal. In this latter, Blandford had, with grim inevitability, provoked Lord Randolph into – very nearly – destroying his own reputation in an attempt to save his brother's. Everything arose from the scandalous flight of the Marquess with his lover, Lady Aylesford, to Paris in 1875. There they lived as Mr and Mrs Spencer, producing an illegitimate son in 1881. Things worsened critically when Lord Randolph tried to blackmail the Prince of Wales into taking Blandford's side against the wronged Lord Aylesford. Intimate correspondence between the Prince and Lady Aylesford somehow got into Lord Randolph's hands; he menaced the Prince with exposure. In prompt response to his son's insane act of partisanship, the 7th Duke was forced by the royal family clean out of England and, in 1876, to take the post of Viceroy of Ireland. At great expense he transported the entire Blenheim household, including Lord Randolph, over to Dublin, where they were sufficiently out of the public gaze. By this means, Blandford and Lord Randolph were granted a reprieve, eventually returning, not a bit chastened, to England.

And sometimes there was simply the ineffable tedium of the English to cope with, Jennie Churchill suffering from the well-bred American woman's propensity to believe herself axiomatically more brilliant, accomplished and full of *savoir-vivre* than the English: complaining, among other things, that other house-party guests were intimidated by her talents and by her erudition, and that 'There is no doubt that English people are dull-witted at a masked ball, and do not understand or enter into the spirit of intrigue which is all-important on such occasions.'[13]

The point has been well made, though, that the education of daughters in nineteenth-century America was more often than not

ornamental and centred around accomplishments which would win a husband: such as music, dancing and foreign languages, and these were usually acquired with the aid of governesses or at one of the few fashionable schools for young ladies. In the nineteenth century the wealthier classes did not take seriously the education of daughters: governesses and finishing schools were more a proof of parental income and pretensions to gentility than an attempt to give daughters a thorough academic training.[14]

Jennie was not a Vassar or Bryn Mawr girl. Her gifts were as much spontaneously native as rigorously acquired. George Cornwallis-West argued (not without bias; he was her second husband, after all) that

Like many well-bred American women, she had the will and the power to adapt herself to her immediate surroundings. She was equally at home having a serious conversation with a distinguished statesman, or playing on a golf-course. A great reader, she remembered much of what she had read, and that made her a brilliant conversationalist, but although gifted with extreme intelligence, she was not brilliant in the deepest sense of the word. She was not a genius.[15]

Nor, for that matter, were all well-bred Englishwomen dullards. Indeed, the American writer Richard Henry Dana, making a tour of England in the mid-1870s, was often refreshingly entertained by the level of discourse on offer, declaring, 'I continue to be surprised at finding how much the English ladies know of, and how well they talk on, national and political questions in comparison with the American ladies I have known.'[16] What Jennie found so irksome, and what led her to believe herself especially gifted, was the cultural horror the upper classes expressed towards any undue advertisement of cleverness – that uniquely dingy interpretation of good manners that led another American writer to recoil, many years later, from 'the spectacle of English gentlemen being conscientiously banal under the impression that it represents a magnificent discipline'.[17] Jennie was a product of New York and Paris, after all, and had grown up surrounded by more expressive social conventions. How could she have enjoyed the perversity of not wanting to seem clever?

Nevertheless, she persisted. The marriage survived. British society's larger concerns were also well served. However you looked at it, the Churchill–Jerome marriage entirely subjugated Jennie Jerome and her fortune to the values of the aristocratic world in which Randolph Churchill operated. There was no challenge to taste or propriety. She had given way to the dominant principle; the States, in its feisty way, had yielded like a surly novitiate to Britain and the correct relationship had been maintained.

So far, so good. Then, a few years after the Churchill–Jerome marriage, Miss Mary – usually known as Minnie – Stevens of New York hitched herself to an untitled relation of the Marquess of Anglesey amid scenes of such tremulous and extravagant optimism that it looked as if the concept of the Anglo-American marriage could scarcely fail. Minnie, the daughter of a well-to-do New York hotelier called Paran Stevens, was tall, dark-haired, handsome and possessed of a firm aquiline nose, betokening a powerful will. Later, the 9th Duchess of Marlborough would write bitterly and critically of Minnie's 'hard green eyes' and their worldly reductiveness, but in 1878, the year of her marriage to Captain Arthur Paget, she was still busily concerned with assuring herself of her place in European society.

Her background did her no favours. Paran Stevens, who died in 1872, had indeed been a prominent figure in New York. His Fifth Avenue Hotel (one of several he owned) was both practical and chic, as this extract from a letter from Francis Charles Lawley to Lord Rosebery implies: 'As regards Hotels in New York, it is customary for young English swells, to whom money is no object, to go to the Breevort House. It is a good but old-fashioned and very costly Hotel, and I should counsel you to go *par préférence* to the Fifth Avenue Hotel which is a typical American caravanserai.'[18] On the other hand, Mrs Paran Stevens, Minnie's mother, was twenty-one years Paran's junior and widely believed to have been one of his chambermaids. Keen to escape the provincial opprobrium of New York, the two Stevens women left the year Paran died, to find Minnie a fit husband somewhere, anywhere, in Europe.

Minnie knew what was out there and what she wanted. Initially, she and her mother drew a blank with the Duc de Guiche (who found out that Minnie wasn't as wealthy as he'd been led to believe); then with Lord Rossmore; finally, with Lord Hay. But with Captain

Paget, a floridly successful army officer, grandson of the 1st Marquess of Anglesey and close friend to the Prince of Wales, they hit, if not the target of their original ambitions, at least one that would do. By this stage, Minnie was in danger of losing her lustre. She was in her mid-twenties; for five years, she had been fairly openly and unsuccessfully touted around Europe; her mother lacked breeding. But Minnie's native attributes sustained her. Entertaining and physically glamorous, she had become a favourite with the Prince of Wales and many others in society. Ralph Nevill, son of Lady Dorothy Nevill, observed years later, in a simmering mixture of prejudice and envy, that 'Only within the last thirty years have Americans found it easy to get into English society. Like the representatives of the Hebrew race, they largely benefited by the affability of the late King, who had a particular liking for visitors from across the Atlantic, especially if they were rich or beautiful.'[19]

This was exactly the chance that Minnie could exploit. She was that kind of visitor from across the Atlantic who most stimulated the Prince of Wales, long before he ascended the throne. Novelty was also on her side. The chronic threat of the Prince's boredom could be countered to some extent with this new, wealthy, voluptuous, American-speaking personage. Lt-Col J.P.C. Sewell, one of the Prince's many intimates, observed that Minnie possessed 'Large and particularly brilliant grey-blue eyes, and a mouth which displayed determination and power without losing its mobility. She had an almost imperceptible American accent, looked English and dressed like a Frenchwoman.' Regretfully he added, 'Mrs. Paget's defect – if she had one – was that, not uncommon among her countrywomen, of unpunctuality'[20] – a general failing duly noted by Ralph Nevill, who protested that 'One objectionable habit introduced by American ladies into English society is unpunctuality, which vulgar people have always been apt to think fine. The Victorians, who had traditions of politeness inherited from another age, had no idea of standing for this sort of thing.'[21]

But Minnie was too worldly, too sexy, too smart to be brought low by her own unpunctuality. She fitted perfectly into the *louche* international environment of Marlborough House. The 6th Duke of Portland knew her, yearningly, as 'a beautiful American lady'. The Prince-King enjoyed an almost excessively long correspondence with her and was prompted to admit that he enjoyed the company of American women so much 'because they are original and bring a little fresh air into Society. They are livelier, better educated and less hampered by etiquette.'[22] When the time came for her to marry Arthur Paget, she was so well entrenched in London society that she could be warned by that same society of the deficiencies of her British husband-to-be: specifically the vice of gambling. Two weeks before the wedding, the Duchess of Argyll took the trouble to write to her, 'Let me congratulate you; you know that my one wish is you should be happy, & I trust you may be so. The love of gambling is terribly strong I have always heard & you will have to use all yr. influence to make your husband keep to his promise.'[23] There was, without a doubt, the uneasy possibility that Captain Paget was marrying Minnie for her money ('She was, it is true, wealthy; but wealth in those days was not the *passe-partout* it has since become', Lt-Col Sewell carefully noted[24]). But Minnie was shrewd enough and tough enough, tempered in the exigencies of the preceding years, to be able to cope with anything a mere husband could throw at her. July 1878 duly saw the marriage of Captain Paget of the Scots Guards to Mary Stevens at St Peter's, Eaton Square. Both the Prince of Wales and the Duke of Connaught were present. The Domestic Chaplain to the Queen officiated and Arthur Sullivan played the organ.

The real surprise – and more startling than this cheerful acceptance of an American adventuress by the London *ton* – was the way in which the Stevens–Paget wedding affected the consciousness of New Yorkers and of the *New York Times* in particular. 'Miss Stevens', began the *New York Times*, with an exquisite mixture of decorousness and asperity,

has, indeed, had a career socially which vies with that of Lord Beaconsfield politically, and points, like his, to the signal success attending well-directed efforts toward an object ardently desired. The man or woman who, 15 years ago, should have predicted that the daughter of the late Paran Stevens would have been married under these conditions, and that his widow would, on the day of the wedding, receive a visit of congratulation from the Prince of Wales, would indeed have been deemed as visionary as one who predicted for Disraeli, in his *Vivian Grey* days the Premiership of England.

This was gratifying enough. But then, going on to nod to those Americans who took advantage of the fact that it was now easier to travel abroad than ever before – easier to visit Europe and 'catch its tone' – the paper announced that foreign travel 'is producing a class – rapidly increasing, too – of persons who are at odds with their own country. There is no denying that to wealthy idle people Europe offers advantages which it is impossible at present to command here. While it is easier for the average man or woman to rise in life here, there is more to be got by those who do rise there.' Following this tentative echo of Lord Bryce's philosophy ('The same man having a higher point to reach to find himself among the first . . . eventually makes more of himself'), it continued:

> 'What is there for a woman to achieve here?' said a clever, ambitious American woman to an Englishman. 'Nothing, absolutely nothing' . . . The rich brilliant American woman thus labors under a sense of the absence of an end to achieve which satisfies her imagination, whereas the same woman would, in England, not merely have social aims to satisfy, but further, would probably be keenly interested in her husband's political career, which here is probably confined to recording an annual vote.

This was radically shocking. At a time when America was entering the first great phase of its maturity, when its economic power was becoming truly exceptional, when its position as the world's greatest republican democracy made it a beacon for the dispossessed and the progressive, how could the *New York Times*, America's single most prominent publication, entertain these seditious thoughts?

It was caught in a dilemma. In words that might as well have been written by Elizabeth Drexel Lehr or Edith Wharton, it argued,

> Rich American men, more especially New York men, are essentially commercial. Their wives and daughters, on the other hand, are not, and the cultivated among them are apt to find a more sympathetic and congenial companion in a foreigner who

has left college only to travel and cultivate his mind and body than in a young man who has been stuck down to business at sixteen.

It then added, 'Here, then, we have the history of the wave of Anglo-mania which has swept over fashionable society, and is to be seen in fifty ways in Fifth-avenue mansions in Winter and Newport cottages in Summer.'[25] A dismal truth had been articulated. American society was not only dull; when it came to the question of those privileges available to women of good breeding, it was inegalitarian.

The relationship between England and America was even more equivocal than it first appeared. The attraction of England was not simply reducible to a title, in return for which one was stripped of one's fortune. There was – unbelievably – an opportunity for emancipation and self-actualisation that didn't exist back home. As it happened, this lopsidedness in the structure of American smart society was still evident two generations later. Harold Acton para-phrased a rich, 1920s, American wife, complaining that though rich American wives

Were given all the money they desired, they could not help being miserable . . . because they lived among women. All their time was taken up with women's lunches, clubs, societies and charities, and they had nothing in common with their husbands. And while the American husband provided amply for his wife's material welfare, he had no real contact with her. He knew that she was far more cultivated and intelligent than himself so he put her on a pedestal. This lady was in favour of less money and more contact.[26]

Harold Nicolson, ten years on, inveighed against the habits of American hostesses:

Chatter, chatter; interrupt, interrupt. If I understood the explanation of this, I should understand more about American civilisation. Is it utter frivolity of mind, or merely a complete lack of all sense of real values? I suspect it has something to do with the position of women, or rather with the vast gulf which separates the male and the female in this continent. Women are supposed to discuss art, literature and the Home. Men are supposed to discuss business. Whatever it may be, it irritates me beyond words.[27]

Meanwhile, as Minnie Paget went on to have four children with Colonel Paget and delight the fashionable world with her gorgeous Cleopatra fancy-dress costume (its shoulder-straps made of emeralds and diamonds; the headdress studded with uncut rubies and emeralds), her mother, riding the tide of her daughter's success, returned to New York and became known for her *salon* on Fifth Avenue. After years of waiting, Arthur Paget was created Sir Arthur Paget in 1906, and Minnie could at last style herself Lady Paget. In short, the Paget relationship was, for all its workmanlike overtones, an advertisement for the apparently happy blending of American verve and finance with British caste superiority. 'I am looking forward so much to my visit to America', wrote Prince Louis of Battenberg to Mrs Paget in 1905, yielding to the temptation – late in the day – to write to this mesmerising woman in her native American: 'I shall be all October at New York . . . If I were 20 years younger I shd. expect to have a real good time with your fascinating countrywomen.'[28] The Pagets made it possible to believe that the marriage of an American heiress to a hard-up British grandee might well be an exercise in happy mutuality.

Indeed, the 1870s was the defining decade of the Anglo-American marriage. All the hard work had been done by its end: the respectability of marrying an American woman was established; the chances of the marriage persisting were seen to be reasonable; the Prince of Wales approved. In the next two decades, as the exotic became commonplace and the transatlantic steamship routes more efficient, scores of such marriages would take place.

FOUR

Behaving Badly

The trouble really started with George Victor Drogo Montagu: Viscount Mandeville, subsequently 8th Duke of Manchester. George Victor Drogo was born in June 1853, into a family whose dukedom dated back to 1719 and whose territorial holdings never quite provided the income subsequent dukes felt they deserved. By the 1870s, it was clear to the young Mandeville that he was no longer in any way financially autonomous. He would have to find money quickly and from a source without tricky complications or conditions, so that the dukedom could survive. He decided that he would go to America and woo one of the rich heiresses about whom there was beginning to be so much talk in society.

This showed an unusual degree of enterprise: rather than wait for a Jerome or a Stevens to step off the boat at Southampton, he actively went in search of a rich mate. And, as schemes went, it was a highly attractive one. First, it meant that he would enjoy the benefits of being a lone English aristocrat in a sea of young American women, and not have to fight off other, more attractive, less plainly insolvent, titled rivals. Second, the American rich were known to be prodigiously rich; and were correspondingly generous to their offspring. Third, under existing marriage laws, every single item of cash and property belonging to the woman became that of the husband, once the pair were married. Even gifts from a parent to his or her daughter after marriage became the husband's property. The Married Woman's Property Acts of 1882 and 1883 would address this iniquity – much remarked upon by the American press – but Mandeville's timing was good. He was going to have it all and be able to support himself in the style to which he was accustomed, so long as an indulgent American father saw to the needs of his wife.

It took him a few months of travelling before the 22-year-old nobleman finally met the 17-year-old Consuelo Yznaga del Valle at

the United States Hotel, Saratoga Springs, New York, in 1875.
Among the palms of this marginally second-rate resort – Rhode
Island the more chic – love grew. Consuelo was the daughter of a
New England mother and Cuban father, whose wealth was
principally expressed in the form of a plantation in Louisiana which
held 300 slave workers; and in a New York town house on 37th
Street, west of Fifth Avenue. There was evidently money in the
family, although not at Astor or Stuyvesant level and much more
prone to market upsets. Still, Consuelo was vivacious, musical,
charming and pretty. According to the 9th Duke, Consuelo's mother
was 'devoted' to music, displaying a fine mezzo-soprano voice, while
Consuelo, 'who played the piano divinely, used to accompany her'.[1]
Pictures of Consuelo reveal melting brown eyes surmounted by a
cloud of fair hair; and a humorous mouth increasingly scored by
strain and sadness as the years pass. The American press noted that
Mandeville 'has been brought before the public by the interest he
has taken in polo, and by his skill in playing that game',[2]
emphasising his talents both as a man of leisure and as one able to
find the most extravagant ways in which to waste whatever money
was available to him at the time.

His father, former Lord of the Bedchamber to Prince Albert,
allegedly expressed horror at the prospect of his son marrying 'a
little American savage'. But on 22 May 1876, Viscount Mandeville
and Consuelo Yznaga del Valle were married at Grace Church,
Manhattan. The ceremony was performed by the Revd Morgan Dix,
DD, and the bride wore a white satin damask brocade, richly
trimmed with lace. Diamond stars sat in her hair. Minnie Stevens
was a bridesmaid. No fewer than 1,400 people attended and, as the
New York Times observed, 'One of the most brilliant affairs of the
season was the marriage at Grace Church, yesterday, of George
Victor Drogo, Viscount Mandeville, to Miss Consuelo Yznaga. Lord
Mandeville is an English nobleman, who has visited the country
several times.'[3]

Unfortunately, Mandeville was also a gilded fraud: dissolute,
spendthrift, incorrigibly selfish. No sooner had he sired the young
William Drogo Montagu, Lord Kimbolton ('Little Kim', as he was
known; eventually to become Lord Mandeville and finally, the 9th
Duke) than he disappeared into a netherworld of partying, gaming

and drinking from which only self-interest and a need to stay ahead of his creditors would occasionally extricate him. A mere two years into her marriage, Consuelo Mandeville felt obliged to reply thus to a dinner invitation from Frances, Countess Waldegrave: 'Mandeville is yachting with the Gosfords and his movements are so erratic that I think I had better say he won't come with me on Sunday, nor on the 13th either. He so often disappoints me that I generally make my mind up to go without him.'[4]

Twin daughters were born after Little Kim, but Mandeville's growing family bored him. His delinquency grew worse. By the turn of the decade, Mandeville (plain 'Kim', as Consuelo addressed him) had begun a highly visible affair with the music-hall singer, Bessie Bellwood. Her signature song was 'What Cheer Ria', and in a vigorous display of fealty she once punched the nose of a cabman who was demanding that his Lordship pay an outstanding bill. Mandeville ended up in court as a witness.

It seemed to make no difference to him that he had married a woman who was talented, glamorous and exotic in her own right, and profoundly popular with the Marlborough House set. 'One of the first ladies I knew who came across the Atlantic (God forbid that I should call it the Herring Pond!) was Consuelo, Duchess of Manchester', wrote the Duke of Portland, affectionately. 'When she arrived in London, as Miss Yznaga, she took Society completely by storm by her beauty, wit and vivacity, and it was soon at her very pretty feet.' Consuelo was a favourite of the Portlands, to the extent that no party was complete without her 'dear and witty presence. Looking back, I can still see everyone crowded round her at tea-time, all happily laughing at her continual flow of witty and amusing stories delivered in a charming, soft Southern voice, for she was a native of Cuba.'[5]

Consuelo's virtues only served to point up Mandeville's deficiencies. Fidelity and the pleasures of home continued to disgust him. Poor Consuelo's letters to him became more desperate. The mid-1880s saw her obliged to write to her husband care of The Pelican Club, Denman Street, off Shaftesbury Avenue: 'Dear Kim [began one letter], Although I feel it is quite useless to write to you and expect an answer yet I cannot bear to let month after month go by without hearing anything of you. There is not a day that I do not

think of you and long to see you and the children and I talk of you. I
want them to love you and remember you though they can see so
little of you.' She ended pathetically, 'Yr. Loving Wife, Consuelo'.[6]
Occasionally, the Viscount condescended to spend time with his
children, usually at the Tandragee residence, in County Armagh. But
his presence was scarcely restful. The 9th Duke recalled how his
father taught him to ride, while on one of his fleeting visits. 'Father
ordered Jelly' – the head coachman at Tandragee – 'to bring an
unsaddled pony round. He lifted me up, put me on its back, and
then gave the astonished pony a resounding slap to make it gallop.'
Inevitably, the Viscount's young son fell off the animal. His father
showed no sympathy but rather gave him a 'hearty smack' by way
of teaching him to hold on tighter and not not be so stupid as to fall
off. Then he struck the horse again. His son fell off. This happened
several more times until at last, 'In sheer self-defence I clung so
tightly to the pony that it was impossible to unseat me; and that was
how my father taught me riding.'[7]

Then Mandeville would be off again, having pocketed some more
of the income sent to Consuelo by her father and, at the same time,
having failed to give any indication of his future movements.
Consuelo loathed the chill, damp and awful solitude of Tandragee ('I
am like Marianna in the Moated Grange, did you ever read that old
fashioned romance?' she wrote to Lady Desborough; 'This place is
the most lovely romantic but melancholy spot on earth miles from
civilization of any kind'[8]) and dreaded any obligation to stay there,
especially if such an obligation was open-ended and impossible to
quantify. 'Why haven't you answered my last letter', she begged
Mandeville as one solitary August stay drew to its close. 'It is very
unkind as you must know how anxious I am to hear from you,
besides I must make some plans for the winter. I cannot endure it
alone at Tandragee I should die of loneliness. You blame me for
sending yr. letters around to friends but where on earth can I send
them when I don't know yr. address. If one of the children were
dying I could not telegraph to you.'[9]

By 1886, after ten years of marriage, the Mandevilles were leading
separate and increasingly desperate lives. Consuelo's principal
function was to bring up the children and, mothering her own
husband, act as proxy banker to Lord Mandeville's excesses. 'Here is

your allowance due tomorrow', she began, stoically, in a letter she wrote to him from France. 'If you will leave instructions how to send it to you I will endeavour to arrange it. I was sorry you would not say goodbye to me the other day when you were going away for so long and I wish you had seen the children.' Despite everything, she signed herself, 'Affecly yours, Consuelo'.[10] The son and heir, Little Kim, similarly yearned for his father's affection and, after the event, tried to memorialise the shambles of their family relationship. 'I always cherished a profound admiration for my father', he wrote, 'and he did his best to inspire me with some of his indomitable courage and pluck.'[11] But the terrible sadness of Consuelo's position remained like a cloud. And in 1889, the courageous, plucky Mandeville was declared a bankrupt, his address at the hearing given uncertainly as 'Charlotte Street, Bedford Square, late of Victoria Street, Westminster'.

What made matters worse was the fact that he was not alone in his depravity. What might have passed off as a peculiar instance of deplorable human failing became, instead, the perceived characteristic of an entire class, once it had been repeated. And in the case of the Marquess of Blandford – subsequently 8th Duke of Marlborough – the iniquities at the heart of the marriage trade were every bit as bad as those displayed by Mandeville.

Blandford had already destroyed what was left of his reputation a year after the marriage of his brother, Randolph Churchill, to Jennie Jerome: the Aylesford Scandal of 1876 and its resultant dreary banishment and social stigmatising more or less enshrined Blandford's unfitness as a human being. In 1883, three years after the return from Ireland, Blandford's wife 'Goosie', having suffered his cruelties long enough – and borne him four children – divorced him. That same year, Blandford succeeded to the title and, as the 8th Duke of Marlborough, continued the programme of frantic material depredations initiated at Blenheim by his father – because, as with the Devonshires at Chatsworth, or the Baths at Longleat, or the Manchesters at Kimbolton, you could never escape the importunings of the family seat.

More or less built by 1724, Blenheim Palace is a huge, amber-stone Baroque masterpiece, as extravagant as a dining-table centrepiece and overwhelmingly large, its sense of drama generated by Vanbrugh, its adventures in architectural form and scale courtesy of Hawksmoor. So wonderful is it that over the first 150 years of its existence, it became an authentic and iconic national monument. It also became colossally expensive to maintain. Even before the arrival of the profligate 5th Duke in 1817, Blenheim – with over 200 rooms, hundreds of staff and thousands of acres of associated land – had become a fiscal nightmare. Once the 5th Duke had squandered the family fortune on books and plants, there really was nothing left for subsequent generations but retrenchment. The 5th Duke himself ended up, in 1840, 'living in utter retirement at one corner of his magnificent palace, a melancholy instance of the results of extravagance'.[12] The 6th Duke did nothing to buttress the Marlborough finances other than try to sting visiting tourists for a five-shilling entrance fee. By the time the 7th Duke assumed the title in 1857, the Spencer-Churchills were suffering an extreme form of that punishment visited on so many aristocrats: having to reconcile their place in society with a shamingly inadequate income.

So, in 1881, having thoroughly squandered the proceeds of the Waddesdon sale and the Marlborough gems disposal, the 7th Duke began the wholesale dispersal of the magnificent Sunderland Library, which had been in the family's possession since the mid-eighteenth century. By the summer of 1882, he had managed to auction off some 18,000 volumes, netting himself nearly £60,000. But this prodigious assault on the Marlboroughs' heritage was trumped in 1886 by the 8th Duke's sale of 227 of Blenheim's finest works of art, including paintings by Titian, Rembrandt and Rubens. Even Lord Randolph was scandalised by his brother's vandalism, but to no avail. The sale raised around £350,000, all of which was duly spent on introducing electricity into Blenheim, putting up orchid houses, wiring in an experimental telephone system. By 1888, the 8th Duke was involved in an affair with the torrid Lady Colin Campbell and had effectively created a world shaped entirely after his own murky inclinations: a world consisting of arcane scientific experiments, running repairs to Blenheim, orchid-breeding, and daring sexual high jinks. It was all extremely costly. He needed still more money in order to satisfy his manias. As with Lord Mandeville, America beckoned.

In the summer of 1888 the 8th Duke sailed for New York, ostensibly to pursue a scheme to recover gold by the 'transmutation of metals'. Some of his contemporaries in England by now regarded him as a truly brilliant man, hobbled only by the lurid shortcomings of his personality. Lord Redesdale claimed that the Duke was 'a youth of great promise marred by fate, shining in many branches of human endeavour, clever, capable of great industry, and within measurable distances of reaching conspicuous success in science, mathematics and mechanics'.[13] Others, by way of contrast, simply wrote him off as the 'Wicked Duke'. When he arrived at New York, the American press correctly identified him as 'badness personified'. He was supposed to have brought with him no fewer than thirty-five distinct pieces of luggage, prompting the additional comment that 'Everything his Grace brought with him was clean, except his reputation.'[14] None the less, Leonard Jerome took it upon himself to introduce the 8th Duke to the New York sporting set, with the fateful consequence that the Duke encountered Mrs Lillian Hammersley, widow of a wealthy New York businessman and distantly connected with the New York Patriarchs. In a display of typically relaxed candour, Leonard Jerome then wrote to his wife that 'The Duke has gone off this morning . . . to the Adirondacks trout fishing, to be gone a week. I rather think he will marry the Hammersley. Don't you fear any responsibility on my part. Mrs. H is quite capable of deciding for herself. Besides I have never laid eyes on the lady but once. At the same time I hope the marriage will come off as there is no doubt that she has lots of tin.'[15]

Mrs Hammersley, although conventional enough looking in many ways, with a pleasantly straight nose and her dark hair neatly piled up, was reputed to weigh as much as 160lb and to wear a beard and moustache. She was also believed to be worth $5 million, which fortune enabled her to feed her pet spaniels on chicken fricassee and macaroons. Marlborough closed in, and by the end of June 1888, the couple were wed. 'Well', wrote Leonard Jerome, 'Blandford is married! I went with him to the Mayor's office in the City Hall at one o'clock today & witnessed the ceremony. The bride was looking very well & all passed off quietly . . . I shall go down to the *Aurania* in the morning to see them off.' There was a hitch in that nearly all the local priests, of whatever faith, refused to marry Blandford, a divorcé. 'However they found a parson of the Methodist persuasion who consented to perform the service. An hour ago it was all done.'[16] Back the new Duchess came to Blenheim, where the Duke promptly spent £40,000 of her fortune on re-leading the roof, electrifying more of the palace, and installing central heating, even in the stables and the dairy. She paid for the vast Willis pipe organ that now towers over one end of the Library and, necessarily, for some more of Marlborough's journeys to Lady Colin Campbell.

It was calamity for the new Duchess. Her East Coast vanity had made her yearn after the title of Duchess; her desire as a woman to take a man she found attractive and perfect him led her to the altar. But once at Blenheim, she was treated every bit as badly as the Duke of Manchester had treated Consuelo Yznaga. She was now merely a cash cow with an American twang and unappealing facial features. Marlborough shut himself in the laboratory he had had built at the top of the palace, before occasionally removing himself to Venice and physical sin. Lily, Duchess of Marlborough – she had repudiated the name 'Lillian' on account of its discomforting chime with 'million' – suffered the quiet mockery of the English upper classes, among whom, inevitably, was Lord Randolph Churchill. He commented to his mother, during a visit, 'I don't think the Duchess Lily looking at all well in health, and the moustache and beard are becoming serious.'[17]

By now, though, the Randolph Churchills' own marriage was starting to come apart. The family may have done their penance in the wilderness of Ireland, but it was Jennie Churchill who had used her special skills of seduction and flattery to mend relations with the Prince of Wales on their return. Her reward, for a while, was to take comfort in Lord Randolph's increasing political success. By 1880, his oratorical skills had led him ever more securely into the heart of government. He made a speech about Bradlaugh, the atheist MP, which was, as Jennie wrote, 'a tremendous success. Everyone was full of it and rushed up and congratulated me to such an extent that I felt as tho' I had made it. I'm told that Tumtum [the Prince of Wales] expresses himself highly pleased and the result is that we have been asked to meet both him and the Princess tomorrow, at a dance Lord Fife is to give.'[18]

Lord Randolph's workload increased. Jennie was left to repine at Blenheim, from where she stoically wrote, 'Dearest Randolph, you must not be unhappy about me, for I shall soon get used to my solitude, particularly now that I have taken up my music & painting.'[19] In 1882, he suffered an illness so severe that Jennie took him away to the States for a holiday. From there, Leonard Jerome expressed his loyalty to Randolph in this touching message to his wife: 'I think Jennie is wonderful for him, he draws on her strength . . . I love having them here. I believe completely in R.'[20] By 1884, the Randolph Churchills and the Prince of Wales were able to dine in the same house without undue hostility. By 1885, Randolph was Secretary of State for India and by 1886, he was Chancellor of the Exchequer, Leader of the House of Commons, and both he and Jennie were dining at Windsor with the Queen, who observed that 'Lady Randolph (an American) is very handsome and very dark.'

But Randolph Churchill could never live a fulfilled life: like his brother, he was essentially cursed. At this point in his life, restored to intimacy with the royal family, enjoying a position of genuine power at the heart of government, married to one of the most glamorous women in society, he was also suffering from chronic syphilis, and was beginning to lose his marbles.

Frequent arguments broke out at the family home in Connaught Place. In 1886 it was rumoured that the couple, whose social existences independent of each other had long been remarked upon, were due to separate. Physically estranged from her diseased husband, Jennie took Count Charles Kinsky as a lover; but she managed the affair – as she did the rest of her numerous *amitiés amoureuses* – with just enough correctness to placate the scorn of her friends and acquaintances. Randolph consumed great quantities of potassium iodide and mercury. Jennie pursued her doomed relationship with Kinsky, maintaining a smiling face most of the time. The burning attraction of the first years was long gone; Randolph – wayward, self-obsessed, increasingly unhinged – was behaving more and more like a Churchill.

And at the end of December 1886, he talked himself out of government for ever, resigning on a specious point of principle. This stroke of ineptitude at once crippled an already strained family budget, which at that point had to accommodate his living expenses,

the expenses of his socially prominent wife, and the costs of bringing
up two sons – young Winston Churchill and his brother, Jack.
Fleeing the scene of the disaster, Randolph immediately went on a
trip to Italy, during which time Jennie wrote to her sister Leonie,

> I feel very sick at heart sometimes. It was such a splendid position
> he threw away. In the bottom of my heart I sometimes think his
> head was quite turned at the moment & that he thought he cd. do
> *anything*. However, 'It is an ill wind that blows *no* good' and R
> has been so much easier and nicer since that I ought not to regret
> the crisis. He writes most affectionately & very often & I hope all
> will be righted when he returns.[21]

It was not. His salary as Chancellor of the Exchequer had been a
munificent £5,000 per year. Now, that was gone; and, with it, many
of the lines of credit the Churchills had grown to depend on.
Moreover, his illness was worsening.

One might argue that the Churchills were victims; that Blenheim
was the real villain: insatiable and capricious, a mistress that no one
could abandon, an avid and morality-free third party in every
marriage. Indeed, the economic problems that gripped the British
aristocracy in the second half of the nineteenth century expressed
themselves over and over again in the Gainsborough-like image of
lovely but useless broad acres (which brought in savagely shrinking
profits) lapping against the steps and terraces of a great house
(which swallowed immense sums, both in capital expenditure and in
day-to-day running costs). The alarming disjunction between income
and outgoings took visible shape in the stone and mortar of the
family seat.

But what if one worked back from the single biggest predicament?
What if one could fix the family home? Wouldn't one then stand a
chance of fixing everything else? Marlborough was not the only one
who tried. Consider, by way of comparison, the relatively sane
Hesketh family. The marriage of Sir Thomas George Fermor-
Hesketh, Bart, to the delightfully rich Florence Emily Sharon of San
Francisco, two years after the Paget marriage, was either a cynical
exercise in propping up the family fortunes or, more reasonably, a

heroic rearguard action, taken in order to preserve an exquisite Hawksmoor house at Easton Neston, Northants, plus the land that went with it.

The situation was, after all, quite straightforward. Easton Neston pre-dates Blenheim by a few years, and is somewhat smaller. But Hawksmoor's genius animates it just as much as at Blenheim. His original double-height Great Hall was a work of art in its own right. The Great Staircase is still a mildly crazed exercise in unfolding volumes. The Garden Hall is light-filled and sweet. Even the basement has charm. It is a masterpiece, and it was clear at the end of the 1870s that, left to his own devices, Sir Thomas George Fermor-Hesketh was perfectly incapable of generating the kind of money that he and Easton Neston needed in order to live in an appropriately high style. What was he to do? In order to think more clearly, in 1880 he went on a round-the-world cruise. The answer came to him as he reached San Francisco: he would, of course, marry a rich American girl. Everything seemed to point that way. As one of his travelling companions wrote at the time, 'Nothing could exceed the Kindness and Hospitality of everyone we met . . . I met a Miss Crocker, a very nice girl with heaps of the needful. Francis got hooked on and has landed her I think. Hesketh has two on hand, both very nice . . . Can't make up his mind . . .' Time went by. Hesketh's friend continued: 'I must say American girls are very pretty, dress well, have good feet, lots of fun & very sharp. Some have lots of money.' At last, 'To my astonishment Hesketh has been making love to Miss Sharon, a most charming girl, daughter of Senator Sharon. The engagement was announced in the *Chronicle & Newsletter*.'

Sir Thomas George had chosen well. Florence Sharon was both beautiful and tremendously wealthy: her father, William Sharon, had made a fortune in mining stocks and real estate, and lived in one of the biggest private houses on the West Coast. Hesketh married the girl at once, along with a dowry estimated at $2 million, and transported her back to Easton Neston, where she spent much of her father's wealth on reviving the house with wood panelling, Corinthian pillars, Spanish wrought iron, comfortable chairs, chinoiserie, a suspended-domed tester bed, and the lowering of the ceiling in the Great Hall. Two sons were born in quick succession. A stuffed bear that Sir Thomas George had shot in Canada was placed terrifyingly by the front door. The idyll grew stale, however. Lady Hesketh was bored with Northamptonshire and began to spend more time in London. Sir Thomas stayed at Easton Neston, tinkering in his workshop and constructing what may have been the first motor car to have been made in England. The marriage never ended, as such; it merely persevered, with both parties living independent lives. But at least the house and grounds had been saved for the next generation.[22]

Or, at the other end of the scale of celebrity, consider George Nathaniel Curzon, who married Mary Leiter, daughter of an American retailing millionaire, in 1895. Curzon's hunger for money was every bit as fierce as that endured by the Dukes of Marlborough and Sir Thomas George Hesketh. He had considerable personal outgoings and a passion for old buildings. His marriage to Mary was written off by many at the time as a piece of gross opportunism, enabling him to refurbish the family home (Robert-Adam-designed Kedleston Hall) and live as Viceroy of India in high pomp. Famously, though, Curzon's relationship with Mary was intense and heartfelt – shot through with Curzon's own brand of monomania, but sincere. She submitted to him completely ('Wholly absorbed in her husband's career, she had subordinated her personality to his to a degree I would have considered beyond an American woman's power of self-abnegation' was the 9th Duchess of Marlborough's appalled footnote[23]) and he ended up loving her for it. The day before he left for India to take up the position of Viceroy, at the end of 1898, he made a speech to those friends and acquaintances who had thrown a farewell banquet in his and Mary's honour. In it, he drew attention to the way Lord Elcho had paid warm compliments to Mary in his, earlier, speech, speaking of her as

typifying the Anglo-American alliance. I care not tonight to speak of the alliance of nations or the national flag. All I know is that the American flag for me is all stars and no stripes. Enough for me is the alliance of individuals – that alliance by which I have now been honoured for nearly four years – an alliance which in its wider manifestations has added to English society many of its greatest ornaments, and has endowed a number of English husbands with the most incomparable of wives.[24]

Typical of Curzon, his peerless oratory both concealed and revealed a deeper truth: he adored his wife. After her death in 1906 – her life given in the service of his viceroyalty – he could not look on a picture of her without bursting into tears.

On the other hand, once she had died, he blatantly helped himself to the contents of the trust funds the Leiter family had established for the three Curzon daughters and began buying, leasing and renovating properties all over the country: Hackwood House in Hampshire; Tattershall Castle, Lincolnshire; Montacute in Somerset; Bodiam Castle, Sussex. Tattershall was being menaced by American property developers. Its fireplaces had been torn out and were sitting in an antique shop in Bayswater, awaiting shipment to the States. Montacute needed proper plumbing and central heating, as well as the presence of Curzon's mistress, Elinor Glynn. Bodiam had to be shored up and left to the nation. It was all expensive. Some of this frenzy was to appease his anxieties about his own status, about his true greatness, by acquiring what amounted to a parody of a grandee's landed entitlement. Some of it was an authentic compulsion to save Britain's heritage for the future. And the money needed to keep up this mixture of imposture and charity then led him to foully betray Miss Glynn in order to marry a second rich American, Grace Elvina Duggan – 'a queer mixture of *naiveté* and *malizia*', according to the 27th Earl of Crawford – in 1917.

Grace was, on the face of it, a celestial retribution for Curzon's light-fingeredness with his first wife's money. She was very rich, very attractive and spent most of their marriage away from him. She failed to produce a son and heir. She stopped Curzon's monthly cheques from time to time. And she traduced him, starting a long affair with Sir Matthew Wilson. 'You never write and I hardly know if I have a wife', Curzon appealed pathetically to her in 1924.[25] Her energetically shabby treatment of the former Viceroy of India was thus a repayment for the rapine he had inflicted on the Leiter fortune; and, indeed, could be seen as a kind of revenge on behalf of an entire generation of American cash cows. But, as he would have countered, it was his contribution to the architectural and historic fabric of the nation that justifed whatever fortunes were spent in his name. When he and Mary Curzon were both entombed at Kedleston, the buildings would persist. Property was unsentimental.

FIVE

The Americans Settle In

Given the increasingly chaotic state of many great country seats, country-house living in England was becoming an increasing test of endurance. Part of its discomfort was a straightforward by-product of the agricultural depression of the last decades of the nineteenth century. Part of it was down to the realisation that, over the preceding years, the traditional English country house had become, sensuously speaking, something of a liability. Evelyn Waugh's novel *A Handful of Dust* is, among other things, a meditation on the last days of such houses. In it, Tony Last, the sentimentally indulgent owner of a Victorian Gothic extravagance known as Hetton Abbey, is well aware of the issues. 'In some ways, he knew, it was not convenient to run; but what big house was? It was not altogether amenable to modern ideas of comfort; he had many small improvements in mind, which would be put into effect as soon as the death duties were paid off.' The ceilings are penetrated by damp; there is an 'antiquated heating apparatus' that fitfully warms part of the house. Elsewhere, there is only 'the cavernous chill of the more remote corridors where, economizing in coke, he had had the pipes shut off'. The great hall is lit by a hideous brass and wrought iron gasolier, modified to take 'twenty electric bulbs'. A large, permanent and ageing staff is needed to keep the place going. Everybody other than Tony Last hates the building. In short, Hetton symbolises folly, obsession, discomfort, a futile expense of energy and capital. It is a legacy without value and its Victorian values are what make it impossible to defend to the modern world.[1] And, as with all Waugh's caricatures, it has a pertinent grounding in reality.

The Victorians tended to see draughts, large, inefficient fireplaces, oil lamps, distant kitchens and an absence of bathrooms in a house as moral virtues in themselves. Although gas and electric lighting made their mark in the cities, Colza oil lamps were simple, cheap, provided a clean, clear light and provided work for the lamp man of the countryside. Even when electricity became commonplace, it sometimes hit a buffer of personal prejudice among the owners of great houses. Sir Ambrose Elton, owner of Clevedon Court in Somerset and director of the Clevedon Gas Company, refused to allow electricity into the building out of loyalty to his chosen source of energy. The exquisite Tudor Melford Hall, in Suffolk, had to wait until after the First World War to get electric lighting – and then only in three of the rooms.

Down in the servants' areas, a sprawling, smoky, black-leaded kitchen range – as opposed to a tidy suburbanised cooker – was taken as a sign of good character. It is a mark of the sorry decay of Waugh's Hetton Abbey that, by the end of the book, 'most of the kitchen quarters . . . were out of use; an up-to-date and economical range had been installed in one of the pantries'.[2] The only proviso was that if one stuck to the old, baronial kitchens, one had to have servants energetic enough to rush the congealing food down yards of passageways into the dining room before it became completely inedible. Central heating, similarly, was nothing other than a perversion of the natural order. John James Stevenson, author of *House Architecture*, wrote in the 1870s that central heating produced a 'close and unwholesome atmosphere'; while Lord William Cecil opined that 'When one is putting in a central heating system, comfort must go to the wall.' Even the Rumford Stove – invented by the American Count von Rumford at the end of the eighteenth century and capable both of concentrating heat and reducing fuel consumption – was mean, middle class and lacked honesty. Instead, householders struggled with a mixture of badly drawing open fires and chronic fumes, necessitating the addition of a Dr Arnott's Chimney Ventilator ('Truly invaluable advantages: SMOKEY CHIMNEYS – NO CURE – NO PAY') or a Grant's Patent Rotary Windguard for the Prevention of Downward Draughts and Smokey Chimneys. And these pointless verities persisted. As one diehard Victorian survivor expressed it in 1910,

Old panelled rooms and the ancient floor-timbers understand not the latest experiments in electric lighting, and yield themselves to the flames with scarce a struggle. Our forefathers were content with hangings to keep out the draughts and open fireplaces to keep them warm. They were a hardy race, and feared not a touch or breath of cold. Their degenerate sons must have an elaborate heating apparatus, which again distresses the old timbers of the house and fires their hearts of oak.[3]

When it came to washing themselves, traditionalists preferred the intimacy of a tin bath brought up to their dressing room or bedroom and toilingly filled with water from cans. They preferred solitude and familiar surroundings to the dank horrors of a corridor leading to a bathroom used by others – strangers, even. They liked fairly hot, hand-transported water, rather than tepid, unreliable water from a distant boiler. They preferred 'the round bath tub placed before the fire with its accompanying impedimenta of hot and cold water jugs, soaps and sponge bowls, towels and mats'. They liked, above all, to follow their own proclivities. Even when an enlightened household did have the money to install and enjoy bathrooms, the barbarity of old habits could still show through. Lesley Lewis grew up in the Edwardian comfort of Pilgrims' Hall, Essex, a substantial Regency house, with gardens, a park and servants, in which her parents had converted a small bedroom into a private bathroom. Nevertheless, 'If you had seen it just after my father had used it in the morning you would have got a shock, and the governess once nearly fainted.' His regime involved a wooden bowl of soap nearly a foot across, as well as a stiff brush made of vegetable bristles. Using the brush, he then worked up a mountain of lather with which he covered himself, as if to shave his entire body. This done, he got into the bath to remove all the foam.

He explained the process to me once in some indignation when I ventured to ask him how he made such a mess. The idea of doing the soaping in the bath and then wallowing in the same water would, he said, be unbelievably disgusting. The lather flew everywhere, often reaching the ceiling, and was a delicate pink if he had cut himself shaving, or spinach-green if he had been using a plaster for lumbago.[4]

The Victorian and Edwardian upper classes enjoyed various complex relationships with the body – distrustful, self-indulgent, austere and voluptuous – which contemporary ideas of hygiene found difficult to modify.

Such spartan appointments could, in other words, be a product of choice, of Victorian rectitude – or of reduced funds. The 9th Duke of Manchester ('When it became my turn to succeed to the title, and a balance sheet was drawn up, it showed a debit balance of two thousand pounds a year'); the 7th Duke of Marlborough (pushing through an Act of Parliament to deprive the Marlborough heirlooms of their protected status, so that he could sell them); the 4th Duke of Sutherland ('mooning about like Scrooge and muttering about money') were just the most visible and visibly titled of that newly indigent aristocracy to whom only the last option was available. Right into the 1930s, the 8th Duchess of Buccleuch was being forced to come to terms with the hopelessly retrogressive Drumlanrig Castle in Dumfriesshire; and felt herself 'lucky enough to have one or two bathrooms . . . because the house had been a hospital in the 1914–18 war, so that it had been given a certain amount of hot water. We wouldn't have had bathrooms otherwise. Electric light was just coming in . . . but not many bedrooms had bedside lights; one had a light in the middle of the ceiling.'[5]

But at least these dukes and duchesses had properties to inhabit. A more worrying difficulty came in the form of those landowners who simply abandoned, sold off or, worst of all, destroyed their ancestral homes. It was becoming clear that not only were most of the great London palaces – Devonshire House, Dorchester House and so on – facing extinction; many lesser manorial country properties were facing ruin. Between 1870 and 1919, some seventy-nine mansions were destroyed in England, Wales and Scotland. Others were got rid of as expeditiously as possible. The Earl of Westmorland sold off Apethorpe Hall in 1904. The Phelipses were reduced to offering Montacute House 'for scrap'. Oxburgh Hall was locked into a cycle of decline that would see it being sold in its entirety after the Second World War. Hengrave Hall was bought cheap by a cotton-spinner from Lancashire. Houghton Hall was offered for sale but found no buyer, before being rescued by the 5th Marquess of Cholmondeley and the Sassoon millions. As Diana Mosley wrote, of the Mitford family home at Batsford, Gloucestershire, 'We all knew that as soon as war was over Batsford was going to be sold because we were too poor to live there. We hoped the war would go on forever.'[6] Or, as Tony Last's egregious brother-in-law puts it, determinedly articulating the worst fate in the world, 'You'll find it quite easy to sell [Hetton Abbey] to a school or something like that. I remember the agent said when I was trying to get rid of Brakeleigh that it was a pity it wasn't Gothic, because schools and convents always go for Gothic. I daresay you'll get a very comfortable price and find yourself better off in the end than you are now.'[7]

The preservation of a great home, conversely, was an event of some note. When Lady Sackville came into money at the start of the 1900s, she at once enlisted the help of Jeffrey, the Knole estate carpenter, and began to tear apart Knole's Elizabethan wooden panelling in order to furnish the place with electric light. The great house had had some kind of steam central heating since 1825, but Lady Sackville managed to extract some cash from her hapless lover, Sir John Murray Scott, with which to plumb in a more up-to-date central heating system, as well as install a tricky butterfly-pattern ventilator in every window in the palace, allowing fresh air in but not the freshly centrally heated air out. 'I enjoyed immensely installing the electric light at Knole [she later wrote, cheerfully], and putting in all the modern improvements I could. I made bathrooms with old Jeffrey (and his Son) who was an admirable carpenter – Everybody says that I made Knole the most comfortable large house in England, uniting the beauties of Windsor Castle with the comforts of the Ritz.' Marvellously enough, 'I never spoilt the old character of Knole. I insisted upon having Electric Light about 1901. And we were the second house which had a motor-car.'[8] So startling was this programme of modernisation that other, less well-off owners of great houses visited her to pick her brains for practical advice as to how to make their own improvements.

This was the situation: a mixture of ongoing terminal threat broken by fitful investments and renewals. But what if one evaded the conventional procedures altogether? What if one cut the Gordian knot and, instead of searching vainly for an American heiress with money enough to refurbish the family seat, simply sold one's share of England's heritage directly to an American?

For an American to buy up an old English property was both a boon and an invitation to disaster. On the one hand, it meant that a great house, even if acquired by a tasteless Midwesterner, would be saved. On the other, it meant that the same house would quite likely be heartlessly modernised, perhaps vandalised, to suit deracinated American tastes. And – worst of all – an updated, comfortable, modernised great house would act as a slinking reproach to all the impoverished, run-down houses in the neighbourhood. True, the number of properties involved was small, especially in comparison with the numbers of young women who came over as brides for the British aristocracy. But the impact was real. An American bride could always be justified as a functional import into the mainstream of an old family; absorbed into the rest of society and diminished accordingly. But a great house that fell into the hands of an American was both a territorial loss and a metonymic reminder of the shifting power relationship between the two countries.

One of the first to take advantage of the British aristocracy's declining fortunes was American-born William Dodge James. James was an explorer, big-game hunter, yachtsman and the inheritor of two American fortunes – one in railways and one in metal-broking. He had travelled to Somaliland (now Somalia), Arabia, Afghanistan and the west coast of Africa. He had climbed Mount Tchad-Amba in Abyssinia (now Ethiopia) and mapped the upper reaches of the Khor Baraka in Sudan. He was also a thorough-going Anglophile, a member of the Royal Yacht Squadron, and had built almshouses for the poor seamen of Cowes, on the Isle of Wight. By 1891, he was ready to settle down, buying himself West Dean Park, near Chichester, for £200,000.

The modestly handsome house at the centre of the 8,000-acre estate had been built by James Wyatt at the start of the nineteenth century. Ninety years later, the fashionable architects Ernest George & Peto remodelled it for James and his late-Victorian sensibilities. At once it became an advertisement for the transfiguring power of wealth. The house acquired a tower, a *porte-cochère*, a whole wing of bachelors' rooms. Inside, a comfortable, vaguely Jacobean oak hall was installed, with a minstrels' gallery in which Cassano's Orchestra could play. Instead of draughts, dim lighting, cold food, occasional hot water and a nagging sense of physical deprivation, all was ease and comfort. Two steam engines, hidden in a building behind the stables, powered the generators. These, in turn, lit no fewer than 364 incandescent light bulbs. The American Elevator Company put in a hydraulic lift to bring the food up from the kitchen to the dining room. There was central heating, constant hot water, an automated steam laundry and built-in water pumps with hydrants throughout the house in case of fire. There was also, in later years, a transatlantic electric telegraph button which Edward VII ceremonially pressed to signal the opening of a sanatorium in Montreal. In the time it took the builders to move in and move out again, the house was translated wholesale from a substantial Regency villa into a modern mansion.

Luckily, this turned out to be a broadly tolerable reinvention of the English country house, partly because it was done with a degree of good taste; more importantly, because it was in the service of English high society. The Duchess of Marlborough may have voiced the paradox – some years later – that while 'Englishmen marry American women . . . hardly any Englishwoman can be induced to marry an American man'; but in a reversal of the conventions governing British titles and American inheritors, William James had actually married Elizabeth Forbes, daughter of baronet Sir Charles Forbes and niece of the Countess of Dudley, in 1889. 'Mrs James', *The Times* noted, 'is considered one of the best actresses in society, and is distinguished for her charm and wit.'[9] The wedding was in Knightsbridge; the Prince and Princess of Wales gave a sapphire and diamond brooch as a wedding present. Thus James's tastes and enthusiasms were almost wholly reinterpreted in the English idiom; he was married into the British aristocracy; and, to confirm the relationship, the delicious Mrs James became one of Edward VII's mistresses.

Moreover, James's additions to West Dean were no worse than those imposed on, say, Polesden Lacey, by that other Edwardian favourite, Mrs Ronnie Greville. If anything, they were slightly less shocking. Mrs Greville's genius was to cause only moderate offence by taking a respectable eighteenth-century Surrey house (which had recently been worked over by an Edwardian architect) and in 1906, getting White, Allom & Co. to put a reredos, plundered from a Wren church, in the hallway; and an entire *salone*, of *c.* 1700, torn from a Venetian *palazzo*, in the saloon. A mock-Jacobean picture corridor was created on the top floor; a Louis XVI-style tea-room sat in one corner of the ground floor. There was proper central heating and plenty of bathrooms. The overall effect was opulent, wildly variegated and, in its sybaritic warmth and convenience, usefully and anachronistically contemporary. William James was enterprisingly restrained in comparison – an example of the kind of new American landowner who would cause the otherwise infallibly stern Ralph Nevill to admit that 'Though there is much abuse of the New Rich at the present time, they alone seem able to keep alive the ancient glories of old-fashioned country life.' In truth, 'The incursion of wealthy Americans has undoubtedly saved quite a number of old English country houses.'[10]

So appealing was the mixture of *calme et luxe* that James negotiated into the fabric at West Dean that Princess Alexandra stayed there alone – the first time she had spent the night in the house of a commoner – in 1896. The magazine the *World* sourly commented that

> Until this surprising 'end of the century' not even a Prince had stayed in any but the most important houses. At one time the visit of a monarch or an heir-apparent made the greatest of great ladies, great statesman or great courtiers, greater. But by degrees the line has been drawn lower and still lower, until at last of very few rich people it can be said that they have never had Royalty under their roofs.

Its Parthian shot was especially vindictive: 'Mrs James fulfills the conditions of her time – she is amusing.'[11] Tumtum didn't care. He even redoubled the royal approval by snubbing the 6th Duke of Richmond during Goodwood Week, 1899, and staying at West Dean in preference to Goodwood House. The 6th Duke was a prude; but the Jameses were suitably relaxed about the presence of two of the Prince's *petites amies*. West Dean Park represented the virtuous modern principle. It was possible to modify without transgressing the limits of taste. It was possible to be American, but to assimilate oneself into the English country house-owning classes.

Not everyone was like James, however. A mere 50 miles away, there was one super-rich American immigrant whose talent to unsettle derived in particular from the way he combined all the worst possible characteristics of an American invader with an ardent desire to be lovingly accommodated by the society he had invaded. He was deeply Anglophile, historically minded, powerful, artistically sensitive, fantastical, crass, ruthless and unerringly offensive. He was the greatest and most difficult of all the transatlantic accumulators of property: William Waldorf Astor.

'Since 1863, when Anglo-Americans became the fashion', wrote T.H.S. Escott at the end of the century, 'millionaires from the New World have often appeared among us . . . But it is comparatively seldom that the father makes, as Mr. Astor has made, England his family home.'[12] Indeed. But much remained to be added to this observation. The great-grandson of John Jacob Astor, founder of the family fortune, William Waldorf was born in 1848 and, as heir to the $170 million Astor estate, grew up in conditions of scrupulous emotional austerity. He had prominent, slightly staring eyes, a well-defined jawline and a wide mouth over which a walrus moustache draped like a pelmet. He was not immediately handsome. He also had a genius for causing, and taking, offence. A series of excursions into American politics had left him disenchanted as well as widely disliked by the electorate of New York. 'Apart from his money', wrote the New York *Sun* after one of his dismal attempts to win a seat in local government, 'Mr Astor is one of the weakest aspirants who ever sought the suffrages of a New York constituency.'[13] Escape from the shame of Tammany Hall came in the form of a posting as American Minister to Italy, in the course of which he fell in love with European culture and its time-aged guarantee of authenticity. It was there that he realised – like Henry James – how much in thrall he was to European notions of civilisation, added to which his wife, Mamie, was a radiant social success at the court of King Umberto I. But when his posting came to an end in 1885, he was forced to return to New York and its stifling contemporary nullities: the Knickerbocker and Tuxedo Clubs; the straining one-upmanship of Newport, Rhode Island; his Aunt Caroline Astor (as in Mrs Astor's 400) who would not yield in her belief that she was, Vanderbilts notwithstanding, the queen of New York society. Mocked covertly by his social peers and explicitly in the yellow press, he may well have said around this time that America 'was not a fit place for a gentleman to live'.

Filled with grievances, he decided to export his wife and four children to England in 1890. He returned to Newport the next summer, only to become entangled in a preposterous feud with his Aunt Caroline over who, exactly, had the right to style themselves 'Mrs Astor': Caroline, the old Mrs Astor, or William Waldorf's wife, Mamie, the new Mrs Astor. This spat – parochial, meaningless, stiff with wounded *amour-propre* – was entirely characteristic of his relationships with the rest of the world. It also marked the end of his time in America. Having suffered at the hands of the society magazine *Town Topics* – its Olympian scorn generated by the spectacle of Astor unsuccessfully battling with his own aunt – he went back to England in the autumn of 1891, the same year that William James settled on West Dean. Here Astor vowed to begin a new life, publicly asserting that he was emigrating so as to keep his children safe from kidnap threats; inwardly furious at the lack of respect accorded him by his own countrymen.

Italy would have done as well; better, perhaps, given his responsiveness to Italian refinement and his acceptance by the court in Rome. But Italy was small time. England, for all its artistic limitations and dismal weather, was none the less the *omphalos* of a great empire and blessed with a caste system whose complexities and taxonomies would have been endlessly fascinating to a man whose capacity for strict mental organisation allowed him to play chess blindfolded. Before long, he was renting Lansdowne House in London and Taplow Court in Buckinghamshire, while he pondered his next move.

This was to take him to a first-class address at 18 Carlton House Terrace, and, more conspicuously, to Cliveden, which he bought from the Duke of Westminster. 'The possession of the Duke of Westminster's Cliveden by an American millionaire symbolises the other social changes effected at several points on the Thames shore', said Escott, noting that, following a fire in 1845, Cliveden 'was raised up again by its ducal owner [then the Duke of Sutherland], himself to be succeeded by another duke, his Grace of Westminster, who in 1890 sold it to the inevitable money-king from the States. In

Mr. Astor's hands Cliveden has become the riverside social center for the fashion and intelligence of the Anglo-Saxon world.'[14] Better than that, even: 'Nor is there any Yankee plutocrat who has dominated republican Paris to the same extent that Mr. Astor sways monarchical London, Sutherland house and Cliveden.'[15] What Escott's typically uncritical résumés failed to point out was that, among other things, Astor was engaged in a fierce quarrel with the Duke of Westminster over the return of the Duke's Cliveden guestbook; that he had publicly humiliated Captain Sir Berkeley Milne RN at a musical evening – a slight that ostracised him from the Prince of Wales's circle and led the *Saturday Review* to write, 'We only regret that the gallant servant of Her Majesty [Sir Berkeley] so far forgot his dignity as to accept a second-hand invitation to the house of this purse-proud American whose dollars could not save him from the contempt of his countrymen';[16] had tried to sue the *Daily Mail* for defamation and had lost; and had, in 1892, absurdly given out the news of his own death so as to garner hypocritically fulsome tributes (adducing his 'learning, his talents, and the noble qualities of his heart which were his most distinguishing characteristics') from the American press.

Astor was fulminating with interior conflicts. Cliveden was one attempt to settle them. He was believed to have spent $6 million on refurbishments and alterations to his newly acquired Charles Barry Italianate sprawl with its magnificent Thames prospects. As part of the renovation scheme, and in a portent of future trends, he inserted a rococo dining room taken entirely from a French palace built for Madame de Pompadour. At around the same time, he was establishing himself more permanently in London. He bought a house at 2 Temple Gardens, on the Embankment. This he dismantled, before erecting – at a cost of $.5 million – the tangible exerior representation of the inner life of a super-wealthy aesthete with well-developed paranoid fixations. Designed by John Loughborough Pearson and completed in 1895, Astor's new version of 2 Temple Gardens was an exuberant Tudor–Gothic fantasy filled with more security devices than an average bank. Thus, on the one hand, it was an exercise in self-centred whimsy: the newel posts on the main staircase were provided with carved figures of characters from *The Three Musketeers*, as well as from Astor's own novels,

Valentino and *Sforza*; while the Great Hall which served as Astor's office was 35 feet high, surmounted by a frieze depicting fictional and historical characters whom he admired – Lorenzo Medici, Bismarck, Captain Cook, Dante, Pocahontas – and overtopped by a romantically ornate hammer-beam roof in Spanish mahogany. On the other hand, in response to the real-world threats that Astor perceived to be all around him, the place had an elaborate electric alarm and integrated locking system which he could operate from a single button beside his bed. He also habitually slept with two loaded revolvers on his night table and when Daisy, Countess of Warwick, came to visit, he led her to a strongroom containing bags of sovereigns. 'I keep ten thousand pounds in cash in this room', he said. 'You never know when you may want money or when cheques may be difficult to cash. A man who succeeds as I have done has many enemies, and if he is wise he avoids all risks.'[17] The Countess of Warwick was determinedly forgiving ('In spite of his fierce hectoring manner and harsh questionings, I felt that he really liked me and was anxious to be friendly'[18]), but the fact of the matter was that Astor's behaviour, as often as not, was bizarre, solipsistic and rebarbative.

He did, at least, feel safe and reasonably fulfilled in Temple Gardens: an office-cum-town house built entirely to his own taste. The castellations, massively solid woodwork and deep, ashlared walls spoke of security; the historicist's level of architectural detailing confirmed his sense of taste; the often breathtaking levels of craftsmanship expressed his wealth back to him. And, unlike Cliveden, it owed nothing to any previous owners. Cliveden, conversely, was a problem. It was big in the wrong kind of way; it was too flashy; it didn't look English enough. The impulse to dig deeper remained within him. When his wife died in 1894, any last impulse to reconnect with the States went. His children were marked down for Eton and Oxford. By now he owned the *Pall Mall Gazette*, the *Pall Mall Magazine* and the *Pall Mall Budget* – getting the *Pall Mall Magazine* to publish a complex and essentially spurious genealogy proving his connection to the Spanish counts of Astorga. In 1899 he became a British subject, appalling his former compatriots. *Cosmopolitan* called him a 'blot on the escutcheon'; while *Town Topics*, his tormentor over the 'Mrs Astor' crisis, found him guilty of 'amazing caddishness and snobbishness . . . the richest man that America ever owned and that disowned America'. He was burnt in effigy in Times Square, a placard reading 'Astor the Traitor' hanging round the dummy's neck. His riposte was to buy the flag from the United States frigate *Chesapeake* and present it to the Royal United Services Institution. This act was at once decried as a 'deliberately malicious affront' and caused the *North American Review* to argue that for the British authorities to go further than mere citizenship and 'confer a peerage on this gentleman would, perhaps, do more after this episode to weaken their cherished entente cordiale with America than any other small mistake they might make'.[19] Fretting about Astor's chances of getting a title was, as it turned out, premature. Having alienated many members of society, he went on to conceive a fierce antipathy towards the stupendous Mrs Keppel, the King's last mistress. 'When Mrs George Keppel had sunk to the life of a public strumpet [he subsequently wrote], I no longer invited her to my house. She was then commencing her relations with the King to whom she reported my omission. When I speak of her relations with the King it is only fair to add what all the world knows, that the King has been physically impotent for more than twenty years.'[20]

There was a helpless perversity in the way Astor pursued his dreams. He wanted an English title and an English nobleman's country seat, while disapproving of the ways of the nobility. 'I don't like your English aristocracy', he once announced with startling candour to the Countess of Warwick. 'They are not educated, they are not serious, but they do interest me. I want to find out all about them; I should like to be able to explain them to myself. I don't think anybody understands them, and I want to do so.'[21] He wanted a great house, but got bored with his properties and moved out of them almost before he'd settled in. He wanted a life of tasteful privacy but kept picking vulgar public fights. And he was, despite his wealth and his evident largesse, fatally ungenerous when he felt his own interests were compromised. 'Walled-off Astor', as he was known, was a prime representative of those American estate owners who were 'fond of elaborate stone work, terraces and walled gardens, have little respect for ancient trees', according to Ralph Nevill, 'and are apt to aim at producing a spick-and-span effect not in character with old country mansions. Where possible they divert old rights of way and are too often intolerant of allowing visitors privileges which in old days they enjoyed without molestation. All this is curious', Nevill concluded, yielding to the bait of cheap sarcasm, 'considering the reputed democratic tendencies of citizens of the United States.'[22]

Plainly, having a neighbour such as William Waldorf Astor would pose many an interesting challenge to the more established families of the area. Nevill, again, lamented the disappearance of the traditionally benign countryside autocracy. The 'rich city men' and 'American millionaires', increasingly making their mark on the countryside, were 'but seldom in touch with those living in the neighbourhood of great mansions'.[23] Even William Waldorf's own grandson was unable to give him the benefit of the doubt, describing a meanly inflexible dullard who would have made the Duke of Wellington seem spontaneous and carefree in comparison. 'His weekend parties in the country', wrote Michael Astor, 'planned many months in advance, lacked that sense of *joie de vivre* which the word "party" is supposed to suggest.' Guests were told exactly at what time to arrive. When they did arrive, a secretary (or Waldorf's daughter) met them, showed them their rooms and told them 'where, and at what time, they would assemble before meals. The rest of the weekend was according to a schedule, short periods set aside for walking, driving, resting, eating, and finally sleep.'[24] T.H.S. Escott's assessment that Astor was pre-eminent among Yankee plutocrats in Victorian and Edwardian society was right, in the sense that he had invested more and striven harder than any of his coevals; and dramatically wrong, in the implication that Astor enjoyed popularity or, indeed, much social influence. His monomaniacal struggle to transform himself into a landowning English gentleman was, effectively, doomed by its own willed intensity. And his greatest purchase, Hever Castle, in Kent, was still to happen.

Meanwhile, the marriage trade went on. Within twenty-five years of the Paget wedding, there were so many marriages between well-heeled American women and British grandees that it became difficult to enumerate them all. An American publication called

Titled Americans listed – at the start of the First World War – over 450 American women who had married into European aristocracy. According to Nevill, *Titled Americans* 'was a sort of "stud book" to the eligible aristocracy of our continent, the names, characteristics, antecedents, and money qualifications of a selected number of young men being most fully set forth within its pages'. It contained a useful rubric of additional breeder's notes, such as: 'Family very poor', 'Enjoys a small allowance' and 'Has sown his wild oats' and could be used as 'a species of catalogue to the desirable young men in the Continental and English marriage markets'.[25]

Despite Nevill's deferences to continental marriages, the majority of these alliances were British–American. Lord Willoughby de Eresby (subsequently 2nd Earl of Ancaster) married Miss Eloise Breese of New York; Lord Alastair Innes-Ker married her sister, Anne. Lord Sholto George Douglas, son of the 9th Marquess of Queensberry, married an American actress, Miss Loretta Mooney, while in the United States. His family, already staggering under the weight of the Bosie–Wilde affair, had him clapped in jail, pending tests on his sanity. The marriage lasted a quarter of a century, none the less. The 6th and 7th Viscounts Exmouth married Americans, while the 19th Earl of Suffolk married Margaret Hyde Leiter, sister of Mary Leiter, Lady Curzon. Pennsylvania girl Ava Willing first married an Astor, then divorced him and married the 4th Baron Ribblestone. New York beauty Miss Adèle Grant married the Earl of Essex. Pauline Whitney, daughter of the Secretary of the US Navy, married Almeric Paget, Baron Queenborough. The 2nd Marquess of Dufferin and Ava married Florence Davis of New York, in 1893; she later divorced him and went on to marry the 4th Earl Howe in 1919. And the 4th Marquess of Anglesey married Mary Livingstone King, from Georgia.

Minnie Paget, entrepreneurial and socially mobile as only a beautiful American could be, was credited with arranging the marriage of Alice Thaw of Pittsburgh to George Francis Seymour, Earl of Yarmouth and son of the 6th Marquess of Hertford. The Hon. Lyulph Ogilvy, son of the 5th Earl of Airlie, married Edith Boothroyd of Colorado. The 5th Baron Camoys married Mildred Sherman of New York City. The 5th Baron Decies married two rich Americans in succession: a Gould and a Drexel. The 9th Earl of

Sandwich, Lord George Cholmondeley, the 7th Earl of Essex and the Hon. Alfred Anson all married Americans. And so it went on.

With hindsight, of course, the indefatigable Ralph Nevill saw it for what it was. Writing at the very end of the great age of the Anglo-American marriage, he said,

> At the present day marriages between young men of ancient family and young women of none are regarded as being highly desirable, provided that the latter has plenty of cash. This has been largely produced by the American invasion, which really dates from the days of the Second Empire, when the Empress Eugénie showed herself well disposed towards ladies from the United States, for which reason the Imperial balls were sometimes called by the envious 'Bals Américains.'

An old-fashioned romantic snob, like his mother, Nevill clung to the idea that the upper classes should enjoy higher standards of self-discipline than their inferiors; and was hurt when they failed to do so.

> Curiously enough, though in England laments at the Americanization of society are often heard, the Transatlantic invasion seems on the whole not to have affected the habits of the people at large. It has however had a certain influence upon the English aristocracy, a considerable portion of which has unconsciously assimilated various American ways and notions, especially as regards money being the main object of life. If, as Carlyle said, the modern hell is the hell of not making money, the making of money to an unlimited extent is certainly the modern Yankee heaven.[26]

But, as Edward VII so well understood, an aristocracy without money was scarcely worth the effort. Much of the perverse deliciousness of the patrician way of life came from its imperative to make ends meet, wrestling with its craving to appear above all things financial. The main thing was somehow to maintain the pretence that America was submitting to England: that the headlining depravities of the Dukes of Marlborough and

Manchester, Curzon's wily plunderings, were justified in that they reminded the world of who was really in charge.

But then, did bad initial motives invariably lead to a bad marriage? Was there any relationship between initial affection and subsequent happiness, when a British nobleman married an American heiress? The insistence modern culture places on the primacy of romantic love would have seemed wilfully fastidious in 1880. Love was something of a luxury in all classes, whose marital choices frequently had to combine a degree of attraction with a substantial interleaving of utility. The worst that anyone could claim was that marriages among the patrician orders sometimes took the ingredients of pragmatism and necessity to unusual lengths. Besides, spontaneous love affairs, when they did occur, could only happen in an environment rich with chaperones, busybodies, prigs and minders – a situation in which the young couple might spend no more than a few hours alone in each other's presence before finding themselves walking down the aisle. Even if you were in love, the opportunities you had to get to know your beloved before marrying him or her were heavily rationed; a great deal had to be taken on trust.

When an Anglo-American match clearly sprang out of true desire, rather than a need to get one's hands on the money, it could either stumble on – as with the Randolph Churchills – or prove every bit as disastrous as a marriage of convenience. Lord Francis Pelham-Clinton-Hope, brother to the Duke of Newcastle-under-Lyme, notoriously fell for the 'piquant' soubrette, Miss May Yohé, towards the close of the nineteenth century. Originally from Chicago, Miss Yohé, whose singing voice was famed for its thrilling loudness as well as its extraordinarily narrow range, was pert, brunette, un-moneyed, liked to announce of her parentage that 'I can trace clear descent from the brave Nagarasette tribe of Indians'[27] and was living and performing in London when Lord Francis fell for her. Fresh from her appearance in *Dandy Dick Whittington*, she secretly married the 27-year-old aristocrat in a Hampstead registry office in November 1894, the year he was declared bankrupt as a result of gambling misadventures. For several years they were happy enough as man and wife, before, in late 1900, 'Madcap' May returned to the States to appear in a New York theatre production. The adoring Lord Francis came with her, but was soon encouraged to enjoy some tourism around the rest of the country. A well-known lothario and dry-goods millionaire, 'Colonel' Putnam Bradlee Strong, moved in on Miss Yohé (now Lady Hope) and an affair began. Lord Francis found out; the divorce proceedings took place in March 1902. The hapless nobleman had to remain seated throughout the divorce hearing, having recently shot off his own foot in an accident. Later, May Yohé married a nephew of General Smuts, while Lord Pelham-Clinton-Hope inherited the title of Duke of Newcastle – at least having the satisfaction of knowing that May would never become Duchess.

Beyond the personal interactions of husband and wife, there was a larger awareness of what this gradual inflow of American capital meant to society. Thousands of dollars were being spent on repairs and renovations to great houses, on the re-equipment of stables and coaches, on the provision of fresh pieces of patrician hardware. These were the living expenses that went with a title; and as such, they could somehow be asborbed into the general pattern of life. Once they had been dealt with, they became invisible, taken up into the general nimbus of entitlement that surrounded the aristocracy.

But the costly physical reality of a live American at a dinner party, or house party, or ball, could not be overlooked; nor could her immediate personal possessions. American women stood out. Lady Susan Tweedsmuir, granddaughter of Lord Ebury and cousin to the Duke of Westminster, noted tartly that 'Some eldest sons of peers married Americans and other heiresses, which buttressed the family fortunes at the cost of bringing in much higher standards of smartness in clothes and equipages.'[28] Or, as Lady Violet Greville put it, writing of fashionable ladies' garments being packed for travel: all

> are laid carefully in huge trunks, with their appropriate lace petticoats, silk stockings, and shoes, trunks that are like little houses in size, and sometimes divided into drawers, where all the necessary garments lie at their ease, and can be pounced upon at a moment's notice. Our American cousins have introduced this custom; and the enormous baggage of a New York belle is indeed a sight wonderful and fearful to behold.[29]

Mabell, Lady Airlie, wrote to Ettie Desborough in 1888 that she had given up trying to improve her appearance 'as a bad job – I used to be able to dress, at any rate without exciting *ridicule*. Now the very plough boys, in the fields, fall into furrows, to hide their shrieks.' This is the kind of social nervousness brought on by the company of other, smarter, brighter, less inhibited, materially wealthier, people. 'Do you ever feel', she implored, 'how much you wish you had been better educated; I so so often – . If I ever read anything that isn't pure groundwork, I am out of my depth at once . . .'[30] Jennie Churchill, quick to spot an affront, claimed that 'If an American woman talked, dressed and conducted herself as any well-bred woman would, much astonishment was invariably evinced, and she was usually saluted with the tactful remark, "I should never have thought *you* were an American" – which was intended as a compliment.'[31] And when the Countess of Warwick said about her 'coming out' in the Season of 1880, 'I was that rare thing – as rare as any *oiseau bleu* – a great heiress, for America may scarcely be said as yet to have assaulted the fastnesses of English society',[32] her nostalgia, however genteelly expressed, was for a less compromised time, a time when the competition was marginally less stiff.

There was, in short, a new social pressure being imposed by American women, with their brilliant *trousseaux*, their tendency to play the piano really well if they could, their lack of *pudeur*, their fathers who could buy swathes of Asprey's jewellery. How much of Lady Airlie's plaint was for a world free of the dollar? With the best will in the world, it had to be admitted that, however great their determination not to cause offence, American women couldn't help but wear the differentiating sheen of transatlantic wealth.

This was true even in London – a 'nation not a city', the richest metropolis in the world, a place containing 'the observed of all observers at Court and Drawing-Rooms . . . the peerless beauty and the most engaging of men at a *déjeuner dînatoire*, a *thé* or a picnic'.[33] New York wore its wealth massively and with a kind of industrial sense of organisation. The great avenues that ran down Manhattan were channels for the energy which kept the city going. London, by way of contrast, was a confusing sprawl, but there was no doubting the levels of privilege on display when the Four-in-Hand Club massed in Rotten Row; or when society paraded in

Hyde Park on a Sunday morning, filling it with drawling men in tails and top hats shone to an enamel gleam, their women sauntering behind them in yards of tulle and damask, the 'insolent carriage' shining down Rotten Row, according to the 1890s poet Theodore Wratislaw, holding as it does a London beauty whose 'heart is hard and hot with triumph'.

London's public buildings may have lacked charisma, but its private palaces – the great aristocratic London town houses filled with Lady Eastlake's 'buzz of voices from the gay crowd' – were stunning. New York may have had the drowsy heat and brilliant sunshine of Rhode Island to escape to, but London society had the entire pantheon of country estates at its feet, with their endless cycles of shooting and dinners and riding and periodic, hair-raising visits from the Prince of Wales. London had much going for it.

Yet even London society sometimes had difficulty accommodating the new arrivals. Lt-Col J.P.C. Sewell's note that Minnie Stevens 'was, it is true, wealthy; but wealth in those days was not the *passe-partout* it has since become', typically enough tiptoes round the issue before giving in and lamenting the fact that 'American hostesses of the type now inevitable in every European capital were unknown in London during the early 'seventies'.[34] That word *inevitable* carries all the weight: the certainty that not only were American women everywhere; they let you know that they were everywhere.

Lady Dorothy Nevill similarly had trouble deciding whether Americans were a good thing or not. Sometimes she adopted a fairly tolerant line. 'It was in the 'seventies', she wrote, 'that two new and powerful forces began to make their influence felt in society, for about that time Americans – of whom formerly comparatively little had been seen – began to come to London in considerable numbers, and then began those Anglo-American marriages which are now quite common.' How acceptable was this?

> On the whole, I think the influx of the American element into English society has done good rather than harm, whilst there are many old families which, both in mind and pocket, have been completely revivified by prudent marriages with American brides. At the present day, so close has the union between ourselves and

the United States become that Americans are hardly looked upon as foreigners at all, so many people having American relatives.

Naturally, the caution with which Lady Nevill voiced her approval bespoke a greater anxiety: 'In the old days things were quite different, and we rather dreaded the social influence of a people whom we did not know. Bright and vivacious, it may be with justice said that it is by the American girls we have been conquered, for she it is in reality who has brought about the excellent understanding which now exists with the great people beyond the Atlantic.'[35] As is the case with Sewell, her language gives her away. 'Bright and vivacious' the American girl may be, but Lady Nevill's dread of 'a people we did not know' sounds both excessive and at the same time all of a piece with her use of 'conquered' to describe a process of social subjugation. She sounds like a hostess grimly assuming a kind of forced levity; she sounds like someone very much in two minds.

American writers also saw the bright and the dark sides. Thanks, in part, to the Marlboroughs and the Manchesters, it became a reflex in American journalism to rage against the despoliation of honest republican fortunes by layabout grandees – to the extent, even, of impugning the royal family. At one point, the *New York American* angrily listed all the 'American Capital Being Spent to Amuse His Majesty', which it estimated at nearly $500 million – adducing some intriguing and speculative numbers, arbitrarily attached to a handful of prominent Anglo-American names:

Duchess of Manchester (feeding the peasantry) – $8m
Duchess of Roxburgh [sic] (country house parties) – $20m
Duchess of Marlborough (charities, public bazaars) – $15m
Countess of Granard (dinners and parties of all kinds) – $6m
Mrs A.H. Paget – $10m.[36]

The American journalist William Chambliss routinely complained about the 'foolish fashion' of sending the nation's dowries overseas; about the 'barter of American girls', and the 'insignificant appearance' of the average European nobleman. The *New York Times* noted that 'Dislike of the English is, on the whole, justified.'[37]

And even a group as affable and well disposed towards the British as the American Society in London could not help but applaud a writer speaking at one of their dinners, who, noting some contrasts between English and American life, lit upon the concept of aristocracy: the Americans 'had not got that. They knew its price, however, and were capable of getting all of it they wanted . . .'[38]

On the other hand, T.H.S. Escott – at one time editor of the *Fortnightly Review* – had been living peaceably in London for several decades when he declared at the start of the new century that 'Within half a generation of King Edward's instalment at Marlborough House, *la belle Americaine* had taken her place in that front rank among social forces which she has never since for a moment lost.' Warming to his theme, he claimed that, 'Historic English homes, to-day shelter bosses and billionaires from the Far West. In Mayfair, Chicago duchesses patronise blue-blooded dames, sprung from a stock old in Norman days. Surely the land of the Tricolour flag has witnessed no such transfers of tenure and of authority, no such structural transformations as these!' At last he concluded, '"Before the century is out, these clever and pretty women from New York will pull the strings in half the chanceries of Europe",' happily quoting an uneasy Lord Palmerston from 1860. But the 'Tricolour' reference, despite its genial tone, was highly charged, giving with one hand and taking away with the other. 'Across the Channel, indeed, the success may not have been maintained at the same high point as the banks of the Thames. The Americans only hold their own in the best society of France when they have well-dowered daughters to marry.'[39] Where exactly did that leave the British? Less likely than the French to marry for money, but increasingly beholden to the United States in other ways? Increasingly subject to Escott's 'structural transformations', whatever the state of the marriage market?

Part of the problem was precisely that marriageable American heiresses were, in themselves, usually so docile, pliant, obliging. They embodied, in every way, the feminine virtues. Being women in England at the end of the nineteenth century, they had no choice but to be incorporated into a society whose rules were unfamiliar and in which they had no special leverage, given that their family money went straight into the hands of their titled husbands. How could they have posed a threat?

But the very amiability of these trophies seized by marauding British grandees heightened the disquiet which they provoked. Despite the accommodating femininity of the women themselves, it was clear that society was under siege from something more relentless and unforgiving. Pleasant manners and pleasant dowries made up a seductive exterior concealing an invasive decadence. It became a part of Britain's increasing mood of self-doubt to protest, as did the Victorian bestseller Marie Corelli, that 'There is always a British title going a-begging – always some decayed or degenerate or semi-drunken peer, whose fortunes are on the verge of black ruin, ready and willing to devour, monster-like, the holocaust of an American virgin, provided bags of bullion are flung, with her, into his capacious maw.'[40] When one looked at the Manchesters or the Marlboroughs, it was difficult not to see them as evidence that the marriage trade was sordid, exploitative and proof that if it went on this way, the British nobility was doomed. Comparisons with the French, acceptable to Escott, were unhelpful to Lady Nevill.

> Whilst the English aristocracy [she claimed] were undoubtedly well advised to profit by the lesson of the ruling caste across the Channel, whose complete downfall at the time of the Revolution was largely brought about by their indiscriminating exclusiveness and insolence towards all not of noble birth, it would seem an open question whether they have not gone too far in the direction of welcoming and pandering to wealth, no matter how acquired.

This was, indeed, a threat: 'The forces of mammon have absorbed and are still gradually absorbing the influence which rank and long lineage once enjoyed. Birth to-day is of small account, whilst wealth wields an unquestioned sway.' Worst of all, as an unintended by-product of the financially advantageous Anglo-American marriage, 'An impecunious man married to a rich heiress is not infrequently reduced to something of the status of a first footman.'[41]

Lady Violet Greville knew exactly where she stood when it came to the intrusiveness of stray Americans (among others) in London society. Unlike Lady Nevill she felt no need to act even-handedly:

Now, there is no rule or reason for attendance at Court. Rich merchants, people in business; country squires; American cousins; people of no estimation except in their own; people who are never under any possible circumstances likely to be invited to State balls or parties – all these crowd and press and gather together, and think their season in London utterly wasted unless they have made their bow to the Sovereign.[42]

This was briskly dismissive enough; but it sounds positively genial in comparison with the strictures voiced by the 1st Baron Ponsonby of Shulbrede. Bemoaning the tendency of latter-day aristocrats to 'fall back on money as power they can wield with some effect', he went on to express horror at the way 'American and commercial wealth are brought in to bolster up their declining fortunes, and they welcome into their ranks many whose sole claim to prominence is the magnitude of their riches. Thus the contagion of vulgar commercialism spreads.' Worst of all was the way the miscegenated Anglo-American marriage could be seen to adulterate the blood line. The offspring of such a relationship, according to Lord Ponsonby, was a terrible kind of cross-breed, a mule aristocrat who 'has formed himself and his relations into a caste, and boasts, when it is not too palpably absurd, of his noble blood. In the direct line his mother may be the daughter of an American tradesman, and both his grandmothers and one of his grandfathers may be people of low and humble origin, but he inherits the name and can talk freely of "old family", "good birth" and "noble blood".'[43] Baron Ponsonby was the son of Sir Henry Ponsonby, Private Secretary to Queen Victoria. He was a liberal MP, representing Stirling Burghs, before becoming a Labour MP for Sheffield Brightside, as well as writing *Falsehood in War-Time* – the book that contained the maxim 'When war is declared, truth is the first casualty'. In other words, his opinions may have been vehemently held, but he could scarcely be called eccentric – any more than Ladies Nevill and Greville. The fact of the matter was that for all their vitality, dazzle and grace, the American heiresses also brought with them the dull rumour of disorder.

SIX

High Water

Having something phenomenal about it, the new influx of rich Americans naturally made its way into fiction and drama. Indeed, it was a phenomenon too well known and too much remarked upon *not* to become material for fiction. Edith Wharton famously enjoyed herself in her unfinished novel of 1937, *The Buccaneers*, in which she quietly savaged the naiveties of American womanhood and the venality of the British upper classes. Henry James just as famously discoursed on the tensions between the New World and the aristocracy of the Old in – among so many other writings – *The Portrait of a Lady* of 1881. Frances Hodgson Burnett – Manchester-born, Tennessee-raised – published *The Shuttle* in 1907: a more-or-less sanguine account of Anglo-American relations binding themselves more firmly together by means of the mystic transatlantic shuttlings of the title. The Californian proto-feminist Gertrude Atheron furiously dispatched the Anglo-American marriage trade in *American Wives and English Husbands*; and again, in *His Fortunate Grace* in which the shiftless 'Duke of Bosworth' seeks a convenient fortune at the hands of a credulous heiress. It was a fairly rich seam to work.

Anthony Trollope came at the problem with the help of numerous interrelated perspectives. He was an Englishman. He was a novelist whose work frequently existed to examine the operations of a class not his own but which persistently fascinated him. His mother, Frances Trollope, had lived in the States in the first part of the nineteenth century and published a notoriously vituperative piece of anti-Americanism, *The Domestic Manners of the Americans*, in 1832. He himself had visited the States several times during the 1860s and 1870s; there, he nurtured a great fondness for the American writer Kate Field. And in his own *Autobiography*, he demanded,

Who can but love their [Americans'] personal generosity, their
active and far-seeking philanthropy, their love of education, their
hatred of ignorance, the general conviction on the minds of all of
them that a man should be enabled to walk upright, fearing no
one and conscious that he is responsible for his own actions? . . .
Where is there wider hospitality? Where can the English traveller
find any more anxious to assist him than the normal American,
when once the American shall have found the Englishman to be
neither sullen nor fastidious?[1]

This complex of influences produced understandably mixed
results. In 1869, he had an unresolved mid-career attempt at the US
question with the relatively harmless young American, Caroline
Spalding, in *He Knew He Was Right*. The character of Miss
Spalding is counterpointed by that of her aggressively modernising
companion and fellow-American, Miss Petrie, whose attitude to
male British aristocrats is encompassed in the line 'They are
dishonest, and rotten at the core.' Nevertheless, Carry Spalding is
too decent to pass up a nobleman, and goes right ahead and marries
the somewhat underpowered Mister Glascock, subsequently Lord
Peterbrough.[2] At this point, the novel ends on a note of mild
irresolution.

Six years later, when he came to write *The Way We Live Now*,
Trollope's attitude had hardened. This time, American womanhood
was represented by the mature, defiantly plain-dealing, sometimes
rapacious, Mrs Hurtle. The mistress of limp Englishman Paul
Montague, Mrs Hurtle is described as 'a witch of a woman'. As with
Wharton's equally deracinated Countess Olenska, Mrs Hurtle is a
poisonous exotic in a room full of domestic breeds. Her baffling
admixture of charm and charmlessness manifests itself almost at
once in her observations about the English Channel ('How very
English it is – a little yellow river – and you call it the sea! Ah – you
never were at Newport!'), the scale of life in England ('things are so
small') and her own ambitions ('I hate little peddling things. I should
like to manage the greatest bank in the world, or to be Captain of
the biggest fleet, or to make the largest railway'). But she is also
magnetising. Paul Montague yields to her sensual allure, is
compromised by a visit to Lowestoft and has to fight his way out of

this unforeseen squalid romantic entanglement so that he can pursue the sensible Hetta Carbury. 'How full of beauty', thinks Hetta to herself, 'was the face of that American female – how rich and glorious her voice in spite of a slight taint of the well-known nasal twang – and above all how powerful and at the same time how easy and how gracious was her manner!'[3] Mrs Hurtle is both delicious and representative of a malign condition – sympathetically tragic, a woman whose narrow grasp of materiality proves both a weapon and a fatal flaw.

By 1880, Trollope had finished *The Duke's Children*. The American invasion was now in full swing. Some of its shocking novelty had worn off. A different kind of woman was required. This time it was to be Isabel Boncassen, the personification of the virtuous principle – at least in comparison with Mrs Hurtle. The daughter of an American who was 'a man of wealth and a man of letters', Isabel is not only inordinately pretty – 'the prettiest young woman either in Europe or America' – but possessed of an astonishing vitality:

The way in which she could speak with every feature, the command which she had of pathos, of humour, of sympathy, of stature, the assurance which she gave by every glance of her eye, every elevation of her brow, every curl of her lip, that she was alive to all that was going on – it was all this rather than those feminine charms which can be catalogued and labelled that made all acknowledge that she was beautiful.

Moreover, she speaks 'with no slightest twang'. Young Lord Silverbridge is captivated, generating the heat necessary to move the plot forward. Completely English Lady Mabel Grex – poor, uncertain of her own desires, lumbered with a collapsing family seat, attracted to Silverbridge but hopelessly emblematic of the dwindling material status of the British nobility – spits that 'I should not have been a good friend to him if it ends in his marrying this Yankee'. Silverbridge's father, the staggeringly hidebound Duke of Omnium, similarly declares to his son: 'You are acting in opposition to my advice – and my wishes.'[4] But what happens? Lord Silverbridge woos Miss Boncassen, wins her and marries her. Trollope – in an

especially woozy and forgiving mood in this, one of his last novels –
makes it clear that in the modern world, the inherent nobility and
incorruptible beauty of Isabel Boncassen counter her humble family
origins and the native Republicanism found in all representatives of
the United States. A compromise is reached between the vital life
force and the need to defer to a civilisation which Mrs Hurtle
dangerously refers to as 'effete'. There is a new dispensation at work
and Trollope welcomes it.

Henry James's assessment of all this was only cautiously
approving. 'The American girl', he wrote, 'was destined sooner or
later to make her entrance into British fiction, and Trollope's
treatment of this complicated being is full of good humour and of
that fatherly indulgence, that almost motherly sympathy, which
characterizes his attitude throughout towards the youthful
feminine.' On the other hand, and damagingly, 'He has not mastered
all the springs of her delicate organism, nor sounded all the
mysteries of her conversation . . . "I got to be thinking if any of
them should ask me to marry him", words attributed to Miss
Boncassen in *The Duke's Children*, have much more the note of
English American than of American English.'[5]

For all Trollope's geniality and fairness of address, in other words,
he cannot help but betray the essence of America. But at least his
efforts are more fully rounded than Oscar Wilde's. When we turn to
Wilde's 1893 drama *A Woman of No Importance*, we are
confronted with Hester Worsley: a strident American heiress
embodying Wilde's feelings about Americans and the British
aristocracy in a single package – a stick to beat the upper classes
with. As Hester puts it, 'The English aristocracy supply us with our
curiosities, Lady Caroline. They are sent over to us every summer,
regularly, in the steamers, and propose to us the day after they land.'
Which is one thing, but not nearly as bad as the truth that 'With all
your pomp and wealth and art you don't know how to live – you
don't even know that. You love the beauty that you can see and
touch and handle, the beauty that you can destroy, and do destroy,
but of the unseen beauty of life, of the unseen beauty of a higher life,
you know nothing. You have lost life's secret.'

Hester's denunciatory rhetoric is unstoppable: 'Oh, your English
society seems to me shallow, selfish, foolish. It has blinded its eyes,

and stopped its ears. It lies like a leper in purple.'[6] Wilde later removed this last phrase, apparently keen not to cause offence. But the fact remains that Hester's social vitality is all of a piece with her moral sensibility and never gets much further beyond it. American puritanism is as dynamic and puzzling as its capitalism: that is what Hester's Americanness amounts to. Isabel Boncassen, on the other hand, coming from the pen of a more benign and Establishment writer, is a much trickier proposition ('She took a prolonged gaze at him, wondering whether he was or was not such a fool as he looked'); and in every way a more worthwhile prize. She is also a closer approximation to the real thing: irresistible, and, in her controversial way, an adornment to her new husband.

Had Edith Wharton ever finished *The Buccaneers*, how would it have compared? Following an opening half almost as genial in tone as Trollope's, *The Buccaneers* progressively darkens. Conchita Closson is mainly a teasing fictionalisation of Consuelo Mandeville ('Tied tight in one of these awful English marriages, that strangle you in a noose when you try to pull away from them') with seasonings of Minnie Paget. The Duke of Tintagel is the wretched 9th Duke of Marlborough, pinned and dissected. Annabel St George has a suggestion of the (American) 9th Duchess of Marlborough. Marriages turn sour. American high society is boring and rife with prejudices and restrictions. Unhappiness seeps through everything like a gas. The American girls – the Buccaneers – flee the barbarous tedium of East Coast America, make faltering successes in England, and find themselves trapped, unable to find contentment in their new home, but incapable of returning to America, corrupted as they are by the desirability of English society. 'I wouldn't go for good and all on any terms – not for all the Astor diamonds!' cries Conchita, rubbishing the idea of a strategic retreat to New York.

I'd rather starve and freeze here than go back to all the warm houses and the hot baths, and the emptiness of everything – people and places . . . ask Jacky March, or any of the poor little American old maids, or wives or widows, who've had a nibble at it and have hung on at any price, because London's London, and London life the most exciting and interesting in the world, and once you've got the soot and the fog in your veins you simply can't live without them; and all the poor hangers-on and left-overs know it as well as we do.[7]

The projected ending, according to Wharton's own notes, was to be sharp, unsatisfactory, embittered. She was writing some fifty years after Trollope: she had all the benefit of hindsight.

Back in the real world, the frightful Lord Mandeville was still busy traducing his wife Consuelo; and it was only on the death of his father in 1892 that, with the assumption of the dukedom, George Victor Drogo started to regularise his life, his financial affairs and his relationship with his martyred Duchess. Despite any initial dismay at his son's miscegenated alliance, the 7th Duke of Manchester had long been won over by Consuelo. She recalled after his death how 'He was the only friend I had in the family, from the day I arrived an absolute stranger in England he received me kindly and never changed.'[8] His son, it seemed, was now trying to access something of the same responsible decency. He attempted a reconciliation with Consuelo, breaking off his relationship with singer Bessie Bellwood. The latter promptly brought a suit against him for the return of money she claimed to have lent him before his accession to the dukedom. The new Duke rebutted the claim and the action dragged, typically, through the law courts, involving a scandal rag called *The Dwarf*. But no sooner had this farrago come to a conclusion than the 8th Duke died, worn out at the age of 39.

Instead of having to rebuild a catastrophic marriage, Consuelo was now left to enjoy a widowhood more pleasurable than married life had ever been. When her brother Fernando died in 1901, he left her nearly $5 million in a mixture of real estate and personal items, mindful of the outrages she had suffered at the Duke's hands. Consuelo's mother and two sisters (one of whom was now married to the baronet Sir John Lister-Kaye) received nothing. Consuelo insisted on redistributing the money among her family. What she kept for herself went on paying the many debts she had accumulated while deploying her charms on a willing British aristocracy (winning over not only the Duke of Portland, but even the hypercritical Lord Randolph Churchill, who teasingly wrote to her in 1892, soon after the death of the 8th Duke, 'My Sweet and Dear Consuelo, It was ravishing to me to get a letter from you & I spent upon its perusal several hours. Whether this length of time was occupied by innumerable thoughts & memories of the charms of the writer or by indefatigable efforts to get at the true significance of the calligraphy I will not decide . . .'[9]).

What Consuelo lacked was any business sense at all. As Little Kim noted, 'Neither my father nor my mother seemed able to grasp the salient fact that to be economical in small things and liberal in large is not true economy', and the estate was not only hopelessly impoverished when he succeeded to the title – despite a quarter of a century of erratic cash subventions from the United States – but remained that way. When Lady Randolph Churchill sent a note to Lady Desborough in May 1892 announcing that 'I have just come down here' – Kimbolton Castle – 'for a night, to see Consuelo', the good news was that, recently and happily widowed, Consuelo 'is very flourishing & in the best of spirits'.[10] The sting in the tail was that entertaining Lady Randolph Churchill on an uncertain budget – this was long before brother Fernando's gift – brought together two measureless Anglo-American spendthrifts, with no one to curb their respective enthusiasms. Still: combined with her musical gifts, her looks, her flirtatiousness, and – not least – her manifest, even saintly, submission to an alien code of aristocratic behaviour, this financial incompetence made her even more widely loved. It made her seem less American.

Then, in November of the same year, Mandeville's counterpart, the Wicked Duke of Marlborough, expired in his laboratory, aged only 48. He left behind a mass of scientific impedimenta and a demonic presence in some of the rooms. One guest at Blenheim made a point of spending the night in a haunted bedroom, claiming in the morning that 'I was in bed with a corpse and it was giving me electric shocks.'[11] Duchess Lily tore to shreds the voluptuous portrait (by Whistler) of Lady Colin Campbell which had been the 8th Duke's pride, before posting the pieces on to her Ladyship in Venice. Lord Randolph fretted that his hideous brother might have bequested all his personal possessions to his lover – 'I do trust there is no foundation for this as it would make a great scandal'[12] – but without foundation. Astonishingly, Lily was generous enough to dust off the taint of the Marlboroughs and wed another member of the British aristocracy: Lord William de la Poer Beresford VC, in 1895. This time the marriage was a happy one, the once-unconsidered Mrs Hammersley becoming a mother at the age of 43. Latter-day visitors to Blenheim Palace are often puzzled by the scarcity of any visual representations of the 8th Duke. His treatment of Lilian Hammersley – to say nothing of 'Goosie' Blandford and Lady Aylesford – has much to do with it.

Jennie Churchill had, as one American to another, often been kinder to Duchess Lily than the rest of society. Her support was duly noted by Randolph Churchill in a letter to her at the time of Marlborough's death: 'I had a long talk with the poor Duchess while the post mortem was going on. You were really quite right about her & I quite wrong. Nothing could exceed her goodness & kindness of disposition, & my belief is that she means to do nothing but what is right liberal & generous by the heir.'[13] Lily's decency was mirrored by that of Jennie, the difference being that while Duchess Lily compressed all the anguish of her relationship with the Marlboroughs into the space of four years, Jennie had to put up with a protracted rising level of turmoil and unhappiness, from the time of Lord Randolph's febrile interventions in the Aylesford Scandal to his death, early in 1895.

The Randolph Churchills were now in the last phase of their drama-filled relationship. By 1891, Leonard Jerome had died – in Brighton – and the increasingly sick and wayward Randolph was off in Mashonaland (Zimbabwe). In 1894, he made a last, ruinously incoherent, speech in the House of Commons, after which A.J. Balfour and Sir Michael Hicks Beach came to Jennie to beg her never to let him near the House again. Increasing privations forced the Churchills out of their town house in Connaught Place and off to live with Randolph's mother in Grosvenor Square. Then, in June 1894, Jennie took the disintegrating Randolph on a world trip – to forget his failure as an MP, to escape their mountain of debts, to salvage some last vitality from their twenty-year-old marriage. A doctor and a lead-lined coffin went with them. Randolph was entering the final stages of syphilitic dementia but Jennie did her best to tolerate his behaviour, as she wrote to her sister Leonie:

Of course the journey has told on him but I feel it is always going to be so. As soon as he gets a little better from having a rest &

being quiet he will be put back by this travelling – *& nothing* will deter him from doing what he likes. He is very kind & considerate when he feels well – but absolutely *impossible* when he gets X & excited – & as he gets like that 20 times a day – you may imagine my life is not a very easy one.[14]

They persevered through North America, then on to Japan, Hong Kong, Singapore and Burma, before cutting the trip short in India and returning to England for the end. Screaming and gurgling with pain, Lord Randolph Churchill finally died on 24 January 1895. He was 45 years old. Far from making provision for his wife and children, he left debts amounting to a staggering £75,000 – fortuitously covered by the sale of some Rand Mine shares he had bought while on his Mashonaland trip.

And that was the end of the first great Anglo-American marriage. Randolph had been intemperate, high-handed and arrogant all his life; Jennie was intemperate, passionate and casually indifferent to those – her children, for instance – who failed to fit in with her immediate needs. Yet, despite their infidelities and absences, despite Jennie's unease with the starchier representatives of British high society, each answered the other's needs. He was clever enough not to be intimidated by her; she was self-willed enough not to be intimidated by him. He had prestige and brilliance; she had glamour and passion. The celebrity surrounding their marriage was not, for once, predicated on mere bad behaviour.

These were busy times for the Marlboroughs. The year Lord Randolph Churchill died was the year that Randolph's nephew, Sunny, now the 9th Duke of Marlborough, married Consuelo Vanderbilt. The contrast between the two marriages was not just one of personality – the bold, assertive Randolph Churchills versus the grander, yet more inward, Marlboroughs. It also signalled an essential change in the dynamic relationship between the United States and England, between wealth and social standing, between the assimilationist tendencies of Consuelo Yznaga and Jennie Jerome, and something more distinctly willed, more intensely conscious of its own power. It symbolised an irreversible shift in the balance – and it was embodied in the graceful form of Miss Consuelo Vanderbilt.

Everything converged on this, the greatest of all the transatlantic marriages: greater than the Manchesters, the Randolph Churchills, the Curzons, the Pagets or any number of Cholmondeleys, Dufferin and Avas or Angleseys. Consuelo was the beautiful, swan-necked, raven-haired daughter of the thrusting Alva Vanderbilt, scourge of the Astors of New York. Consuelo Yznaga had been one of Alva's bridesmaids, then lent her name to young Consuelo, as well as standing godmother to her. As the 9th Duke of Manchester later wrote, complacently, 'There have been considerable alterations in New York society since the days of the original Four Hundred, and people who were outside its magic circle then are well inside now. Some of them have been assisted by the efforts of my mother and myself, and it was she who helped to launch the W.K. Vanderbilts on the social sea.'[15]

Minnie Paget, who had been bridesmaid to Consuelo Yznaga, in turn effected the introduction between Consuelo Vanderbilt and the young Duke of Marlborough, who had only recently ceased to have an American stepmother in the form of Duchess Lily. Alva Vanderbilt may have clawed her way to the heart of New York society; but she had also just divorced William Kissam Vanderbilt, thereby casting a fresh stain on her pedigree. She saw the wedding of her daughter to the Duke as a foolproof way of protecting herself from the detractions that divorce inevitably brought with it. It was, in fact, to be another ratcheting up of the Vanderbilt name, greater even than her trouncing of Mrs Astor in 1883.

Consuelo, 17 at the time, first met Marlborough, six years her senior, at a dinner at the Pagets' house in Belgrave Square. The connection, the centrepiece of a nexus of relationships and ambitions, was formally made. The Marlboroughs, despite Lily's generous interventions, still needed a fortune to keep up Blenheim. The Vanderbilts had that fortune. There was a dreadful inevitability about it all. Marlborough came to America, stayed with the Vanderbilts and was arrested in Central Park for riding a bicycle with his feet off the pedals. At the Marble House, the Vanderbilts' Newport, Rhode Island, home, Marlborough proposed and Consuelo accepted. In the wedding to end all weddings, the two young people were married at the St Thomas Episcopal Church, Fifth Avenue, on 6 November 1895. Consuelo's dress was white satin trimmed with Brussels lace; her train was embroidered with seed pearls and silver; a wreath of orange blossoms held her veil to her head. Sunny Marlborough's cousin, Ivor Guest, was best man. May Goelet – heiress to the vast Goelet property fortune, second only, indeed, to that of the Astors – was one of Consuelo's eight bridesmaids. A mob on the street outside struggled to see the participants. The whole event was rumoured to have cost the Vanderbilts $1 million. And from the moment the marriage was solemnised, it began to unravel in a manner that caused the Duke of Marlborough to become almost as reviled as his own father, or, even, the Duke of Manchester.

The root of the problem lay in Sunny's sense of destiny. His father, his grandfather, his great-great-grandfather, had all plundered Blenheim and left it diminished. Both hampered and empowered by the demands of the palace and his famous title, he determined to express his sense of destiny and history by restoring Blenheim, and by being a truer Duke of Marlborough than any of his predecessors. The gap, however, between Sunny's aspirations and his effectiveness resembled the gap between Trollope's young Duke of Omnium and his uncle, the legendary Old Duke, in the novel *Phineas Redux*. As one of Trollope's characters puts it, speaking of the Old Duke's ways, 'There is nothing left like it now. With a princely income I don't suppose he ever put by a shilling in his life. I've heard it said that he couldn't afford to marry, living in the manner in which he chose to live. And he understood what dignity meant. None of them understands that now.'

And the new Duke? Even his own Duchess of Omnium finds it hard to raise much enthusiasm, admitting that he 'considers himself inferior to a sweeper while on the crossing, and never feels any pride of place unless he is sitting on the Treasury Bench with his hat over his eyes'.[16] The familiar theme: the best is past, the present a torpid imitation. The 1st Duke of Marlborough (or, at a pinch, the 7th) had carried himself with an apt dignity now lost to his descendants. It had been a long and public decline from then on.

But Sunny's imperatives were all to do with defying that commonplace, turning it on its head, ensuring the succession, maintaining the palace, re-gilding the Marlborough name. He had been in love before his marriage to Consuelo was arranged; he had given up his love for the sake of history, just as Consuelo had been obliged to give up hers (a New Yorker called Winthrop Rutherfurd, relation of one of the original New York Patriarchs). People were apt to express surprise that Sunny – this stuffy, status-obsessed homunculus – could have been so close to his cousin, the toweringly creative and energetic Winston Churchill. But both were fully alive to the unseen potency of history and its influence on the present; and both loved Blenheim. They both appreciated that larger forces were at work and that they must bow to them.

So the newly married couple settled uncomfortably into Blenheim, seeking to spend the immense dowry W.K. Vanderbilt had settled on them: $2,500,000 in Beech Creek railroad stock, yielding 4 per cent per annum – $100,000 – for the Duke's sole use. Consuelo struggled to learn the palace routines. She had to distinguish between the operations of the thirty or so domestic staff and face down the tall, loutish footmen. She made a big thing of adapting the practice in which all the leftover food from a meal was scraped into undifferentiated tubs full of mixed hot, cold, sweet and savoury, and given like pig feed to the poor of the estate. This she turned into something more consumer-friendly, in which the main courses and the puddings were at least put in different containers. Every morning began with prayers in the chapel at half-past nine. Every evening, dinner was taken in silence, Consuelo seated at one end of the table, knitting; the young Duke at the other, twirling his signet ring abstractedly and brooding on the contents of his plate. Eighteen months earlier, she would have been living in conditions of the highest material comfort; relatively indolent, despite the presence of her over-bearing mother; left to pursue her own whimsical amusements in the warmth of Rhode Island or amid the colossal material riches of the Fifth Avenue mansion built in the 'French Renaissance style' and whose dining room 'had at one end twin Renaissance mantlepieces and on one side a huge stained-glass window, depicting the Field of the Cloth of Gold on which the Kings of England and France were surrounded with all their knights'.[17] Now it was 1896 and she was in Oxfordshire, with its own special, penetrating dampness and sense of enclosure, living in a real palace, not a Fifth Avenue parody, and facing the prospect of a panic-inducing, hugely expensive, visit from the Prince and Princess of Wales.

Tumtum and Princess Alexandra came and went. The standard shooting-party photograph taken at the time shows the Prince sprawled in his usual armchair posture, next to the pleasantly smiling Mary Curzon, with, two places to his right, Consuelo Marlborough, looking like a visitor from another world entirely. The rigidity of the young Duchess's pose is only matched by that of poor Princess Alexandra on her left; Consuelo's painfully elegant slimness contrasting with the beefier builds of her lady guests; her dark eyebrows arched in the set position of unhappy disbelief which they always adopted, giving her face the look of a Japanese Noh player. To Consuelo's right sits Jennie Churchill, her arm pressing against Consuelo's shoulder, either to give her the emotional comfort only a compatriot could, or because the recently widowed Jennie needed reassurance, now feeling herself 'without a friend in the world and too old to make any more'.[18] Sunny (as in the Earl of Sunderland, one of his lesser titles) sits on the ground at the feet of Princess Victoria, looking like a schoolboy back at his parents' house for the holidays.

Two sons were born. Consuelo grew into the role. The Marlboroughs attended balls at Holland House, Grosvenor House, Devonshire House. They drove to Ranelagh, Roehampton, Hurlingham. They attended debates in the House of Commons and the House of Lords. Shortly after the Prince of Wales's visit to Blenheim, the Curzons found themselves together with the Marlboroughs at Hatfield House. Mary Curzon – rich and pretty herself, the cynosure of many eyes – wrote:

Everybody raves about Consuelo, and she is very sweet in her great position, and shyly takes her rank directly after Royalty. She looks very stately in her marvellous jewels, and she looks pretty and has old lace which makes my mouth water. I never saw pearls the size of nuts. In a grand party like this, George and I have rather to tag along with the rank and file, but we are very happy and don't mind being small fry.[19]

The Duke bought quantities of jewellery to adorn Consuelo and ordered a little mail-phaeton for himself as well as a crimson state coach. And he started to plan his improvements and alterations to the Great Court at Blenheim, the Library, the Grand Avenue. French granite replaced the rustic mess of grass which had grown up at the front of the palace. The Library, having been denuded of books, now started to reacquire them. The architect and designer Achille Duchêne started work remodelling the Court Yard and the old Victorian shrubbery on the east front. A massive replanting of trees took place in the grounds.

This – after ensuring the succession – was really the point of the marriage. As ever, there were three participants in the relationship: Sunny, Consuelo and Blenheim Palace – that extravagant, troubled, demanding mistress, the embodiment of Sunny's own sense of prestige. All three had to be placated, and Blenheim was the most urgent. And Sunny might well have argued that, as things went, his lavishing of the Vanderbilt fortune on an English title and its possessions was a relatively virtuous occupation. Unlike the Duke of Manchester – or his own father – he was preserving and improving a great national treasure. He was obeying the dictates of history, rather than his own selfish interests. Indeed, he was aiming higher even than Lord Curzon and his architectural projects – toiling only for the good name of the Marlboroughs, with none of Curzon's foxy promiscuities, nor his towering self-love.

And, when all was said and done, who had any right to complain? The only other interested party was the Vanderbilt family itself, the source of all this money – and what were the Vanderbilts doing with it, back in the United States? They had their Fifth Avenue hunting lodge; they had the Marble House at Newport, Rhode Island, where Sunny had proposed to Consuelo; they had The Breakers, also in Newport; they had the Hyde Park mansion, overlooking the Hudson river; they had Biltmore, North Carolina – the largest private house in the United States. They were furiously squandering the family millions on yachts, racehorses, motor cars, parties, building works, mistresses, furnishings, drink, carriages, continental trips, works of art and wardrobes full of clothes. In fact the Vanderbilt family had now made itself a byword for novel and astonishing levels of profligacy, amounting to 'forthright stupidity'. Sunny was a model of self-denial in comparison.

The young 9th Duke of Manchester, conversely, was staring at financial ruin following his accession to the title in 1892. Little Kim had not, of course, been helped by his own lazy imprudence. 'When I went up to Cambridge', he complained, 'the trustees gave me an allowance of four hundred a year, out of which they expected me to keep myself, to pay for my clothes and subscriptions and everything.' He quickly found himself running out of money: when he left Cambridge, he was a staggering £2,000 in debt. 'It is fatally easy', he admitted, 'for a young man to borrow at the Varsity.'[20] Thus his career started as it meant to go on. Faced with thousands of pounds of debt accrued both at university and on the underperforming estates at Kimbolton Castle and Tandragee – and with no capacity for earning a living on his own – he at once decided to emulate his father and went across to the States to look for a fortune.

This was less degrading for him than it might have been for other British noblemen. After all, the Duke was half American; his godfather was William K. Vanderbilt – Consuelo Marlborough's father; he had spent much time in the States as a boy, some of it on the Yznaga plantation; he had every right to be there. Mere aristocratic poverty was not his only calling-card.

But the trend was no longer in his favour. Times were changing and, soon enough, he began to make a nuisance of himself. By 1897, having conducted some initial researches, he was on his way to press his suit with May Goelet. However, he was already known for having made the injudicious claim that he would have to marry an Astor or a Vanderbilt in order to straighten out his financial affairs. It was also rumoured that he had left Kimbolton Castle in a hurry, a livery bill of £46.10s outstanding, the housekeeper unpaid and no food in the larder. 'England's Poorest Duke After Our Richest Heiress – The Young Duke of Manchester Who Couldn't Pay His Livery Bills Coming to America to Win Miss Goelet', announced an American newspaper.[21] The Duke was not pleased:

This transatlantic bad habit of 'making a story' at any cost, regardless as to whether there were a grain of truth in it or not, and ignoring the objections to publicity of those most nearly concerned, has always been beyond my comprehension, especially as the average American seems a level-headed sensible sort of fellow, not in the least addicted to sensationalism as revealed in the shrieking headlines that adorn most of the daily Press.[22]

Nevertheless, on 10 July 1897, the papers trumpeted 'Duke of Manchester to Wed. Marriage said to be arranged between him and the Daughter of Ogden Goelet.' This turned out to be a false alarm. The next day, 'The Duke Denies It. His Grace the Duke of Manchester Says the Report of His Engagement to Miss Goelet is Untrue.' Then, two days later, it was decided after all that May Goelet 'is Engaged to the Young Duke of Manchester in Spite of Denial'. But there was more to it than that. 'It is understood in society that the two mothers arranged the match. Mr. Goelet is supposed to regard the arrangement with some disfavour, because, although the estates of the Duke are large, his income is comparatively small.' For a while longer, he pinned his hopes on Miss Goelet. And then it was all over. Despite Consuelo Manchester's best efforts, the match came to nothing, and the 9th Duke was left again to prowl across the United States, hopelessly searching for money.[23]

The atmosphere of farcical desperation persisted for another two and a half years. By 1898, he had gone back to England and, amazingly, discovered a British heiress willing to consider him. She was Joan Wilson, daughter of a wealthy northern shipowner, and their engagement was announced in May of that year. The *New York Times*, which now dogged the Duke as assiduously as any of the Yellow Press, reported his betrothal with the observation that,

> The Duke, from time to time, has been reported to be engaged to almost every heiress to whom he has shown any attention in society, and to some who were neither heiresses nor in society. Last Summer, when Miss Ethel Barrymore and William Gillette, who were playing in *Secret Service* in London, were invited to visit the Duchess, the engagement of her son to the young American actress was at once rumored.[24]

Miss Wilson seemed plausible enough at the time, especially in comparison with Ethel Barrymore. But Manchester's reputation was as dreadful in England as it was in the States; this liaison too came to nothing.

By 1900, he was 23 years old, still drifting – worse, had been declared bankrupt with debts of $135,000 – when something extraordinary happened: he married an American heiress. Helena Zimmerman of Cincinnati was the attractive young daughter of Eugene Zimmerman, Vice President of (among other things) the Cincinnati, Hamilton & Dayton Railroad Company and one of America's richest and most recondite millionaires. That she agreed to have the Duke says much about the essential optimism of human nature and the remnants of charm which hung about a dukedom. In November 1900, they were wed in New York – 'One of the most interesting marriages between American heiresses and representatives of the British peerage'.[25] The young Duke, blessed with a four-square posture inherited from the Yznaga family and an expression of idle condescension from his father, was no Adonis. It was thought that he had done well to secure Miss Zimmerman.

Almost immediately, Helena found herself plunged into the nebulous chaos of Manchester's world. The wedding ceremony had barely finished when, as the Duke recalled, 'A reporter got hold of my wife's maid, and with the assistance of two thousand dollars' worth of palm-oil persuaded her, in the absence of my valet, to lend him all my underclothes. The diligent man had these garments photographed, and they duly appeared in the newspapers under the surprising headline: "Wedding Trousseau of a Duke".'[26] (His genius for attracting bad publicity is even more evident when it is realised that at the same time as Manchester was humiliating himself, the similarly scapegrace Earl of Rosslyn managed a New York trip in complete harmony: 'I had been lucky in making good with the Press, with their sensational headlines and exaggerated stories. The reporters looked on me as a "sport", and I once got the better of a disingenuous member by interviewing *him* and having a whole page illustrated in *The Sunday Herald*, against his couple of columns in a rival newspaper! He was terribly chaffed about it.'[27]) Still, the young Duke and Duchess overcame this embarrassment and sailed for England at the beginning of March 1901.

No sooner had they landed than a writ was issued against the Duke for breach of promise – a certain Portia Knight alleging that he had already sworn to marry her. Miss Knight, it turned out, was an American actress (previously a member of the Kendall Weston

Stock Company) who, having been 'on the stage in New York for a short time', was now 'living privately in London'. Surprisingly, it was 'evident that she is in earnest, and that the suit was brought without any idea of gaining publicity'.[28] Nevertheless, the Duke managed to deal with this crisis, only to be sued both by an American jewellery company and by Duveen's, the art dealer, for unpaid bills. A while later, he found himself broke once again, and had to get a job as a newspaperman. Eugene Zimmerman had bought the couple the vast Victorian pastiche that was Kylemore Castle, Connemara, as a present, but it was not enough to keep the Duke happy. He went off the rails once more and, in 1924, a warrant for his arrest was issued in Montreal, on a false pretences charge.

At last he divorced Helena in 1931, before marrying Kathleen Dawes, of Connecticut, in the same year. By this time, what cachet there was in being Duchess of Manchester must have been worryingly insubstantial, given the aggravation the position clearly entailed. Decades earlier, the American critic James Jarves had written of the horrors attending unwise marriages between American girls and unscrupulous European aristocrats. He concluded that

> No American woman ever should enter into the solemn engagements of matrimony with a foreigner of any nation without duly considering all the changes in her modes of daily life and thought that she must submit to in order to be in harmony with her new conditions. If the primary inducement be the prestige of something new in social rank, which in itself is an illusory phantom at the best, so much the more reason for a cautious sounding of all the depths of the new waters before venturing in them.[29]

It was a warning that could have been addressed, word for word, to both the 8th and 9th Duchesses of Manchester.

But not to Jennie Churchill, who, by this time, had slumped gratefully into the arms of George Cornwallis-West, with whom she was enjoying a relationship of lively sexuality, spiced with a strong sense of illicitness and a seasoning of persecution. George was twenty years Jennie Churchill's junior – indeed, was only sixteen days older than Winston Churchill. He had no title and no fortune. But when, in 1898, Daisy, Countess of Warwick introduced him to Jennie, the mutual attraction was irresistible. Overpowered with desire and a need to be worshipped, she gave up an affair she had been pursuing with the sensationally attractive 'Beauty' Ramsden of the Seaforth Highlanders, and embraced George.

Both George's family and the Prince of Wales tried to stop it. The Prince had long enjoyed a relationship of quiet carnality with Jennie and corresponded with her affectionately and at length. The thought of slim, pretty George coming between them was too much for him. They quarrelled. 'My dear Lady Randolph Churchill', he subsequently wrote (not '*Ma Chère Amie*', his usual form of address),

It has been my privilege to enjoy your friendship for upwards of a quarter of a century – therefore why do you think it necessary to write me a rude letter – simply because I have expressed my regret at the marriage you are about to make? I have said nothing behind your back that I have not said to your face – You know the world so well that I presume you are the best judge of your own happiness – but at the same time you should think twice before you abuse your friends and well-wishers for not congratulating you on the serious step you are going to make! I can only hope that we shall all be mistaken.

Then, instead of the '*Tout à Vous*', with which he habitually closed his letters, he signed off with a frosty 'Believe me, Sincerely yours – A.E.'[30]

George Cornwallis-West's father, meanwhile, wrote to Jennie's sister, Leonie, requiring her to take steps on his and her sister's behalf:

I wish seriously to ask you [he began] if you consider a marriage which I am told is again talked of between Lady Randolph and my son can possibly lead to the happiness of either? To begin with she is older than his own mother. She will lose the name in which she is best known to the world and its rank and position and she will find herself married to a young man of such an impressionable nature that only a few weeks ago he proposed marriage to a young and pretty girl who refused his attentions – notwithstanding his protestations of love and his repudiations of your sister.

(This may well have been a reference to May Goelet. Like half of London society, George had flirted with May, and she with him. 'Such a dear, attractive, good-looking boy', she wrote, 'and quite the best dancer in London. Anyway he fancies himself very much in love with me. So foolish of him. I am so sorry about it – what can one do? I like him ever so much as a friend – but why they have always to wish for something more, I can't imagine.'[31]) Colonel Cornwallis-West went on, struggling for adequate expression, 'The life of a couple so ill-assorted is doomed, is painful to think of – and the marvel to me is that a woman as talented and experienced as your sister could coolly contemplate it as nothing out of the common. I can only add that if this marriage takes place, it will estrange the whole of my family from my son and so I have told him.'[32]

None of this made any difference. In an echo of the tempestuous correspondence Jennie and Lord Randolph Churchill had enjoyed a quarter of a century earlier, George bombarded Jennie with love-letters dense with guileless sincerity:

I love you Missie darling, as I have never loved, or ever shall love another woman. I have given you all that I had to give, and all that was best in me, and shall never regret it until the day of my death. I cant tell you what a trying time I am having at home, when my mother was here it was alright, but now she has gone to be with Daisy. I am alone with my Father who never loses an opportunity [*sic*] of dropping hints about financial difficulties and how easily they could be overcome if I married an heiress, he also takes a pleasure in abusing all your friends, though he knows he dare not mention your name thus to me.[33]

Or again: 'My Precious I missed you so last night, it seemed so lonely to be curled up by oneself, without your dear little warm self next one. Ah Missie mine I love you so, if I tell you so often will you tire of me, or doesn't your rule apply to yourself . . .'[34] This made Jennie feel young again. It also made her feel needed in a helpless, uncritical way – rather than with the normal affectless chill of the philandering English upper classes. As a consequence, George and Jennie were married on 28 July 1900, at St Paul's Church in Knightsbridge. Sunny, Duke of Marlborough, gave Jennie away. None of George's family turned up.

Not the least intriguing element of the wedding day, however, was the realisation that the new Mrs Jennie Cornwallis-West had so far transformed herself from the Jennie Jerome of twenty-five years before. Instead of a sensual, fresh-faced American heiress being fed as a treat to one of England's grandest and most reprobate families, she was now an Anglo-American society matron – familiar, predictable in her eccentricities, no longer 'a strange and abnormal creature, with habits and manners something between a Red Indian and a Gaiety Girl'.[35] On her honeymoon, she took with her the stack of unpaid bills which sat permanently on her like an incubus. 'Of course I was eager to put her affairs in order', George later said, 'but I found it a bit thick when expected to pay for Lord Randolph Churchill's barouche purchased in the 'eighties.'[36] This was a typical penurious English grandee's gesture on Jennie's part: a recognition that she had no money, that she knew she had no money, and that she knew no way of getting any. What's more, it hadn't stopped her from throwing her time, energy and non-existent funds into grand society-inflected projects such as the *Maine* hospital ship (at the start of the Boer War) and her pauperising literary quarterly, the *Anglo-Saxon Review*. 'It was at one time one of Lady Randolph's amusing foibles to be regarded as literary',[37] noted the Countess of Warwick with spry malice. But the project – the *Anglo-Saxon Review* – was less significant than the fact that Jennie was pursuing it so actively. No passive Yankee millionaire's daughter, she was a doer, an enabler, a fixture in the world, an indication of the way things were going.

In fact, just about the last of the great money-for-title marriages came not long after Jennie's betrothal to George Cornwallis-West; and it involved May Goelet. Staying at Bad Homburg some years before, she had written a famously voluble letter to her Aunt Grace, detailing her marriage prospects and the activities of her various

suitors. 'I must give an account of my proposal', she insisted to her
aunt. The litany of the titled and the well-born that followed was
both comprehensive and startling. Lord Shaftesbury was first,
having 'popped almost as soon as he returned to London'. Having
come round to Miss Goelet's one afternoon, he cleverly waited until
May's mother had to leave the room for a few minutes: 'Off he went
– like a pistol.' She told him at once that his proposal was
'ridiculous' as he had only known her for three weeks, couldn't
possibly know his own mind and, as the capstone to her argument,
had famously been in love with an English noblewoman ('Lady N').
Shaftesbury apparently fought a determined rearguard action,
claiming that the affair had long been over, that he did know his
own mind, and that he wanted to marry Miss Goelet. 'I like him
very much only I have no intention of marrying him or anyone else
at present', she concluded, thrilling both herself and Aunt Grace
with the gossipy insight that her mother was 'terribly afraid' that
Shaftesbury would weaken her resolve and win through to the
money. Shaftesbury dealt with, she moved on to the Duke of
Roxburghe, who 'is the man that everyone says I am engaged to'.
Quiet, undemonstrative, the Duke 'never goes to balls', but did
accept a dinner invitation at the house of Mrs William Dodge James,
where he and May Goelet had a proper conversation, very nearly
continued the following night at the Curzon house, where both were
guests. As it turned out, though, Lord Castlereagh – the
'Londonderry boy' – got hold of May and fixed his attentions on
her, 'so I didn't have a chance of saying a word to the Duke'.
Charley Castlereagh – later to become the Hitler-appeasing
Marquess of Londonderry – was already an accomplished seducer of
women, and May was lucky that he made no assault on her
character. Next,

> Mrs Benson is crazy to make a match between Captain Holford
> and myself! And Lord Grey who married Captain Holford's other
> sister is very anxious to arrange it too. The Prince said to Lord
> Grey, 'It's quite time George (Captain H.) was getting married. I
> know just the right person for him – a charming girl, Miss Goelet.
> It really must be arranged.' Now the funny part is that Capt.
> Holford has never said a word for himself. He wants to find out,

you see, if we are willing before he commits himself in the least. Dorchester House, of course, would be delightful; and I believe he has two charming places in the country. Unfortunately, the dear man has no title, though a very good position – and I am sure he would make a very good husband.[38]

The final offer, as we now know, had come from George Cornwallis-West – that 'dear, attractive, good-looking boy'. Plainly, Miss Goelet was relishing her position. If she felt ambivalent about the fact that her charms were heightened by her great wealth, it didn't matter. There was a teasing equilibrium between her status as an heiress and the social positions of those who paid court to her. In her letter she limned her power by accommodating everyone from the Prince of Wales to George Cornwallis-West, via a duke, an earl and a viscount. She enjoyed the cynicism that went with being young, rich and beautiful, and there was evidently no suggestion that she might want to settle down or devote herself to one nobleman above all others.

Her decision to marry the Duke of Roxburghe in November 1903 – and her subsequent devotion to him – could not easily have been foreseen. Even more unpredictably, she settled down as the chatelaine of the sprawling and underheated Floors Castle, near draughty Kelso, where, a lifetime away from the society, sun and comforts of Newport, Rhode Island, she amply fulfilled her duties as the Duchess. And, yes, a small part of the Goelet fortune duly went on heating, plumbing, redecoration, carpeting and electricity. Even the light switches were done in a Louis XVI style. Surprising it might have been; but, like the marriage between Isabel Boncassen and Lord Silverbridge, it was, in many ways, a partnership of equals and owed its resilience to that equality. Roxburghe was a great estate-owner (admittedly in largely illiquid and depreciating Border acres) and a great duke. He had wealth, a vast nineteenth-century castle and a title which included the Marquisate of Bowmont, the Earldom of Kelso and the Barony of Wakefield. He also – unlike the Duke of Manchester – had held on to his dignity and had no need to grovel to Miss Goelet merely in order to save his patrimony. May Goelet, on the other hand, had been through the gamut of aristocratic proposals and had arrived at a mature decision. It was a marriage to hold up as an example to the most virtuous of British aristocrats. But it also, coincidentally, marked the beginning of the end – the point at which the British aristocracy could no longer take American riches for granted, nor the robust acquiescence of an American wife. Things had been changing for some time, now. The Golden Age that began in 1874 was coming to a close. The heiresses had more or less been used up.

SEVEN

Astor

It was in the same year as the Roxburghe wedding that William Waldorf Astor's determination to embody the active principle of the American in society reached its climax. It was 1903 when he bought Hever Castle, in Kent – a monument, not so much to his own vanity, as to the impossible dream of reinventing himself as a respected gentleman of means and taste.

When Astor first set eyes on Hever, it was a tiny, square, moated, semi-ruined, battlemented castle, rich in history but reduced to the condition of a farm outbuilding – filled as it was with livestock on the ground floor and tenant farmers on the upper levels. About the last time it had been properly appreciated as a piece of architecture was in the summer of 1866. Then, it had been taken over by a group of earnest young painters – Philip Calderon, W.F. Yeames, David Wynfield, all members of the St John's Wood clique, who disported themselves amid the stonework and timber beams, striking postures of such keen medievalism that *Punch* spent weeks satirising their pretensions. Before that, the castle, which dated back to 1270, had been the home of Anne Boleyn and had played host to Henry VIII on many stressful occasions. Its diminutive size told against it, though. Having passed through the hands of the Waldegrave family, from 1749 until 1903, it rested with the Meade-Waldos, who could find little to do with this charming, pointless curiosity, other than let it fall into desuetude.

Then Astor, following two whole years of negotiations, acquired it in July 1903, along with 640 surrounding acres. According to his own *Pall Mall Magazine*, he

wished to live in comfort in his medieval stronghold, having no desire to call up from the past the phantoms of the Plague, the Black Death, or the Sweating Sickness, and other deadly dwellers in the castle of the Middle Ages. Again, he naturally wished to entertain his friends, but to house them in his Castle would necessitate the most radical changes in the very chambers he was bent on preserving intact.[1]

What this meant in reality was an uncompromising reinvention of Hever – a process that would turn out, depending on one's point of view, as a daring yet sensitive transformation of a historically important country seat, or as a predictably over-assertive American traducing of an English cultural artefact.

Certainly, the material forces involved were enough to make any traditional landowner uneasy. By December 1904, no fewer than 800 workmen were toiling away at Astor's new home. As well as 30 acres of landscaped gardens, 3,000 rose bushes, a rockery and several grottoes, the new Hever was to enjoy a blustery 35-acre lake, overlooked by a loggia at the end of Astor's finely wrought Italian Garden. This same lake was largely hand-dug by 748 navvies over the course of two years. One man had the sole responsibility of transporting 45 gallons of beer to his co-workers every day. The Italian Garden itself expressed Astor's unresolved yearning for Mediterranean culture (which led him to buy a villa at Sorrento in 1905 – another property acquired and then largely ignored) but the rest of the project was entirely fixated on the Tudor–medieval aesthetic of the castle.

Astor's sensitivity to the structure wrestled with his need to establish a high order of convenience and modernity. Central heating was ducted through concealed gratings; electric light switches made little of themselves against the panelling; the sewage had to be pumped 2 miles away; a labyrinth of white-tiled cellars was constructed under the castle and beyond in order to give access to the services; an electricity-generating house was built. Finally, an entire Tudor village was painstakingly conjured out of the land, so artfully styled by the architect F.L. Pearson that, with its quaintness and mildly distressed informality, it appeared to have been there all along.

In fact, the Tudor village became one of the definingly controversial elements of Astor's Hever. Was it a brilliantly thoughtful solution to the problem of where to put guests and servants when the castle itself was too small to hold much more than Astor himself? Or was it not only intolerably overblown and whimsical but an affront to the notion of aristocratic sociability – given that an essential function of this village was to allow Astor at the end of the day to banish all guests and encumbrances to beyond the moat, after which he would pull up the drawbridge and retire to the castle's one bedroom? Astor himself wrote, 'I cannot imagine a more natural way of providing guest-rooms. It is impossible to add to a castle; a village street in the medieval style would savour of the stage; and yet if the rites of hospitality were to be exercised at Hever, some considerable extension was, of course, necessary.' In his eyes, naturally, the 'considerable extension' was a wholly satisfying exercise in lordly pastiche: 'For a moment I could not believe that they [the houses in the Tudor village] had been built a few short months ago, they seemed so old and crooked, and possessed such individuality as though they had grown up one by one in various ages, as those old villages did which we sometimes see on our travels, sheltering themselves under the walls of the overlord.'[2]

The permanent platoon of eight private detectives, employed to keep out prying strangers, the broken glass embedded in the estate walls, and the dispiriting sight of Astor's brougham disappearing reclusively under the portcullis gave the lie to this companionable image – as did another of his provocations – aimed at the Countess of Warwick: 'I live here to be alone', he said, 'and nobody is admitted to Hever without invitation. Even my own children must be asked before they come.'[3]

Then there was the interior. In one sense, it was a modern masterpiece of re-creation: an advertisement for contemporary British craft skills. In it, the drawing room was surrounded by a delightful inlaid panelling of oak, bog-oak and holly. The library was panelled in a wood called sabicu – harder and denser than ebony and exquisitely carved by W.S. Frith; its ceiling bore a delicate moulding copied from Hampton Court. Elsewhere, the ceilings were decoratively plastered with armorial devices and quaint motifs, scrupulously using only those materials and techniques that would have been familiar to the Tudors. Where there were appropriations and introductions from other buildings – the panelling in the morning room, most of the furniture, the odd fireplace – they were done discreetly and fastidiously.

But in another sense, it was a pedant's interior, an essentially heartless simulacrum of a dignified home environment, causing the architect Philip Tilden to write with easy contempt, 'Hever Castle might indeed have been another Bodiam, infinitely alluring as it sat as I first saw it in the 'nineties, with its grey skirts sweeping the waters of the moat, set around with the blue swords of the wild flag; but instead it has now become a miniature Metropolitan Museum of New York.'[4] Why the scorn? What was so offensive about Hever – especially given Tilden's cheerful complicity in the monstrosity that was to be Hengistbury Castle, designed for Gordon Selfridge two decades later? It seems unfair. The pastiche is uniformly excellent. There's nothing over-ambitious or overweening in it – even the dining hall, traditionally the place where good taste is menaced by the need for a sense of occasion – manages to avoid any grating excess. The scale and proportions of the original building are diligently respected. About the worst of it is a feeling that, in striving to perfect every surface, Astor might have managed to expunge the real sense of character, of gaminess, that a medieval castle would normally be expected to exude – that, in attending to, and enriching every detail, Astor has somehow managed to reduce Hever's personality rather than increase it; giving it, in the end, the hint of a very finely appointed country house hotel. Or, as Patrick Balfour, later Baron Kinross, sagely expressed it,

> In seeking luxury we lose comfort. There is one thing for which America has always secretly envied the English: an elusive, personal quality, an easy-mannered intimacy, a sense of the peacefulness inseparable from the conception of the English gentleman. Hence, traditional English hospitality is different from any other hospitality. The reason for this is simple: it is that we understand – or understood – comfort . . . Comfort is an essentially personal thing. It means taste. That is where it differs from luxury. The two could not be further apart. Luxury can be fiendishly uncomfortable. Comfort is often quite unluxurious.[5]

Astor was, as ever, in two minds. He strove for a kind of feminine principle, an interest in good taste, a desire to respect the prevailing tone, a keenness to integrate and to be seen to be integrating. He wanted the house to be both an articulation of good manners and a demonstration of authorial taste. But he couldn't help advertising his vigour, his thoroughness, his masculine need to assert his own presence.

For all its latent uneasiness, Hever looks much more like a success if one turns to someone who really exhibited the masculine principle – the lust for self-advertisement; the need to impose on the landscape; the tendency to think in terms of sheer scale. For really unarguable ostentation, one had to look for a different kind of plutocrat. One had to turn to an irresistible, entrepreneurial figure, not a mere inheritor. One had to turn to Andrew Carnegie, in fact.

Where Astor's dream was to use Hever to announce his absorption into English culture, and William James's ambition was to place his house at the service of society, Carnegie's Skibo Castle was a monument to the self-esteem of the man who built it. And in the case of Skibo, there was no gainsaying the high – indeed, embarrassing – level of pretension and *mauvais goût* it incorporated. It was diametrically opposed, in form and intent, to West Dean or Hever. It was an essay in vastness.

Carnegie may have been born in Dunfermline, the son of a weaver, but when his father took the Carnegie family off to Pittsburgh in 1848, the 13-year-old Andrew Carnegie became more or less perfectly Americanised. Just like an early Astor or Vanderbilt, he fought his way up from nothing, establishing the Carnegie Steel Company, and selling it to J.P. Morgan at the end of the century for $480 million, thus, temporarily, becoming 'the richest man in the world'. He also turned heads by writing a tract called *Triumphant Democracy*, a eulogy to his new home. 'The British race, all equal citizens from birth, will be a very different antagonist to the semi-serfs you have so far easily excelled', he told his American readers. 'Assuredly the stuff is in these Island mastiffs. It is only improper training and lack of suitable stimulating nourishment to which their statesmen have subjected them, that renders them feeble.'[6] At this point he turned his back on business in order to reinvent himself as a philanthropist. His tireless autodidacticism and his retiree's sentimentality towards the land of his birth saw to it that in 1898 he bought Skibo, a dilapidated castle near Dornoch in Easter Ross, with a view to housing his library, spending his summers in Scotland and overseeing his philanthropic works.

Skibo had once been a tenth-century Viking stronghold in Sutherland, just north of Inverness. By the time Carnegie saw it, it had become a middling-sized Victorian Highland fastness, mildly improved by its previous owner, Mr Evan Sutherland-Walker, 'a dapper little gentleman, often attired in Highland dress of kilt, balmoral bonnet and buckled shoes'. Sutherland-Walker had bought the place in 1872, at which time 'his driving-out equippage of carriage and pair was first class, with liveried coachman and groom on the dicky'.[7] But financial mismanagement and a wilderness of litigation eventually forced Sutherland-Walker out. At this point, Skibo was balanced uneasily between traditional discomfort and low-key modernity. Carnegie saw his chance, bought the estate and on 1 May, he, his American wife Louise and their daughter Margaret paid their first visit. An organist was hired to play Beethoven's Fifth Symphony as they arrived. Louise wrote,

> We are all very pleased with our new home. The surroundings are more of the English type than Scotch. The sweet pastoral scenery is perfect of its kind. A beautiful undulating park with cattle grazing, a stately avenue of fine old beeches, glimpses of the Dornoch Firth, about a mile away, all seen through the picturesque cluster of lime and beech trees. All make such a peaceful picture that already a restful home feeling has come. The Highland features to which our hearts turn longingly are not wanting, but are more distant.[8]

This last reference was a coy reminder that the Carnegies had already spent some time holidaying further inland in a smaller, wilder, rented lodge: getting a taste for Scotland, which could now only be satisfied by buying something outright.

Having inspected the property, the Carnegies left, so that Skibo could be rebuilt – indeed, massively inflated, into a kind of parody of a Scottish baronial stronghold. Carnegie's motives were, inevitably, affected by the fact that he was a returning emigré – a poor boy who had made good, who had embraced a new nationality, who was coming back to prove a point to the people he'd left behind. Like the rich, score-settling, property-buying deracinated Irish-American Malone, in Shaw's *Man and Superman*, Carnegie had business to finish – with his inner drives, if not with the inhabitants of nearby Dornoch. In Malone's words, 'I was starved out to America in me mother's arms. English rule drove me and mine out of Ireland. Well, you can keep Ireland. Me and me like are coming back to buy England; and we'll buy the best of it. I want no middle class properties.'[9] Carnegie was similarly preoccupied with the demands of the past, but was less aggressive in his delivery. He let the staggering bulk of Skibo argue on his behalf, while sentimentally insisting on his own homespun half-truths: 'I'm a Celt, not a prosaic Englishman',[10] he liked to say.

Such Scottish pieties are less convincing than the evident need to make a grand statement. Carnegie's business partner, Henry Phipps, had actually used the highly tasteful architectural *pasticheur* George Crawley to decorate his new house in New York. But Crawley's sweet, painstaking historical whimsy would not have done at Skibo. Carnegie went instead to the rather tougher Ross & Macbeth, of Inverness. They designed him something that was externally colossal, over-busy, and yet austere; and which was internally palatial. Between 1900 and 1903, he spent an estimated £100,000 on the property. The result was later described as having the effect 'of a grand hotel, the architecture purchased by the yard'. The structure which was Skibo went from being conventionally daunting to being absolutely immense. Two hundred tons of steel were shipped over from Carnegie's own Pittsburgh steelyards to provide a new inner framework. Twenty-one principal bedrooms were gouged out of the existing building or built on to it. A fireplace as big as a boxroom was fitted into the predictably vast dining room. The library – the moral heart of the new Skibo – was laboriously panelled in light oak and topped with a pale yellow moulded ceiling. Above the 12-foot-high bookcases (which had space for 7,000 volumes) ran a 2-foot-high frieze of carved oak bearing all the coats of arms of all the Scottish cities that had given their freedom to Carnegie: among them Edinburgh, Glasgow, Aberdeen, Dundee, Perth, Dingwall, Tain, Dumfries and Wick. All were bound together by intricate Celtic designs based on the flora and fauna of Scotland. The entrance hall – a symphony of Jacobean-flavoured parquetry,

balustrades, panelling and loosely gothicised stone arches –
contained stained-glass windows depicting scenes from Carnegie's
life: his birthplace; the ship that took him to America in 1848; the
ship that brought him back; Skibo itself. An indoor swimming pool
stood near the castle, its fresh sea-water heated by the same boiler
that heated the greenhouses. (Swimming pools were not necessarily
pernicious in themselves, but they did arouse suspicion. The Duke of
Richmond and Gordon recalled that when Gordon Castle acquired a
pool, 'Everybody disapproved of it, thought it was rather fast . . .
When we had built the swimming pool and my father's brother,
Esme Gordon, was staying with us, we said "Uncle Esme, you must
come and see the swimming pool." "No, thank you," he said, really
quite shocked, "as far as I'm concerned, water is a thing you get
fishes out of".'[11] A guest at Skibo, on the other hand, luxuriously
observed how 'We have all been in the new swimming bath, a sort of
Winter garden with a marble bath of warm sea water – men and
women all tumbling about like seals in the American fashion.'[12])

Carnegie's pool was not the worst of his alterations; but the boiler
was a problem. On first firing up, it was found that the pool boiler-
house had been placed in precisely the right spot for the prevailing
winds to blow the smoke back over the castle. A tunnel therefore
had to be built at great additional expense, to convey the boiler
smoke underground to the main furnace inside the castle. From
there it could escape harmlessly through the furnace chimney. After
due investigation, it turned out that there was no waterfall anywhere
on the Skibo estate. So Carnegie bought an immense tract of land
from his neighbour, the 4th Duke of Sutherland – who, as a pinched
traditional landowner, was soon to embark on a protracted disposal
of many more of his assets. These additional acres had a fine
waterfall, which was at once co-opted into the Skibo experience.
'Walkers' were employed to tramp along the miles of estate roads to
check for bumps and ruts. The 'Monk's Walk' led from the castle to
Carnegie's private nine-hole golf course. And so on. It was a
masterpiece of dour profligacy. Unlike such great houses as
Blenheim or Knole, whose tenants were always subjugated to the
history of the structure, Skibo, a new pastiche built over the traces
of somewhere forgettable, took its meaning entirely from its creator.
It was a testament to Andrew Carnegie's super-abundant self.

In 1902, when the building works were nearing completion, Carnegie wrote to John, later Viscount, Morley, biographer of Gladstone, 'Skibo never so delightful; all so quiet. A home at last . . . the average American wouldn't like our life at Skibo. There aren't enough of "other people" to go around – no casinos, no dancing, and all that. But we love it . . .'[13] This was a typically Carnegie gloss on an awkward situation. The problem was that while Skibo Castle was an irrefutable gesture of potency, it was also too big to be in any way satisfactorily domestic or home-like. Despite his claims that 'There aren't enough of "other people" to go around', it was in reality a vast, zoo-like clearing house for Carnegie's powerful friends – constantly full of tireless industrialists, Liberal politicians and writers: Lloyd George, Rudyard Kipling, the Rockefellers. Everyone had to be active, all the time. At eight o'clock every morning, a bagpiper woke the household from the terraces. The castle organist played selections of Beethoven, Bach, Wagner, while the company ate breakfast. Carnegie then compelled his guests (with the exception of John Morley, who held special sway over his affections) to walk, play golf, fish, sail or drive, as long as the weather held out. Every Fourth of July, he held a fête, blessed by a Siamesed standard made up of the Stars and Stripes and the Union Flag sewn together. The swimming pool could be turned into a ballroom. A massive dance floor was once erected, 'Huge electric arc lamps and chandeliers glittered overhead', Logan's dance band from Inverness played on the balcony, alternating with the castle piper. Edward VII came for lunch and Carnegie got the celebrated poetaster Joaquin Miller ('The Byron of the Rockies') to produce some verse in honour of the visit. Miller's poem contained the deathly line 'Hail, fat Edward!', which Carnegie roguishly underscored by saying 'That's you, Sir!' to the appalled King. Notionally created as a summer retreat, Skibo became what it looked like: a great, bustling five-star resort and, worse, a test of endurance for Carnegie's long-suffering wife.

By 1904, Louise was shattered by Carnegie's mania for socialising. He therefore had a smaller country house set up not far from Skibo, at Auchinduich. Retreating from his original retreat, he wrote to Morley, 'The family go into retreat July 22 – to Aug. 10th away up the high moors . . . Madam thinks higher air for two weeks best for

Baba [their daughter Margaret]. She also gets a rest preparatory to shooting season. It is an experiment we are to try. I think a wise one.'[14] This was marginally better, and Louise felt able to carry on hostessing at Skibo. The Carnegie family visits finally stopped with the outbreak of the First World War. Daughter Margaret subsequently kept the place up, but when she died, the castle, having no meaning other than to memorialise an individual and – unlike Blenheim – being too ugly to justify itself in any other way, lapsed, like many Highland strongholds, into disrepair before being rejuvenated as a real, working, hotel.

'To those who were privileged to know him', wrote one Scottish devotee, Carnegie's 'memory has a fragrance which the passing years never seem to take away, but lingers indefinitely like the fragrance of crushed petals in a pot-pourri bowl.'[15] The sense of evanescence is not misplaced: for all its immensity, Skibo had a paradoxically disposable quality about it, a very American kind of expendable newness. It was built to look as eternal and unbreachable as the Pyramids; but it was in use for scarcely more than a decade. And yet Carnegie genuinely identified with the place. While Ralph Nevill opprobriated the expatriate American owners of country houses – 'Though wealthy Americans spend large sums on acquiring old country houses and on doing them up in elaborate fashion, they seldom spend much of their time there, and often get rid of them after a short space of time when the novelty of house decoration and garden planning has worn away'[16] – Carnegie was, in his way, sincere. It was the castle that was phoney.

At least Skibo seemed to give Carnegie some kind of pleasure. W.W. Astor, conversely, was miserable, with or without Hever, the jewel in his crown. He employed psychic researchers to track down Anne Boleyn's ghost; they failed. He built a maze and 'discovered' a smugglers' cave. It did not make him happy. Another ill-fated trip to the United States in 1904 only worsened his sense of persecution. Journalists and gossip-mongers dogged him. 'I do not believe', he wrote the following year, 'that anything would avail to change the ordinary acceptation in America of my great grandfather's life and character. He will go down as a "Dutch sausage peddler" and my fate promises to be the same if the American press can make it so.'[17]

Back from the States and brooding on his dignity, he oversaw the final stage of the work at Hever, before abruptly losing interest in it – much as he had lost interest in Cliveden. His daughter Pauline had been acting as hostess for him; but she married Lt-Col. Herbert Clay in 1904 and in 1906 Astor handed Hever over to his oldest son. He moved down to Brighton, where he bought a villa and busied himself with creating yet another Italian garden.

Late in the day – 1913, in fact – he surprised himself by embarking on an affair with Lady Sackville, the result of 'a splendid hour's excitement' at Hever. He gave the needy Baroness £10,000 in cash and they made more assignations at the fortress house on the Embankment, where Astor felt most at ease. It all fell apart, naturally enough, as Lady Sackville wrote in 1914, having just visited Astor at his home in Sorrento: 'He has become hard on everyone, even against his own children and so self-centred and unfeeling about everything . . . We are parting perfectly good friends, but things have changed, alas.'[18] Finally, having concluded that not just America, but virtually the whole world, was not a fit place for a gentleman to live, he retired once and for all to his Brighton villa, devoted himself to the prodigious consumption of food and drink and died on 18 October 1919 after a fine meal of roast mutton and macaroni. His body was found, slumped in the lavatory, replete and dead.

What more could he have done, though, to make himself tolerable to English society? He was generous to a wide variety of charities and hospitals. His donations to the Red Cross and other forms of war aid during the First World War were lavish and gratefully welcomed by the British government. The universities of Oxford and Cambridge between them received $250,000 in gifts. In 1916, he was made Baron Astor of Hever, in recognition of his services; a year later, his title was bumped up to a viscountcy. How better could he have ingratiated himself?

In the end, the buildings he owned came to define him more closely even than the personality with which he met the rest of the world. As with Andrew Carnegie, the grandeur of his architectural projects served to distance him, rather than incorporate him. For Carnegie – a tourist, a play-actor – this was not so much of a problem. For Astor, always searching for confirmation, assurance, justification, the great Hever project, for all its many felicities, only emphasised his awkwardness, his aura of wrongness. The great house gave physical shape to the limits of American ambition.

The Marlboroughs were likewise entering the new century with a mixture of bold conviction and gathering uncertainty. Consuelo had by now added to her portfolio of successes by making a ravishing attendant to Queen Alexandra at the 1902 Coronation. She was one of four pretty duchesses who acted as pall-bearer to the Queen at the moment of coronation: dressed with almost oriental magnificence, dripping with pearls and diamonds, a huge pearl choker accentuating her slender neck, an underdress of antique lace revealing itself between layers of velvet and ermine, she bore aloft a pall of yellow silk on the end of a silver staff as the new Queen knelt. It was hardly surprising that J.M. Barrie should have made his declaration that he would stand all day in the street just to watch the beautiful Duchess get into her carriage.

Using a gift of money from W.K. Vanderbilt, the Marlboroughs confidently built themselves a new town house in London, calling it Sunderland House and decorating the exterior with stylised stone carvings of their own faces. Sunny's adventures in politics saw to it that he became Under-Secretary for the Colonies. There was no apparent affection between the Duke and Duchess; but this was not a difficulty in itself. He had her money; she had his great title. That was enough. In the Edwardian scheme of things, the next step would have been for each to take a lover, while leaving the relationship nominally intact – like the façade of a great building, behind which all kinds of secret alterations and underminings were taking place.

And so it happened, with Sunny starting surprisingly early – at around the time his first son, John Albert Edward, was being born, in 1897, a scant two years into the marriage. But then, the woman he fell for was Miss Gladys Deacon – another American beauty and very possibly the most desirable creature in Europe at the time.

The daughter of a temperamentally unhinged Bostonian who had shot his wife's lover in a hotel room in Cannes, Gladys was barely out of her teens when she came to stay at Blenheim in 1901. Her profile was exquisitely Grecian; her wit, learning and gaiety were unequalled. The 'Toast of Paris', she was the friend of Marcel Proust and Edgar Degas. She was also romantically pursued by Bernard Berenson, the Duke of Norfolk, Lord Francis Pelham-Clinton-Hope (after his divorce from May Yohé) and 'Little Willy', the German Crown Prince. Gladys and the Duke had first met in 1897, when she was still 16 years old. It says much for the Duke's taste as well as his powers of attraction that over the years he had managed to establish himself as first among Gladys's suitors.

In return, Gladys was nothing if not comprehensively charming. She regularly came to stay at Blenheim, where she seduced Consuelo emotionally as well as Sunny, physically. Quite soon, both Marlboroughs were besotted with this exotic creature. In January 1901, Consuelo wrote to Gladys, 'Whenever I am depressed I imagine myself in Italy with you – not with the Italians – just reading, contemplating everything beautiful and breathing in the spirit of the universe in great deep breaths – uplifting and refreshing. Dont laugh at me! I think I should like to have been a Vestal Virgin & forever nourished the fire of life & rejoiced as such! or else Cleopatra –.' Faced with Gladys's beauty and accomplishments, Consuelo betrayed her nervousness, imploring Gladys not to laugh at her pretensions and cloaking herself with the defiance of the insecure: 'I hate the middle course.'[19] Consuelo's pet name from childhood was 'Coon'. Gladys allowed Consuelo her little outburst and asked her to send a lock of hair. Consuelo promised a 'Coon ringlet'.

Sunny wrote to Gladys a few months later, rather more elegantly quoting La Rochefoucauld: 'L'absence diminue les médiocres passions, et augmente les grandes, comme le vent éteint les bougies et allume le feu.'[20] Gladys was drawn both by Sunny's title and his apparent erudition. In August she came to stay at Blenheim for six months and for a while both Consuelo and Sunny were happy. The tripartite relationship intensified. In July 1904, when Gladys was temporarily lying sick in Italy, Sunny and Consuelo unwittingly wrote her loving notes of sympathy and condolence on the same day. Sunny referred to the 'kindness which I believe few men have received at a woman's hands'; while Consuelo, belying the air of New World primness which sometimes hung about her, sang to 'Dear little Gladischen', that

My heart is very full of kindness for you . . . I love you & feel for you and you want love and sympathy, women can give to each other what no man gives us – for their love is interested & is often in opposition to self interest . . . I want you too, I long for your clever and deep thoughts, for all that makes you so attractive and dear and I feel very silly writing this, but it is quite true & I have never cared for any other woman like you – I feel as if you were my sister . . . just be your nice self while you read this & think of the Coon who is fond of you . . .

This appeal plainly worked, as Gladys replied, 'Dearest Coon, your letter went straight to my heart & awakened there new echoes of love for you.'[21]

Had Consuelo been content to pursue her own love affairs while acting the complaisant wife, then the marriage might have staggered on for decades. The problem was that she felt herself insufficiently bound by the conventions of her class. Not only was she nurturing a passionate affection for Gladys Deacon, she felt able – having satisfied the future of the Marlboroughs by producing an heir and his brother – to embark in 1905 on a preposterously visible fling with the notorious Charley Castlereagh. Having emoted to 'Dear little Gladischen', she then ran off to Paris with Charley – a move of such incandescent boldness that not only did it spell the end of the Marlboroughs' marriage, it also very nearly ruined that of the Castlereaghs. Society, used to the moral deficiencies of the Marlboroughs, would have taken their bad behaviour almost as a matter of course. But the Castlereaghs – and, more pointedly, Charley's parents, the Marquess and Marchioness of Londonderry – were too prominent for the rest of the world to let the matter go. Despite Charley's already substantial history of womanising, it was felt that eloping to Paris with Consuelo was too big, too irresponsible. Sunny wired to Consuelo in Paris that he didn't want her back; the royal family leant on Charley to return and give up his luscious prize. Charley gave in to royal pressure and returned.

One reason, of course, that he felt able to devote himself to a lifetime of promiscuity was because he had let himself be dragooned into marriage at the age of 21 with a woman he knew he could take advantage of. Edith, Lady Castlereagh, was big, hearty, pleasant-looking, snobbish and energetic. She was not a society beauty, despite her sexy tattoos (done in the manner of the royal family) and her cultivation of a wryly knowing half-smile for the photographers. She was also besotted with Charley and stayed besotted with him for the rest of their marriage, constantly reminding him how 'I never cease to love you more than anyone else in the whole world.'[22] This was just the kind of wife he wanted. In between tutting over his latest affair and bringing up the children, she could pour out her devotion on him ('I don't blame you because the women hunt you to death. You are so beautiful and so attractive')[23] at the same time as she fulfilled her part of the larger dynastic contract by producing an heir – the young Robin Castlereagh – and translating herself into the notional Queen of London society, as her mother-in-law had done before the war. Thus she would not only sustain the lustre of the family, but put herself in the best position devotedly to further whatever career Charley thought might begin to suit him: starting with the viceroyalty of India and working his way down. She was the obverse, therefore, of Consuelo. The Londonderrys were rich, but Edith's father, Henry Chaplin, was a quintessential pleasure-loving grandee, who ate, drank and sported his way through the family money with prodigious efficiency, leaving Edith as one of those big, pink, underfunded English girls to whom the rich, highly finished Americans were such a threat. She was bound to Charley Londonderry by adoration and by money. Consuelo neither cared for Sunny nor needed his money, given that his money was her money, anyway. Edith was beefy; Consuelo was luscious. Everything about Consuelo held a capacity for danger, for dislocation.

Edith, housebound with her small children, could not sustain the mask of tolerance with which she had greeted his other infidelities. This time she felt entirely humiliated; and let her feelings show. Charley was penitent on his return. 'My own darling Edie', he wrote, genuinely unnerved at her new horror of him, 'I feel you are beginning to hate me. I don't think I have been nice to you. I have been cruel and unkind to you and now I believe you do not care about me at all.' He vowed that he felt a real sorrow; he recalled how her face used to light up when she saw him; he mourned the terrible rift that had opened up in their marriage and the iciness in

Edith's manner. 'You never want to see me and you never want to talk to me and you seem to want me to go away from you', he wrote, as if her revulsion could not have been anticipated: 'Forgive me, my darling, and do love me again.' Consuelo was just too powerful a threat for horsy, English Edith to affect to scorn. She replied,

> I did experience a real deep shock in the early summer and it showed me with a clearness and abruptness how foundations which one imagines to be firmly built on rocks seem as nothing when a great wave of – what shall I say? – feeling anything you like, comes along . . . God alone knows what I expected in the summer when I felt that everything was slipping and sliding away from me.[24]

Consuelo's easy alacrity in running off with Charley Castlereagh not only poisoned the Castlereagh marriage (and gave Charley a taste for rich American aristocrats which he indulged again with the Countess of Ancaster); it revealed the extent to which she felt herself outside the order of things. The Countess of Warwick and Lady Randolph Churchill (to name just two) were both flamboyant enough in their affairs and yet, beholden to smart society, usually managed to pay lip-service to the conformities of the time.

Consuelo, on the other hand, bored to tears by her marriage, simply took off with a wholly conspicuous philanderer. And while Charley subsequently fell into line, Consuelo carried on in her own way. Tempered by the rigidifying *ennui* of Blenheim and inured to the ways of the British aristocracy after ten years of the Marlboroughs, she had arrived at a new conception of her own position and responsibilities. When Joseph Chamberlain married Mary Endicott, daughter of the American Secretary of State for War, in 1888, Beatrice Potter (later Webb) wrote that Mary 'will draw him closer to the aristocratic party. She is . . . an American aristocrat and like the aristocrats of a new country is probably more aristocratic in her tastes and prejudices than the aristocrats of the old country.'[25] What was true of Mary Chamberlain was even more true of Consuelo. Having overcome the adminstrative headaches of running Blenheim, she was in no sense cowed or intimidated by her position as a duchess. There was a parity in her own mind between the status she enjoyed as a Marlborough and the status she enjoyed as a Vanderbilt. She enjoyed a high degree of self-determination and personal autonomy. She had all the indifference to others' feelings one would expect of a rich princess – whose smile sometimes worryingly bore the empty, unfeeling, quality of a pretty doll's. What's more, thanks to the provisions of the Married Women's Property Acts, she had no terrors about losing her fortune – unlike her beleaguered godmother, Consuelo Yznaga. Last of all, she managed her separation from Sunny – in itself quite a daring act – in such a way that public opinion gave her, rather than Sunny, the benefit of the doubt, even though both were by now practised adulterers, both without a leg to stand on.

Instead of merely agreeing to let the marriage die a natural death while both parties got on with their lives, Consuelo insisted on a legal separation, enshrining her right of access to the children and to Blenheim itself. Although the Infants' Custody Act of 1839 had gone some way towards addressing the iniquity whereby a divorced or separated woman had *no* right of access to her own children, its provisions were limited. Consuelo therefore had to be determined and well organised in order to make sure that she got what she wanted. The separation became widely known within the family by October 1906. Winston Churchill, confidant to Sunny but ever on good terms with Consuelo, wrote to Jennie Cornwallis-West from Blenheim. Busily, he told her that Sunny had definitely separated from Consuelo; and that Consuelo had moved down to Sunderland House, in London. He then went on to explain how he had volunteered Jennie's offices to Consuelo as a companion and helpmate in her darkest hours, and suggested that Jennie should take herself down to Sunderland House at once and be a prop for Consuelo to lean on.[26] He was genuinely upset by the split and, buoyed by his native ebullience as well as an inability to sense the ferocity of Consuelo's mood, thought that things might be managed with civility, at least. Later that year, he would assure Consuelo that he would always strive to defend her (incontrovertibly damaged) reputation in the eyes of the world and praying that within a year she would be both united with her children and legally sorted out with respect to Sunny.[27]

Sunny's position remained more or less the same, to the extent that he still enjoyed the $100,000 per annum settled on him by his father-in-law. His detestation of Consuelo, however, grew with time. By the end of 1906, Consuelo's letters to him from Sunderland House were pure legalese, dictated by her lawyers and written in her own, surprisingly confident, hand: 'The Duchess's legal advisors have not a shadow of a doubt that having regard to the conclusive evidence against the Duke the Court would give the custody of the children for at least ½ the year to their mother.'[28] This display of chilly tenacity made Sunny furious. He was even driven to offend his beloved cousin. The start of 1907 found him writing a long letter of expiation to Winston, beginning, 'I hate to quarrel with you' and 'I will imitate your suggestion not to enter into a long argument.' The problem at the heart of their rupture was, of course, Consuelo and the children. 'I appeared to estrange myself from you all. There was policy in my method', he explained, declaring that Consuelo 'intimidated you and relied on your influence to work on me. The moment that she was informed that I had broken communications with you . . . she dropped all her nonsense . . . and accepted at once the terms of separation.' There was more. 'You must forgive me . . . I had to pretend to be estranged from you. It was the only way I could triumph over that Old Hag. She is now utterly defeated, and she can stuff up her – ' here a black line appears in the manuscript, marking the spot where he would have put a torrid anatomical expletive, ' – her intimidations.'[29]

Sunny's confidence that 'she is now utterly defeated' was misplaced. Lord Hugh Cecil wrote to Winston,

The Christians feel that whatever his wife may have done, at any rate he is to blame as himself unfaithful; the fast set do not like a fuss made about such a matter and the implied rebuke at their own lives. His position, that his wife is unfit to live with him because she went wrong before he did and because the standard for women in these things is higher than for men, is not defensible either before the Church or the World. I am sure he will do himself harm.[30]

The US President, Theodore Roosevelt, wrote to his ambassador in London, meanwhile, 'The lowest note of infamy is reached by such a creature as this Marlborough, who proposing to divorce the woman when *he* at least cannot afford to throw any stone at her, nevertheless proposes to keep and live off the money she brought him.'[31] Even George Cornwallis-West's amenable sister, Princess Daisy of Pless, felt a kind of pitying disdain towards him. Staying with her at Avignon, in the company of the American-born Countess of Essex, Sunny managed emblematically to reduce a dining table to rubble. The Princess wrote in her diary:

> After dinner we wanted to have the table moved so the Duke pushed it and down the whole thing went. Dessert, wine, butter, olives, dates, plates; the corner of the room into which everything fell looked like a pigsty . . . it really was rather funny as nothing was left on the table but the cloth. The Duke was miserable; by the way he looked at the debris one might have thought he was peering at his own life, which at the present moment is in much the same state.[32]

It is just possible to feel a degree of sympathy for Sunny in the middle of these humiliations. As John Singer Sargent's great family portrait of him, Consuelo and the children reveals, his crabbed demeanour and physical unimpressiveness left him hopelessly out-classed by Consuelo's irresistible bodily charm and aristocratic bearing. Consuelo herself – the 'Old Hag' – was perfectly capable of wilful and destructive behaviour. But she could get away with it; and knew that she could. All Sunny could do was try to pick up the pieces of his great scheme.

Consuelo's move to London had not only given her the elbow room with which to pursue an affair with the Hon. Reginald Fellowes (whose mother was a daughter of the 7th Duke of Marlborough); it also gave her the freedom to distance herself – quite uncompromisingly – from her old transatlantic companion, Jennie Churchill. Having given so much to society, Jennie was now a more marginal figure – a result of, among other things, her marriage to George Cornwallis-West; her increasing age; her increasing lack of funds; and her insistence on seeing herself as a literary and artistic celebrity. Ettie Desborough went to see her at her house outside St Albans and missed no opportunity to poke fun at her afterwards. As she wrote to A.J. Balfour:

I motored over to see Jennie West – she was all alone in *frowning* vein, in her Moated Grange, like a rather fat Mariana – but *absolutely* undefeated, I never saw anyone show such spirit & dignity in that hopeless position of being tied up to a young flagrant second-rate husband. She was absolutely alone, dressed in some hideous pale mauve cloth, working away with a mildewed (female) secretary at that indescribable rubbish! I looked at a page of the M.S. – it was an interview with Queen Victoria.[33]

In this reduced state, Jennie happily took the opportunity – as Winston had urged her – to move into Sunderland House in the autumn of 1906. There she would help Consuelo ride out the storm; not, however, without a certain *Schadenfreude* of her own.

Poor Consuelo is utterly miserable [she wrote in mid-October], but dignified & quite calm – The whole thing is out so it is no use hiding it . . . I feel as sorry for Sunny as I do for her – & I am obliged to say that he is justified in taking the course he has – it does not make it any the easier for all that she has brought the whole thing on herself – How the women who have had 20 lovers – & are kept by rich Jews et autres will be virtuously shocked![34]

But after a fortnight, Jennie's muscular interventions had palled and Consuelo had frozen her out. Jennie decamped to Bolton Street, from where she wrote

I have left your home *deeply* wounded & hurt at your inexplicable conduct – I make every allowance for the frame of mind you must be in during such a terrible crisis in your life – but that you should turn on *me* who have not only been a true friend to you, but had you been a sister could not have shown you more loyalty & affection, is indeed an unexpected blow – You have not even had the courage to have it out with me. I am in utter ignorance of your strange conduct. My conscience is *absolutely* clear. You needed my friendship & I gave it unhesitatingly. I do not regret it – God knows you are not in a position to alienate a friend.[35]

This was more than just a disagreement between friends at a difficult time. It was a breach between two generations of titled Americans. Jennie Churchill/Cornwallis-West had committed herself to the world into which she had married: despite her reservations and intolerances, she subscribed to it, had built her life around it and was its apologist. Twenty years her junior and with an entirely different view of the world, Consuelo Marlborough was cool, indifferent and felt no loyalty to the caste into which she had married. Determined to put still more distance between herself and her immediate past, she then took to a life of mixed philanthropy – in the manner of the American rich – which ultimately took in the Children's Jewel Fund, the Women's Municipal Party, and becoming a county councillor for Southwark. She worked hard to establish a new identity for herself, distinct from the role she had played as Sunny's wife, keen to create the impression that she had depth. Several years later, Herbert Asquith found himself at lunch at the Duke of Rutland's house in Arlington Street, seated 'between 2 Duchesses – Rutland and Marlborough. The latter by the way was more sensible than I have seen her lately . . .'[36]

She also, as a Parthian shot, took the trouble to torment Sunny one last time by backing Lord Lansdowne for the job of Lord Lieutenant of Oxfordshire – a position that Sunny had set his heart on. So incensed was he, indeed, that he went round to Lansdowne's house in Berkeley Square specifically to berate him. Eventually, Sunny did get the post. 'I do not often complain', he complained to Gladys at the time, 'but few men have been plagued with such a woman as C [Consuelo] – truly her life is spent in doing harm to the family whose name she bears.'[37] But the family whose name she bore was, *au fond*, that of the Vanderbilt family, not the Churchills.

A few years after her separation from Sunny, Consuelo decided she needed a country retreat in order to manage some time away from all her highly visible charity works in town. In her words, mediated by her biographical assistant, the American writer and socialite Stuart Preston (memorialised as the 'Loot' in Evelyn Waugh's *Unconditional Surrender*), 'I wanted a small house not too far from London, and on a wonderful summer day I found it. It was called Crowhurst and was a little Tudor manor house lost in the gold of

the North Wolds. With its high roof of Horsham stone, its walls
half-timbered with silvered oak, its stone chimneys and leaded
casements, it had the charm of an old engraving.' For Consuelo, it
seemed, it was the realisation of a dream. What's more, it had a
past, having belonged to a Revd Mr Gainsforth, 'whose family had
owned it for four hundred years . . .'[38]

First, the tell-tale phrase 'not too far from London' is significant.
In 1910, when Consuelo bought Crowhurst Place – near Lingfield in
Surrey – it was becoming more and more apparent that the country
house ideal was shifting away from that of a large family home,
splendid in its isolation, to that of a convenient weekend retreat.
Some gardens, a few guest rooms, an hour or so by car or train from
the city, were all that was needed. Second, and more important, is
the fact that Crowhurst was not a 'little Tudor manor house' which
had been snugly in the ownership of the Gainsforths for four
centuries. It was, instead, a very good modern pastiche, built by the
designer and architect George Crawley, around the wreck of a fine
timber hall dating from 1432.

Crawley – who had previously worked for Andrew Carnegie's
business partner George Phipps – had actually bought Crowhurst
for himself and his wife in 1907. At that time, it was not much more
than a decaying farmstead reached by a wooden bridge thrown
across an overgrown moat. The 'walls half-timbered with silvered
oak' didn't exist; nor the 'high roof of Horsham stone', nor the
'leaded casements'. All these had to be painstakingly added by
Crawley over the years. His first winter there was so bare of
comforts that snow blew in through holes in the roof. By the time he
had finished, however, the place was transformed into a delicious
and civilised fantasy of a Tudor building, at which point his wife,
made ill by the exigencies of all the building work, could no longer
live there. Luckily, Crawley found Consuelo as a purchaser. Even
more luckily, she kept him on as consulting architect in order to
enlarge the place further with a servants' wing built on to the
ground floor of the north-east corner in the same half-timbered
medieval–Tudor style which Crawley had romantically elaborated
over the rest. 'The hall reached from the ground to the raftered
roof', said Consuelo, 'in which an opening still showed that it had
been built before the days of chimneys.'[39] Which was true, given

that the hall was the only really old part of the house. What was also true was that, in diametric opposition to Blenheim Palace – which, despite all the Hammersley and Vanderbilt money that had been poured into it, was never going to be anything less than a breathtakingly expensive and inconvenient aesthetic monolith – Crowhurst was neat, fully modernised and largely inauthentic. What Consuelo wanted, in her directed, American way, was a charming simulacrum of traditional English country life; not the endless compromises of the real thing. What she wanted – and got – was a Hever in little.

More than that: Crowhurst underlined her independence, her personal sovereignty and her ability to pick and choose those elements of English life that appealed to her. She was now a very long way from being a glamorous adjunct to a great English family. Instead, she was a property-owning transatlantic freewoman of uncertain talents, considerable social standing, and a conviction of her own worth. W.W. Astor strained to achieve precisely such a state in Hever, and failed. Consuelo, with her admixture of independence, taste, selfishness and femininity, had more or less achieved it. Title, American wealth and English land came together in one person: the most complete realisation of the Anglo-American ideal. Which was not at all what Sunny had had in mind for her, back in 1895.

Eventually she tired of Reginald Fellowes (whom the Duke had stumbled across at Beaulieu-sur-Mer and cursed as 'a dark swarthy looking mulatto') and took up with an old flame, M. Jacques Balsan. Balsan was a wealthy French *haut-bourgeois*, with whom she found greater happiness than she had ever experienced with Sunny. This had much to do with the fact that Balsan treated her tirelessly like a lady. In 1920, she and Sunny finally divorced. In 1921, she married M. Balsan and went to spend her time in the south of France. Clementine Churchill subsequently wrote to Winston from the Balsan house, where she was staying as a guest, that Consuelo was blooming: rosy-cheeked, bright-eyed, constantly plied with treats and gestures of endearment by 'her Jacques'.[40] *Il n'y a rien plus belle qu'une femme aimée*, in fact.

EIGHT

The War

By 1910, and with the death of Edward VII, the Anglo-American project had stalled. The supply of heiresses was drying up; and, anyway, it had become clear that no American dowry on its own, however large, could shore up the fortunes of the British aristocracy, jointly or severally. The horrors of Lloyd George's 'People's Budget' of 1909, with its death duties, its land taxes and its supertax, merely hastened the end for many landowners. Even a grandee such as the 9th Duke of Bedford found himself disposing of great parcels of land, regarding it as 'modern and up-to-date to sell off landed property and buy stocks and shares because the return was greater'.[1] At the same time, King Edward's enthusiasm for all things foreign was replaced by George V's smothering insularity. 'The nearest I ever got to the United States', he announced, 'was when I walked half-across Niagara, took off my hat and walked back again.'[2] American wives had either disappeared into the mainstream of society, or, like Jennie Cornwallis-West, were battling to maintain a position they had grown used to.

In 1908, Jennie produced a volume of memoirs which managed to be relatively low on mealy-mouthed *politesse* and relatively high on old grievances – not least of which was the position of the American in society. Harking back over thirty years, to the time when she was still an *ingénue*, she recalled how 'American men were myths, few being idle enough to have leisure to travel. But they were all supposed to be as loud and vulgar as the mothers were unpresentable and the daughters undesirable – unless worth their weight in gold.'[3] Richard Henry Dana had expatiated on a similar issue a generation earlier, wincingly describing an American tourist who had barged into a reception in Paris:

She had too much paint on her face, spoke in a loud voice, wore the extreme *décolletée* fashion, and was plainly common and eccentric . . . Altogether she did and said so many strange things that she made me blush for my country, and the good French people stared in amazement. She had left her husband in New York, her children in Germany, and is in Paris, as she says, to 'amuse herself'. It is by such women that foreigners judge American society. These queer people inform their new acquaintances that they are of the best families; of the 'high aristocracy' of America; and the poor foreigners swallow this information with astonishing credulity and afterwards tell their friends of the *Américaine*, so none but the most eccentric get talked about and it becomes generally believed that our American society is made up of just such people; while the well-bred, cultivated Americans escape observation altogether.[4]

As for Dana, so for Jennie Cornwallis-West:

The innumerable caricatures supposed to represent the typical American girl depicted her always of one type: beautiful and refined in appearance, but dressed in exaggerated style, and speaking – with a nasal twang – the most impossible language. The young lady who, in refusing anything to eat, says, 'I'm pretty crowded just now', or in explaining why she is travelling alone [and here Mrs Cornwallis-West stole a joke from *Punch*] remarks that 'Poppa don't voyage, he's too fleshy', was thought to be representative of the national type and manners.[5]

Mercifully, with thanks to Jennie's tireless efforts and flawless integrity as a human being,

A great deal of water has flowed under the bridge since those days. The steady progress of American women in Europe can be gauged by studying their present position. It is not to be denied that they are sharing many of the 'seats of the mighty', and the most jealous and carping critic cannot find fault with the way they fill them. In the political, literary, and diplomatic world they hold their own. The old prejudices against them, which arose mostly out of ignorance, have been removed, and the American woman is now generally approved of.[6]

A year after her *Reminiscences* came out, Jennie staged her play, *Borrowed Plumes*. This ran for two weeks in July at the Haymarket Theatre and starred Henry Ainley and, fatally, Mrs Patrick Campbell, who seduced away George Cornwallis-West. *The Times* quietly remonstrated that Mrs Campbell 'had to be exasperatingly passive, a kind of patient Griselda, meekly suffering . . . when one longed for some outburst of *furia Campbelliana*'. It then recorded that 'At the fall of the curtain the authoress was compelled to acknowledge with curtseys the cheers of the audience', before the society ladies who had made up the bulk of the crowd 'again put on their Directoire hats, and, as they prattled their way out into the rain, declared that, after all, it had been much better fun than Henley could possibly have been'.[7] Less fun for Jennie, as it turned out. 'Jennie had written a play', George later wrote, in his guilt, 'and was anxious for Mrs. Campbell to produce it and to play the principal part; consequently the latter became a constant visitor to the house.'[8] George pounced; Mrs Campbell yielded. Separation hung over the Cornwallis-Wests, but no matter: Jennie defiantly wrote to her sister, Leonie, 'After all, and I say this without conceit but as a fact, if I were to die tomorrow, of all the "Souls" lot, I am the only woman who should leave a record behind her. The Primrose League, the Maine Hospital ship, the *Anglo-Saxon Review*, my book, my play!'[9] And then, in 1912, the year in which George asked for a divorce, she organised the 'Shakespeare's England' exhibition at Earl's Court, causing the *Daily Mail* to describe her as 'the busiest woman in London'.

This was a long way from the hopes and ambitions of 1874; a long way from the dreams of plunder which the Mandevilles and Blandfords had entertained. What society was now getting was energy, dynamism; not the hard cash that was its by-product. It drew one's attention inexorably back to the idea that America itself was the source of power and influence, and that Britain's job was now, increasingly, to look across the Atlantic in puzzled wonder. In an echo of those blithe aristoratic excursions of fifty years earlier, the Countess of Warwick set off to the United States – at the same time that Jennie Cornwallis-West was establishing Shakespeare's England in west London – to deliver a series of lectures on the question of women's suffrage. But it was not a happy experience.

Countess Daisy was upset before she even got off the boat: 'The first trial that faced me was the odious way that I was beset by reporters. They did not even wait for the arrival of the liner, but scrambled on board from a boat and swarmed around me. It was plain that whatever I said would be exaggerated, and I was warned by friends that if I said nothing these men would write up sham interviews and supply me with opinions.' Then she found that all her patrician high-mindedness counted for nothing with the common people of New York:

> The Carnegie Hall was crowded for my first lecture, but I soon discovered that my audience was lusting for Society gossip and were in no mood for serious subjects. They wanted to hear anecdotes about high life and royal palaces, not about women workers. They had paid big prices for their seats and I had to do my best to satisfy them. After that experience I hurriedly sketched out a few talks on Society with a big S, and gave five lectures in different cities. But this was not what I had come to America to do, so I took legal advice, and broke my contract.[10]

This was a personal humiliation; it was also a clear sign that high birth and an aristocratic title carried no special benefits, exacted no larger respect. The opposite, in fact. They were frivolous, an invitation to the cheaper side of human nature to come out to play. The Countess of Warwick was no longer a person of significance, but a circus sideshow, an entertaining oddity. Something had happened during the intervening generation to make the whole, perfect, British caste system seem far less enticing than it had done before.

And then, of course, there was the First World War.

Georgiana, 5th Duchess of Devonshire, had set a trend for aristocratic women to take an interest in warlike matters at the time of the American War of Independence. With the British Army mobilising against the threat of a French attack, and troops massing at Coxheath in Kent, she organised a female auxiliary corps that had more to do with stylish dressing and less with practical assistance. 'Her Grace the Duchess of Devonshire', wrote the *Morning Post* in

1788, 'appears every day at the head of the beauteous Amazons on Coxheath, who are all dressed *en militaire.*'[11] Excited by this contact with the world of fighting, the Marchioness of Granby then bought a half-share in a sixteen-gun ship. A precedent was established.

Lady Randolph Churchill had taken things a step further during the Boer War. With her sons and her lover – George Cornwallis-West – all involved in the action, she had determined to do something other than repine helplessly in London. She therefore decided to finance a hospital ship, fully equipped with doctors, nurses and medical orderlies, and send it down to South Africa to bring relief to the British forces. Installing herself as Chairman of the Executive Committee, she argued and cajoled until she got an American millionaire, Bernard Nigel Baker, to come up with an old cattle boat called the *Maine*, which was pressed into service. Minnie Paget was on the committee, stirring up further interest among the Marlborough House set. Louise, Duchess of Argyll, wrote to her in December 1899, 'I am *most anxious* to *know* about the American Ship for Africa. It is a splendid thing to do, and I hear it is being done most thoroughly . . . You know I always want to do all I can for the amity of England & America'[12] – as were both Duchesses of Marlborough, Consuelo and Lily. By the end of 1899, the *Maine* hospital ship was ready, the Duke of Connaught mellifluously sending it off: 'Never before has a ship sailed under the combined flags of the Union Jack and the Stars and Stripes; and it marks, I hope, an occasion which brings out that feeling of generosity and affection that the two countries have for each other.'[13]

Fifteen years later, the politics had moved on. The Boer War had been viewed largely with disfavour by turn-of-the-century America, as Jennie Churchill knew. The *Maine* had had to be financed entirely with 'American money' in order to make the contribution tell. On the other hand, 'It would be useless to deny here the fact that the war was viewed with disfavour by my countrymen. They had a fellow-feeling for the Boer, fighting, as they thought, for his independence.' Luckily, 'The plea of humanity overran their political opinions, and the fund once started, money poured in.'[14] Now, though, there was a greater degree of equivocation, even though the United States did its best to cling to a professed neutrality.

The moment war broke out, polyglot New York was riven with competing charitable efforts, supporting wounded Russians, displaced Serbians, French prisoners-of-war, British amputees and, of course, Germans – combatants, refugees, starving families. Thus the British–American War Relief Fund, based in Manhattan, took in a gift of $905 one month, $2,000 another (for the supply of a recreation hut 'near the battlefront in France'),[15] and organised a concert whose souvenir programme showed 'Miss America carrying a basket laden with food toward the scene of the European Conflagration'.[16] By way of contrast, a German bazaar, held in Madison Square Garden, raised a staggering $26,000 in a single March night, to aid 'widows and orphans of the Fatherland'. The problem was that for all its attempts to remain disinterested, the United States was, overall, rather less in favour of the Germans than it had been of the Boers. And when it turned out that one Teutonic bazaar had included a rifle range in which the targets were dummies dressed in French, Russian and British military uniforms, even the *New York Times* was moved to protest.[17] There was a licence to side with the Allies.

If this was true in New York, it was doubly true in London. Lady Churchill's coyness about approaching Americans for money in the Boer War no longer applied. Expatriate American women seized the chance to occupy themselves on Britain's behalf. Some, like Mrs Almeric Paget, started off bold and unconventional, founding the Almeric Paget Military Massage Corps to treat wounded officers and men. Others, like Lady Churchill, drifted into *bien-pensant* artistic works with a view to boosting morale and maintaining standards. Working with Mr A.G. Temple, normally Art Director of the Corporation of London, she began 1915 by helping to organise a show of naval and military paintings at the Manchester Art Gallery.

Consuelo Marlborough, in contrast, set to work on a comprehensive programme of charitable acts. Tempered by her work for the Women's Municipal Party and on Southwark Council, she began January 1915 by chairing a meeting of the American Women's War Relief Fund in Park Lane. This was attended by the Duchess of Roxburghe, Cora, Countess of Strafford, Jennie Churchill – taking a break from picture-hanging – and Minnie Paget. The rift between

Jennie and Consuelo at the time of Consuelo's separation in 1906 had been patched up, although it was never quite sound again, as Jennie revealed in a letter frantically dashed off in 1915 to Lady Lister-Kaye (Natica, sister of Consuelo Manchester) in which she wrote,

I understand from Consuelo Marlborough that you are supposed to have told Flora Guest that I 'abused the Vanderbilts'. As I have never done *anything of the kind* to you or to anyone else, I would be very grateful if you would write & deny this, as it seems incredible that you could have said such a thing – Consuelo Marlborough & I are on valued terms of friendship – we work together, & such a statement if true would make our position towards each other difficult – therefore I sincerely hope that you will be able to contradict it . . .[18]

By March of 1915, Consuelo Marlborough was writing to *The Times* to inform subscribers to the Domestic Servants' Red Cross Fund (whose administrative HQ was Sunderland House) that the ambulance which it had sent to the Front had 'carried no less than 185 wounded soldiers'. The twenty beds which the fund had endowed at Netley military hospital in Southampton had also 'been fully occupied the whole time'.[19] In May, she held an 'At Home' at Sunderland House in aid of L'Oeuvre du Vêtement des Soldats Belges, with poems by de Musset. She followed this a month later with another 'At Home', in aid of the British Red Cross Society. The Duke of Marlborough was stung into retaliating with some mildly publicised wartime 'farming experiments' at Blenheim, only for Consuelo to hold *another* 'At Home' at Sunderland House to promote the Crusade of the United Workers for Self-Denial by Non-Combatants During the War: an aristocratic attempt to encourage thrift among the working classes.

Minnie Paget had, like Jennie Churchill, done sterling charitable work in her day. A masque of Peace and War, organised by her at the Haymarket Theatre during the Boer War, had raised over £7,000. A bazaar in aid of the Charing Cross Hospital had raised a startling £17,000. Age and accident had diminished her by the start of the First World War, but she still threw herself into 'Russia Day',

18 November 1915, in which teas, dinners, concerts and entertainments were provided in support of the Russian allies, along with a matinee at the Alhambra, London, attended by Queen Alexandra. The following year, she organised a jumble sale in June to raise funds for the Wounded Allies Relief Committee, the event taking place at the Caledonian Market, Islington. She even committed herself to raising £1 million to provide homes for soldiers blinded in action. And Lady Lowther, wife of Sir Charles Lowther, Master of the Pytchley, opened an agricultural gift sale for war funds by offering for sale a 3-year-old Shire colt. He was, she said, 'a beautiful horse, gentlemen, he has four legs and can see with both eyes'.[20]

This was very much where things remained. Partial but somehow marginal, the Americans could scarcely involve themselves too thoroughly in anything manifestly national: the emergent Women's Royal Naval Service, or Women's Auxiliary Army Corps – or, for that matter, the Women's Volunteer Reserve. For the braver members of the British aristocracy, their duty was straightforward and inescapable. Lady Diana Manners trained at Guy's Hospital; her mother turned their London home – 21 Arlington Street – into a hospital. The Duchess of Westminster ran the No. 1 Red Cross Hospital at Le Touquet; Lady Dudley organised the Australian hospital nearby; Lady Norman ran No. 5 Red Cross Hospital at Wimereux. Millicent Sutherland organised the Millicent Sutherland Ambulance which went to Namur. And so on.

As women, civilians and expats, the old American heiresses were necessarily at several removes from the heat of action. It took a second generation – as in William Waldorf Astor's son, John Jacob; or Consuelo Marlborough's two sons, John and Ivor; or Minnie Paget's sons Arthur and Albert; or Jennie Churchill's younger son, John – to be English enough to take the fight to the enemy. And when the Americans finally entered the war in 1917, the question of who deserved whose support, and how, became a non-question.

The final year of the war ground on. Peace was negotiated under the umbrella of President Woodrow Wilson's Fourteen Points. The League of Nations came into being, the men who survived came home, and for the British aristocracy, life after the First World War could be anything from just about tolerable to entirely desolating.

At the most personal level, there were many who were living through the intolerable loss of a generation of sons and fathers in the trenches. This generated a deep and chronic anguish in the surviving relatives; and a deep and chronic unease among those contemporaries of the dead who had survived. Then there was the irksome reality of having to rebuild life and society after the catastrophe. And – an issue strictly for a once-privileged minority – there were the landed posessions: the state of the land itself.

Rich families such as the Londonderrys had managed to keep their multiple homes in reasonable shape. So had the Marlboroughs, buoyed up by their American investments. Elsewhere, home parks had been hopelessly vandalised, turned into makeshift farmsteads or troop training grounds. Studs and stables had lost most of their horses to the cavalry; packs of foxhounds had been run down to nothing. Many great houses, both in London and the country, had been ill treated, having been turned over for military or hospital use; or were simply neglected on account of the Great Interruption. Servants were no longer quite so easy to find. And, of course, money was increasingly problematic: a situation not helped in 1919 by Austen Chamberlain's imposition of 40 per cent death duties on estates worth £2 million or more.

What to do? Well, there had been land sales before the war, and these started up again with renewed urgency. In fact it was the year 1918 that cut the tape on a fresh race to market, with one firm of estate agents alone disposing of nearly half a million acres of land during the course of the year (a quarter of a million of those acres belonging to the increasingly desperate Duke of Sutherland). By the start of 1919, the Duke of Westminster, as well as Lords Aberdeen, Aylesford, Beauchamp, Cathcart, Tollemache and Yarborough, were all putting up land for sale – as well as Sutherland, who, braced by his success in the previous year, offered not only another 144 square miles of the Highlands, but the decaying Dornoch Castle as well, not far from Andrew Carnegie's gallingly deluxe Skibo.

By the end of March it was estimated that there were around a thousand square miles of land on the market. Lord Aylesford sold off sections of his Packington Estate, in Warwickshire, and raised £65,000. The Earl of Yarborough sold a mere 350 acres of prime Lincolnshire arable farmland and netted £41,000. The Duke of

Sutherland managed to dispose of his Trentham Estate in Staffordshire for £333,000. And still it went on. The Duke of Rutland sold nearly half of his Belvoir estate in 1920 for a shattering £1.5 million; as well as his entire Scarisbrick estate in Lancashire, for around £1 million. The Duke of Beaufort and the Marquess of Bath were also in the marketplace, while the Duke of Devonshire sold Devonshire House, his magnificent eighteenth-century London home, for £1 million to a developer called Sibthorp. 'I may be called a vandal for pulling down Devonshire House', Sibthorp declared shortly after, 'but personally I think the place is an eyesore. My new super-cinema restaurant, dance hall and tea rooms will be far more beautiful and are much needed.' The Duke and Duchess, meanwhile, moved to Carlton Gardens. 'It will be interesting to see what the pictures look like in a small house', announced the Duchess, valiantly.[21]

New plutocrats had been helping out by buying landed estates since before the war – men such as Lord Leverhulme the soap king, Lord Cowdray the banker, Sir James Buchanan the distiller – and, for a while, they kept the postwar market going. But 1921 saw both the collapse of arable farming when the government reversed its policy on guaranteeing corn prices, and a collapse in industrial production which put nearly a quarter of the labour force out of work. So furious were the property transactions up to this point that the *Estates Gazette* reckoned a quarter of England had changed hands in the space of four years. After this, the terrible silence of inactivity, as a full-scale depression fell on the country. Lord Leconfield declared that being a rural landlord was 'no longer the fun it used to be', while the Duke of Portland threatened to leave his family seat, the bizarre, semi-subterranean Welbeck Abbey, swearing that it was only the crippling hand of government that could make him act in such a way: 'With the present enormous weight of taxation and the extremely onerous incidence of death duties, the future has become uncertain for all landed proprietors.'[22] The Marquess of Linlithgow began 1922 by closing his magnificent Adam residence, Hopetoun House in West Lothian, on account of taxation levels. He mournfully told his estate workers that although he did not care to dwell upon personal aspects of the case, 'Obviously to leave a house which has been in continuous operation from father to son since 1705 is a terrible wrench.'[23]

The disappearance of the old London houses continued. Soon, Lady Michelham would sell her thirty-bedroom mansion in Arlington Street for a mere £75,000; Dorchester House, in Park Lane, would be knocked down to make way for a hotel; the Duchess of Rutland was about to sell off the family mansion – also in Arlington Street – to a property syndicate and move out to the lodge. At the same time, she disposed of Lady Diana Cooper's Italian bedstead for £58. The Duchess of Sutherland liked to throw an annual ball (Sunny Marlborough's heir, the Marquis of Blandford, turned up at one dressed as a female cross-Channel swimmer) but would quickly find that the money had run out and that the balls must cease. All over Britain, it was a long litany of anxious retrenchment.

Against the trend, some more business-minded landowners had managed to improve their finances. The Duke of Northumberland artfully managed to dispose of some land in Surrey and Yorkshire, while, in a brief mid-twenties revival of the market, Lord Portman, Lord Middleton and Lord Brownlow all made sales. The Duke of Sutherland, now cash-rich, snapped up Lord Northcliffe's stately home, Sutton Place in Surrey, using some of the proceeds of his Highland disposals. Lord Leverhulme acquired Grosvenor House in Park Lane, just round the corner from where Devonshire House was being razed to the ground. Those who had held on to their territorial possessions found that some of them could be made to pay through tourism. Indeed, grouse shooting became an industry geared almost entirely towards rich Americans, one of whom paid £35,000 for a five-year tenancy of a famous grouse moor. Others forked out as much as £7,000 for three months' shooting. The Cunard Line took leases on whole tracts of countryside, installed electricity in the cottages, rebuilt the roads and then transported the shooters across the Atlantic. It was said that some American sportsmen brought with them 450 pairs of bedsheets to cut down on the laundry bills. Others were believed to offer $1,000 bills as tips.

But whether you were solvent or impoverished, this much was true: a charmless, postwar world was gradually coming into being, in which the few landed aristocrats who could afford it stayed on comfortably in their family homes, pitying the rotting, servantless country seats of their neighbours, while the rest sold up and moved into aseptic modern flats being built over the ruins of the great town houses. There, as Ralph Nevill put it, 'Many a landowner, having had to exchange his luxurious mansion for a small London flat, sits bewailing that Radical legislation is ruining the country – by which, of course, he means himself.'[24] All of this was duly chronicled by Patrick Balfour – causing Evelyn Waugh to protest later on to Diana Cooper, 'Pauper Balfour wrote a book saying all rich people live in blocks of flats which doesn't seem to me to be true.'[25]

At the same time, the peerage itself – its identity, its quintessence – was being compromised by the arrival of an increasing number of spurious and unsatisfactory titles. This process had been gathering pace since the end of the nineteenth century, and was now becoming a visible embarrassment. By 1890, families who had made their fortunes out of business or commerce comprised a quarter of all new peerages granted. Cubitt the builder, White the chemist and Cunliffe-Lister the velvet king all acquired their titles at this time. Bankers and brewers had been given an earlier dispensation by society to elevate themselves, but even so, the Barings and the Guinnesses took the opportunity at this time to improve their existing titles. Between 1886 and 1914, some two hundred new peers were created. A distressing half of these were from non-landed, non-traditional families. But there was worse to come. Lloyd George's antipathy towards the entrenched aristocracy, combined with a highly opportunistic approach to the granting of new titles, saw to it that in the course of his administration more peers were created annually than had ever happened before. Between 1917 and 1921, he oversaw the creation of four marquessates, eight earldoms, twenty-two viscountcies and no fewer than *sixty-four* baronies.

All of this put Anglo-American marriages in a new light. It was estimated that by 1914, 12 per cent of the baronetcy and 17 per cent of the peerage had some kind of American connection; and that American money had enriched the British aristocracy by well over £40 million. And yet this now seemed to be of merely historical interest. The late-nineteenth-century commonplace that a British peerage could be bought by any sufficiently motivated rich American heiress was replaced by the twentieth-century commonplace that a peerage could be bought by anyone at all. The aristocratic scramble for American wealth – and the agonies that went with it – now seemed so distant, so expressive of a different, more solidly rooted time, that it was almost quaint. Even Ralph Nevill, brooding on the problem of those rich Americans who had settled in England, came up with this gallant admission: 'Some . . . have married and developed into quite passable imitations of English squires – the third generation in such cases is, it must be confessed, usually English to the core.'[26] The awful rupture of the First World War, and its dreary aftermath, made the question of the American in society appear dangerously footling.

In fact, amid all this upheaval what *had* happened to the original American invaders and the great wave of pre-war transatlantic marriages?

They had died, divorced, disappeared into the fabric of society. Middling transatlantic couples such as the Earl and Countess of Yarmouth, the Marquess and Marchioness of Dufferin and Ava, and Lord and Lady Cholmondeley had all divorced. Lily Hammersley, one-time Duchess of Marlborough, stepmother to the current Duke, subsequently Lady Beresford, had died at the beginning of 1909. Consuelo Manchester died at the end of the same year. Beautiful young Consuelo Vanderbilt was in the process of becoming a cosseted, middle-aged, pan-European aristo whose first grandchild would be born in the mid-twenties. May Goelet, Duchess of Roxburghe, was in her forties and had long settled into a peaceful Scottish anonymity.

William Dodge James had died in 1912. Henry James died in 1916, proud bearer of the Order of Merit and holder of British nationality. This he had gained after writing, touchingly, to Asquith in 1915, seeking to affirm what was for him an article of faith during a time of national threat:

I desire to offer myself for Naturalization in this country, that is, to change my status from that of American citizen to that of British subject. I have assiduously and happily spent here all but 40 years, the best years of my life, and I find my wish to testify at this crisis to the force of my attachment and devotion to England, and to the cause for which she is fighting, finally and completely irresistible.[27]

Three years after Henry James, William Waldorf Astor died. A friend noted in grudging tribute, 'He found himself involved in more than one unfortunate controversy or feud. He never doubted that he was right. Autocracy was the inward essence of him . . . In the end, he seemed an almost inaccessible personality – an imprisoned soul immured within walls of his own making.'[28] That same year – 1919 – Minnie Paget died. In 1905, she had had a terrible accident, falling down a lift shaft and breaking her legs. But as *The Times* graciously observed, 'The lameness from which she suffered as a consequence did not diminish her spirit or benevolent activity.' She struggled on, 'beautiful, clever, ready-witted and tactful', before making her last exit in Paris.[29] Her gorgeous Cleopatra fancy-dress was sold at auction, an act as final as the scattering of funeral ashes.

Jennie Cornwallis-West was in a state of terminal decline. At the start of the war, she had divorced George Cornwallis-West, following his affair with Mrs Patrick Campbell. At the end of the war, she married yet another eyebrow-raising husband – the unconsidered Montagu Porch, over twenty years her junior. By now, all her energies were directed towards maintaining her status as a *grande dame* of the British Establishment. She had already dealt with the question of Anglo-American relations in her *Reminiscences*, and declared them purged of all deficiencies. But she wanted something more. In 1919, she wrote to her sister, Leonie Leslie,

> I had a talk with with trustees about my name. I want so much to have it regularised – legally until I revoke my deed poll, I have a right to call myself Lady R.C. as a favour – *just once*. As you know I have worked war-work since the beginning of the war, *arduously* and have never had the slightest recognition and it would be a great favour if the King gave me permission (by receiving me) to stick to my name which as you know my boys have asked me to. I have no snobbish feeling about it. I have made a name for myself and it is undoubtedly an asset. Give me your advice. I wrote my name at B. Palace the other day Lady R.C.[30]

Now aged 65, she was obsessively brooding on what posterity might make of her, as well as having to come to terms with her falling off from a Churchill, to a Cornwallis-West and, ultimately, to the vacancy that was Porch. She was facing a crisis of vanity that only the British caste system – which she had spent decades alternately exploiting and chiding – could help to resolve.

As it happened, she was dead by 1921: she slipped in her stylish new shoes while staying with Lady Horner, broke her leg, contracted gangrene, was forced to have the leg amputated and died of subsequent complications. She was buried next to Randolph Churchill, in the inexplicably modest cemetery near Blenheim which does duty for several of the Churchill family. Sensing the emblematic nature of the death, *The Times* drew attention to her 'American birth – a circumstance perhaps more piquant 40 years ago than it is now'. Combine this with 'a particularly vivacious personality which made itself felt as a social force as soon as marriage gave it high status, and', as *The Times* duly noted, 'the figure of Lady Randolph Churchill becomes one of the most interesting of the time'.[31] If there was a note of hesitancy just audible in its eulogy, then that was *The Times*'s way of reminding its readers that Jennie Jerome had always been rather a handful.

Sunny Marlborough, now in his fifties, was one of the dwindling representatives of those easier, prelapsarian times. In 1908, Winston Churchill wrote to Clementine that Sunny's life had been sorely deranged; and that if only a woman of sufficient wisdom had taken charge of him, he would survived and prospered, happy. Revealing something of his own inability to relate to feminine psychology, Winston argued that Sunny understood women completely, empathising with them at once, and that without a woman's presence in his life, he could never achieve inner peace.[32]

But Sunny was, of course, not without the company of a woman. Gladys Deacon had long been his mistress. In fact, he had been keeping her in some luxury in an apartment in Savile Row since 1910. In her youth, she had had wax injected into the bridge of her nose in order to achieve an even more perfect Grecian profile. Not long after the war, this infill appeared to detach itself from its anchorage and start to slide down the internal structure of her face, bulking out her jawline and giving her mouth a 'curious twist'. Undeterred by the gradual disintegration of Gladys's beauty, Sunny stayed obscurely committed to her. And, when his divorce from

Consuelo came through, he went ahead and married Gladys in June 1920, at the British Embassy in Paris, where Jennie Jerome had married Lord Randolph Churchill back in 1874. Five clergymen refused to officiate and it was only with difficulty that a chaplain was brought over from Blenheim at the last minute.

Amply bolstered by Vanderbilt money and assisted by the great French designer Achille Duchêne, Sunny was now well on the way to realising his dreams for Blenheim. His confidence in his gifts as a patron was growing. He even, through Gladys's agency, met Marcel Proust in Paris and very nearly enticed the author to leave France and make his first trip to England, in order to view the splendours of the palace and bless it with his presence. 'You can go to bed immediately at the Gare du Nord', he murmured to the wavering hypochondriac. 'You can have a bed on the boat, and you can stay in bed while you are at Blenheim.'[33] Proust would have made an intriguing and diametric counterpoint to the ubiquitous, noisy, H.G. Wells, who turned up at Blenheim in 1922, but in the end he could not be moved. He might even have responded to the 'majestic silence' and 'mute corridors' of the monumentally burnished palace; other guests felt chilly, bored and intimidated.

As did Gladys, soon after her marriage. By the end of 1922, she was nursing thoughts of rebellion. 'Most interesting to me', she wrote at the time, 'is Sunny's rudeness to me. Not very marked in public yet – but that will come. I am glad because I am sick of life here. Convention & commonplace & selfishness alone voice themselves over us. *Quelle vie*! But we will separate perhaps before long & I will then go away for good & ever.'[34] Sunny was fussing over less transient things: his new terraces on the west front of the palace, as well as the Marlboroughs' new London address at Carlton House Terrace. Gladys was, for him, as much a piece of living, breathing statuary as a marital companion. He even took the logical step of immortalising her as a lead sphinx on the Water Terrace at Blenheim. She had no larger intrinsic purpose – other than, perhaps, to produce some more Marlborough heirs. After three miscarriages, even that was no longer possible.

By now, her looks were becoming unmistakably grotesque, so cancelling out her usefulness as an art object. Consuelo had the money and the *hauteur* required to break away. Gladys didn't. She was forced to live with an aristocrat whom she concluded was being eaten away by 'black vicious personal pride like a disease'.[35] Fights broke out. Sunny punched Gladys and gave her a black eye. As a provocation – and with a distant memory of her deranged, pistol-waving father confirming her actions – Gladys took to placing a loaded revolver beside her dinner-plate each evening. Nervous guests asked why it was there. 'Oh! I don't know', she said, 'I might just shoot Marlborough!'[36] Evelyn Waugh found himself dining at the Marlboroughs' London home, where the Duchess was 'very battered with fine diamonds. The Duke wearing the Garter: also a vast silk turban over a bandaged eye from which his little hook nose protruded.' As he was about to leave, Gladys took Waugh to one side and said, '"Ah, you are like Marlborough. He has such a mundane mind. He will go to any party for which he is sent a printed invitation."'[37]

Gladys took to breeding spaniels and let them roam in packs through the great house. They chewed the furniture, defecated on the carpets and urinated on the hangings. It was clear that Gladys had started to cross the line between vigorous eccentricity and outright madness. And the more unhinged she became, the stronger she became. Sunny couldn't take any more. He gave in, left Blenheim and set up permanent residence in London, staying at a hotel in Woodstock whenever business dragged him back to Oxfordshire. Gladys, meanwhile, was left to drift alone through the Long Library, the Great Hall, the reeking Saloon, her face in ruins, her stunning blue eyes bulging, her clothes covered in dirt, 'a moving carpet of King Charles spaniels' rippling around her ankles.

The gradual dwindling of the patrician economy and the gradual evolution of the American incomers from *parvenus* to comfortably tolerated (and indeed, comfortably expired) quasi-Brits pointed up a larger truth – that Britain was no longer vital or energetic; that it was an increasingly frayed Garden of the Hesperides, a place of passivity and decline. It was, in short, a place that could do less and less unilaterally to prop up its own finances, precisely because the world had shifted its economic centre of gravity from Europe to the United States.

Not only had America been militarily essential to the Allies in the latter stages of the war; it had also racked up a huge credit balance –

in munitions and foodstuffs – with Britain. Now, in the 1920s, it had taken over Britain's rôle of creditor nation to the world, while Britain had entered the twilight of debtor status. Britain's share of global commerce was in the process of plunging from 14.15 per cent in 1913 to 10.75 per cent in 1929. The United States had already overtaken Europe in manufacturing production by 1919 (hardly surprising, given Europe's preoccupation with the battlefield) and by the end of the decade, would have over 40 per cent of the world's manufacturing output, in comparison with Britain's less than 9 per cent.

The USA didn't *need* the world as much as Britain had in the nineteenth century. It simply became huge, in a markedly autogenous, solipsistic way (in 1921, its visitors to England spent half the amount – £18 million – they had spent in 1913). It was, on the one hand, the world's largest exporter *and* importer and thus tied vitally to the world's finances; on the other, its internal market was so vast, so dynamic, that it could create growth without paying undue attention to anyone else. When it fell, at the end of the 1920s, it fell further than everyone else, not least because of its disregard for any larger questions of global stability. But, until then, it was inordinate and unstoppable. John Adams, the second President of the United States, had written at the end of the eighteenth century that it was the destiny of America to 'beat down' the pride of John Bull. That destiny was now being fulfilled; and the British loathed it. Before the war had ended, the 27th Earl of Crawford found himself fulminating against the American President, Herbert Hoover, claiming that the British authorities who had to deal with him were uniformly 'prejudiced by his shifty hangdog manner, by his refusal to look one in the face, and by a general craftiness of manner and phrase which are most discourteous and extremely unsavoury'.[38] By the 1920s, America was pitilessly insisting on the fullest repayment of its war debts, while at the same time offering Germany a loan of 800 million marks so that it could more easily manage its reparations payments. The fact that the Dawes Plan was backed by the British government only made the situation more shaming: American money was flowing into Germany, which promptly paid it to Britain, which was then obliged to repay it to the United States. The 6th Earl Winterton felt obliged to point out, halfway through his lengthy career in Parliament, that 'Half the difficulties which arise in the relations between Great Britain and the United States come from the illusion of a common standard between the two countries',[39] which was another way of characterising the impossibility of the relationship. But this would have cut no ice with Stanley Baldwin, who had been given the unlovely job of negotiating the settlement of the British war debt. After months of wrangling it was reported that he had got to loathe the Americans to such an extent that he could not bear so much as to be in the same room as them.

There was more, though: there were at least two United States, equally menacing. There was the globally dominating United States; and there was the domestically invasive United States. America was international; and it was local. In the most parochial ways, the productive hand of America was becoming increasingly visible in British life – from Singer sewing-machines to Remington typewriters to American-made vacuum cleaners (the Hoover Company of Ohio pencilling in plans for its landmark factory on the Great West Road) to the Woolworth's retail chain, to the J. Walter Thompson advertising agency, to wondrously competent Frigidaire refrigerators. As Diana Cooper wrote to Duff Cooper in October 1925 from Cincinnati, where she was on tour with the American production of *The Miracle*,

> In the afternoon I was taken off to a cooking demonstration . . . a crowded theatre of women and a stage covered with ovens, refrigerators etc . . . There was on show the Frigid-Air machine that makes the ice by electricity in your house – I covet it a lot. There was one being lotteried and they gave me some tickets – so may be I'll come home with my ice-box. The woman said if I didn't win it she thought they might give me one as English advertisement. They are very expensive.[40]

Then, six months later, 'Tell Holbrook to get all the information about a *Frigidaire* machine. I must have one – it's expensive – but I'm too spoilt for cold foods. It costs over £100 but please don't thwart me, we make our own ice and everything is made good.'[41] America made things that people didn't even know they wanted.

And in the great new defining industries of the century, especially the automobile industry, America was pre-eminent. On the one hand, Cadillac and Packard cars were well-made, surprisingly sophisticated luxury products for the richer motorist. On the other hand, go-ahead American industrial production techniques made the manufacturing processes of mainstream British motor companies look primitive: a discrepancy that was rubbed in when the Ford Motor Company acquired an immense site at Dagenham in 1924, thus heralding its intention to become the UK's biggest car manufacturer; with General Motors buying up Vauxhall cars the following year.

The entertainment industry hit hardest in purely cultural terms. Fully internationalised, insidious, wonderfully attractive and inventive, it again made Britain's home-grown products seem unambitious. Hollywood was a household word by 1925. Jazz, which hadn't existed before 1914, defined an entirely new kind of music and a new kind of social expression to go with it. The Duke of Portland, naturally, objected. Recalling the 'sweet music' which used to be played at balls, he sorrowed that 'All this is changed and, in my opinion, changed very much for the worse: for, at the few balls I have attended since the War, I found couples of all ages, young, middle-aged and definitely old, solemnly performing what seemed to be flat-footed, negro antics, to the discordant uproar – I will not call it music – of a braying brass band.'[42]

Elsewhere, Douglas Fairbanks, Clara Bow and Lillian Gish did for Hollywood what the Paul Whiteman band and Eddie Cantor were doing for the newly arrived record industry. Together, they painted a picture, not of some freakish goliath, but of a modern, expansive, sunlit other world, filled with dance, motor cars, labour-saving devices and an abundance of good living. When Lady Louis Mountbatten, granddaughter of Sir Ernest Cassel, invited Mary Pickford and Douglas Fairbanks to stay at Sir Ernest's Park Lane mansion, Brook House, the stars left behind a signed photograph: 'To duckie Edwina, from Mary and Doug'. This was prominently displayed: witness to a peculiarly irresistible kind of colonialism.

And, at last, at the end of the decade, the new US ambassador to Britain, Charles G. Dawes – as in the Dawes Plan – scandalised the Court by refusing to wear knee-breeches for a presentation to the

King. Many years before, Lord Rosebery had arrived at Windsor Castle wearing trousers instead of silk stockings and knee breeches. 'I presume you have come in the suite of the American Ambassador', said Edward VII, big with scorn. Rosebery withered. But there was no scorn fierce enough to make the American ambassador change his apparel, no leverage that could be used on his feelings. The Prince of Wales cunningly suggested that Dawes might wear trousers for his journey from the American Embassy to Buckingham Palace and change into breeches when he got there, thus satisfying both parties. Dawes, who looked like the hard-nosed banker he was, refused to compromise. He turned up wearing trousers. Queen Mary blanched, but the trend stuck. Trousers became acceptable. However one approached it, the truth was increasingly hard to get away from: America was beholden to no one. It had its own kind of aristocracy now, and felt no need to pander.

NINE

Castles and More

Quite how little the new postwar Americans felt they needed to bow to an older culture could be seen in the case of William Randolph Hearst and his dalliance with St Donat's Castle. Hearst was a supreme instance of transient American interference with the fabric of old society. His was the most superficial, most twentieth-century kind of play, heedlessly contrary to the earnest integrations of the previous century – to the ethos, indeed, of William Waldorf Astor who came, remained, struggled, failed to overcome his native obsessions and so made Hever into a tastefully hamstrung American reinvention of the Middle Ages.

Ralph Nevill managed to foretell the effect of W.R. Hearst on St Donat's in the very year that he purchased the castle:

> Wealthy aliens [he wrote] who have become domiciled in England are rather fond of acquiring ancient or historic mansions and restoring them to what modern taste or the lack of it believes to be their original state. Very often a venerable mansion which has been untouched for hundreds of years, after being gutted and practically rebuilt, is filled with elaborate panelling stripped from somewhere else, hung with gorgeous tapestries or old Spanish leather which form a background for expensive furniture, some old, some new, but all supposed to be of the exact period chosen by the owner, or more often the decorator whom he employs.

The problem with this was not just that it represented an assault on an historic structure, but that it brought with it an undignified attempt at organic heterogeneity: 'The costly jumble of museum pieces brought together by fashionable dealers never produces the same effect as does what has well been called "the dear jumble of a home".'[1] This was 1925, and Hearst had decided that he needed an authentic medieval fortress to accommodate some of the cultural artefacts which he had bought over the years and which were littering warehouses throughout the United States.

The 62-year-old Hearst owned newspapers, magazines and newsreel businesses in San Francisco, New York, Chicago, Seattle, Los Angeles and Boston. He had been working on San Simeon, his grotesque micro-city on the 'Enchanted Hill' in southern California, for six years; he was also a perfervid art kleptomaniac, rifling Europe for treasures as if he meant to relocate the whole of the Old World in an earthquake-proof concrete structure on a West Coast hilltop. But the collecting was running out of control. By the mid-1920s, he had hundreds of thousands of things but an increasingly finite amount of space to put them in.

A ready-made castle offered the perfect solution. As he told the *South Wales Echo*, 'I had seen some of your great castles, such as Caernarfon and Conwy, and they made such an impression on my mind that I decided to acquire something in the same way, only smaller and more domestic, as it were.'[2] The search had in fact been going on for several years. Hearst's representative in the UK, Miss Alice Head, the boss of the National Magazine Company in London, had been seconded to the detective work. 'WANT BUY CASTLE IN ENGLAND', Hearst originally cabled her. Leeds Castle, in Kent, came up, but as Miss Head cabled back to Hearst in California, 'NEEDS EXPENDITURE LARGE SUM TO MAKE IT HABITABLE NOT A BATH IN PLACE ONLY LIGHTING OIL LAMPS SERVANTS QUARTERS DOWN DUNGEONS'. She then travelled to St Donat's, near Cardiff. This impressed her more: 'PERIOD PLACE IN EXCELLENT REPAIR WITH CENTRAL HEATING MODERN SANITATION. DONT WANT MISS IT.'[3] Hearst took her at her word and by October 1925 the castle was his. Rather – and this hints at the cracks that were beginning to open up in Hearst's personal finances – it was carefully signed over to the books of the National Magazine Company.

The great difference between Hearst and, say, Andrew Carnegie, in respect of their properties, was that Carnegie effectively built himself a new castle at Skibo, whereas Hearst, turning his back on his practice at San Simeon, and somewhat in the pattern of W.W. Astor, preferred to mangle an existing structure until he was happy with it. Unlike Astor, he had no interest in steeping himself, however awkwardly, in the culture in which he was investing. At St Donat's, he had much to work with. The earliest parts of the castle dated from the second half of the thirteenth century. A flourishing in the Tudor period had been followed by a slow decline, until the Williams family bought the castle at the start of the twentieth century. They made some small improvements before selling the property on. In May 1921, *The Times* carried a forcefully worded advertisement announcing the sale of ST DONAT'S CASTLE – AN HISTORICAL, ORIGINAL MEDIEVAL CASTLE, which was not only 'finely placed in its sea-girt park, high up on the spur of a wooded glen, commanding magnificent marine views', but could be ranked 'with the finest examples in the Kingdom, with perfect gatehouse, inner and outer Baileys, Towers and Battlements, &c., and upon which vast sums have been spent with great skill and knowledge upon restoration and the formation of A COMFORTABLE AND LIVEABLE OLD-WORLD HOME OF THE FIRST IMPORTANCE'.[4]

It was huge, imposing and already boasted an armoury, a long gallery, five entertaining rooms, thirty bed and dressing rooms, electric light, central heating and modern sanitation. As such, it was snapped up in 1922 by its first American owner, a diplomat called Richard Pennoyer. Pennoyer (in another reversal of the rules governing Anglo-American marriages) was husband to the Dowager Countess of Shrewsbury. She ought to have been able to advise him against the mistake he critically made: he bought the castle without the accompanying estate, which, it was generally held, would have paid for the upkeep of the whole property. A couple of years passed, and Pennoyer discovered to his chagrin that, minus the income from the surrounding land, he could no longer afford his dream by the sea. He therefore had to sell, and in 1925 Miss Head made her move. Hearst at once proposed 'to furnish the place in period style, chiefly gothic, and to bring some fine old tapestries here. I have', he went on, 'a lot of beautiful things which I shall put in. My first objective of course, is to make the place habitable.'[5]

In fact it took him three years to get round even to visiting the castle which he had so ardently searched for. His wife, Millicent, was the first member of the Hearst family to come to St Donat's, in

June 1926. W.R. Hearst Jr turned up in 1928, followed by younger brother George. He was followed, at last, by William Randolph Hearst in September 1928. Hearst and Mrs Hearst never actually visited St Donat's at the same time. In reality, it was to be a fantasy Celtic hideaway for Hearst and his lover, Marion Davies. Hearst's sense of the due weight of history only extended as far as the topmost layer of anything that interested him. In so far as St Donat's could be made into another San Simeon – pre-existing and hewn from medieval stone as it was, rather than engineered *ab initio* – it would depend on how far it could be corrupted to suit his tastes and provide a backdrop for his girlfriend. A good deal of the enduring legend of William Randolph Hearst depends on the disparity between his energies, which were prodigious, and his sense of reality, which was conditional. Nothing much, apart from Marion Davies, seemed to exist for him on more than a purely cosmetic level. The world was one huge film set. On his second visit, he caused further distress by announcing, 'We shall just increase its historical interest by bringing tapestries, ceilings, panelling screens, pictures – every one of which will be genuinely antique.'[6]

His accomplice in the refurbishment to which he subjected St Donat's was the otherwise well-respected designer, Sir Charles Allom. Allom's knighthood had been granted in 1913 as the reward for his work on the royal palaces. A keen cricketer, golfer and yachtsman, Allom had the sort of colourful, unabashed character that would have appealed to Hearst. And, as his magpie interventions at Polesden Lacey twenty years earlier had suggested, he was unfussed by the notion of eclectic thievery. Indeed, he appeared to share Hearst's frankly brutal approach to the problems presented by St Donat's.

His public announcements were emollient enough:

St Donat's is to become a great national museum, the repository of the most important objects gathered from all quarters, that represent the architectural genius of England from Norman times up to the days of Inigo Jones. Mr Hearst is one of the world's most generous and most modest hosts. He will have learned societies to visit St Donat's in order to see the country's choice of historic treasures within its walls.

But he added, menacingly, that Hearst was 'arranging the interior so that it will provide bedrooms, each with its own private bathroom, for over 100 guests'.[7] It already had space for thirty guests, albeit with typically modest British bathroom arrangements. Now, visitor accommodation was going to be tripled in a massive building programme, involving huge quantities of masonry, radical re-plumbing and rewiring and with necessary and related increases to the servants' quarters and the common parts.

Hypertrophy of stately homes was not, in itself, a crime. Skibo Castle was huge; St Donat's was set to go the same way. But the eighteenth-century mansion known as Wentworth Woodhouse in Yorkshire, home of the Earl of Fitzwilliam, was even bigger: it was the largest private house in England. And it only just beat the huge intemperately Gothic 1870s folly that was Alfred Waterhouse's Eaton Hall, built for the 1st Duke of Westminster – 'a Victorian monstrosity in which you could lose yourself quite easily', according to Daisy, Countess of Warwick.[8] So big was Eaton Hall that it very nearly put Loelia Ponsonby off her marriage with the 2nd Duke. 'As I turned a corner', she wrote, reminiscing about her nightmarish first stay there, 'there was this enormous long corridor seeming to go absolutely out of sight. Suddenly I saw two figures advancing down it like tiny little marionettes from the other end . . . I walked tremblingly. It was frightfully difficult to know when to start smiling.'[9] Eaton Hall was believed to have cost £600,000 to build, and visitors to it complained that staying there was like breakfasting in a cathedral. There were precedents for Hearst's dream.

Not only was big acceptable; one's architect didn't have to be a barbarian to contemplate building on such an overweening scale. Consider, for instance, the reaction of the highly fastidious Philip Tilden to the commission given to him just after the war by Gordon Selfridge, which was to build the biggest castle in the country. Tilden's strictures about Astor and Hever Castle ought to have applied to Selfridge in spades, especially given the fact that the latter was already living uncomplainingly in Highcliffe Castle in Hampshire, 'a bastard place in itself, built up of a thousand odds and ends'[10] – and given his general disapproval of Americans anyway. Tilden wrote:

I had already been amazed at the way in which the Americans, save for the few, stood before pseudo-gothic buildings with a sort of gasp, not in the least differentiating, as far as I could see, between buildings of the mightiest of gothic periods, and those produced during the pseudo-gothic phases: the Walpole gothic of the eighteenth century – that which was fostered by Gray's *Elegy* and all that it stood for in the way of church towers, ruins, owls and ivy.[11]

But Selfridge was apparently different, even though his project was steeped in just as much folly and self-worship as Carnegie's at Skibo and Hearst's at St Donat's.

Selfridge, Wisconsin-born, had once worked for Levi Leiter, father of Lady Mary Curzon, in the Chicago firm of Field, Leiter & Company. Graft, determination and business flair saw him work his way up the commercial ladder to the point at which he made a trip to London in 1906, which left him decisively unimpressed with the quality of shopping in the world's greatest city. Seizing his chance, he opened Selfridge's department store in 1909, and the rest was history. His Anglophilia was, unlike Hearst's fleeting romance with Celtic history, deep-rooted and long-lasting. By 1919, at the height of his wealth and social zestiness, he had decided he wanted to build a monster castle on Hengistbury Head – a low finger of rock projecting into Christchurch Bay – a Gothic-Norman fantasy of unbelievable proportions. The essentials of the proposed Hengistbury Castle kept changing, but soon Tilden was having to use an extra-small scale of 1 in 64 in order to fit all the components on to a single sheet of paper.

Selfridge demanded 'mighty vistas, balance, and the co-ordination of parts'.[12] At various times, the castle was to contain 250 suites of rooms for guests, each with its own bedroom, dressing room, bathroom and sitting room; a Gothic hall; a 300-foot tower; a private theatre; a winter garden; a covered lake.

The whole plan was strung on one great vista, more than a thousand feet long, and widening centrally at the main entry. The hall of this was to be domed, and from its marble floor wide sweeping stairs were to rise and hide themselves in a hundred arches on either hand where galleries led forth in diverse directions . . . To give some idea of the scale of this central feature, the dome was to be internally but ten feet less in diameter than the dome of St Paul's.[13]

And yet, in Tilden's own words, this monster was to be 'a sign of the times, a sign of hope that fear had been strangled, that culture was to be fostered, that men and women were to be happier'.[14]

But Hengistbury Castle was never built. Selfridge managed to erect a much smaller building on the same piece of land, from which to oversee the great creation; but even as Tilden redrafted the design throughout the 1920s, adding and subtracting, but mainly adding, so Selfridge squandered his fortune on the erotically charged Dolly Sisters before being reduced to penury by the Depression. Like Hearst, he was free to speculate on the grandest of personal monuments; Tilden was there to help him dream.

All architects are to some extent mercenaries. Tilden's enthusiasm for Gordon Selfridge's unfeasible plan suggests that the nicest tastes could take pleasure in the outrageous. Sir Charles Allom was scarcely worse than Tilden. The Hearst project was big, expensive and appealing. Allom knew about Americans, anyway, having designed the interiors for the Frick Collection on Fifth Avenue. He went to it with a will: 'I sometimes think that what I know about Mr Hearst's plans and dreams are a fairytale, they are so remarkable. But happily they are true',[15] he confessed, yielding to the enchantment of the project.

And it was an enchanting project. On his first actual visit in 1928, Hearst had been so delighted by St Donat's that he scurried round it from late afternoon to ten at night, emerging from the cellarage covered in cobwebs and dust. He returned to the States and from New York drafted a 25-page memorandum of his plans for the building. Using the same rapacious *pasticheur*'s art with which he had encrusted San Simeon, Hearst got Allom to build in a collection of eighteen chimneypieces and fireplaces garnered from all over Europe. A fifteenth-century screen plundered from a Devon church was set at the entrance to the banqueting hall. A fireplace was removed from a château in Beauvais, cut down so that it would fit under the low ceiling, and stacked on top of a pair of jambs from a different medieval source altogether. An English State bed from Lord Vernon's collection was pushed into one bedroom; a Queen Anne State bed into another. Two whole barns were pressed into service to accommodate bits and pieces that Hearst had accumulated over the years with a view to incorporating them into some bastardised architectural scheme, somewhere in the world. Thirty-three wooden cases held a tracery window from St Albans Cathedral, 'returned from Los Angeles'. The worst of it came when, under Allom's covert direction, a team of labourers was sent to Bradenstoke Priory in Wiltshire to dismantle an entire tithe barn and reassemble its double collar beam roof in a specially built hall at St Donat's. The Society for the Protection of Ancient Buildings was understandably incensed: much of the dismantled priory simply disappeared. 'To confess myself to you', Hearst blandly ventured, 'I am tremendously keen about St Donat's. Its beauty overwhelms me, and I have not yet found anyone who does not like this place. One feels the throb of romance as one walks in the grounds around its wondrous castle walls.'[16]

About the only thing that Hearst introduced to the property which did not involve the partial or wholesale vandalism of another building was a swimming pool. This was 150 feet long, lay at the bottom of the ornamental terraces overlooking the Bristol Channel and, in the manner of Skibo, contained fresh, heated, sea-water. There was that, and mains water services. Miss Head wrote later:

> The water came from our own reservoir, which also had to supply the village of St Donat's, and I was informed that it frequently went dry in the summer. If it could not cope with three bathrooms, what was going to happen when it had to supply sixty bathrooms, showers, as well as tub baths? I got in touch with the local authorities and we had a water-main laid from Bridgend, a matter of several miles. And the same with the electricity.[17]

The South Wales Electricity Power Company had to run a cable from the main road, a couple of miles away, in order to service the quantities of electrical equipment Hearst required. As well as endless lights, there were to be electric clocks, thermostatic controls, refrigerators, examples of 'private hairdressing apparatus', toasters, fans, underwater lights for the swimming pool and floodlights for the castle exterior – the first such lighting Wales had seen. As the rebuilt castle took shape, so the staff moved in. A permanent team of forty kept the place in order, day to day; chefs were sent down from the Savoy and Claridges to cook for Hearst and his guests when they came to stay.

Hearst's relationship with St Donat's was at one end of the absolute spectrum of possible relationships between a plutocratic American and an old building. It was believed that he had spent £45,000 buying the castle; and a further £250,000 reinventing it. He owned it from 1925 to – effectively – 1937, when his personal finances collapsed and the National Magazine Company was given the impossible job of selling the property on. He probably spent no more than four months there in total, each time with Marion Davies and a thin retinue of Hollywood two-bit celebrities: Constance Talmadge, Dorothy Mackaill, Eileen Percy, Buster Collier. The money and effort Hearst put into the castle were only equalled by the indifference he showed when it came actually to enjoying his property and all its luxurifications. There was something unhinged about it; as if he didn't really know what buildings were *for*; as if the incredible demands of always living in the present tense – that very American tense – had deprived him of any way to interpret the past.

In the end, with the castle never quite finished, Charles Allom deserted him, unsuccessfully attempting to sue him for unpaid work. St Donat's sat there for the next thirty years, more or less unused – apart from a moment in 1951 when National Magazines lent it to Bob Hope, who was appearing at the British Amateur Golf Championships at Porthcawl.

There was something unnerving about every American purchase of England's heritage, whether it was by an Anglophile aesthete or a brutalist or a fantasist. Ralph Nevill's niggardly praise once again catches the tone: 'It must be confessed that without the intervention of the restorer many a fine old building, like the Campanile at Venice, would have been liable to collapse. The persons in recent years who have expended the largest sums in averting catastrophes of this kind have hailed from across the Atlantic, no one else having now the money to spend.'[18] The pleasant delusions of the late nineteenth century were mauled every time an English or Scottish or Welsh great house fell to the US dollar. When an estate changed hands, it was an assertion of new and frightful powers from overseas. But life was now like that: without the occasional stray American buying up impossible historical properties, many ancient buildings would never have made it past the mid-century.

Was it odd that Americans of any taste or disposition should have wanted to settle in England at this time, apart from the fact that, as time wore on, there was no Prohibition, and a fractionally less brutal Depression, in southern England? Edwardian society had been as opulent and provocatively ostentatious as any in the world. Postwar society was not. The patina of relative disadvantage that had descended on Britain not only extended to the buildings, the streets and the restaurants; it extended to the people themselves, who, in comparison with the greedy Jazz Age sensation-seekers of the American big cities, were dowdy, repressed, supercilious, envious and captious. London was still, in its way, a beautiful city. But its ambitions had slipped. And it was a long time since Richard Henry Dana had so kindly remarked on 'the fine voices the English had' – this with especial regard to the son and daughter of Lord and Lady Clifden – presuming spoken English to be 'a product of the climate. I asked about this and they told me that all the well-to-do English children were carefully taught to speak, almost as people are taught to sing, and to avoid all nasal or harsh utterances.'[19]

Modern casual visitors such as the American writer Margaret Halsey were more likely to recoil from the noise of 'English gentlemen being conscientiously banal', or of two women in a smart tea-shop: 'Tall, currycombed, fashionable creatures they were, and the bodiless staccato of their well-bred English voices was like the sound of typewriters borne on the wind.' She was also depressed by the antique plumbing, the chaotic shop window-dressing, the damp, the service, the trains, the minuteness of everything, and the apparent lack of self-esteem with which Englishwomen dressed.

The fundamental difficulty is that they are ashamed of having legs and waists and breasts, and so they muffle themselves up as if their bodies were something that had to be smuggled through the customs. I suppose the English reply to this criticism is that American women spend too much time and energy on their clothes, which I think is true. But what do Englishwomen spend their time and energy on instead? I ask it, who have eaten their cooking.[20]

Scott Fitzgerald, whose cultural ambitions pre-war had been so heavily infected by the idioms of the Old World, found himself racked with ambivalence during the early 1920s. 'You may have spoken in jest about New York as the capital of culture', he wrote to Edmund Wilson, 'but in 25 years it will be just as London is now. Culture follows money. We will be the Romans in the next generations as the English are now.'[21]

Indeed, the only tolerable thing about England was its architectural heritage and its native sense of good taste. 'The English of the gentlemanly persuasion . . . seem to me only remotely human', said Miss Halsey, 'but their houses look far more human than comparative American homes. American interiors tend to have no happy medium between execrable taste and what is called "good taste" and is worn like a wart.' The better-bred English, on the other hand, simply used the tallboys and writing desks left to them by their parents, with an ingratiating ease and lack of pretension. They also enjoyed a kind of native good taste, not being influenced by 'shiny pictures in magazines. In England, magazines do not have the green-bay-tree aspect that they do in America, and no English advertising, in any medium, is likely to put ideas into anybody's head.' In fact, 'I thought that the rooms we saw when we were dining and house-hunting in Exeter were, in general, full of distinction and individuality. They made the Schrafft-like interiors at home seem, looking back on them, floridly imitative.'[22] It was one of the few advantages England had left. And while Miss Halsey was giving an inch to the English, Harold Nicolson, in the United States, was writing to Vita Sackville-West (also in the States) on the contrasting vacuity of American domestic culture. 'Nobody seems to have anything behind their front', he explained. 'Poor people, they feel it themselves, and hence all those pitiful gropings after Manor Houses in Wiltshire and parish registers and the Daughters of the Founding Fathers.'[23] There was still a material appeal – one reaching beyond the dubious *arcana* of the peerage, and into broader, more universally appealing areas concerning taste, authenticity, visual sophistication.

Thus Hearst's rampages contrasted dynamically with the more discerning interventions made by, among others, Nancy Lancaster, who translated herself from Charlottesville, Virginia, to the Home Counties and successfully hybridised a form of Anglo-American decorative *bon goût* in her various English houses; or Major Lawrence Johnston, who came from a family of Baltimore stockbrokers and transformed Hidcote Manor Garden, in Gloucestershire, into a masterpiece of fragrant invention; or Huttleston Broughton, the 1st Lord Fairhaven. The son of both an expatriate Englishman who had made an American fortune in mining and railroads, *and* a New York heiress, the super-wealthy Broughton began his life in the States, moved to England to continue his education at Harrow, served with the Life Guards in the First World War and, in 1926, bought the semi-derelict Anglesey Abbey in Cambridgeshire. Ralph Nevill's claim that 'The incursion of wealthy Americans has undoubtedly saved quite a number of old English country houses' was justified precisely by Broughton's revivification of Anglesey from a medieval wreck into a quietly imposing country house of consummate taste and charm (though not without some wincing preciousness: guests were expected not to precede Broughton into the library before dinner, since he hated the sight of other people's footprints on the passage carpet – which he had re-brushed every evening). In 1929, he became Lord Fairhaven and, having restored the Abbey, dedicated himself to creating a superb garden to go with it. Sir Arthur Bryant later wrote, 'Huttleston Fairhaven must be almost unique in having created in the middle of the twentieth century a garden which can compare with the great masterpieces of the Georgian era . . . He has endowed the England of tomorrow with a landscape garden worthy of her past.'[24]

Then there was Lady Olive Baillie. Lady Olive, daughter of Almeric Paget – 1st Baron Queenborough – and Pauline Whitney, the American heiress, was an Anglo-American hybrid who had the nerve to take on Leeds Castle in Kent after Hearst had passed it over. Under her guidance, Leeds Castle was thoroughly modernised in the late 1920s, but not to the point at which it could be said to have lost all meaning. She threw many a sleazy party within its tolerant medieval walls and among its tasteful ameliorations; guests included the Prince of Wales, Joachim von Ribbentrop, Errol Flynn and Douglas Fairbanks.

Also present at Leeds from time to time was Barbara Hutton, the Woolworths multimillionairess, who, in turn, declared herself less of an architectural assimilationist at heart and more of a strident American statement-maker. Having married the brilliantined Count Haugwitz-Reventlow and produced a baby son – Lance – the original Poor Little Rich Girl decided that she needed somewhere in London secure and modern enough in which to bring up her child and fight with her husband. In 1936, she bought what was left of St Dunstan's Villa, in Regent's Park. This Decimus Burton-designed stuccoed mansion had previously been owned by the Marquess of Hertford and Lord Rothermere. By the 1930s, it was disintegrating in the midst of its 14-acre park-within-a-park. Hutton got permission from the Crown Estate Commission to tear the semi-ruin down and replace it with something smart in neo-Georgian red brick. Leonard Guthrie did the designs, 'Johnny' Sieben – who had refurbished the Woolworth town houses in New York – and Sheila Lady Milbank were in charge of the interior decor. Between them, they did an aptly lavish job. As well as some conventional oak parquetry, marble bathrooms, a couple of Canalettos, a collection of Louis XV furniture and some plundered eighteenth-century French panelling, the new house contained a nursery wing fitted with padded pink calf-skin walls. Thousands of trees and hedges were planted; a 10-foot-high steel fence ran round the perimeter. Hutton moved in, in 1937. By 1939, war was looming and she was divorcing Count Reventlow. She left St Dunstan's Villa and never lived there again.

Thus, Americans came and went. Some stayed; others were in an increasingly transient or holiday-making frame of mind. The fact was that they liked the artefacts produced by and for the English upper classes, without necessarily liking the upper classes themselves. The old heiresses somehow had to like both; later generations could exercise more options. England was less an end in itself and more a resort, somewhere to play at being a grandee. It was as real as theatre and as axiomatically disposable. The results, for anyone keen to sell or let to a passing American, were a matter of chance. As the 8th Duchess of Atholl glumly noted, 'By 1928 money difficulties were beginning to weigh on us. An American lady's six-year tenancy of the castle had come to an end.'[25] The stately homes of England were becoming Noël Coward's *Stately Homes of England*: quaint period possessions, kept up mainly for Americans to rent.

TEN

Changes

Halfway through 1926 came a last reminder of the great Anglo-American marriage trade from before the war: a return to a lost age. It was Sunny and Consuelo's crisis of Catholicism, dragging them back into the public gaze and adding yet another chapter to the tale of the complex, unedifying and essentially doomed bargain they had entered into thirty years earlier.

The situation was this. Consuelo Vanderbilt was now happily Madame Consuelo Balsan; but Jacques Balsan's family was composed of devout French Roman Catholics, who were unable fully to welcome a Protestant divorcée in the form of Consuelo, however impressive her credentials. Sunny, on the other hand, was following his own desires, being inexorably drawn into the Roman Church by its gratifying mixture of austerity, voluptuousness and snob appeal. His civil divorce and his prompt remarriage hung over him: a stain he would wish removed. Both Sunny and Consuelo needed to have their old marriage expunged in the eyes of the Catholic Church, so that they could proceed to the next stage of their lives. What followed was, at the time, mildly scandalising; in retrospect, a further instance of Consuelo's – and the Vanderbilts' – un-English gift for detaching themselves from the turgid constraints of the aristocracy by whatever means necessary, and getting their own way, even if at a cost to themselves.

When Sunny formally applied in 1926 for admission to the Roman Catholic Church, to be followed by the full solemnisation of his marriage to Gladys, it was announced by an official that 'our Church does not do the sort of thing the Duke desires unless there is really just cause'. Moreover,

The whole matter is held up for the present. If the marriage with the present Duchess [Gladys] is to be regularized it will be done privately by a priest. Before the Duke can be received into the Church the stain of his divorce will have to be wiped out and he will have to undergo a period of informal preparation and instruction. Nothing more can be done for a Duke than for a tramp.[1]

But as it happened – a fact of which the same official seemed unaware – the stain of divorce *had* been wiped out, following a hearing at the Roman Catholic Diocesan Court of Southwark (where Consuelo had been a county councillor) in July of that year.

At this farcical event, Consuelo and her mother, Alva, had established that the foundations of Consuelo and Sunny's marriage were inherently undermined, since Consuelo had been forcibly coerced into marrying the Duke in the first place. These were, in fact, about the only grounds for annulment that the Roman Catholic Church would recognise. Here it was, in south London, that Alva, Consuelo and several of Alva's friends and relations, including Mrs Jay and Mrs Tiffany, of New York, swore in the most colourful terms that Consuelo's heart had belonged to Winthrop Rutherfurd in 1895; and that Alva Vanderbilt had threatened and bullied Consuelo into marrying a duke whom she had determined as a more suitable match.

Mrs Tiffany, Consuelo's aunt, testified that 'My sister was continually making scenes and tried to soften her daughter by saying she was suffering from heart disease and that she would die if she continued to cross her.' Mrs Jay likewise swore that 'This marriage had been imposed by my sister on her daughter, who wished to marry another man.' Alva, displaying all the robustness with which she had dispatched Mrs Astor's pretensions back in 1883, declared on record that 'I forced my daughter to marry the Duke. I have always had absolute power over my daughter, my children having been entrusted to me entirely after my divorce. I alone had charge of their education. When I issued an order nobody discussed it. I, therefore, did not beg, but ordered her to marry the Duke.' Her methods were boldly straightforward. 'I asked the Duke to come and stay with us at Newport. He came and stayed about a fortnight. I told Consuelo he was the husband I had chosen for her. She was very much upset and said she could not marry him. I considered myself justified in over-riding her opposition, which I considered merely the whim of an inexperienced girl.'

Mrs Tiffany added that once Consuelo had helplessly given in to Alva's demands, 'Her mother, fearing that Consuelo might at the last minute change her mind and retract her consent to marry the Duke, which had been extracted from her, placed a guard at the door of her room on the day of the wedding so that nobody could speak to her or even approach her.'

Consuelo's own testimony was even more heart-wrenching:

My mother tore me from the influence of my sweetheart. She made me leave the country. She intercepted all letters my sweetheart wrote and all of mine to him. She caused continuous scenes. She said I must obey. She I knew very well that I had no right to choose a husband, that I must take the man she had chosen, that my refusal was ruining her health and that I might be the cause of her death. There was a terrible scene in which she told me that if I succeeded in escaping she would shoot my sweetheart and she would, therefore, be imprisoned and hanged and I would be responsible.

As if this litany of savagery weren't bad enough, she went on:

Mother told me she had chosen a man for me whom she considered suitable in all respects, that he was about to arrive in America as her guest and that she had already negotiated my marriage with him. I insist on declaring that I married the Duke of Marlborough yielding to the tremendous pressure of my mother and following her wish absolutely. In addition to the threats of which mention has been made, mother told me several times if I insisted on opposing her will it might easily kill her. This was also the opinion of a doctor whom I met through a friend of mother's, Mrs. Jay.

Love letters that had been exchanged between Consuelo and Winthrop Rutherfurd some thirty years earlier were miraculously produced. The similarly antique testimony of the witnesses was taken in uncritical good faith. No one was in any way challenged or cross-questioned. Even Sunny, *in absentia*, made a statement to the effect that Consuelo 'came very late to the wedding and appeared much troubled'.[2] The Catholic tribunal had no choice, in the face of this deluge of evidence, but to declare the Marlborough marriage an act of singular coercion, and, therefore, null in the eyes of the Church.

Four things flowed from this incredibly convenient outcome. First, Consuelo and Sunny were truly free of each other. Second, it allowed the Episcopal Bishop Manning of New York to initiate a small public war against the Roman Catholic Church, which, after all, had just seized two glamorous converts from under his nose at the same time as it announced its primacy over all forms of Protestant Christianity. 'Many who were present at the marriage, and were associated closely with the Marlboroughs at the time, have informed me that they saw no sign whatever that the bride was acting under any compulsion, but quite the contrary', Manning seethed. He went on to add: 'That any woman of middle age [Consuelo was looking at fifty] after years of married life, should be willing to swear that her parents sold her for worldly gain, and against her will, is in itself a scandal, and the more so when one of her parents is not here to deny such an accusation.'[3] This latter was, of course, W.K. Vanderbilt, who had died in 1920. Alva, who had separated from Vanderbilt in 1894 and married Leonard Jerome's old friend, Oliver Belmont, in 1896, promptly left New York when news of the annulment broke, sailing for the South of France on the *Berengaria*. 'Plainly preoccupied, Mrs. Belmont takes her meals alone at a small table', the *New York Times* reported; 'Mrs. Belmont avoids all the other passengers and spends considerable time alone in the saloon, reading.'[4]

Third, the annulment marked the point at which the story of Consuelo's coercion became formally established. Up to November 1926, the Marlborough marriage had been seen as an exceptionally grand, cynical liaison between American wealth and English title: the greatest and most theatrically doomed of all such Anglo-American marriages. Neither party came out especially well, but there the matter lay. Only now, it seemed, the marriage had not only been a sham, but a protracted assault on the liberties of the bride.

Having announced herself as the victim of what amounted to a slave auction, Consuelo went on to cling tenaciously to the identity she had fashioned. She even made it her official history a quarter of a century later when she produced an autobiography of sorts, *The Glitter and the Gold*. Scornful, vitriolic and self-serving, this memoir was diligently co-produced by Stuart Preston – 'The Loot' – to whom Consuelo makes the cautious genuflection 'I am greatly indebted to Mr. Stuart Preston for his careful scrutiny of the proofs' in the Foreword.[5] Preston was an interesting choice. Having become a London society personality during the Second World War, when he was known as 'The Sergeant', he had impressed, among many others, John Lehmann – a noted literary editor and one-time employee at the Woolfs' Hogarth Press. Of Preston's arrival one day at the home of society grandee Lady Cunard, Lehmann wrote:

The Sergeant appeared in person, to cries of delight reminiscent of the clamour of sea-gulls when you throw them a biscuit. His name was Stuart Preston, he was American, and with his boyish charm, his detailed knowledge of the world of social and other celebrities that seemed to stretch a good deal further than Who's Who, and his well-stocked mind and excellent taste in the arts, he was more unlike the conventional image that the word sergeant still called up, than I could have believed.[6]

Preston conquered London society before returning to New York after the war, where he largely failed to live up to his astonishing early promise. Too charming, too sociable to be a great writer, this ultra-obliging Boswell, under Consuelo's imperious direction (and that of her editor, Marguerite Hoyle of Harper & Brothers), helped construct *The Glitter and the Gold*, which set in stone the notion that Alva was a near-psychotic bully, bent on the aggrandisement of her family name; that Sunny was heartless in every possible sense (which did ring true); and that she, Consuelo, had had her freedoms as an American citizen cruelly molested.

Thus the tragedy of Consuelo's early life, as drawn in *The Glitter and the Gold*, epitomised all that was wrong with the transatlantic marriage trade. According to the book, Consuelo's mother was uniformly brutal: 'A born dictator, she dominated events about her as thoroughly as she eventually dominated her husband and her children', while dealing with minor infractions by thrashing Consuelo with a riding crop. It was Alva's desire, apparently, to create in her daughter a kind of simulated perfection and, having done that, to make it clear that Consuelo's 'person was dedicated to whatever final disposal she had in mind', as a consequence of which 'I spent the morning of my wedding day in tears and alone; no one came near me.' Sunny wasn't violent, but he was monotonously unpleasant: 'A few days later M[arlborough] departed to see something of a country [America] he then announced he would never revisit.' Sarcastic and belittling, the Duke jeered at America, then took it upon himself – in the absence of Mrs Alva Vanderbilt – to exercise full editorial control over Consuelo's wardrobe. 'Unfortunately, his taste appeared to be dictated by a desire for magnificence rather than by any wish to enhance my looks.' Back at home, he carped, chastised, and kept everybody waiting at meal times. Blenheim itself was magnificent, but a drag. The young couple began life in a frigid north-facing apartment carved out of some unusable rooms before moving into the quarters usually occupied by the Duke and Duchess. These turned out to be 'equally uncongenial'. There was a crucial shortage of bathrooms and modern plumbing. This not only bothered Consuelo's 'American sense of comfort', but also left her conscience-stricken and filled with guilt 'towards my housemaids whose business it was to prepare something like thirty baths a day'. Typically, Sunny did nothing; it was only with the arrival of the 10th Duke that Blenheim got enough bathrooms. The kitchens 'were at least three hundred yards from the dining-room'.[7] And so on. Like a character in a fairy tale, she was betrayed, scorned, imprisoned. It is a tragic and pitiable account, informed by a strongly Manichean division of the world into pro- and anti-Consuelo factions. Naturally, everything stands or falls by its authenticity.

But what if she never really was the Rapunzel-like figure she tries to evoke? Bishop Manning of New York denied that Consuelo was in distress on her wedding day, while New York gossip in the 1890s tended to portray Consuelo as whimsical, airy, prone to fall in and out of love matches, capricious in her favours – not the solemn votary of love, the soul partner of Winthrop Rutherfurd whom she portrayed in *The Glitter and the Gold*. What if she *had* been less the latter and more the former? What if she had decided in 1895 that she quite like the idea of being a splendid duchess, of queening it over great Manhattan and little England, even if there was no way for her to foretell the consequences of that decision? And if she really had been such a natural victim, forever subjugated to the bullyings of mother and husband, how did she summon up the cool determination to extricate herself from her marriage as efficiently as she did in 1906?

When, in November, the news leaked from the Catholic Tribunal of her alleged coercion, she at once gave a press interview to the *People*, undermining her story still further. In it, she confusedly assured the world that

> I say, once for all, that the suggestion of undue pressure is the foulest slander that could have been uttered against my father and mother, both of whom thought only of my happiness. I may have been a little romantic and consequently over-enthusiastic at the time. To that extent, perhaps, I was easily persuaded in my own heart when the glamour of first love was upon me, that it was for my happiness that I was taking the step; but I want you to be clear that the step was mine and that I alone was responsible for it. Disillusionment came soon, and probably I paid for my girlish enthusiasm.[8]

So what, precisely, was all this? The inconsistencies simply pile up. On the one hand, this was this Mme Consuelo Balsan, formerly the Duchess of Marlborough, nearly 50 years old, a mother of two grown-up sons, being badgered by her 73-year-old mother into issuing a face-saving disclaimer when the ugly truth about her first marriage (and the mother's part in it) emerged. On the other, it was an act of spontaneous kindness on Consuelo's part, to spare her mother's feelings. But it also sounds like an unpremeditated admission of the truth, prompted by guilt at the fabric of deceptions she had just woven before the Tribunal. It can't help but pose awkward questions. Which was true: her statement to the Tribunal that she had been coerced? Or her statement to the press that she hadn't? Was the Tribunal a scrupulous examination of the events leading to a disastrous marriage? Or an elaborate piece of expediency to tidy up her life in retrospect? And, having gone through all the business of a papal annulment, did she decide to stick to that story years later in *The Glitter and the Gold*, because it better suited her *amour-propre* to paint herself as a victim, rather than someone who merely changed her mind?

This brings us to the fourth by-product of whole annulment scandal: a reiteration of Consuelo's candid tendency to go after whatever seemed desirable to her at any given time. For all her apparent sad-eyed passivity, Consuelo, like her ruthless mother, had an American utilitarianism and lack of sentiment in her dealings with the world. Her wealth, beauty and hard practicality had now been proven to be every bit the equal of her title. She married a duke, didn't like it, abdicated from the great position she had in society, and ordered her life accordingly. She ran off with Charley Londonderry, came back, separated from Sunny, secured her legal rights with the children, and settled in some style in London and Surrey. She was still immensely rich, still beautiful, and with the body of public opinion on her side – a condition she made enduring with *The Glitter and the Gold* and the novelettish prose stylings of Stuart Preston. She married M. Balsan and pleased herself, spending much of her time in the warm French sunshine. Sunny, in contrast, went gradually downhill and is remembered as the man who saved Blenheim's greatness but destroyed his own reputation. Consuelo emerged, and still emerges, as the victor.

But did Consuelo, the exquisite American import – far from sadly capitulating to the narrow exigencies and exploitations of the British aristocracy – finally win? Or did she betray herself on this one occasion, revealing just a bit too much American directedness, a clumsy lunging at the prize, a lack of *finesse*? Having laid herself open to accusations of, at the very least, not knowing her own mind, she can't help but reveal her *apologia*, *The Glitter and the Gold*, as a piece of highly expedient retrospective face-saving. She had displayed a weakness and had to cover over the tracks: this book was her attempt to marshal history.

If the Marlboroughs' final lurch into the public eye signalled the end of an era, it was at least accompanied by the beginning of a new one. The year 1926 was also that in which Lady Maud Cunard changed her name to Emerald. For some, such as Patrick Balfour, this was a moment of high significance. Why? Because it meant that (the new) Lady Emerald Cunard was now so confident of her powers that she could brashly rechristen herself in order to draw attention to her place at the very peak of the new wave of American imports. But who was she, anyway?

In brief, the late nineteenth century had been the age of the American heiress; the early twentieth was the age of the American hostess, and Emerald was the most successful American society hostess of all. She had once been mere San Francisco-born Maud Burke: nobody very special in 1900, but now a woman who would become, depending on one's point of view and level of paranoia, the Tsarina of London society; an unprincipled, roving anarch; and one of the principal architects of the constitutional crisis of 1936.

She was born in 1872, into a city that had been no more than a few square miles of redneck gold-rush anarchy twenty years before, but which, with the discovery of the Nevada Comstock Lode in 1859, became so wealthy and so cosmopolitan that it could reinvent itself as a metropolis very nearly as swaggering and prosperous as Philadelphia or Boston – as Thomas George Fermor-Hesketh had discovered, back in 1880. A broad undertow of danger was still present, inevitably: Rudyard Kipling claimed, after a visit in the 1890s, that 'San Francisco is a mad city, inhabited for the most part by perfectly insane people.' And it was, for all its fashionable moral looseness and interest in the cult of the aesthetic (led by Addison Mizner, later to become architect of the huge, unedifying Boca Raton in Florida), monstrously local, a teeming, affluent outpost perched on the very edge of the known world. This was where Maud Burke began her life.

Her parentage was mildly complicated. A millionaire named O'Brien may have been her natural father; her legal father died when she was young and her mother was subsequently courted by an assortment of rich speculators. Finally, Mrs Burke married a stockbroker, while Maud herself became the enthusiastic pet of a wealthy bibliophile called Horace Carpentier, who enjoyed the company of bright, pretty, teenage girls, whom he furtively referred to as his *nieces*. From some or all of these sources came Maud's inherited wealth. It was part of her mystique that not only did she come from one of the most distantly knowable cities in the United States, she could not provide an obvious explanation for the money which sustained her, on and off, for the next fifty years. The mistiness of her background and her finances also encouraged a tendency in her to reinvent, to disguise, to mythologise. This, coupled with her mental quickness and her deeply felt responses to literature and music, resulted in a personality that was analytical, fantastical, obfuscatory, amorally inventive and terrified by boredom.

It also happened that she was, physically, the type known as a Pocket Venus: diminutive, fair-haired, pert, bosomy, with small, graceful hands and an artful laugh. She made a certain kind of man weak with lust. So, armed with an imagination and the physical qualities to frame it, she decided early on that San Francisco was stifling and that she would be better off seducing men from more interesting cities.

The problem was that she could get the wrong men to fall in love with her, but the ones she really wanted would never properly commit themselves. By 1894, she had travelled to London, where she met George Moore – the celebrated writer – and seduced him. Moore's reputation has now almost completely evaporated, but at the turn of the century, the author of *A Modern Lover*, *Esther Waters* and, later, the Hail and Farewell trilogy, was a major literary figure. His sexually provocative table-talk and his self-advertising disregard for convention were predicated on an authentic bohemian prank-sterishness, rather than mere foul manners. His comments on modern society and modern morals were attended to, however badly he behaved. A lonely giant, he fell hopelessly for the fairy-like Maud, and when she left London to return to the States, he wrote, 'Thinking of her my senses grow dizzy, a sort of madness creeps up behind the eyes – what an exquisite despair is this – that one shall never possess that beautiful personality again, sweet scented as the May-time, that I shall never hold that oval face in my hands again, shall look into those beautiful eyes no more, that all the beautiful intimacy of her person is now but a memory.'[9]

She, on the other hand, was keen on Prince André Poniatowski, grandson of the late King of Poland, whom she had met in New York. While George Moore languished, she allowed herself to believe that

Poniatowski was engaged to her. He wasn't. In fact, he was in love with the sister of Mrs Harry Crocker – Mrs Crocker being, effectively, the Mrs Astor of San Francisco high society. To Poniatowski's horror, a local newspaper announced his engagement to Maud. He at once asked her to make a public denial; she did so, then, humiliated, returned to New York, miserably looking for a suitable husband of any sort. There she met the bovine but well-connected Sir Bache Cunard and, in 1895, married him on the rebound.

Sir Bache was titular head of the famous shipping line, which had been founded by his grandfather. This latter was made baronet in 1859 and now Sir Bache enjoyed the proceeds of Cunard's business, as well as the title. He was 43 when he met Maud. He was also a bone-headed squirearchical sportsman with a sprawling half-medieval estate at Nevill Holt, in Leicestershire, once described as 'a long range of mediaeval battlements and a "tame church on the lawn" tethered behind it like a ship's dinghy'.[10] He had been at the wedding of Consuelo Yznaga and Lord Mandeville in 1876 and was evidently comfortable with the idea of an Anglo-American relationship. She seduced him in a relatively perfunctory manner and their marriage was, after a few administrative snags, settled for April 1895, in New York. One gossip-monger claimed that 'With moderate luck Sir Bache Cunard will get some two millions of old man Carpentier's accumulation of dollars, as his bride, Miss Burke, is the Outland Capitalist's favourite niece and should come in for a large slice of his estate',[11] but Sir Bache was rich on his own account and was, besides, so infatuated with his 22-year-old fiancée that money was never an issue. Knowing that Maud would be as unhappy in Leicestershire as Sir Bache would be in Belgrave Square, Bache's sister begged Maud to call the marriage off. Maud doggedly insisted that 'I like Sir Bache better than any man I know',[12] and the wedding went ahead.

Then followed some twenty years of marital drudgery and mild emotional blackmail, as the new Lady Cunard wrestled with the confinements of life in some of the best hunting country in England. She was an uneasy, transitional figure – American, lively, pretty, but not an heiress in the same mould as Consuelo Vanderbilt or May Goelet, any more than Sir Bache was in the same league as the Dukes of Marlborough or Roxburghe. She had to work harder for what she wanted, striving not to fall back into the parochialism of New York or, worse, San Francisco. The Cunard family house, Nevill Holt, gave her an aesthetic challenge: she dressed up its masculine interior with rugs, *bibelots*, bowls of potpourri. She produced a daughter in 1896: the clever, intractable, mildly unhinged poet and sexual radical, Nancy Cunard. From the moment she was old enough to hold an opinion, Nancy disliked her mother intensely. Maud – too egotistical to dredge up any real sympathy for her child, but preoccupied with her well-being, none the less – would later go on record as describing motherhood as 'a low thing: the lowest'. In between spats with Nancy, she threw out Bache's clubland-style furniture and armorial clutter, and had the walls painted white, to his fury. He rode, hunted, fished and did metalwork in a tower above the gateway to the house. After days of work there, he lovingly gave his wife a cup carved from a coconut shell, with a scalloped silver border containing snowdrop heads made of seashells. Later, he produced a decorative metal gate in which the words 'Come into the Garden Maud' were spelled out in pony-sized horseshoes. Both of these gifts annoyed and depressed her.

She wanted society and she wanted to live in London. She could play the piano well, read Balzac and Zola in the original French, could sing, had a sharp wit. With difficulty, she persuaded a solid assortment of names – Harry Cust, A.J. Balfour, Herbert Asquith, F.E. Smith, Somerset Maugham, the Duchess of Rutland, Vita Sackville-West, Lord Howard de Walden and Jennie Cornwallis-West – to make the trip out to the romantically windy, damp, scarp on which Nevill Holt stood and to whose interminable surrounding countryside she was becoming increasingly antipathetic. 'In later life', as one acquaintance put it, 'she developed an almost Gallic aversion from the open air.'[13] Her determination to get a better class of person to come through her front door at first told against her; she was seen as pushy. At last, contact with Edward VII overcame the resistance of the snobs and she was tolerated. When Sir Bache went to Scotland for the shooting, Maud drafted in singers and musicians to expunge any traces of his presence. One hot August night, all the windows were open and no one could sleep. Eventually, a guest sang forth the Valkyrie's cry. Someone else answered with a call from

Götterdämmerung. Then everyone joined in. An atmosphere of mild frenzy (Maud called it *Love*) was still detectable when Sir Bache came back a few days later. 'I don't understand what's going on in this house', he said, 'but I don't like it.'[14]

Maud had seized the initiative. Gradually, she peeled herself away from her husband. More importantly, she also exploited her new friendship with Herbert Asquith – who, like Edward VII, could always be swayed by an attractive woman – to get the thing she really wanted: a town house in London. This was the Asquith house at 20 Cavendish Square, left vacant after Asquith's move to 10 Downing Street in 1908. Cavendish Square was on the margins of smart London, being north of Oxford Street, but would do. In 1911 she moved in and had the place fashionably tricked out in *Ballet Russe* style, following the sensational arrival in London of what was then still known as the Imperial Russian Ballet. Nevill Holt's interior had been conventional enough, after she had worked it over, albeit with a twist of intuitive *bon goût*. Cavendish Square, on the other hand, became modishly provocative in her hands, with (in particular) a dining room hung in arsenic-green *lamé*, against which stood a black lacquer screen of carved porcupines, with a lapis blue circular dining table in the centre. The hallway contained a huge Chinese incense-burner. The drawing room was littered with *bibelots* and rare books. The whole was an advertisement, a statement of intent – and also a means with which to engage her prey. An authentic bibliomane, she used books to consolidate her relationship with Asquith, as he wrote to Venetia Stanley, in 1914:

> You will be amazed at the result of Maud Cunard's mission to buy me a Xmas present, for wh. she had apparently received *carte blanche* from Alice Wimborne [the First Viscountess Wimborne] – She asked me at lunch whether I would like a 'nice' Petronius or Apuleius, and she evidently went off post haste to Quaritch (the most expensive bookseller in the world). For by tea time there appeared a wonderful copy – in a beautiful old red French binding – of Apuleius' *Golden Ass*, printed at Vicenza in 1488! and once, as the book plate shows, in the Sunderland library at Blenheim . . . And inside (to keep up appearances) a little slip 'with very best wishes & love from A.W.'[15]

A year later, and 'Maud Cunard has just appeared with 2 new books for me: a Terence & a Sallust both printed by Baskerville & in good condition. She is a wonderful woman, & one never knows what is the latest hare that she is pursuing.'[16] The hare, plainly, was Asquith himself – along with everyone else who interested her. Her snobbery was deep-rooted ('naïve and unashamed') but oddly inclusive. She liked politicians, musicians, writers, aristocrats, pretty people, smart people and clever people: Mrs Patrick Campbell, Somerset Maugham, Lady Lavery, the Weymouths, Lord Berners, Winston Churchill, the Londonderrys, the Prince of Wales . . . It was a dynamic snobbery, a volatile thing in comparison with the hefty, entrenched bigotries of the British upper classes.

Naturally enough, this dynamism could reveal itself to be crass, childish and infuriating whenever it was placed in the service of an obsession or mere temper. Diana Cooper – usually a fan of Maud's – fulminated against her when they were both stuck in a hotel in Salzburg in 1925: 'Maud got stung by a wasp and made a scene in the lounge, screaming and spitting with rage, Morris Gest [impresario of Diana's play *The Miracle*] was a looker on, and was disgusted, not knowing her, at her lack of breeding etc.' Two days later, stuck in the same hotel:

> Maud Cunard is a pest. She really is unbearable, always in a towering rage and threatening to go that night if the wasps won't leave her alone. I must say they beset her. I think it must be that Orestes' unguents [Dr Orestes made face creams and pomades] are concocted of wasps' vomit and they return to it. She weighs very heavily on us all. We are always trying to dodge her, and always haunted by her désoeuvréness, and spoiling our plans for her. Gerald Berners is always shrieking 'O I've been stung' and sucking his finger, while Maud swallows the bait without fail.[17]

Later Evelyn Waugh (who first met Diana Cooper at Lady Cunard's dining table) complained to Mary Lygon how Maud was pestering him for better seats for the stage version of *Vile Bodies*, claiming that 'Lady Cunard (whom God preserve) has just been given seats in the 18th row and is gibbering down the telephone saying "How can

Jennie Churchill, not long after her marriage to Lord Randolph Churchill. *(Hulton Archive/Getty Images)*

Edward VII enjoying himself at a house party at Mar Lodge, built for the Duke of Fife. On his right side is Miss Emily Yznaga, sister of Consuelo, Duchess of Manchester; on his left is Minnie Paget, social phenomenon and one of the architects of the Vanderbilt/Marlborough marriage. (*Hulton Archive/Getty Images*)

Andrew Carnegie relaxes on the terrace of
Skibo Castle, his Sutherland retreat.
(Hulton Archive/Getty Images)

Viscount William Waldorf Astor, who
died Oct. 18, 1919, gave $46,000,000 to
his two sons two months before. On this
they paid $10,800,000 taxes in 1922 to
the Treasury which claimed the transfer
had been made in anticipation of death.
When they lately sought to recover
this, plus nearly $10,000,000 interest,
a Federal Jury decided against them.

William Waldorf Astor: the stock photo,
given an extra dimension by the news
report attached to it. Even after death,
Astor typically caused controversy – this
time over the avoidance of taxes. *(Hulton
Archive/Getty Images)*

Consuelo Marlborough, photographed in 1911, five years after her separation from Sunny. *(Hulton Archive/Getty Images)*

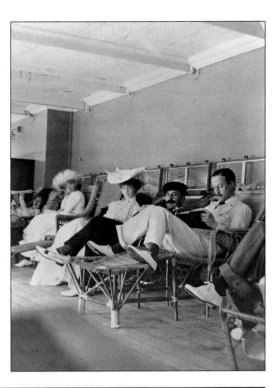

1902: Sunny and Consuelo Marlborough on board a P&O liner to India. Consuelo appeals to the photographer; Sunny, elegant in white ducks, buries himself in a book. *(Hulton Archive/Getty Images)*

1932, and the Prince of Wales and Thelma Furness attend a midnight gala at the Plaza Cinema. Thelma affects the doe-eyed tragic look perfected by her role model, Consuelo Marlborough. *(Fox Photos/Getty Images)*

Lord Decies – who had two Americans wives, Vivien Gould and Elizabeth Wharton Drexel – smilingly accepts an ice from the 26-year-old Tallulah Bankhead at a theatrical garden party. *(London Express/Getty Images)*

Emerald Cunard at the Strauss Ball of 1931, in the company of Sir Jey Singh, Maharajah of Alwar. *(Topical Press Agency/Hulton Archive/Getty Images)*

The Channons' dining room in Belgrave Square. *(Pat English/Time Life Pictures/Getty Images)*

'Chips' Channon and Lady Honor Guinness, leaving St Margaret's, Westminster, after a rehearsal for their wedding. *(Keystone/Getty Images)*

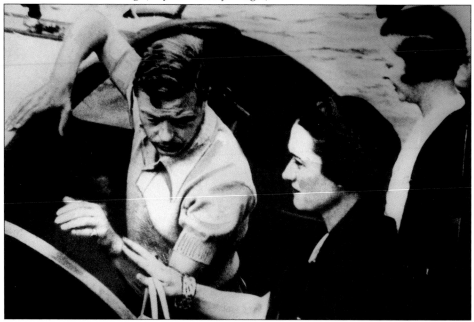

1936: the Prince of Wales and Wallis Simpson, holidaying in the Mediterranean. This photograph, revealing a clandestine moment of tenderness, quickly became known all over the world – apart from in Britain. *(Keystone/Getty Images)*

I take Prince George to the 18th row?" so I have confiscated all Maud Yorkes tickets and given them to the old trout.'[18] Diana Mosley, also a Cunard supporter (Maud 'made her guests perform to the best of their ability, so that the atmosphere was exhilarating and charged'[19]), observed none the less her crassness in perpetually asking, 'Who do the King and Queen *see*? Who is in the King's *set*?'[20] Even Herbert Asquith said, wearily, 'I hear her nasal accents at this moment in the next room, exhorting or threatening or wheedling poor Bongie [Maurice Bonham-Carter, Asquith's Parliamentary Private Secretary]. She is quite undefeatable.'[21] Undefeatable, oppressive and, occasionally, quite wrong-headed.

Many, indeed, never got beyond Maud's brittle exterior, eerie *maquillage* ('Curiously enough, the nearer one got to her the younger she looked; from a distance one could see only paint and wrinkles', according to Kenneth Clark[22]), peculiar physical characteristics and unnatural voice. Most often compared to a bird (the foul Mrs Ronnie Greville called her 'The Yellow Canary'; Virginia Woolf described her as a 'ridiculous little parakeet-faced woman'), she was either an avian freak or, according to the more sympathetic John Lehmann, was slightly built 'with exquisite figure and legs, advantages which were set off by the always impeccable elegance of her dress and the ropes of pearls and the diamonds which . . . she showed no signs of foreswearing'. Certainly, 'Her neatness of body, her incisive profile and high, lilting voice, and a certain way she had of holding her head, produced an often birdlike effect: of an exotic bird from a tropical jungle.' But against that, 'Her eyes were her most extraordinary feature: in the shaded lights of my first evening they seemed to me more like semi-precious stones than human eyes, *trouvailles* applied to the face in whose glaze none of the transitory emotions of the soul could be seen to stir.'[23] For Peter Quennell, while her features could never have been characterised as beautiful – 'The delicate high-bridged nose was accompanied by a slightly receding chin' – nevertheless, 'Even in profile they had a curious bird-like charm that matched her trilling song-bird's voice.'[24] And for a typically over-stimulated Harold Acton, 'Her approach to a subject was delicate and birdlike: with exquisite grace she would wing to the very core of some burning topic and watch the blaze with amused and cynical eyes.'[25]

Photographs reveal little of the Pocket Venus who captivated George Moore and Sir Bache Cunard at the turn of the century, and who was still captivating the more refined onlookers thirty years later. Even Cecil Beaton's portraits make her look like a seafront palmist, for all her inclusion in his *Book of Beauty*. She walked with a strange, mannered, high-stepping gait, and, with her fluting voice – from which much, but not all, American twang had been eradicated – she would deliver aphorisms both meaningless and consciously provocative: 'Only the *banal* need a home'; 'Jealousy is the most terrible of passions, don't you agree?'; 'A gentleman does not blow his nose in public'; 'A lady wears corsets'. She lunged at syllables, especially at the beginnings of words: things were often *on*pleasant; *on*necessary. And, finding reality not enough, she had a weakness for mythologising, for fantastical, whimsical, elaboration. Thus, 'This is Mr Evan Morgan, who looks like the poet Shelley and whose mother makes birds' nests'; or, of Lord Alexander Thynne, 'Miss Winifred Barnes, the musical comedy actress, fell over a very small cliff for love of him'; or, introducing Napier Alington, 'This is Lord Alington, dear. He drives in a taxi at dawn from Paris to Rome wearing evening dress and a gardenia, without any *luggage*'; and Michael Arlen was 'the only Armenian who has not been massacred'.[26] Consuelo Marlborough felt the queasy dislike inevitably experienced by the attractive but intellectually average towards someone plainer but much cleverer. She didn't get the irony that underpinned Maud's reckless hyperbole. 'I used to wonder why she did not herself realise that it was the wrong approach, especially in England', was the Duchess's stern assessment. Forced none the less to recognise Maud's larger social achievements, Consuelo reckoned that whatever successes she did garner were only the kind that any *enfant terrible* might manage: 'Like a restless child she flitted from one interest to another, lacking stability and poise.' Clearly uneasy about everything that Maud represented, Consuelo eventually took consolation in the natural aristocracy of beauty. Whatever her genius, Maud looked, 'I thought, like a little parakeet, with a golden coxcomb on her head, a small beak and a receding chin'. Thus the proper order was restored.[27]

The fact remained, however, that nothing seemed to be able to stop Maud Cunard in her plan to monopolise great tracts of London society. In 1920, she moved to 5 Carlton House Terrace, probably the most exclusive address in London. At the same time she tirelessly and shamelessly boosted Sir Thomas Beecham's League of Opera at Covent Garden – two brand names promoting a third – even persuading the ridiculously superior Londonderrys to subscribe to a box at the Opera House. To Seymour Leslie (nephew of Jennie Churchill) she wrote, '*You* can help with the League of Opera by asking each member of your music society to give a donation and join, anything from a pound upwards. We have 35,000 members. Please help with your vigour and tell me what to do . . . We must establish a permanent opera and it will be given in English, German and Italian – *Manon* in French if given. We will engage all the best singers of the world.' She ended with a pert 'Yrs. ever Emerald', before hurrying off after another project.[28]

Beecham was her greatest love, and he didn't care about her. 'Sir Thomas is quite a Don Juan', she would simperingly announce in those days, willing herself to believe in the primacy of his desire, even though she was now over 50 and he was an incontinent and unreflecting philanderer. She was free to be as clever as she liked, and indeed, to be *who* she liked; but she could not – didn't want to – get over Beecham (who had been knighted in 1916 and succeeded to his father's baronetcy in the same year). He had once been a guest at Nevill Holt: she fell hopelessly for him and moved to London partly so that she could be both private paramour and public fund-raiser for his work at Covent Garden. His busy, sexually enhanced exploitation of her energies and her chequebook (there is a story that he once stepped up to the podium and announced to the musicians he was rehearsing, 'Gentlemen, you will be pleased to know that the future of the orchestra is assured, thanks to the virility of your conductor') not only made her feel desired – however corruptly – but allowed her to frame her life increasingly as a kind of tormented fictional intrigue. After all, as John Lehmann observed, 'An aristocratic (but also American) audacity, intelligence, wit and, beneath it all, an almost tragic sense of disillusionment were the keynotes of her character.'[29] It was this mixture of brains, impertinence and, in the end, rank misery that made her interesting. Her love affairs and her marriage and were all dependably unsatisfactory, her unhappiness galvanising her into action. Her affair with Beecham was, from her point of view, both enchanting and catastrophic. He took what comforts he pleased in her bed and spent her money on his own projects, before eventually marrying a pianist called Betty Humby. Determinedly brilliant, she was too public, too *produced* to be much good at sensual or tender intimacy; too driven to have a clear sense of the truth underlying those relationships – with her daughter Nancy, with Thomas Beecham – that meant most to her.

As she grew older, the penetrating loneliness of her position became unendurable – at night, especially, when all the guests had left: 'At those midnight moments that her mask of diamond heartlessness slipped: one had glimpses of a pathetic and suffering creature below, a woman to whose heart wounds had been dealt that refused to heal. She dreaded being left alone with the night: she slept scarcely at all.'[30] It was common knowledge that 'She detested solitude: she dreaded the hours of the night: insomnia was an old and fearful enemy.'[31] She herself described it as being 'lapped in lead'. The living death of solitude made her work harder at pursuing her desired, social, ends; her belief in the power of love was combined with an equal certainty that love was impossible. She was a romantic, cynical, exotic, who had dedicated herself to English society – a society that had no useful category into which to put her, no way of confining her energies. She was a socially entrepreneurial Anglo-American hybrid; a new kind of figure, without antecedents and without, as far as anyone could tell, any real sense of duty or obligation to anyone but herself.

And while William Randolph Hearst was buying St Donat's in 1925, poor Sir Bache Cunard was dying, having lived alone at the Haycock Inn at Wansford for the preceding eleven years. He was heartbroken that his Maud had never come back to him and could not bring himself to mention her in his will. He requested that his 'funeral may be of the most simple kind and that black horses be not employed. I would prefer', he added, wretchedly, 'to go to my grave in a farm waggon rather than a hearse.'[32] With her husband gone, and to celebrate her emancipation from the man who had given her a title, a daughter and a start in society, in effect, Maud changed her name to 'Emerald' in 1926 (on account of the gems she had such a liking for) and set about moving house from Carlton House Terrace to the slightly cheaper 7 Grosvenor Square. And this, as subsequent events would bear out, was where all the trouble really started.

ELEVEN

The New Wave

The year 1926 was indeed a busy one, Emerald Cunard notwithstanding. July saw the celebrated Mrs Laura Corrigan throw one of her more remarkable parties, in which the guests themselves – unwontedly – provided the cabaret. The programme contained the following items:

On the ukelele . . . Lady Louis Mountbatten singing a plantation number accompanied by Lady Brecknock and Mrs Richard Norton

Exhibition dance . . . Lady Plunket

Double tandem cycle act . . . Daphne Vivian and Lord Weymouth, with Lady Lettice Lygon and Lord Brecknock singing 'Daisy, Daisy'

A satire . . . Lady Loughborough and Poppy Baring

A duet . . . Michael Hornby and Bobby Jenkinson

Mrs Corrigan then danced the Charleston to a number called 'On with the dance, let joy be unrefined', while dressed in a top hat and red shoes. After this, the climax: she stood on her head, having taken the precaution of tying a scarf round her knees so as to stop her skirt falling down. Lady Maud Warrender, daughter of the Earl of Shaftesbury, had hoped to do her plate-breaking act, but called it off in order to protect the fine parquet floor. At the end of the evening, the guests all joined in the game of 'The disappearing aristocrat' and melted blithely away into the dawn. But – who was Mrs Corrigan, anyway, that she could command such breezy complicity?

She first arrived in London (on 1 April, characteristically) in 1922. She was of uncertain early middle age, American, bald, gauche and startlingly rich. Her past was even more opaque than that of Lady Cunard, her money almost as limitless as Consuelo Vanderbilt's. One version of her biography held that she was born Laura Mae Whitrock, the daughter of a lumberjack, who then became a telephone switchboard operator for a fun-loving Ohio steel magnate called James Corrigan. Seduced by her voice on the other end of the line, Corrigan – head of the Corrigan-McKinney Steel Company of Cleveland, tenth largest in the United States – took her on a date and married her the next day. Another account had it that she was the daughter of a carpenter from Waupaca, Wisconsin, who had married a doctor. While working as a waitress in Chicago, she met that same magnate James Corrigan, who instantly fell in love with her, persuaded her to divorce the doctor and marry him. Either way, her brisk elevation from toiler to multi-millionairess allowed Mrs Corrigan to pay tribute to an inner compulsion. She left Ohio and the obliging Mr Corrigan and went on to conquer New York society, which was still tirelessly squabbling over the relative smartness of the Fifth Avenue set versus the Park Avenue set and the relative decline of the Astors and the Vanderbilts. Mrs Corrigan, a hick, got nowhere. She went to Europe and assaulted Paris. That failed. She crossed the Channel and assaulted London. This time, it worked.

Her success is an awkward, intractable thing to understand. 'Short, tight-featured, determined', all that Mrs Corrigan had going for her were wealth and drive. How could these have been enough to win her a commanding social position? And why, given the mixture of *ennui* and desperation that characterised so much of English society in the 1920s, did she bother? Nevertheless, within a month of arriving in town, she had been tipped off by a friendly American peeress – the Countess of Strafford – that the Old King's mistress, Mrs Keppel, was looking for someone to rent her delectable town house at 16 Grosvenor Street. Mrs Keppel had acquired this in 1910 and with her 'instinct for splendour' and a small personal fortune, courtesy of Edward VII and Sir Ernest Cassel, tricked it out with grey walls, contrasting red lacquer cabinets, yielding carpets with matching Angora cats, porcelain pagodas given her by Tumtum. Old Masters queued along the walls and the dining room could seat seventy. All this Mrs Corrigan took over, together with Mr Rolfe the butler and Mrs Rolfe the cook –

both of the pre-war school of excellence and deference – together with twenty indoor servants. She also got the guest book, Mrs Keppel shrewdly raising the rent to accommodate this extra. Mrs Corrigan had just time to shower smart London with invitations, most of which were ignored, before she met up with a social busybody and facilitator called Charlie Stirling, who at once became her social secretary.

At this point, her luck turned. Stirling, who was a friend of the Marquess and Marchioness of Londonderry, got them to appear at one of Mrs Corrigan's functions, and by the second half of May 1922, she was hosting a dinner party for Princess Marie Louise, cousin of the King. After that, she was a tolerated, if unconventional, presence in Society. In 1924, she held a dinner party for 104 guests – all crammed into 16 Grosvenor Street – for which Mrs Keppel's decor had been transformed into a *Jardin des Perroquets Verts*. For another event, she had the curtains sprayed with powdered glass and then carefully lit so that they sparkled like diamanté. She broke new ground by including professional cabarets at parties. Further success attended her when she decamped to the Palazzo Mocenigo in Venice for the summer, wearing a pair of ill-advised shorts. Notwithstanding the shorts, Mrs Corrigan's Venice holidays were graced by socialites such as Diana Cooper, Cecil Beaton, Lady Londonderry, Prince Christopher of Greece. And when she came back to London, she carried on as before, genuflecting to Lady Weymouth, the Duke and Duchess of Kent, the Londonderrys, again.

And yet, for the two decades in which she tended her beat, she was thoughtlessly and unrestrainedly despised. Her baldness was fatal in this respect. Otherwise unexceptional-looking, with a firm jaw, a letterbox mouth and eyes artificially widened by cosmetic surgery (she couldn't quite close them, even when she slept), she was, mysteriously, quite bald. Her eyebrows may have been her own, but the top of her head was believed to be as bare and pink as a knee. She travelled with a selection of auburn wigs in a box known by everyone except her as 'Laura's wigwam'. She had formal wigs for evening wear, airily tousled wigs for active, outdoor wear, a wig with bathing-cap attached for swimming. The *Sunday Express* called her 'The Big Wig of London'. Emerald Cunard, when asked by Mrs Corrigan what she would be wearing for an opera gala, replied *to her face*, 'A small emerald bandeau and my own hair.'

Then there was her difficulty with language and ideas. Mrs Corrigan's infelicities have been sneeringly archived for decades, with the result that over the gap of time she sounds spectacularly uneasy in the realm of speech, a parody of an aphasic American. For her, apparently, fine needlework on a seat was an example of '*petits pois*'; her house in London was her '*Ventre à terre*'; when someone asked her, 'Do you know the Dardanelles?' she is supposed to have answered, 'Wal no. But I've got lots of letters of introduction to them. I guess they're *terribly* nice people.'[1] Forced by the now-geriatric George Moore – still in thrall to his reputation as a terrorist of bourgeois sensibilities – to come up with a reply to the challenge, 'I always think, Mrs. Corrigan, that of all sexual perversions chastity is the most incomprehensible', Mrs Corrigan failed utterly, according to Patrick Balfour: 'Firstly she seemed but dimly aware of what Mr. Moore meant; secondly, her American conscience told her that it was something not quite nice; but thirdly, here she was seated next to the great man, and must play up accordingly . . . "Wal," she said, diplomatically, "I guess I shall have to think over that, Mr. Moore."'[2]

When confronted for the first time by Mrs Keppel's exquisite antique rugs at 16 Grosvenor Street, she said, 'Why, they're not even new.' Staying at the Palazzo Mocenigo, she simply abreacted on the arrival of Prince and Princess Christopher of Greece. On this occasion, according to Diana Cooper ('Mrs. Corrigan of course is the best mirth provoker'), she

> curtseyed on both knees. She took a retinue of men guests and footmen and gondoliers. She said, 'But sir, where are the servants?' – 'We have none,' they answered. It was sad as the house had been turned upside down to lodge them as befitted their service rank. She couldn't help but exclaim, 'But why, mam, I have 2 bodymaids, and Mr. Corrigan never crossed the Atlantic without 2 bodymen.'[3]

When visiting Sunny Marlborough at Blenheim, she asked where, exactly, the site of the battle of Blenheim was. He pointed at the statue of the 1st Duke on its column in the great park and said, 'There'. Duff Cooper simply called her 'atrocious'.

A counter-argument duly went around that Mrs Corrigan knew what effect she was having and merely did it to establish herself as a character. How true was that likely to be? Pre-emptive self-mockery bespeaks defensiveness rather than confidence: a need to draw an inevitable sting. Emerald Cunard's one-liners and capricious sarcasms made people quail. This never happened with Laura Corrigan, who invariably comes across as a hostage to passing thought, to unforeseen vocalisations.

And her lavishness was, after all, a kind of bribery. Her personal virtues may well have included affability, generosity, gusto and a sense of fun; but she ruthlessly dispensed gold trinkets as party favours in order to retain her position in society. Lady Weymouth once got a comb of gold and tortoiseshell in a pink leather Cartier case, 'the first I had ever seen'. Lord Weymouth got some gold braces as a wedding gift. Diana Cooper got a diamond clip for her birthday, which fell into a Venetian canal as she leant over a balcony ('At five a.m.', she wrote to Duff, 'a diver went in after baby's diamonds. I *do* hope he finds them'[4]). When Mrs Corrigan organised a raffle or tombola as part of her party entertainments, the draw was fixed so that the most expensive prizes went to those with the grandest titles. Once, Michael Hornby, married to the daughter of a baroness but otherwise of no great hierarchical significance, accidentally found himself the winner of a gold cigarette case which had been earmarked for Prince George. Thus Mrs Corrigan's entertainments went on, and debilitated London society turned up for them, because she was one of the few people with enough drive, money and indifference to her own dignity to make such things happen.

Instructively, even the Londonderrys, the Marquess and Marchioness, so great and so grand, ended up beholden to her and to her great wealth – even though they, unlike most other members of the peerage, were hugely rich on their own account. This was mainly thanks to the coalmines which they ran in the north-east of England: in the mid-1920s, Charley Londonderry's total assets were estimated to be worth over £2,500,000.

After the war – the 6th Marquess having died in 1915 – Charley and his wife Edith took charge of the five great Londonderry houses, including the residence at Mount Stewart, in Northern Ireland, and Londonderry House in Park Lane. Edith herself took over custodianship of the renowned Londonderry Jewels. As with the 1st Duke of Marlborough and the subsequent Churchills, the reputation of the 2nd Marquess of Londonderry – Foreign Secretary, scourge of Napoleon, architect of mid-nineteenth-century Europe, detested by his Parliamentary colleagues – lay heavily on his successors, the Vane-Tempest-Stewarts. It was impossible not to be aware of his glamour and his twisted repute; impossible to approximate to them. Worse, the new Marquess of Londonderry, like the latter-day Duke of Marlborough, was a walking compendium of deficiencies. Charley was slim, elegant, surgically well turned out and infected with the terrible restlessness of failure. He claimed never to have spent more than ten consecutive nights in the same place. He philandered constantly and pointlessly. He sired an illegitimate daughter, born six weeks after he married Edith. He ran off noisily with Consuelo Marlborough in 1905 and then returned, contrite. He then had a long and blowsy affair with the American-born Eloise, Countess of Ancaster, whose home at Grimsthorpe Castle in Lincolnshire was only a couple of miles from the Londonderrys' hunting box at Oakham. He reflexively made an attempt on Lady Diana Manners, shortly before she married Duff Cooper, in 1918. He was still at it well into the 1930s, with Olive Murray-Smith, daughter of Lord Burnham. It was infidelity on a pathological level.

He longed to be great player on the political stage. As it turned out, boosted by Edith's marathon courtship of Ramsay MacDonald, Charley rose all the way to the position of Air Minister, before being sacked by Stanley Baldwin. Having excited the horror of his Parliamentary colleagues by advocating aerial bombing as a means of subjugating rebellious tribesmen in India and Iraq, he then crowned his political career by publicly attempting to conciliate Hitler shortly before the outbreak of the Second World War.

Edith staggered on, catering for the political classes, but it was increasingly clear that what kept the Londonderrys going was less their talents as individuals and more their exceptional wealth and monumental self-regard. This irked the thrusting Winston Churchills as much as anyone – despite, or possibly on account of, Charley and Winston being cousins. When the idea was being floated of some kind of marital alliance between Robin Castlereagh and the Churchills' daughter Diana, Clementine at once expressed horror at the idea of yoking her destiny to that of the incredibly snobbish, self-obsessed, intellectually negligible Londonderrys. 'Puerile' was one of her descriptions of Edith and Charley; 'futile' another.[5] Hindsight, in other words, characterises the Londonderrys as glittering also-rans. 'I have been a miserable failure', Charley once wrote to Ettie Desborough, examining the debris of his life as it drew to a close. 'I think poor Edie realises this and know Robin does too. But E. is constant in her support and her care for me and I never would know from anything she says or does that I have failed to give her the position she should have had.'[6] In this way, despite their name and their social eminence, almost everything they did had a kind of mediocrity running through it.

Laura Corrigan, back in the perky 1920s, carried none of this potential baggage: she could scarcely have been less like the Londonderrys. Her wealth, unlike the Londonderrys', was uncompromised and directed solely in the pursuit of entertainment: 'She entertains because she is ambitious – to entertain', as Balfour put it. She did not own five houses. Her money was not there to prop up Jimmy Corrigan's name; nor was it entailed to future generations. If it hadn't been for her chance meeting with Charlie Stirling, would she ever have come across the Londonderrys? Would they have given her the time of day? And yet, once the Londonderrys had found her, they stuck with her. As snobs do, they enjoyed having someone to patronise. As rich people do, they felt comfortable in the presence of yet more wealth. Believing themselves destined for an even better existence, they took an uncomplicated, venal, delight in expensive things. The contract was watertight. Whatever Mrs Corrigan's vulgarity as a person, she happily excited Charley and Edith's cupidity and then satisfied it with presents. Among other things, she had Lord Castlereagh's thousands of papers at Mount Stewart bound in calfskin as a gift to Charley. She gave Edith, on her birthday, a Cartier wristwatch and a shooting stick. Then she gave her a gun, followed by a handbag with extraordinarily heavy solid gold handles. In return, they (or at least Edith) went to her London parties, had her to stay at Mount Stewart, stayed with her in Venice. She was so far outside their normal conception of society that they had no idea that they were compromising themselves by dancing attendance on her.

But there was more. The Londonderrys, like the Weymouths, the Mountbattens, the Lygons, the Loughboroughs, the Barings, the Coopers and the living marginalia of the royal family, all liked receiving gifts; but they also liked Mrs Corrigan's vitality, her thoroughness, her resilience – her Americanness. In January 1928, Laura's distant husband died of a heart attack when about to play a game of bowls at the Cleveland Athletic Club. She took a year's sabbatical from London society and then came right back, as industrious as ever. Patrick Balfour could only marvel at her tenacity, her work ethic: 'No one could describe Mrs. Corrigan as informal', was his conclusion.

> Her idea of an intimate little luncheon is a table laid for fifty covers. Nor, in the beginning, was she exclusive. But, through sheer persistence, Mrs. Corrigan is now become wellnigh as exclusive as her compatriot Lady Granard herself [formerly Beatrice Mills, of Duchess County, NY; subsequently the 8th Countess of Granard]. The list of guests not invited to her last party would have aroused the frantic jealousy of many a minor American meteor . . . She does not, like the pre-war hostesses, entertain people from a sense of responsibility or duty or habit; nor from an interest in what they will have to tell her of politics or art or the affairs of the mind. None of these things concerns Mrs. Corrigan. Mrs. Corrigan is, in fact, a very acute business woman, but she prefers to make Society her end in life.[7]

So fascinated was the young Cecil Beaton by Mrs Corrigan's industriousness that, before he became a successful society photographer, he resolved to write a stage play which would feature 'a pushing American hostess, a "Shooting star" closely based on Mrs. Corrigan'.[8] Diana Cooper described her as being 'in a frenzy of thrill'[9] at the anticipation of international royalty. The un-English, unadulterated dynamism of *thrill* lay behind much of her success.

Edith Londonderry, on the other hand, may have inherited the title of Queen of Society from her mother-in-law, but in the end her unique gift to the smart set was The Ark: an institution that, distanced by history, now appears quaint, infantile and almost whimsically unconscious of its own inadequacies. A kind of nursery-flavoured private club, The Ark was started by Edith in 1915, at Londonderry House, as a refuge (it must be conceded) for overtaxed army chiefs and government ministers. It was still going, though, at the end of the war, and continued to suck in the well-connected and the curious.

John the Buck, Arthur the Albatross, Winston the Warlock, Barrie the Bard, John Dory, Nancy the Gnat, Sam the Skate and Orpen the Ortolan were among those who turned up to be served champagne by liveried footmen, and eat canapés. Rather, John Buchan, A.J. Balfour, Winston Churchill, J.M. Barrie, Sir John Lavery, Nancy Astor, Sir Samuel Hoare and Sir William Orpen all arrived, each bearing the playful soubriquet bestowed on him or her by Circe the Sorceress, i.e. Edith. Charley, pointedly, was Charley the Cheetah. Sometimes they all played a game called Chase the Ace in order to win the prize of a box of matches. 'Foreign animals came to roost in The Ark in the shape of Ambassadors and Ministers and a big sprinkling of Cabinet Ministers', wrote Edith. 'One thing about The Ark parties was appreciated, they were small and informal, as only members were invited. Each animal received a separate invitation, whether married or single, and each animal was invited to bring its mate to Circe's den. Married couples very rarely belonged to the same species.'[10]

The Ark worked because it created a condition of prelapsarian forgetfulness at a time of emotional and financial exhaustion; and did it in conditions of authentic grandeur. It was, however, less Madame Récamier and more Eton Pop in its ambitions. Stirred by its undemanding pleasures, members of The Ark wrote poems in praise of it and of Edith Londonderry. For instance:

ARKEOLOGY

Much worse than the Park
In the dark is the Ark
With its tandems of beauty and breeding
That swarm to Park Lane,
In sunshine or rain,
For Antediluvian feeding . . .

No chapell-of-ease
Is as 'go as you please'
As the Ancient Ark, wherein Circe
Our Arkship supreme
With a mischievous gleam
In her eye, plays the *Belle Dame sans merci*.[11]

Not a *salon* in the conventional sense, the deliberately middlebrow Ark thus allowed British men to be as brightly anti-intellectual as they liked. And when, in November 1919, she built on her Ark success by reinstating the traditional eve-of-Parliament reception (last organised by her late mother-in-law and suspended during the war), it became clear that Edith Londonderry was positioning herself as a major social impresario. The Parliamentary receptions were among the biggest, most massively effortful social events of the year, when Edith hung herself about with the Londonderry jewels (wearing a huge tiara known as the 'family fender') and stood, as had the 6th Marchioness, at the top of the stairs of Londonderry House. The 1919 reception had 2,500 guests. Lord Curzon noted that it was 'just like old times, only three times as many people'.[12] It took 20 minutes for some of the arrivals to get from the bottom of the stairs to the top. Sensibly, Edith consolidated her reputation as a social force by letting in representatives of all political parties, rather than a top-heavy mass of Conservatives. Indeed, as the 1920s drew on, she started an *amitié amoureuse* with the increasingly pathetic Ramsay MacDonald – partly to maintain political centrality; partly to give herself some kind of consolation against Charley's endless love affairs; partly in order to cater him into the cabinet.

So she worked at it. But the success she enjoyed had a great deal to do with the fact that she had inherited a complete set of tools with which to be a hostess; and that, by the mid-1920s, there wasn't much competition. As Balfour noted, 'The Duchesses of Portland, Beaufort, Rutland, Devonshire, Buccleuch, Somerset and Richmond no longer entertain on any scale in London. The Duchess of Bedford is concerned principally with aviation; the Duchess of Marlborough with dog breeding.'[13] The upshot was that

Lady Londonderry is the only big political hostess, and her eve of the session receptions, often held in the afternoon, are now no

more than a formality . . . It is a sign of the times that invitations
to many parties at Londonderry House are now worded as
follows:

> YE ARCHAIC ARK ASSOCIATION
> Londonderry House, Park Lane.
> Her Arkship, Circe the Sorceress,
> commands the attendance of –
>
> – at a feast to be held in the Antediluvian
> Dining-Den of the Ark[14]

For all the grandeur of the setting and the prestige of the
Londonderry name, there was a sense of imaginative failure hanging
over the Londonderrys, a lack of zest, an absence of culture. When
Clementine Churchill described them as being both puerile and
futile, it was with the sense that they were victims of their own
massively privileged circumstances, and too dull to imagine a way
out. Was it any wonder, then, that they fell so easily into the arms of
the spectacularly well-motivated Mrs Corrigan, and so obligingly
helped set her up for the next decade and a half? Was it any wonder
that they let her make the running? Was it any wonder that they
were part of the problem, rather than the solution?

Nor were Mrs Corrigan and Emerald Cunard the only American
hostesses to work at being a part of the postwar British smart set.
Maxine Elliot – actress, professional beauty, former mistress of King
Edward VII – came back to England after the war to consolidate the
place she had already carved out for herself and skip across to her
Mediterranean home in France when the mood took her. Mrs
William – Mabel – Corey did the same. A former dancer with the
Ziegfeld Follies, Mrs Corey was a millionaire's trophy wife who was
always detestably pressing trinkets on Lady Cunard (who preferred
to give; hated to receive) and was mainly remembered by Seymour
Leslie as 'an early patient of the infant art of facial surgery. As often
happened in those days, for the surgeons were literally feeling their
way, her mouth had become much diminished and indeed
completely round, so that she appeared to be about to whistle.' Mrs

Corey was not a towering success. '"Ma Belle" as we all called her, was a bewildered amiable figure and one supposed she was pleased to be helpful though how could one be sure as she could not smile and her face was set forever in a dead-pan mask.'[15] And when Mabel complained that the corrupt French police had stolen the beds from her château 'to furnish a brothel', Emerald Cunard protested, 'Mabel Corey, I do not allow such talk in my presence. If you say anything so *on*pleasant again I shall require you to leave the room.'[16]

There was also, from time to time, the exciting presence of New York-born interior designer Elsie de Wolfe, who became Lady Mendl (in 1926) when she married the diplomat Sir Charles Mendl. Nancy Astor, American wife of the properly anglicised 2nd Viscount William Waldorf Astor, was of course a famous MP and hostess of many unhappy teetotal parties at Cliveden, which the first William Waldorf Astor had disowned. Elsa Maxwell, a stray vaudevillian from Iowa, criss-crossed Europe almost entirely for the entertainment of the well-born. She eagerly promoted both Cole Porter and his work. In return he wrote her a song which managed to allude to her 'ninety-nine most intimate friends'. Showing rare genius, she also threw a 'murder party' at American-born Lady Ribblesdale's house in St James's, in the course of which she managed to have the Duke of Marlborough 'arrested'.

There was a terrible sense of ubiquity about the American hostesses – even though there was never more, in reality, than a handful to go round. The problem was that London's sensibilities were so brittle, so conscious of the way the world was changing, that every American voice, every American-inspired amusement, made a double impact. For some, the only way to compensate for this dreary truth was to embrace a kind of louche gaiety, a modern version of the Hogarthian debauch.

Without a doubt, the Bright Young People, assisted by the young Prince of Wales and his brother, Prince George, did their best to generate a sufficiently steamy top-dressing of fun. The Jungman sisters, Brian Howard, Lady Eleanor Smith, Lady Diana Cooper (drinker, *morphinomane* and leader of the 'corrupt coterie'), Loelia Ponsonby, Cecil Beaton, the Lygon sisters, Tom Mitford (in his guise of 'Bruno Hat', avant-garde artist and tormentor of the intelligentsia), the world-weary Patrick Balfour – all strove to shock. Brian Howard blithely threw a party at St George's Swimming Baths at which guests were asked to bring a bottle and a bathing-suit: a black orchestra provided the music and a 'bathwater cocktail' was served. Lady Ellesmere had her party at Bridgewater House, Green Park, gate-crashed by several hundred completely unrepentant young things. Mrs Rosemary Sandars threw a party at her house at Rutland Gate for which everyone had to turn up dressed as a baby. Lord Howard of Effingham had to appear at Bow Street Police Station following a minor riot outside Mrs Meyrick's notorious 43 Club. The Hon. Stephen Tennant had a party for which the guests had to dress as shepherds out of Watteau. A Mozart party found its early-morning stragglers dressed as eighteenth-century Viennese aristocrats, digging up the road in the West End. And when not invited to a private party, the young smart set could go public. The Embassy Club in Old Bond Street was for fashionable people to get drunk in with an element of decorum; Mrs Meyrick's '43', a quarter of a mile away in Gerard Street, was for the same people to get drunk in when they decided to slum it; Rosa Lewis's Cavendish Hotel was a kind of halfway house. There was drug-taking (some of it thanks to the efforts of Mrs Meyrick's acquaintance, drug-dealer Brilliant Chang) and overt sexual ambiguity – Reg Batten and the Savoy Havana Band singing about *Masculine Women, Feminine Men* ('Which is the rooster, which is the hen? It's hard to tell them apart today'). The Dean of St Paul's, Dr Inge, declared that 'We are threatened with a great outburst of licentiousness such as that which disgraced the country in the reign of Charles II and again during the Regency.'[17]

Some young people even defied convention and bowed to the exigencies of postwar living by getting jobs. Mrs Barbara Innes, niece of Lord Lonsdale, was found selling cars in a Bond Street showroom. 'I intend to specialise in salesmanship', she said. 'I shall miss a certain amount of hunting but foot-and-mouth has stopped most of that so I cannot really grumble.'[18] The Hon. Henry Lygon, brother of Earl Beauchamp, took to running a pub near Smithfield, and was on record as describing the everyday working man's pub as 'nothing less than a drink den'. Lady Ossulston started a laundry, telling reporters that she was trying to abolish the use of laundry marks. Other members of society, even more excitingly, went into serious commerce. A Moore-Brabazon became a director of Kodak; a Lyttelton became manager of the British Metal Corporation; the future Earl of Drogheda got a job with the American Smelting and Refining Company. Everyone did the best they could in the strange, disorientating circumstances.

As a result, an entire generation of older patricians found itself having to make uneasy accommodations with the postwar world. No one – from the 6th Duke of Portland, born in 1857, to the relatively youthful Edith, Marchioness of Londonderry, born in 1879 – could think of a good thing to say about social trends. For the 1st Marchioness of Aberdeen and Temair, born in the same year as the Duke of Portland, it was a nuanced loss, expressed by way of appeal to a happier past. 'London Society in those days', she argued, harking back to the old Prince of Wales and the *Belle Époque*,

> embraced a very definite and a very limited class. First and foremost, there were the landed proprietors from all parts of the kingdom who considered it their natural duty to spend some months in London every year, their wives and daughters attending the Queen's Drawing-room and themselves the Levees, and they and their families accepting and returning a certain number of set dinners and parties . . . Then there were the permanent Government officials, a select number of London residents, and a few literary people; also artists and musicians whose reputation brought them within the charmed circle.

So hermetic was this scene that while 'Captains of industry and local magnates were beginning to be recognized', it was the case that

> their appearance at a Society function would still excite comment, and explanations of how important they were in their own circle and in matters of finance would be passed round in reply to queries as to the newcomers. It was a stiff, ossified world, and the dead hand of nostalgia lay heavily upon the 65-year-old Marchioness. 'The London season as it was in those days, with its customs, its etiquette, its unwritten laws, then seemed one of

those fixed institutions in the life of the country, which gave the impression that it would go on indefinitely. There was a sense of solid security about it – it was part of the very life of the people who had the largest stake in the country, who counted for something. Nobody could well come to the front without participating in it to some degree. People might scoff at London Society and its conventions, its artificiality, and its apparent devotion to pleasure as the main object in life; but there it was: it represented the élite of the governing classes of the British Empire, and to be recognized as 'in Society' was (and indeed perhaps still is) the goal of many ambitions.[19]

Very well. Diminishing the present by reference to what it is not was an innocent enough, and predictable, pastime for an authentic grandee such as the Marchioness, who, as well as being the daughter of Lord Tweedmouth, was a former Vicereine of Ireland, founder of the Victorian Order of Nurses, Dame Grand Cross and President of the International Council of Women. But even the 9th Duke of Manchester, with all the cynical effrontery of *his* life behind him, felt able to adopt a tone of weary disparagement when contemplating the reduced world left for younger generations to experience.

The difference [he declared] between society in King Edward's day and society now, to anyone who has known both periods, is that there is no society at present. What has happened is that society no longer exists as it did, and there is a twofold reason for this: firstly, there are only a few people nowadays who have any pretensions to be labelled 'society' and secondly, those that have a claim to the title have not money enough to keep up their estates and open their houses, and so are forced to economise by living on a much smaller scale. As a natural result of such economy [and this from a notorious ex-bankrupt and social scrounger] what little entertaining is still done is conducted in a scrappy sort of way in restaurants and cocktail bars.[20]

This plaint is then taken up by Edith, Marchioness of Londonderry, who, having clumsily acknowledged that things were not always perfect when she was a girl ('Society was very restricted compared to

modern ideas') nevertheless felt able to carp about the course events
had taken:

> Society, as such, now means nothing, and it represents nothing
> except wealth and advertisement. The Peerage, to a great extent,
> has replenished its waning fortunes from the ranks of those who,
> before the War, would not have formed part of what the Press is
> pleased to term 'Society'. Therefore, it also does not represent
> what it formerly did, and it is well that this should be
> understood.[21]

For her, the Duke of Manchester would have been precisely one of
those degenerates who had reduced select society to such a degraded
state. The irony was that the Marchioness herself, with her fondness
for patronising rich postwar *arrivistes* such as Mrs Corrigan, was
busily helping to replenish the waning fortunes of the peerage
precisely 'from the ranks of those who, before the War, would not
have formed part of what the Press is pleased to term "Society"'.
The tone of parched derision – shared both by the Queen of Society
and a world-class layabout – is essentially the same, as is their
absolute lack of self-awareness.

Only Mabell, Countess of Airlie, Mistress of the Bedchamber to
Queen Mary and quintessential Establishment figure, did her best to
manage her gloom at the passing of the old ways by introducing a
note of perspective – quoting in her memoirs a letter written to her
by her brother, the 6th Earl of Arran.

> The days of family pedigrees are over. I always think it rather
> pathetic when I see people who have been turned out of their
> country houses by taxation stick up their family portraits in small
> London flats [the Earl observed, facing facts]. They are clinging to
> the past and will not realize that an old family only remains such
> as long as it continues to own the family house and landed
> property. [The past, meanwhile, needed reassessment.] I look back
> on my life before 1914 when I had everything the world could
> give me – brilliant London seasons, two lovely country houses and
> continual coming and going of people. I turn nostalgically to
> those halcyon years with delight and remember how much I

enjoyed them. Yet I understand that even were I able to afford to live again as I did then it would be impossible owing to the march of democracy. To live that life demanded that domestic servants should be slaves and contented with their slavery. It was only by slavery that the old regime could be carried on.[22]

Patrick Balfour looked at things with a similarly lengthy purview when he identified those historical forces that had been at work for some fifty years.

The Victorian Court [he explained] especially in the last half of the century, was never 'smart' or amusing. Only the middle classes followed its fashions, and the greater number of Queen Victoria's friends were drawn from the middle classes, not the old aristocracy. The latter gathered round the Prince of Wales, whose circle was considerably leavened by the introduction of numbers of the new rich whom he could not afford to disregard.

It was, in effect, an assault on two fronts. The middle classes rose; the old aristocracy reached down into the rockpool of 'American and South African millionaires'.[23] The upshot? 'Society in its old sense has ceased to exist. The social climber changed in character; for Society has climbed down.'[24]

And the Duke of Portland? His horror was provoked – among other, worryingly specific, things – by the tobacco degeneracy of the modern woman. Writing about life at the end of the nineteenth century, he observed that 'In those days, very few ladies smoked in public, though if they did so in private, it was their own business and nobody else's!' A devotee of the sweet and docile Consuelo Manchester, he found the assertiveness, the flavour of masculine self-determination hinted at when women smoked in public, repellent; especially if it encouraged them towards an equally masculine laxity about all aspects of their personal appearance. For him, a part expressed the whole.

I am all for ladies smoking cigarettes, cigars, pipes, or anything else, if they really enjoy them; but surely it is neither becoming nor attractive for an otherwise pretty and charming young woman to appear with a half-smoked cigarette hanging from her vividly painted lips, and with henna-coloured nails at the end of yellow, nicotine-stained fingers. In my youth I was taught that pearls fell from ladies' lips; but that has all been altered of late and, instead of pearls, a half-chewed and dirty cigarette seems only too often to take their place.[25]

Just in case anyone was tempted to think that the Bright Young People had at least escaped complete annexation by some terrible lumbering American widow, or triumphal ex-pat Charlie Chaplin, or Douglas Fairbanks and Mary Pickford, or indeed anyone glowing with the nimbus of American glamour, along came something quite unexpected – a, young, sleazy Mrs Corrigan, a desirable Elsa Maxwell, an embodiment of exoticism made super-real by her American vitality and lack of *pudeur*.

This person was Tallulah Bankhead: born in Huntsville, Alabama, daughter of William Brockman Bankhead, Speaker of the House of Representatives and notionally an extremely minor member of the American upper classes. Trying her luck as a stage actress, she found work in New York hard to come by, and in early 1923, at the age of 20, moved to London to appear with Sir Gerald du Maurier in *The Dancers*. This was her first piece of good fortune. She was strikingly good-looking, with abundant red hair; she was also a libertine, who drank, argued and copulated her way through life with a barely sane rapacity, and, as such, found a ready foothold among the fast set. Indeed, she was already friends with several fringe members of society, thanks to the relationships she had begun while struggling in New York – with Noël Coward; with Jeffrey Amherst, the 5th Earl Amherst, who was working as a staffer on the New York *Morning World*; and, most significantly, with Lord Napier Alington, the 3rd Baron Alington, who was in the States to learn about high finance. Alington was sensual, permissive, evasive. His mother, the 2nd Lady Alington, had once appeared dressed as 'India' in a gown of red and gold gauzes, her dimpled chin prominent, her broad, creamy arms bound in gold, at *The Masque of War and Peace* organised by Minnie Paget in 1900. She worried about the 'wildness' of her children but did nothing to restrain it. While in New York, Napier lived in an appropriately scurrilous apartment known as Naps's Flat.

Despite a history of rackety disappearances, he spent most of the winter of 1922 with Tallulah, who found herself in love with him. Part of his appeal lay in his selfishness, his indolent refusal to commit himself – the kind of personal characteristics that Tallulah, forever testing the limits of her own desirability, found irresistible. When she left New York in 1923, he barely cared.

But then she became a star in London, vigorously enjoying the attentions of a fan club that seemed to erupt from nowhere – shopgirls and secretaries who filled the cheap seats and yelled 'Tallulah Hallelujah!' while she was on stage, articulating their desire for emancipation. She also re-established her connection with Napier Alington (who promptly gave her a peke called Napoleon) and got to know more of Naps's bohemian friends: Lady Diana Cooper, theatrical designer Ned Latham, and the idiotic Baronet, Sir Francis Laking, who became a shambolic private secretary to Miss Bankhead until his death in 1930, following an excess of yellow chartreuse. Having watched the procession of the Duke and Duchess of York after their wedding in 1923, she promptly wrote to her father, 'The people rode in Golden Coaches more beautiful than in Fairy Tales. Daddy dear, having a King and Queen makes *such* a difference!'[26]

Tallulah's bad behaviour was a kind of raddled inverse of Mrs Corrigan's assiduously good behaviour. Where Mrs Corrigan took on the Keppel house and staff and pressed gold toys into the hands of her guests, Tallulah Bankhead took a lease on 1 Farm Street, where she used to open the front door stark naked and hold cocktail parties in her bathroom. While Mrs Corrigan was enjoying the residual acclaim from her *Jardin des Perroquets Verts* dinner, Tallulah Bankhead was readying herself to star in Coward's *Fallen Angels*, subsequently described as 'vulgar, obscene and degenerate' and a huge commercial success. On the last night of the run, Mrs Charles Hornibrook, a notoriously unhinged agitator for public morality, stood up in her box and shouted, 'I wish to protest. This play should not go unchallenged.' While the pit orchestra played 'I Want to be Happy', Mrs Hornibrook was thrown out.[27] In 1926, Mrs Corrigan threw the party in which the Weymouths sat on a tandem bicycle and sang 'Daisy, Daisy'. A couple of months later, Sir Francis Laking turned up with Tallulah at a Bright Young People party, dressed as a woman; he then provided his own, personal, cabaret by stripping stark naked and attempting the charleston. While Mrs Corrigan was dreaming of the arrival of Prince and Princess Christopher of Greece to the Palazzo Mocenigo, Tallulah was dining with Sir Gerald du Maurier at the Savoy Grill – where a woman rushed up to her and slapped her hard across the face. Miss Bankhead betrayed no emotion, unhurriedly turned to Sir Gerald and said, 'What were you sayin', Dahlin?' While Mrs Corrigan was making up to the Londonderrys, Tallulah was playing mah-jongg with Beverley Nichols and Diana Cooper and saying 'Well, dahling, you've got my wind.' She opened as Iris March in the stage version of *The Green Hat*: the Prince of Wales, Napier Alington, the Marchioness of Milford Haven and Lady Tweedmouth were all present on the first night. She went on to give 128 wildly successful performances. She then capped this by appearing as the promiscuous wife of a British Cabinet Minister in *Scotch Mist*, a play so scandalising that the Bishop of London wrote to the Prime Minister on behalf of the London Public Morality Council. Years later, Cecil Beaton would witness her '*Walpurgis* night', in the course of which 'Tallulah danced frienziedly, throwing herself about in a mad apache dance with Napier Alington. After she left, she wept and bemoaned the fact that he had never married her' – he had, in fact, married the more appropriate Lady Mary Ashley-Cooper, daughter of the Earl of Shaftesbury, in 1928 – 'Then she threw off all her clothes, performing what she called "Chinese classical dances"'.[28]

In the space of ten years, she defined a way of behaving, an absence of self-restraint, that was only possible because she was American. Her looks, her accent, her otherness, the unknowability of American conventions, all worked in her favour. Like Laura Corrigan, she was outside the familiar. Unlike Laura Corrigan, it was impossible to place her actions within a moral context; she was a Rousseauesque natural. When he died, Sir Francis Laking bequeathed 'To my friend Tallulah Bankhead all my motor cars'. It turned out he did not own a single one.

TWELVE

The Prince

Neither the money, nor the parties, the golden gifts, the intrigues, the bad behaviour, the gradual annexation of London society by American energies would have greatly mattered, despite everything, if it hadn't been for the Prince of Wales. It was when he began his affair with Lady Furness at the end of 1926 that what had been seen as a mildly distressing, mildly amusing, social trend suddenly hardened into a crisis in the making. At that point, the American way finally engaged with the British monarchy: and the effect was to reveal even the most amiable and entertaining aspects of the American invasion as menacing and, finally, destructive.

Thelma Furness was born Thelma Hays Morgan in 1905; she had a twin sister called Gloria. The girls' father was a moderately wealthy peripatetic American diplomat. At the time, he was Consul at Lucerne. Not long after, they decamped to Amsterdam and from there, kept on moving. Thelma claimed that both she and Gloria ended up speaking English with a kind of patois accent inflected with both French and Spanish.[1] Both girls were vividly good-looking – Thelma in particular adopting for photographers an expression of the same kind of exquisite saucer-eyed melancholy so popular with Consuelo Marlborough a quarter of a century earlier. Indeed, she wrote that Madame Balsan – first cousin, indeed, to the man who married her sister Gloria – was one of the most beautiful women she had ever known, and that if anyone should ask her whom she would most wish to resemble in all the world, 'I would unhesitatingly say Consuelo Balsan'.[2]

Both girls – like Consuelo Vanderbilt/Marlborough/Balsan herself – were not only beautiful but mildly solipsistic and prone to unsuitable relationships. While she was still sixteen years old, Thelma married a lothario called James 'Junior' Vail Converse, a divorcé with a seven-year-old son called Petey. Junior Converse spent a lot of time trying to broker outlandish business deals; when these fell through, he drank heavily and took his anger out on Thelma. In 1924, she divorced him and moved to Hollywood with the vague idea of becoming a film star. She was lovely enough, but she couldn't act. She settled for a brief affair with Charlie Chaplin, then drifted across to Europe, where she was photographed – with her sister – for Cecil Beaton's *Book of Beauty*. And then she met the appalling Marmaduke, 1st Viscount Furness, who immediately fell in love with her.

Furness himself was a widower whose first wife had died in 1921, leaving him with two children – Averill and Dick. He was 42, small, leathery, foul-mouthed and rich, being one of the grandest shipowners in Britain. Despite being a viscount, he was commonly known as Duke, as in (Marma)duke. Thelma dutifully observed that while his offensive language at first shocked her ('It was more characteristic of the stables than the drawing-room'), the better she got to know him, the easier it became to explain away his profanities as a 'mask for shyness' rather than a 'sign of vulgarity'.[3] This was a remarkably tolerant line to take. Everyone else simply knew Furness as inveterately sweary – a tendency in no way disproved when he came to pick up his 20-year-old bride-to-be from Southampton in the middle of the General Strike of 1926. Riding at the the head of a fleet of Rolls-Royces, Duke drove her back to Claridge's, keeping a loaded revolver in his lap all the way. 'I'd like to see any bastard try and stop this car', he said. His friends called him 'a lucky dog'.[4]

Unsurprisingly, this alliance didn't last. Even though Thelma produced a son for Duke in 1928, the marriage was bound to go sour. She argued that he was bored with her and was spending time with the glamorous American multiple divorcée, Peggy Hopkins Joyce, in Monte Carlo. He might well have countered with the fact that Thelma was now seeing the Prince of Wales and that there was little, morally, to choose between them. But whereas Peggy Hopkins Joyce was an astonishingly predatory ex-Ziegfeld Follies girl who would eventually work her way through six husbands and scores of lovers, the Prince was a confused youngish man due, in the fullness of time, to became King Emperor. Duke's affair was merely an affair. Thelma's was very nearly a constitutional issue.

In fact, Edith Londonderry had played an unlikely central role in bringing Thelma and the Prince together. In the same year that Thelma married Duke Furness, the pair were invited to Londonderry House for a royal dinner. The Prince was there, still attached to his lover, the 'tiny, squeaky and wise and chic' Freda Dudley Ward: 'Very pretty', according to Duff Cooper, as well as 'really very nice too and quite amusing.'[5] The Prince, according to Thelma, 'looked younger than I had pictured him and very handsome'.[6] He was chattering with Lady Londonderry, who then made the introductions and the Prince duly stored the image of Lady Furness in the back of his mind. Two years later, he had lost interest in Mrs Ward (whom he had started seeing as long ago as 1918) and transferred his attentions to Thelma. The Prince was on tour in East Africa in the autumn of 1928; there he met up with the Furness party, who were failing to amuse themselves in Nairobi. A year after that, he decided that Marmaduke Furness was scarcely in a position to object if he, the Prince of Wales, took his wife out.

By offering her cocktails at St James's Palace, followed by dinner and a dance, he wooed her. She offered no resistance, finding him 'winsomely handsome', and 'the quintessence of charm'. Better yet, he had none of Duke Furness's tendency towards swearing incontinently or slapping Thelma on her bottom, managing instead to appear both shy and glancingly seductive.[7] Her allure lay partly in her physical presence; partly in her hedonism, her uncomplicated enjoyment of gratification; partly in her lack of deference to the crushing structures of society; partly in her capacity for self-reinvention. Freda Dudley Ward had done her best to modify the Prince's drinking, smoking and nightclubbing. She had a sense of propriety, no matter how far the Prince tried to lead her astray. Thelma Furness had no such agenda. She was free, liberated by her nationality and Duke's wealth from the nightmare of royalty, from 'Buckhouse prison', as the Prince called Buckingham Palace. She could be anything from an ingénue movie actress, to a pan-European socialite, to a somewhat detached representative of the British upper classes. She was also married and a mother – both conditions that appealed to the Prince, who had not only loved Freda Dudley Ward for the forbidden quality her marriage lent her, but adored her little daughters (while referring to her as 'My very own darling beloved little mummie'[8]). Now Thelma appeared to provide an intriguing contrast: more of the same, only better.

Thelma's Americanness was an irreducible part of her appeal, not least because the Prince had already decided that he himself had a real affinity with the United States. George V's grouchy stolidity had served the nation well enough in times of trouble, but it was a performance ineradicably rooted in the past, in an Edwardian culture now destroyed by war. The Prince, on the other hand, was accessible, unstuffy, attractive, highly mobile. In so far as such a thing was possible, he was an aspirational prince, perfectly made for the New World. What's more, he had been there, seen it for himself and knew empirically what a good thing it was.

He had actually set off on his first North American tour as long ago as August 1919, at once taking Canada by storm and establishing an informal but permanent connection between himself and that continent. He wrote to Freda Dudley Ward from Toronto, 'I've never received such a welcome!! It's been too marvellous for words . . . knocks Cardiff or any place in Great Britain right out.'[9] He insisted on identifying completely with the Dominion, to the point where 'I regard myself as belonging to Great Britain and Canada in exactly the same way.'[10] In fact, 'When I go down to the United States next week', he said, not long after, 'I shall regard myself as going there not only as . . . a Britisher, but also as a Canadian.'[11]

Of course, the United States was a less straightforward destination than Canada. The Prince had already acknowledged the strange, ambivalent, attraction of the young country at the start of the year, writing from the Headquarters of the 3rd American Army in Koblenz: 'These Yanks are generally such d—d good fellows & too fearfully kind & hospitable for words; they've got a sort of fascination for me & Gud how they make me laugh.'[12] Again, a few weeks later: 'I'm liking the Americans more than ever though no-one knows their faults more than I do!! They are quite different to us & one has to realise this before one can like them; I'm just longing to go to the States.'[13] George V was against the US part of the trip from the start, but allowed his ministers to press ahead with the plan. Edward Grigg, one of the Prince's minders on the tour, went ahead from Canada to get a feel for the USA: 'Grigg returned from New York this morning prophesying success for the visit though says there's quite a lot of anti-British feelings in the States just now which we've got to try to live down & propagand against!!'[14] So the Prince went to Washington and visited President Wilson, ill in bed; he partied, conspicuously ('He holds very strongly that he can influence American feeling even better by dancing with Senators' daughters than by talking to Senators, and I am sure he is right', observed Grigg[15]); he turned his sights on New York. A spasm of fear was caused by American press reports that the fun-loving Prince was going to stay at Newport, Rhode Island, that den of waste and intemperance. But no. He cruised straight down to New York City in the battleship *Renown*, using it as a floating hotel for the stay, only returning to it in the dead of night after hours spent dancing and chasing after girls. To Mrs Dudley Ward he wrote,

I had a marvellous welcome here this morning & got through the freedom ceremony & speech all right!! But I've got at least 2 speeches a day here & I really don't know how I'm going to pull through alive . . . I'm just scribbling this last little letter to you before landing for a huge pompous war workers' dinner at the Waldorf followed by a gala performance at the Opera, of all terrible stunts!! Christ it all makes me so tired & sick of life all this useless official balls & it's such a cruel misinterpretation of me . . .[16]

Despite the nervous drudgery of having to perform for eighteen hours a day, the Prince went down astonishingly well. Dull Establishment figures were overjoyed at the way New Yorkers not only tolerated him but seemed delighted with him, giving him a reception every bit as wild as the one he received in Toronto. Lord Reading – newly returned from a diplomatic mission to Washington – wrote to Lord Stamfordham, 'The Prince has proved a better Ambassador than all of us rolled into one. He has caught the American spirit, so difficult to understand quickly, and has done more in America to make their people comprehend the strength of the democratic support to our monarchy than all books and articles and propaganda.'[17] Edward Grey, British ambassador in

Washington, repeated the claim, stating that the visit 'has done more good than any number of political speeches'. In his report to the Foreign Office he went on, 'His Royal Highness has created in New York a feeling of personal affection so strong that, though it may have no direct influence on politics, it must do something to create kindly feeling in New York itself.'[18]

Reading and Grey were actually discussing that nice balance in the Prince's personality which married selfish giddiness with personal congeniality. In order to be appealing to a larger public, to meet people informally and win their sympathy, he had to be so free of any burdensome domestic sense of protocol and formality that, with the brakes off and the Court thousands of miles away, he had no way of stopping himself from sliding into sexual dalliances and reckless party-going. These were all one with his ability to connect with the world. His grandfather had the same characteristic. The old Prince of Wales had made France a second, hedonistic, home; out of that came the *entente cordiale*. The young Prince Edward's ambition (only a decade after Edward VII had occupied the throne) seemed to be much the same with regard to the States. He wanted to be able to relax into the modern, American, world and lose his sense of obligation; out of that, who knew what fascinating alliances might spring?

But much had changed in the intervening ten years. Tumtum's scandalising waywardness and his endless quest for new, boredom-killing pleasures was one of the nagging themes of the late nineteenth century. It was only by luck and a great effort on the part of the Establishment that he survived intact to glorify the Edwardian age. Now, both the monarchy and the Establishment that girdled it were reduced; deference to title had dwindled; the press – especially abroad – was nosier and shriller; the Prince of Wales himself was a more vulnerable personality.

This really started to be a problem when, in 1924, the Prince set off for his second visit to the United States. He had bought himself a ranch in Alberta, went over in 1923 to spend some time there, and decided to return the following year.

The benign after-effects of the first trip could not last. Worse, the second trip was managed with a terrible lack of competence or suavity – the rot setting in at New York, to which he headed first, leaving Canada for the second part of the visit. The Duke and

Duchess of Roxburghe – May Goelet supplying the American connection; the Duke supplying Court propriety – had been sent out on 23 August to meet the Prince on his arrival and keep an eye on him. They had little effect. Even before the *Berengaria* on which the Prince was travelling had docked at New York, he had raised eyebrows by dancing all night long with a pretty St Louis debutante called Lenore Cahill. On arrival, Miss Cahill revealed that 'He was so democratic and easy to talk to that he seemed exactly like an attractive young American, like our very nicest ones. It was wonderful to find him so interested in different things. He is very fond of dancing and dances very well.'[19] The dancing, of course, was the snag. Not because the Prince knew the English steps as opposed to the American ones (although Miss Cahill sweetly remarked on this), but because he was doing it at all. It was a statement of intent made before he had even set foot on American soil.

Things were hardly improved by the presence of the asinine 'Fruity' Metcalfe (who managed to leave some of the Prince's personal correspondence in the apartment of a New York hooker), combined with that of the equally unreliable and highly licentious Brigadier 'G' Trotter. As key figures in the royal entourage, they encouraged the Prince's bad behaviour and did nothing to promote virtuous living. Spells of watching an international polo competition – the ostensible reason why the Prince was stopping at New York in the first place – alternated with ferocious revelry. He was caught dead drunk in public twice, on both occasions having to be taken home before he disgraced himself further. He stayed out late and consorted with graceless social climbers such as Mrs Alva Vanderbilt, Consuelo's mother, at her home in Jericho, NY. His straitlaced Assistant Private Secretary, Alan 'Tommy' Lascelles, complained periphrastically to Piers 'Joey' Legh, another in the Prince's entourage,

> As you know, I've always kept as far away as possible from that side of his life, which is no concern of a private secy *pur et simple*, and only happens to be your concern because, apart from being a p.s., you are also a close friend and adviser of many years standing. But there must come moments . . . when the private pursuits of comets mess up the ordinary public highway which it

is quite definitely the business of the private secy to keep straight and tidy.[20]

At the time of the 1919 trip, the Prince had been boyish, fresh-faced, too youthful to scold. Now he was 30 years old, a young middle-aged man whose truancies looked seamy rather than merely venial. The press increasingly represented the visit as one long callous frivolity, and the hapless Lascelles was obliged to issue a press statement 'to counteract the impression that the Prince was a pleasure lover and a sportsman only, an impression based on the Prince's diversions on his American holiday'.[21] Lascelles then explained that the Prince was in reality something of a *littérateur*, having actually managed to get to the end of *Mark Twain*. Following that, a tea party had to be thrown for several leading newspaper editors, in order to ensure their compliance.

Luckily, the magical personality of the Prince himself, his spontaneity and apparent lack of caste snobbery – 'his absolutely democratic manner', in the words of the *New York Times* – were still enough to beguile the press and the people together. His habit of wearing a cool grey suit surmounted by a grey hat of a similar shade was so widely admired that New York's tailors were deluged with orders for the grey Prince of Wales look. At one polo match, 'The whole stand . . . was a kind of fog bank from thousands and thousands of hats in the Prince's style.'[22] A couple of days later, 'Admiring Throngs' were seen to 'Swamp' the Prince as he toured the city. By the time everyone had visited Chicago, heartland of the normally hostile Hearst press, Tommy Lascelles felt able to write, 'I have never seen a more hearty welcome given to the Prince in any one of the various big towns in England to which I have been with him.' And reporting to Queen Mary, he went on with some relief, 'During the whole day, I never saw or heard a single sign of unfriendliness.'[23] From there, the Prince and his entourage at last went on to spend rather less than a week at the Prince's ranch in Alberta – the original reason for the whole North American visit – having spent nearly three weeks in New York. The weather in Alberta was indifferent and the Prince got the flu, only cheering up on his way back through Ottawa by fooling around with an attractive married woman at the Governor General's ball.

In the end, there was just enough that was positive about the second American trip to make it seem like a success. The 9th Duke of Manchester, speaking with the special insight of a worthless Anglo-American aristocrat, said of American feelings towards the royal family, 'Most popular of all, of course is the Prince of Wales, and often, when I contemplate their enthusiasm for him, I am almost forced to the conclusion that if a free vote of United States citizens could be taken the majority would welcome him as Monarch or President.'[24] However you looked at it, there was something ineluctable about the conjunction of the youthful glamour of postwar America with the youthful glamour of the Prince. 'It was not crowd psychology that swept him into instant popularity', announced the *New York World*, 'but the subtle something that is personality.'[25] It was a meeting of the Prince's character with that of the young country. The Unites States no longer just meant heavy industry and cash-cow millionairesses with their vulgarian families, riding the tidal bore of their namelessly acquired fortunes; it meant youth, openness, freshness, beauty, lack of prejudice and pomposity, eagerness for new things – all the qualities which the Prince of Wales popularly appeared to incarnate. When it wasn't being clumsy, overweening and banally ignorant, America now stood for so many of the best things in life – hopeful and productive change arguably being the greatest.

And when Prince Edward stood beside his hairy, prickly, scowling, catarrhal father, George V (with all his repudiations of change in general), it was impossible not to be moved by a vague hope of some new dispensation for the royal family – a dispensation that, in time, might happily work its way through the whole of society. The obverse was that such new freedoms could, and did, translate into dumb negligence. The Prince – already becoming well known for his resistance to court duty – was equally in danger of becoming a frivolous, American-flavoured, lightweight. And now he had found himself drawn into the arms of Thelma Furness, who, worryingly, embodied and abetted this tendency, while appearing to have no idea of what she was actually doing.

For his part, the Prince was busily embracing further possibilities by shaping a new version of himself as a homeowner. In 1929 he acquired Fort Belvedere, right on the very tip of Windsor Great

Park, some 5½ miles due south of Windsor Castle – as far as it was possible to get from the Court and Castle without leaving the grounds of Windsor Great Park entirely. Famously described by Diana Cooper as 'a child's idea of a fort', Fort Belvedere was a largely eighteenth-century mish-mash, crenellated and Gothicised, enlarged for George IV, and gazing out over Virginia Water one way, Sunningdale the other. It was also semi-ruined and surrounded by a jungle of laurels and rhododendrons. It was of no great architectural merit and it was to the Prince what St Donat's Castle was to W.R. Hearst – a place crying out for intervention and improvement, a hideaway that demanded the imposition of a larger self.

And this the Prince duly managed. In the grounds, he taught himself the correct use of a billhook and began slashing furiously at the laurels, venting his private frustrations on the undergrowth while at the same time making sure there were no gloomy encumbrances around his new tennis courts and swimming pool. In the building itself, he installed electric lights, central heating, hot and cold running water, and his greatest luxury, a private steam bath in which he could relax after hours spent savaging the bushes.

It was here that he could pretend to be yet another kind of prince: domestic, spontaneous, accommodating. Here, he played the ukulele and the bagpipes. Here he drank, smoked and wore a kilt, without reproach. Here he practised his needlework ('my secret vice') and held gatherings of his friends. Here he incarcerated Prince George in order to treat the latter's drug addiction: poor George having gone terribly wrong in 1929 when he was corrupted by another American – Mrs Kiki Preston, sometimes known as 'The girl with the silver syringe'. Through her he became a hopeless drug addict – so hopeless, in fact, that the Prince of Wales was seized by an access of charity and took his favourite brother back to the Fort, there to nurse him better. He even managed to get Mrs Preston to leave the country and write to George that she had decided to settle permanently abroad. Months went by while George went Cold Turkey. He only resurfaced early in 1930 and even then was considered such a liability that when he ran into Mrs Preston at Cannes a couple of years later he had to be physically escorted from her presence.

And here, naturally, the Prince of Wales took Thelma Furness: 'In time, the Prince and I began to spend long week-ends at Fort

Belvedere.' With the benefit of hindsight, she liked to see these stays as long Arcadian moments in a tale that would turn sour through no fault of her own. He would vent his anger on the world by slashing at the undergrowth and playing his bagpipes before turning to his guests, who were invariably 'the people we liked to have around – there were no dignitaries, no representatives of State and Empire'. The intimacy of Fort Belvedere and the primacy of emotion were all that mattered: 'I was in love with a man, a shy, sensitive, charming man.' The fact that he was also Prince of Wales, due in the very near future to become King Emperor, 'were facts only incidental to my feelings; they were elements of history, not love . . .'[26] That this interpretation was partial, highly coloured and deliberately wilful hardly matters. In a world otherwise built around fabrication and performance, Thelma and Edward's private weekends must have had quite a lot of the appearance of reality. For the Prince, they generated the kind of suburbanised intimacy that he generally only glimpsed at second hand. For Thelma, they were an odd but tolerable confirmation that she was indeed the queen-in-waiting whom Hollywood had rejected and Marmaduke Furness had failed to treat like a proper lady.

No one else approved, though. According to Sir Robert Bruce Lockhart, when Millicent, Duchess of Sutherland, was staying with the Prince at Bayonne in 1931, the King telephoned him to discuss the national financial crisis and the need for the Prince to be seen to give up £10,000 a year of public funds – the King himself giving up £50,000. 'The Prince was in a night haunt at the time and was furious: "The King . . . and I are being had for a pair of mugs."' The Duchess of Sutherland and her close friend, Vera, Countess of Rosslyn, claimed that the Prince had become visibly more irresponsible. 'They blame Lady Furness who has a bad influence on him. Freda, at any rate, kept him under restraint. She could get him back tomorrow if she wanted to, but apparently, she does not want.'[27] Chips Channon, another rich American émigré living in London, writing with all the affronted nervousness of one who discerns some of his own failings in the object of his criticism, claimed that it was Thelma Furness 'who first "modernised" and Americanised him, making him over-democratic, casual and a little common'.[28]

But Thelma was, plainly, not the first American the Prince had ever been familiar with. He had been on friendly terms with Emerald Cunard since before the war. Equally, the Prince was well enough acquainted with Chips Channon for Chips to reminisce, 'I first met him in 1920 and I have known him fairly well ever since, but there have been long intervals when I never saw him, or when I did he barely recognised me. At other times he was exceedingly friendly towards me.'[29] The Prince also went to Lady Olive Baillie's seamy Hollywood-flavoured parties at Leeds Castle, he played golf with Nancy Astor and he enjoyed all the American pleasures of cocktails, dancing and nightclubbing. On occasion he could even resemble an American-flavoured heavy, if Harold Nicolson is to be believed. Hurrying into the Embassy Club, Nicolson and Sir Oswald Mosley were 'late, and in running up the steps from the cloak-room, we push into someone whom I at first take to be a slouching ex-prize fighter but then recognise as the Prince of Wales. He flicks cigar-ash at me with a rather sly smile.'[30]

On other occasions, he could be simply the friend of an American heavy – according to Osbert Sitwell, via Sir Evan Charteris and the Earl of Crawford:

> Yesterday Evan told me a story of Osbert Sitwell who found himself in conversation with a young rather tough-looking American who asked about popular estimation of the King. Sitwell made some general remarks and observed rather casually that the public is disturbed that H.M. does not seem to go to church. The American was interested and rather surprised, finally said, 'Wall, I'll put that across him next time we meet,' and Sitwell then discovered that this smart gangster feller is in the habit of meeting H.M. – at Corrigan's house I suppose.[31]

Depending on where you stood, the Prince's American informality, his encroaching American accent (displacing his fashionable 1920s mock-Cockney), his impatience with worn-out ritual, his Edwardian delight in the frankly un-English, were either signs of impending catastrophe, or inherently encouraging. It was still too early to be certain.

Thelma's real weakness lay not in her origins but in her banality. When she and the Prince were photographed holidaying in the South of France, the boredom and lack of affect in both their faces – even allowing for the formalities of the time – seem almost sinister. At Fort Belvedere, she was good at posing appealingly on the ramparts or by the swimming pool, but it was hard to tell what else she was good for. When she went ice-skating on Virginia Water with the Duchess of York – subsequently Queen Elizabeth, wife of George VI – the best she could do to summarise the Duchess's legendary charm was to suggest that if she ever found herself having to live 'in a bungalow in a small town', it was the Duchess of York that she would most like to have as a next-door neighbour 'to gossip with while hanging out the washing in our backyards'.[32] For all her beauty and style, Thelma was a terrible lightweight, light enough even to weary the Prince.

And at last her cause was scuppered – indirectly – by the actions of her twin sister, Gloria Vanderbilt. *She* had married Reggie Vanderbilt – Consuelo Balsan's cousin – in 1922. He died of a brain haemorrhage in 1925, after they had had a daughter, little Gloria Vanderbilt. Gloria senior promptly took off to the fleshpots of Europe with the $3 million trust fund left behind by her late husband and spent it on high living. Eventually the Vanderbilts caught up with her and initiated a battle both for the custody of little Gloria and for access to the trust fund. This became the celebrated Vanderbilt case of 1934, in which Gloria's name was sedulously disparaged by a stream of carefully prepared witnesses. These alleged, among other things, that Gloria senior had been sexually involved with a gold-digging German nobleman; had neglected the upbringing of her daughter; and had enjoyed a lesbian relationship with the Marchioness of Milford Haven. The court found against Gloria senior, gave custody of little Gloria to Gertrude Vanderbilt Whitney and deprived Gloria senior of the income from her late husband's trust. The popular press in America made the most of this farrago of smut and Gloria senior found her life unexpectedly in ruins. Her loyal sister Thelma left England early in 1934, to join her in the States. Thelma's disappearance from the Prince's life was greeted with cries of approval by his courtiers. The problem was that someone even more pernicious had taken her place.

Mrs Wallis Simpson's life in London had a curiously frozen, inert quality to it – especially in comparison with what had gone before. In July 1928, she had married the dull but dependable Ernest Simpson, an Anglo-American who had served fleetingly in the Coldstream Guards and was now working in the marginally prosperous family shipping business. When she moved to London, its rebarbative stony chill depressed her intensely. The crowds were anonymous and unfriendly. The buildings were damp and oppressively ancient. The whole thing 'evoked in me a bone-deep dislike'.[33] The Simpsons lived in a less-than-glamorous flat in Bryanston Court, near Marble Arch, where Wallis struggled perpetually with keeping the curtains clean, hiding worn patches in the carpets, and juggling the food and drinks bills. Their friends were a mixture of moderately flavourless American expats, with a few outlying members of society thrown in. Occasionally the money would be so tight that she and Ernest would stop socialising altogether until their finances had regularised, or her devoted Aunt Bessie had sent a cheque over from the States.

However cribbed this existence might have been, it was at least an improvement on what had gone before. Two years younger than the Prince of Wales, she was born Wallis Warfield, an impoverished offshoot of a respected Baltimore family. Her father died when she was five months old; her mother had to exist on charitable handouts from relations. Alva Vanderbilt may have spent her early life in similarly straitened circumstances and been the daughter of a boarding-house keeper, but at least she married into the Vanderbilt millions. Wallis Warfield had no such luck. Instead she fled from degrading shabby gentility by marrying a handsome, drunk, abusive naval officer called Earl 'Win' Spencer in 1916. Dissatisfied with her new husband, she soon left him and went to live alone in Washington DC for six edgily uninhibited years, before rejoining him in the Far East and finally divorcing him in 1927.

After this, Ernest was a pleasant change, with his moustache, his mild snobberies, his effortful conversation ('He seems full of general information like a Whitaker', observed John Aird, the Prince's Equerry), his Guards tie. The relative modesty of their existence and its lack of excitements were tolerable, at least for now. Life at Bryanston Court was on the absolute margins of smartness, especially when compared with the routines of their grander English friends, some of whom were still capable of throwing 'huge affairs for forty and fifty people, with liveried servants and tables blazing with silver'. The Simpsons' quotidian existence was, on the other hand, 'fairly simple'.[34] Who were the Simpsons seeing at this point? From the start, Benjamin Thaw, First Secretary at the US Embassy in London, was a key figure – not least because he was married to Consuelo Morgan, elder sister of Thelma Furness and Gloria Vanderbilt. Consuelo 'Tamar' Thaw, as she was known, became a regular fixture, through whom the Simpsons were plugged in to a larger society. Indeed, within a few years they had branched out from expat Americans such as the Thaws and Mike and Gladys Scanlon (Martin 'Mike' Scanlon, air attaché at the American Embassy), to include the Sackvilles, Lady Milford Haven, George and Kitty Hunter (well-bred, socialite Brits) and, of course, the Prince of Wales.

But the leap from dowdy nonentities to notorious celebrities was as puzzling to many at the time as it is to anyone looking back from the present day. Wallis's much-remarked talents for entertaining, interior decorating, and presenting herself in the most finished and accomplished way possible hardly account for her rise. Certainly, she stole Mrs Ralph the kitchen-maid from Lady Curzon and trained her up into an excellent chef; she also painted the walls of her drawing room an interesting shade of green. Her hair was, according to Cecil Beaton, of 'Chinese' sleekness. Daphne Weymouth wrote that 'She was capable of eclipsing more beautiful but less *soignées* English roses, who in her presence looked like croquet mallets beside a polished arrow'.[35] But hostessing skills and personal grooming alone are not enough to make one popular.

More importantly, Wallis was highly competent, resilient, stylish, hard-working, brave, determined to better herself and not unduly flustered by the fact that she was (before long) in the presence of the future King of England: all of which properties made her special and, in the eyes of the Prince, cherishable. Few Englishwomen could have mustered such a suite of personal attributes. Even Freda Dudley Ward would have had difficulty. Of course, Freda Dudley Ward was pretty; Thelma Furness even prettier. In comparison, Wallis Simpson was lantern-jawed, spade-handed and tricked out with a sardonic, slot-like mouth. But Mrs Ward and Lady Furness lacked the will to win, the fundamental need to prevail. Freda Dudley Ward much preferred to string along a retinue of male admirers in a playful, Diana Cooperish way, never quite satisfying their demands but doing enough to fire the jealousy of the Prince. Fretting over not one but two perceived rivals, he once wrote to her in self-stimulating anguish that one lover's 'barrage will come down again as soon as he returns to England, though guess it doesn't worry you, sweetheart!!' Then he demanded to know, 'Has Burghie [Lord Burghersh] been as intense as ever lately & has he been following you around any more?!!'[36]

This mild sexual taunting was enough for Mrs Ward. Wallis, on the other hand, did her best actually to claim lovers for herself, to have them and subdue them to her will if she could – 'even men she didn't want, she didn't want anyone else to have'.[37] Despite her lack of evident physical beauty, she was rarely without a man, or even two. In the years when she was separated from 'Win' Spencer, for instance, she took the opportunity to have a wild affair with an Argentine diplomat. When she had landed the Prince of Wales and was certain of his devotion, she still found time – according to Special Branch files – to have an affair with a car dealer called Guy Marcus Trundle. She openly made up to a handsome socialite called James Dugdale, and to the highly desirable Prince George. Harold Nicolson referred to her 'taut, predatory look', while even the normally unflappable Philip Ziegler, official biographer of Edward VIII, describes her as 'ruthless and voracious'. And *ruthless* is a word that readily springs to mind whenever one sees a photograph of Wallis with her iron jaw, her steady, reductive gaze, her stiffness, her aura of discipline.

And yet for every piece of dispraise levelled against her, there is often a countervailing piece of mild approval. Harold Nicolson, despite her tautness and predatoriness, thought her 'virtuous and wise', a 'nice woman'. Chips Channon – not the most disinterested of witnesses – reckoned her 'a woman of charm, sense, balance and great wit, with dignity and taste'. Even John Aird, normally bubbling with detestation, found a way of accommodating her: 'I feel she is basically not a bad sort of tough girl out to get what she can.' Thelma Furness shared in the puzzlement, years later, when confessing all in her autobiography. Harking back to the time when she first met Wallis, she couldn't help but brood on Wallis's physical plainness, versus the gin-dry zest of her personality. 'She was not beautiful; in fact, she was not even pretty. But she had a distinct charm and a sharp sense of humour.' Like Thelma, Wallis wore her hair parted in the middle, creating a tableau in which to set her 'alert and eloquent' eyes. She also carried a little more weight than she would in later years – not that she could have been called fat: 'She was merely less angular.' Her hands, famously large, drew Thelma's attention, moving around with an absence of grace and too much animation whenever she attempted to emphasise a point.[38] The more beautiful of the Prince's two lovers and yet the one who was wronged, Thelma retrospectively drew Wallis closer to her – so as to extract full value from the subsequent treachery – and called her 'one of my best friends in England'.

Wallis was equally and conversely keen to put some distance between them. She claimed barely to have known Thelma Furness during her early days in London, 'except for having exchanged polite greetings with her at one or two parties'. Narturally, Wallis was galled by Thelma's beauty, her slimness, her big brown eyes, her brown hair worn in a seductive chignon, the camellia-like texture of her skin.[39] How could odd, angular Wallis have intentionally seduced anyone – let alone the Prince of Wales – away from such a delicious creature? And even if she had, was it really the betrayal of a best friend? Far from it: 'Our relationship was friendly and easy but scarcely intimate; neither of us was given to exchanging confidences.'[40]

Inevitably, given the differences of perception that separate them, they cannot even agree on how they met; or how the Prince of Wales first met Wallis. Thelma vaguely believes the first event to have taken place some time at the end of 1930 or the start of 1931. Wallis (according to Thelma) had been brought along to Thelma's house at 21 Grosvenor Square (a stone's throw from Lady Cunard's) by sister Gloria, who was supposed to have said, 'Mrs Simpson is fun. You will like her.'[41] According to Lord Louis Mountbatten, the meeting happened at the house of his brother, the Marquess of Milford Haven. According to Wallis's memoirs, it happened at the Furness hunting lodge near Melton Mowbray – Burrough Court – in

November 1930. And according to her own correspondence, it was indeed Burrough Court, but in January 1931: this is now generally held to be the starting point of the relationship, not only between Thelma and Wallis, but between Wallis and the Prince. Wallis wrote to Aunt Bessie on 13 January, 'I got up and spent the entire day on hair and nails etc as Saturday we were going to Melton Mowbray to stay with Lady Furness (Mrs Thaw's sister) and the Prince of Wales was also to be a guest.'[42] The 'entire day' going on hair and nails has the ring of authenticity about it, and it was a suitably enamelled Mrs Simpson who took the train up to Melton with Ben Thaw and her husband; and in that train she practised her curtseys before meeting royalty. The Prince of Wales, accompanied by the reprobate General Trotter, was up at Melton, as were Thelma Furness and Prince George. 'The Prince of Wales, as I remember, had on very loud-checked tweeds', is how Wallis summoned it to mind, years later and with the dates wrong. She remembered thinking, as she stared at the Prince of Wales, that he looked just like the photographs, with his tip-tilted nose, his tousled hair, and, critically, a 'strange, wistful, almost sad look about the eyes when his expression was in repose'.[43] He paid her little attention. She, however, felt satisfied at getting a job done. 'It was quite an experience', she wrote, with a nerveless, ambitious candour that no smart Englishwoman would have dared confess to, 'and as I've had my mind made up to meet him ever since I've been here I feel relieved. I never expected however to accomplish it in such an informal way and Prince George as well.'[44] This was Wallis Simpson, née Warfield, a middle-aged woman of no special beauty or talents with an obscure Baltimore heritage and less than three years' living in London behind her, expressing a matter-of-fact satisfaction at her first encounter with the man who was the social apogee of the Empire. Its coolness is impressive and slightly eerie.

They met for a second time in May 1931. This is the encounter that Thelma remembers as the first encounter, at her house in Grosvenor Square. He came over to Wallis and apparently said 'How nice to see you again. I remember our meeting at Melton.'[45] Innocent Thelma, meanwhile, was simply being nice to Wallis, another expat American struggling with the demands of English society. She claimed that not only were she and Wallis friends, but that Wallis was one of her *best* friends – a friend so valued that she and her lover, the Prince, would go out of their way to include the Simpsons at their Belvedere parties.[46]

Wallis, for her part, was now making significant inroads; she was capitalising all the time, adding to her collection. By April 1931, she was planning a dinner and bridge party for, among others, the Marchioness of Milford Haven, Lady Fitzherbert and Lord and Lady Sackville. In June of the same year, she was presented at Court. The Simpson finances were so precarious that everything had to be borrowed for this key event. 'Tamar' Thaw provided a white satin dress; Thelma Furness ingenuously lent a white satin embroidered train, feathers and a fan. Afterwards, Thelma threw a small party at which the Prince was present. He then gave Mr and Mrs Simpson a lift back to Bryanston Court before driving on to Fort Belvedere in the company of that 'right old rip', General Trotter. A couple of days after that, Wallis was writing to Aunt Bessie, 'I hope I can have HRH here for a KT [cocktail] some afternoon – but you have to work up to these things gradually and of course through Thelma.'[47]

It took another seven months, though, before her plans to get the Prince of Wales over to Bryanston Court could be realised. Having seen in the New Year with the Sackvilles at Knole, the Simpsons at last hit their mark in mid-January 1932, when they persuaded the Prince to come to dinner: he stayed until four in the morning. And then, on 30 January, they were found staying with the Prince at Fort Belvedere, in the course of which they had to attack the jungle of laurel outside his play fort with billhooks, and watch him do his needlework in the evening.

Despite this buzz of activity, the relationship grew relatively slowly. There seems to have been no great explosion of passion between them. Thelma Furness remained the Prince's favourite, the woman most likely to become the Princess of Wales. And money was still tight. The financial chaos of 1931 – whose austerities had led the King to give up £50,000 per year, the Prince to give up £10,000, and forced Ramsay MacDonald to preside over a national coalition government – dragged on. Lady Cunard was starting to sell off her emeralds and her Marie Laurencin paintings and replace them with copies; the Mountbattens had to sell off Brook House with its 'giant's lavatory' marble hall; Sunny Marlborough's heir, the young Marquess of Blandford, was plotting to open a shop in Berkeley Square from which to sell eggs and butter; Ernest Simpson's shipping business was finding the going difficult. 'I could do a lot worse than take on an American', the Prince had once written to Freda Dudley Ward, when discussing his marriage prospects;[48] there was no reason to think that Thelma would not be the American he took on. All the way through the early 1930s, the Simpsons were plagued by money anxieties; and while Thelma Furness was cheerfully organising charity film galas for the Prince at the Plaza in Regent Street and instructing her lawyers to begin divorce proceedings against Duke Furness, the Simpsons were so broke that they faced the prospect of having to sell Bryanston Court and move somewhere cheaper.

Clearly, though, something was being shifted in the Prince's emotional furniture. When Wallis Simpson turned 37, in June 1933, the Prince gave her a surprise dinner party at Quaglino's. There he gave her an orchid plant, which she duly placed on a windowsill at Bryanston Court. Not long after, he came round again for dinner. Wallis got Mrs Ralph to serve up black bean soup, grilled lobster, chicken Maryland and a raspberry soufflé which was so delicious, the Prince asked for the recipe at the end of the evening. And at last, towards the end of January 1934, Thelma Furness made her ruinous mistake: she went to America to visit her sister.

According to Thelma, she and Wallis had lunch at the Ritz, in the course of which the innocent Lady Furness offered to deliver messages to Wallis's friends in the States, bring back gifts, generally devil for her while she was away. To which Wallis tragically replied, 'Oh, Thelma, the little man is going to be so lonely.' Thelma's answer was 'You look after him for me while I'm away. See that he does not get into any mischief.'[49] According to Wallis, Thelma revealed her plan to go to the States, asked Wallis along for cocktails ('We rattled along in our fashion', claimed Wallis, briskly) and then announced, 'I'm afraid the Prince is going to be lonely. Wallis, won't you look after him?' – all the concern for the Prince's well-being coming from Thelma, in fact, not shared equally between the two women.[50]

Convention usually has it that the unsuspecting Thelma boarded her ship, visited her sister Gloria – in turmoil as a result of the custody case concerning little Gloria – and returned to England to find, to her horror, that Wallis had turned predator and thieved the Prince. Such was her faith in the goodness of human nature that Thelma never looked under her own nose to see where the threat might be. The penny only dropped when she came back in March 1934, and went to dinner at Fort Belvedere with the Prince and the Simpsons. She noticed that Wallis and the Prince had started to indulge in private jokes together. She stonily observed Wallis playfully slap the back of the Prince's hand when he picked up a lettuce leaf with his fingers. 'So over-protective of heaven knows what', Thelma caught Wallis's eye and made a small sign of disapproval. But Wallis stared right back, with the candid stare of ownership: 'That one cold, defiant glance had told me the entire story . . .'[51]

To which Wallis, one way or another, would counter that the whole thing was as much a surprise to her as it was to Thelma. The moment Lady Furness had left, it seemed, Wallis was being spontaneously invited over to Fort Belvedere. There was no pressure from her. The mood was intimate but correct. The Prince, grateful to have a woman of maturity and sense to talk to, rather than a vapid sensation-seeker, allowed himself to expatiate on his dreams and ambitions. He talked about his frustrations and his hopes for the preposterous job he was about to inherit. Wallis listened with all the attentiveness and loyalty of a good friend. 'It was as if a door had opened upon the inner fastness of his character.' She also interpreted his interest in the role of monarch, his ambition as being 'not dissimilar to the attitude of many American business men whom I had known'. Unlike the typical successful American businessman, however, he gave off a miasma of gloom – 'a deep loneliness, an overtone of spiritual isolation', to which Wallis vibrantly responded.[52] There was a high seriousness, here, in fact; a fitting respect, not just for the position, but for the inner man, for his complexities. Wallis, so we are meant to believe, was a vessel into which he could pour his solitary deliberations. But things moved on. 'Thelma's absence stretched into weeks', she wrote, as if an important journey to the United States in 1934 could have lasted anything other than weeks. 'Finally, he asked me whether Ernest and I would like to bring some of our friends to the Fort.' The proprieties were ensured, naturally, by the presence of others. She brought along Corinne and George Murray, the Hunters, Mike and Gladys Scanlon, plus some other friends – 'mostly Americans' – to distract him. Time passed. Finally, Thelma came back about eight weeks after she had left, on 22 March. 'The former warmth and easiness of their relationship were plainly gone', and 'Something had happened between her and the Prince.'[53] This estrangement, as it transpired, was to mark a cardinal moment in English history.

Various explanations suggest themselves. Wallis may have decided to launch an assault on the Prince of Wales simply for the satisfaction of winning him, rather than for any larger reason. This would be the 'ruthless and voracious' Wallis, whose romances were driven by pathology rather than by love or honest desire. On the other hand, she may have had no more than a wish to please, no larger plan than to keep her honoured friend amused. She might even have hated the whole situation and was only going along with it out of politeness. The energy might have come entirely from the Prince, in no sense the most rational or stable of personalities. Given his history of becoming infatuated with people only to drop them with terrifying suddenness the moment his mood changed – Freda Dudley Ward; poor Fruity Metcalfe – it's quite possible that he tired of Thelma the moment she left him; then excised her accordingly and battened on to Wallis as the next great emotional project. It may even be that Thelma was aware of this tendency, and, quite independently, had started brooding on some sort of escape from a relationship which was by now very slightly boring her. After all, on the return trip from New York, she began a vivid flirtation with fun-loving lothario Prince Aly Khan before going off with him on a round-Europe trip, less than two months after her tragic dinner at Fort Belvedere in March. Aly Khan, with his dark good looks, his careless charm, his immense wealth and his constant and enjoyable travelling, might well have seemed quite an attractive change from the burdened and anxious Prince.

Wallis was only half-delighted by her new position, if her next letter to Aunt Bessie is to be believed. Fretting as ever about money, she wrote, a few weeks after Thelma Furness's return to England, 'I am much sought after [by the Prince of Wales] and am trying to meet English people through him and he has had different ones every week-end lately. I'm afraid I'll have to give up soon as it naturally takes more money to play around with him. More clothes, week-ends etc – then the tips there and all his friends are so rich – I think I'm the only poor one he has ever had.'[54] Her relative poverty was hardly the worst of it. John Aird was beside himself following the weekend at which Wallis had stared Thelma down, raging that 'his friends' – the Prince's – 'of his own selection are awful and one of the worst examples was there, a couple called Simson [*sic*], she is an American 150 per cent and HRH seems to like her a bit extra; he is a very unattractive and common Englishman.' Taking a breath, Aird then decided, as if in deference to his master, that 'They seem terrible at first and this feeling does not decrease as one sees them more often, although basically, I think, they are quite nice.'[55] As well as being terrible and nice, they were accessible, almost demotically so, given the barriers and protocols that normally penned in the royal family and their circle. They continued to live in their apartment, making ends meet, even as the Prince dragged them off on a trip on Lord Moyne's yacht *Rosaura*, down to the Mediterranean, later in 1934. 'I feel', observed Aird at the time, 'she is basically not a bad sort of tough girl out to get what she can, but unless she is much cleverer than I think, she does not quite know how to work it so as to cash in best.'[56] But the question remained, was it Wallis attempting to cash in on the Prince, or was the Prince so helplessly in the grip of an infatuation that Wallis merely had to *be*, in order to prosper? Rebecca West found herself at a party at around this time, to which

Indeed the Prince of Wales had come, with a party including his new artificial Rac [West slang for woman] who has displaced Lady Furness. She is a Mrs Simpson – about 34 – very smart but very common and trivial. She was a quite low-class American who married a bad lot who deserted her in Shanghai, where she picked up a living anyhow until she married a businessman called Ernest Simpson. Then she came to England and has resolutely climbed and climbed (on the slender basis of an introduction to Lady Sackville) till she attained this objective. The Prince looked dreadfully common and ostlerish and the women he came with were very second-rate, but he was quite sober and seemed very pleasant and amiable.[57]

By November 1934, the Prince was so confident of the rightness of his feelings for Mrs Simpson that he felt able to provoke the King with the reality of this *mésalliance* by getting her on to the guest list for an evening party at Buckingham Palace in honour of the Duke of Kent's wedding to Princess Marina of Greece. At first, the King had furiously crossed her name off the list; it was in all probability the Duke of Kent who reinstated it. The King therefore took his revenge by explicitly banning her from any Silver Jubilee functions, as well as from the Royal Box at Ascot. None of this made any difference to the Prince's feelings for her.

THIRTEEN

The American Set

As 1934 turned into 1935, so the bafflement, consternation and, in some quarters, pleasure at the Prince's choice of lover increased. The closer she got to him, the more it alarmed the stuffier members of the Court; which was most of them. For the Prince, on the other hand, every sign of interest or affection from Wallis was a kind of legitimisation. In a permanent state of conflict about the duties imposed on him by the impending weight of monarchy, and by his ability to carry out those duties – tormented, in fact, by his general fitness as a human being – he was forever in search of someone who could candidly and convincingly reassure him that he *was* useful and that he *did* deserve affection. Fruity Metcalfe – his only real male friend – once did the job, on and off; Freda Dudley Ward, sensible and a bit motherly, did it too. But Freda and Fruity were inevitably compromised by their places in the British social hierarchy. With the best intentions in the world, they could never have shed the layer of deference which supernaturally interposed itself between them and the Prince; they could never quite convince him that their love was for the man himself, rather than for some fraudulent, shifting combination of glamorous high birth and inconsequential personal charm. But American Wallis was not born into this; did not feel any helpless desire to abase herself before her putative King Emperor; was not even sure she wanted to spend all her time hanging around him.

Even better, so far as he was concerned, was the fact that she was a competent, forceful, resilient person in her own right. Her frankly dodgy past – her scrapes with penury and bad marriages – served only to make her seem more real, more authentic: a person who had experienced life, could make something of herself despite her misfortunes and who *still* chose the company of the emotionally underfunded, self-doubting Prince of Wales. Even her stoical ability to suffer endless attacks of gastric flu, tonsillitis and colds proved her worth, becoming at the same time a vote of confidence in him. And when she harried him and berated him – as the staff and servants at Fort Belvedere loved to attest – it indicated the opposite of indifference, of emotionally disengaged *politesse*.

Cecil Beaton once came to photograph Wallis at her house in Regent's Park. The Prince of Wales bounced in and they all ate *hors d'oeuvres*. At last, the Prince, 'like a child whose before-dinner play hour had come to an end', was told that everyone had to get ready to leave. 'Wallis, who had only a few minutes to dress for Emerald Cunard's dinner, was already beginning to unbutton her dress . . .'[1] This was precisely the kind of unembarrassable, domesticated briskness that so captivated the Prince. After all, just as the most zealous Republican might easily wrong-foot himself one day by entertaining a sour-sweet illicit fantasy of what he *would* say were he ever to become an intimate of the monarch, so monarchs sometimes hanker after closeness with someone who isn't a courtier, a toady, or a respectable member of the aristocracy. George V loved J.H. Thomas – railwayman, trades unionist, Labour Party stalwart, working man – because Thomas could make that human connection. Edward VII could only be soothed in his declining years by Mrs Keppel, who, for all her galleon-like stateliness, had the common touch. The Prince of Wales loved Mrs Simpson because, in a world filled with increasingly alienating formalities and ostentations, she appeared to speak with the sweet voice of commonsensical, occasionally chiding, humanity.

So it went on. February 1935 found the Prince on a ski-ing trip to Kitzbühel with Wallis in the party. Just to keep her hand in, she flirted vigorously with the good-looking James Dugdale. The Prince was even more horrified by this than by the amorous 'barrages' that had once been directed against Freda Dudley Ward. His desire accordingly increased. The rest of society and the Court – those who knew, anyway – were increasingly aware of their own impotence. Wallis Simpson was a person without antecedents, family or proper connections. There was no way to get to her except through the same narrow social conduit by which she had reached the Prince. She was, in fact, a wholly social entity, cut free from the strictures of birth and background, which was why the Prince was drawn to her.

She existed in the present, in the experience of the here and now. This was ideal for Edward, who likewise was happiest existing in the excitement of the moment, who had almost no interior culture to draw upon in moments of inaction or reflection, who did his best to fill the time with heedless activity, who was a social creature, and who defined himself as such. Wallis once put her dislike of other Americans down to the fact that 'they have no air'. But in the mind of the Prince, the United States was all good: a place of candour, gratifications, freedom. And Wallis was a little piece of America.

His relationship with her was still amost wholly communal: they met in the company of others, and needed company for their relationship to continue. But who would provide this mediating society? Other Americans, of course. Not burdened by any scruples concerning Wallis and the Prince; not tied by any court ethos or ambitions; sharing a nationality with the Prince's lover – they were happy to oblige. So the Prince started to find the company of Emerald Cunard a refreshing antidote to that of the crushing George V and Queen Mary.

Ensconced in Grosvenor Square, fully recognised (by everyone except Margot Asquith) as 'Emerald' since her name-change of 1926, Lady Cunard was now at the height of her unnerving powers. Testimonials that linger from these times startle with their fervency. Harold Acton claimed that hers was 'a combination of social talents one could only meet once in a lifetime', and that, in causing the dullest and most unpromising of guests – 'the most intractable material' – to deliver the goods, she sculpted new forms of social intercourse. 'Lights glimmered at her house which flickered out elsewhere. She was like a spiritual dowser in a desert.' As if that wasn't enough, 'Having skipped the Victorian age, [she] stepped straight from the eighteenth into the twentieth century. Her wit was Irish, her vitality American, but she was above nationality; intellect denationalized itself in her presence and she set the tune that it danced to. It was impossible to be bored in her house.'[2] If this sounds less like the plausible description of a personal friend and more like the outpourings of a writer carried away by the sound of his own enthusiasm, then compare it with John Lehmann's assessment – Lehmann, part-American himself (his mother a New

Englander), an altogether quieter personality than Acton – when he argues that 'Her capacity for putting her guests at ease, but at the same time for communicating a certain glittering vivacity, for challenging one to be at one's best, was extremely stimulating.' At the same time, her reductive snobbishness, her extreme interest in worldly things meant that 'conversation at her table was often ruthless, sometimes coarse, but never dull; reputations were mercilessly investigated, wealth probed and shrewdly assessed'.

Had this been all, then Emerald Cunard would have been not much more than a more intellectually incisive, less sexually predatory, version of Jennie Churchill. What clinched it for Lehmann was her cultural intelligence. She enjoyed a real and deep intimacy with nineteenth-century fiction, in more than one language, Lehmann often finding himself 'easily outdistanced by her detailed knowledge of the works of Dostoevsky, Tolstoi or Balzac; I listened to her with growing respect when she talked of *The Brothers Karamazov* or *La Cousine Bette*.'[3] She even had Peter Quennell – critic, essayist and noted biographer of Lord Byron – praising her acuity and observing that 'She was a woman of many serious interests – she had a lifelong passion for music, an unexpectedly wide knowledge of French and English literature.'[4] Moreover, 'Her taste was sound, her knowledge of literature wide; her appetite for new experiences had never lost its pristine edge.'[5]

Kenneth Clark – chilly, well-bred, clever Wykehamist – had no trouble finding fault with people; a society hostess should have been mere chaff before his intellect. But in this case, Emerald Cunard 'had a remarkable knowledge of opera, and would intersperse her conversation with arias from Bellini, Verdi, Puccini and even Wagner, very accurately sung'. Better yet was 'when she had some heavy public man to tease. She would whizz round him like a humming bird till he became completely dizzy and began to doubt his own identity.' Thus, by dint of hurling out a rogue scandaliser about incest, followed by a sung snatch of Wagner, a quotation from the *Oresteia* and a learned reference to Pythagoras, she once reduced 'a rich monolithic American named Myron Taylor' – President of US Steel, later an internationally known roving ambassador for the United States – to the point where he was 'sweating profusely. All he could do was to cover his large senatorial face with a table napkin.'[6]

At the same time she was tirelessly and shamelessly boosting Sir Thomas Beecham's opera projects at Covent Garden, even campaigning to save the Opera House from redevelopment. She would take herself off alone to suburban theatres to watch actors she particularly admired. She chased around after Duff Cooper during his campaign in the St George's by-election of 1931. She read and re-read her Balzac late into the night. Or, as the normally world-weary Patrick Balfour was moved to comment, 'Lady Cunard is the modern hostess *par excellence*, and if you hear people say that they do not give a damn whether or not they are asked to her parties, you know that they are feeling sore. They are well aware that Lady Cunard is the one hostess in London worth cultivating.'[7] She was unstoppable.

All of which makes one wonder what, exactly, she made of the Prince of Wales. He may well have been a gifted linguist (speaking German, French and Spanish) as well as possessing the royal family's oddball genius for names, dates and faces, but his idea of high culture was a trip to a musical followed by dinner and dancing at the Embassy Club. He was an aristocratic lowbrow, in other words, whom Emerald Cunard would have made mincemeat of, had it not been for his position.

In fact, he had already known her for two decades, ever since Nancy Cunard was presented at Court in 1914 and he had danced with her at her coming-out ball (where 'She felt sorry for him because he seemed so shy and bored'[8]). Emerald herself had been banned by Queen Mary from attending court balls – thanks to the Queen's quite rational disapproval of her eccentric brilliance and gilded cunning – but had still found a way to add the Prince to her roster of acquaintances, so much so that by the end of the war, he was already quite frightened of her. He wrote to Freda Dudley Ward,

Darling don't be angry wiv [*sic*] me if I implore you to steer as clear as possible of Lady Cunard, though I know she's always worrying you as she does me & that she's vewy [*sic*] kind & all that sort of thing; but I know she's a proper 'beta' & there's always some dark motive behind anything she does camouflaged by kindness!! She's a vewy dangerous woman & not to be trusted

& she terrifies me; do you remember how she used to try & ask us to the opera together last Summer?[9]

Time hardened him thereafter. By the 1920s, he had begun to call on her at her Carlton House Terrace address, so that he might escape the dead hand of his mother, and cheekily hobnob with the omnipresent Thomas Beecham. The Prince also encountered there the painter Alvaro Guevara (who nearly had a boxing match with him), and Wyndham Lewis. Lewis was in one of his more erratic moods at the time, and began toying with a pearl-handled gun which he produced from a coat pocket. Lady Cunard at once snatched it up, saying 'Oh! What an elegant object! Is it loaded with black pearls?' – thus demonstrating presence of mind as well as a familiarity with *The Duchess of Malfi* ('What would it pleasure me to have my throat cut/With diamonds? Or to be smothered/With cassia? Or to be shot to death with pearls?').[10] So there was a history between them. The Prince and Emerald were friends; but not intimates.

This changed somewhat once Emerald became aware that Wallis Simpson was in play. She dropped her usual pretence of finding fellow Americans boring and announced that 'Little Mrs Simpson is a woman of character and reads Balzac.'[11] Wallis read nothing of the sort, but that was neither here nor there to Emerald the fantasist. Before long, she was striving to bind the couple more firmly to her – as Chips Channon observed. Chips had married Lady Honor Guinness, daughter of the Earl of Iveagh, in July 1933, in one of the society weddings of the year. The Bishop of Chelmsford had officiated at St Margaret's, Westminster, where Lady Honor had worn an immense veil of white tulle, held in place by a coronet of orange-blossom, and was attended by no fewer than ten pages (including the Coopers' son John Julius) all dressed in eighteenth-century-styled powder-blue satin outfits. King George of Greece was among the guests, as were the Duchess of Rutland, Lady Desborough and both Ladies Colefax and Cunard. Emerald Cunard gave the happy pair a drawing by Augustus John; Mrs Corrigan and the groom's father both provided cheques. Now, Chips was planning to become an MP, as well as hoping to move from his house at 21 St James's Place to somewhere more palatial: this he would shortly find at 5 Belgrave Square, almost next door to Prince George, who was soon to move into no. 3. For now, though, he was simply pleased to be part of the circle of Americans hungrily clustering around the Prince of Wales.

In January 1935, he wrote that Emerald Cunard had 'swept in to tea and stayed two hours. I had never seen her so brilliant. She now gives off an *ambiente* that completely lights up her pretty, wrinkled, Watteau face. She had had a dinner party last night (to which we were bidden and refused) for Diana Cooper.' Why all the animation and brilliance from Emerald? Because of the intoxicating proximity of the Prince, who at that moment rang Chips's door bell: 'And there was the Prince of Wales accompanied by Mr and Mrs Simpson. It was an *imprévu* visit: the Prince was as charming as only he can be sometimes, and now is so rarely.' Later on, the Prince took them off to the Embassy Club for supper. There, Diana Cooper and the Prince spent two hours talking politics. 'Emerald said, "The little Prince talked like a prophet and drank Vichy water," and then she said to him [alluding to the name by which his family and closest friends knew him] "You are not David, Sir, but Daniel." She is in an excellent mood.'[12] As well she might have been. Less than a week after the Prince's *imprévu* visit to the Channons, Emerald invited Chips to lunch 'to meet Mrs. Simpson', whom he found to be 'a nice, quiet, well-bred mouse of a woman with large startled eyes and a huge mole. I think she is surprised and rather conscience-stricken by her present position and the limelight which consequently falls upon her.' Emerald, conversely, 'dominated the conversation with her brilliance, her *mots* and epigrams, some mild, some penetrating, darted like flashes from a crystal *girandole* . . . '[13]

Naturally, Lady Cunard's social eminence was still being questioned – by the likes of Nancy Astor, for instance, who button-holed Chips on a cross-Channel ferry a couple of months later and accused him of introducing his wife Honor to 'dreadful people like "That Cunard woman", and asked me how it was that I, born of respectable American parents, could have such "Low tastes"'.[14] But Emerald was still quite important enough to loom out of Chips's increasingly breathless diaries a few weeks later, when Chips announced to himself that 'It is war to the knife between the past and the present. Mrs. Simpson has enormously improved the Prince.

In fact I find the duel over the Prince of Wales between Mrs Simpson, supported by Diana Cooper and, strangely enough, Emerald, and the —— camp is most diverting.' The tactful blank was probably earmarked for Freda Dudley Ward, possibly even Thelma Furness. Following the more conventional Aird line – interpreting Wallis as a 'tough girl', as opposed to his earlier assessment of her as a 'quiet, well-bred mouse of a woman' – Chips then confirmed that 'She is madly anxious to storm society, while she is still his favourite, so that when he leaves her (as he leaves everyone in time) she will be secure.'[15] He then trotted round to the Simpsons' 'little flat' for cocktails on Empire Day 1935, only to bump into Emerald yet again – as well as the 1st Viscount Margesson, the Prince of Wales, 'and one or two others. London Society is now divided between the old gang, who support ——' and here, another blank 'whom the Prince now ignores, and Emerald Cunard, who is rallying to the new régime'.[16]

Even allowing for Chips's inevitable partisanship and a natural tendency to exaggerate Emerald's (and by extension his own) importance, it has to be said that only a week later, he was at Covent Garden with his wife to watch *The Barber of Seville*, 'and were joined in Emerald's box by the Prince of Wales and the *ménage* Simpson'.[17] To anyone looking on from the orchestra stalls, it would have appeared that the Prince was entirely and menacingly surrounded by jabbering Americans, with only the beaming vacuity that was Ernest Simpson to prevent him from being completely overwhelmed by them.

But who, then, was Chips? Where had *he* come from? Chips was another variation on the theme of the American in society – this time, the American as rich male gadfly. Where Emerald's past had been foggy and mildly unconventional, Chips's upbringing was relatively more transparent. Henry 'Chips' Channon was born in 1897, the only son of Henry Channon II, a rich Chicago business-man of West Country extraction. Henry Channon the father had made a small fortune supplying chandlers' items to the countless boatmen who plied the Great Lakes; and then branched out into boat ownership himself, eventually running a fleet of ships. Chips described him as 'dull, charmless, uneducated, unexciting', but he did make his son a settlement of $90,000 in the early 1920s: enough to keep him comfortable. When his grandfather left him an additional $85,000, however, Chips was rich. Not only did he never have to work; he also had the kind of capital that allowed him to pursue daring schemes of social advancement as well as glittering architectural vanity projects, together with a programme of stupendous material acquistion: 'We used the new gold plate I bought in New York', as he put it, 'and it was much admired.'[18] The fact that he chose to do this in England – principally London – now seems wonderfully generous, given that by 1919 he had not only travelled across continental Europe and seen all that its culture had to offer, but was an habitué of Paris and friends with Cocteau, Gide, Proust and the Abbé Mugnier.

But the continent lacked something that London had. He came to the city for the first time in 1918, on his way back from Paris to Chicago, and experienced a *coup de foudre*. At the end of that year, he wrote that he was 'in love' with London, 'and feel that it is pregnant with my destiny'.[19] It was to become a Jamesian level of devotion. In March 1925, he wrote, 'Oh, land of freedom, where women are all sirens and men are all gods. What a joy to be with you again!'; and then again, two months later, praising 'one of those London days when one's blood surges within one and one is madly, desperately happy, when one is tempted to spend a quarter's income on flowers, and something puckish impels one to a thousand capers. Oh, this London!'[20] America represented a kind of Id, a self that had to be buried – 'I have put my whole life's work into my anglicization, in ignoring my early life' – and of which he once claimed 'The more I know of American civilization, the more I despise it. It is a menace to the peace and future of the world. If it triumphs, the old civilizations, which love beauty and peace and the arts and rank and privilege will pass from the picture. And all we will have left will be Fords and cinemas. Ugh!'[21]

His horror of the States was so deeply rooted that it even infected his feelings for a country as bland as Switzerland: 'The Swiss are so unimaginative, practical and charmless that they might almost be Americans',[22] he complained in 1924. England, on the other hand, captivated him so entirely that he went to study at Christ Church (where he acquired the nickname 'Chips'), moved back to London with two Christ Church friends – the Viscount Gage and Prince Paul of Serbia – and at once laid siege to society, befriending a heady mixture of Lord and Lady Curzon, the Prince of Wales, Elizabeth Bowes-Lyon and Princess Marina of Greece. His infatuation with England had something of James's earnestness; his love of the high life (including drink, drugs and, as it turned out, ambisexual hedonism) was conversely lacking in American piety; his youthful zeal was a mirror of Lord Rosebery's for the United States, all those years before.

Indeed, the traffic between the two countries had changed so radically that it was now the States that was exporting playful capitalist princelings such as Chips, while England, in return, was sending across enmity-filled scribblers such as Rebecca West ('Everywhere the women are hideous and beyond all belief slovenly . . . Their utter and complete lack of sex attraction is simply terrifying. Not that it matters – for the men seem entirely lacking in virility. They wear spectacles almost as commonly as the Germans – and they are beyond belief slow'[23]); or Harold Nicolson ('What appals me is the sense that the only alternative to these audiences' – for whom he was doing a trans-American lecture tour – 'is either the vulgarity of big business or the morons of the farming community. America seems to have so few alternatives: England so many'[24]); or even Margot Asquith, reduced to travelling to the States to promote a book ('My heart sinks', she wrote to Ettie Desborough, 'as America comes nearer. I *loathe* ships, trains, reporters & platitudes & tho I *like* American men I dont care for *any* of the females'[25]). Chips, conversely, was filled with love, tittle-tattle and money; and, like Emerald Cunard, whom he soon got to know, found easy purchase in postwar society.

He was also like Emerald in that he had moments of lucidity about his own character, observing of his zesty, party-loving Grandmother Libby that while, as a child, he loved her more than anyone else, he inherited from her 'all my most unattractive traits – love of display, grandeur, money for its spending sake, and social position'.[26] And his playfulness was counterpointed by depression. 'I fear I am the saddest of mortals, a rake grown old before his time', he wrote, still maintaining enough distance to transform feeling into rhetoric. 'How empty is success and fame . . . how dull drunkenness, how prosy sobriety, how stale literature, how fatiguing sexual intercourse, how surfeiting wealth, how debasing poverty, and how impossible life and how futile philosophy.'[27] But the closest resemblance between Cunard and Channon lay in their tendency towards fantasy. Chips was someone whose basic irresponsibility connected with a highly cultured tendency to read the structures of fiction into real situations. The Abbé Mugnier claimed that he was 'an extremist, a sensationist, an individualist, an original and half a mystic'.[28] Diana Cooper wrote that, on the one hand, 'Never was there a surer or more enlivening friend . . . He installed the mighty in his gilded chairs and exalted the humble. He made the old and tired, the young and strong, shine beneath his thousand lighted candles. Without stint he gave of his riches and of his compassion'; but that on the other, he saw life 'as a Disraelian fairy story'.[29] When his now-celebrated diaries were published, survivors of the 1930s were appalled to discover how he had imaginatively traduced them. 'Everybody is on about Chips's diary', Nancy Mitford wrote to her lover, Gaston Palewski. 'You can't think how vile & spiteful & *silly* it is. I'm thankful only to be mentioned as having sat next to him at dinner . . . One always thought Chips was rather a dear, but he was *black* inside – how sinister! Of course Diana Coo[per] upholds the book. "If it's so bad why are you all talking about it?"'[30]

For all the high solemnity with which Chips expressed his devotion to England – and which urged him to become a British citizen, before accepting a knighthood in the last year of his life – he had trouble, like Lady Cunard, in spotting the point at which events moved from being merely frivolous to that at which they entailed deeply serious consequences. His love of pretence, of social theatre, made him popular; it also made him something of a liability. And he knew the Prince. In 1924, when the Prince was in Chicago on his second American tour, the two had bumped into each other with cries of friendship. Since then, it had been rather more patchy. But Chips liked Wallis; Wallis wanted to get on, so she encouraged Chips; and anyone whom Wallis was friendly with, the Prince was friendly with, too.

Naturally, the Prince of Wales saw plenty of people who weren't Americans. Fort Belvedere would soon fill up at the weekends with unexceptionable grandees such as the 5th Duke of Sutherland, the 8th Duke of Buccleuch, the 10th Duke of Marlborough, the 6th Earl of Rosebery, and Esmond Harmsworth, son of Viscount Rothermere and head of Associated Newspapers. The Duke of Marlborough ought to have been a vigorous Anglo-American, given that Consuelo Marlborough was his mother. But a wholly English upbringing and reduced contact with Consuelo after the separation had expunged that tendency. Indeed, when his father, Sunny, died in 1934, the grace-note of Americana more or less went with him – poor Gladys having been forced out of Blenheim in the summer of 1933 and out of the Marlboroughs' London residence in Carlton House Terrace not long after. Left to roam London in an increasingly distressed condition, she finally died in 1977, still Duchess of Marlborough: she and Sunny had never got round to divorcing.

The 10th Duke – Bert, as he was known – left all that wearisome psychodrama behind him. He was large, bluff, genially fun-loving, possessed of an uncontrollably toilet-fixated sense of humour. He had seen action in the war and had enjoyed himself chasing after showgirls, especially one called Betty Barnes. When courting her, he said, 'I used to sit in a box every night and one night my mother, who disapproved, was sitting in the next box being courted by Jacques Balsan.'[31] But his family straightened him out with all due expedition and in 1920 he married a tough no-nonsense fellow aristocrat, Mary Cadogan, granddaughter of the 5th Earl of Cadogan. Chips was friends with the Marlboroughs, having been at Oxford with Bert's younger brother, Ivor (whom he called '*chétif* and complaining' and 'a sad specimen . . . at Oxford he was considered the cleverest of us all: he had brains, romantic looks, £12,000 a year; he was a Duke's son with every advantage – he would go far. But what has he done or accomplished? Nothing, except be bored and miserable'[32]). Transferring his affections to the much livelier Bert, Chips found things more to his taste:

It is a long time since I have been to Blenheim, where we are spending the weekend, and where I spent much of my youth under the old régime. This is Honor's first visit to this colossal and very beautiful house, and my first since the present people succeeded. Mary Marlborough has improved the house and has enhanced the atmosphere. It is now gay and healthy, and the long corridors echo with childish laughter and screams, and huge dogs sprawl about.[33]

Bert's great-aunt was Jennie Churchill; his mother's godmother was Consuelo, Duchess of Manchester; Minnie Paget had brokered Consuelo Vanderbilt's marriage to Sunny Marlborough; his mother had been the most spectacular of all the American brides; his stepmother the most beautiful American woman in Europe. Now the tide had quite withdrawn, leaving Bert to enjoy his fart jokes in the English manner, and Mary to chivvy the servants who ran Blenheim. The contrasts between 1895 and 1935 were sharply pointed. Instead of the naked dynastic ambition of Alva Vanderbilt striving to combine with the haughty cupidity of the Marlboroughs, everything now centred on a rich, lovelorn English prince, yearning for an impoverished Baltimore nonentity. Instead of Randolph Churchill pouring out his heart to Jennie Jerome – 'Oh dearest do not be angry with me if I am unjust or accusing you at all, you must rather have pity on me, I get quite distracted at times with worrying myself'[34] – there would presently be the Prince of Wales writing to Wallis Simpson, 'This eanum [little] note to welcome a girl back and to say that a boy loves her more and more and that he will be hurrying back to her very soon now . . .'[35] Instead of the pretence of a tussle between equivalent forces, there was complete submission.

Diana Cooper was an even more constant royal companion than Bert. Indeed, her ubiquity is almost as astonishing as that of Emerald Cunard. 'I suppose it is always the Opera and the American courtiers for you now', Evelyn Waugh once wrote to her, admitting defeat to a superior social force.[36] By 1935, she was a regular at Fort Belvedere and in July of that year found herself staying there with a typical assortment of weekend guests (her husband Duff, the Simpsons, Esmond Harmsworth, Anthony Eden). 'The food at dinner', she noted, 'staggers and gluts. *Par contre* there is little or nothing for lunch, and that foraged for by oneself American-style (therefore favoured, bless him).' Wallis was 'admirably correct and chic'. So was Emerald Cunard, who 'arrived at 8.30 for cocktails, which she doesn't drink although the Prince prepares the potions with his own poor hands and does all the glass-filling'. Eight-thirty was late enough by anyone's standards for cocktails, but Lady Diana excused it by arguing that 'Everything is a few hours later than other places (perhaps it's American Time).' Either way, 'The house is an enchanting folly and only needs fifty red soldiers stood between the battlements to make it into a Walt Disney coloured symphony toy. The comfort could not be greater, nor the desire on his part for his guests to be happy, free and unembarrassed. Surely a new atmosphere for Courts?'[37]

Emerald Cunard was, as it happened, glad still to be in royal favour. A few weeks earlier, she had done duty as hostess for the Prince during Royal Ascot. This party had naturally included the Simpsons, 'but Emerald is wobbling a little bit about Mrs. Simpson', noted Chips at the time, 'because Portia Stanley so attacked her [Emerald] about her [Wallis]'.[38] Given that Portia Stanley had been one of the Prince's earliest and most ardent loves (during the First World War, when she was still Portia Cadogan), *and* was close friends with his sister, Princess Mary, Emerald Cunard might have put two and two together and allowed herself to be less startled by such an assault. Still, she did her duty, not without a certain nervousness, and skipped gratefully back into the fold once Lady Stanley had gone.

The Londonderrys were rather more marginal to the Prince's view of the world. They were well connected enough to be on terms with both Emerald Cunard and Chips Channon, who wrote proudly in his diary entry for 27 March 1935, 'In the evening to Londonderry House, where we found half political and social London at the Londonderrys' old-fashioned, distinguished "do".' Honor, apparently, was 'bored and lovely and splendid', while Chips enjoyed himself: 'For me Londonderry House parties always have glamour.'[39] But the Londonderrys were also close to the King and Queen, whose injunctions not to invite Mrs Simpson to any formal event they, like the Stanleys and the Yorks, scrupulously observed. This infuriated the Prince so deeply that he calculatedly and conspicuously snubbed Edith Londonderry at one of her Wednesday evening dances. He turned up, without Wallis, and had a drink. The music began; everyone waited for the Prince to get up and dance with Edith, his hostess, before which time no one else was allowed to dance. The Prince tarried. Edith and everyone else twiddled their thumbs. At last he stood up, walked straight past her and on to the daughter of the Brazilian ambassador. He bowed low and asked *her* to dance. So much for Edith.

Against this onslaught of vulgarity, Mrs Ronnie Greville (rich, untitled, but snobbish, lurking behind the studded front door of her house at 16 Charles Street, with her brewer's fortune, her drunken butlers and her friendship with the Duke and Duchess of York) and Lady Londonderry fought a rearguard action to sustain the idea that, in the end, breeding would out.

> It would be wrong [Edith Londonderry wrote, cunningly] to imagine that none of the pre-war types exist. They do – but not in the glaring light of the Press. There is still, what shall we call it, an Upper Class, its ranks diminished and impoverished by the war. These people, in pre-war days, never encouraged the limelight on their doings. (That is another American importation.) They still wield a certain influence behind the scenes, and, in times of crisis, their presence will still be felt, something solid and very British and, above all, they are people who were born and bred to the old tradition – that possessions carry duties with them, before pleasure.[40]

The 27th Earl of Crawford grumbled obliquely about the dilution of select society by American fashions, condemning the way 'The vile social columns of the *Mail* and *Mirror* and *Express* describe day by day the extravagance and vulgarities of the smart London set – a positive disgrace. And it is all ascribed to fashionable society whereas the heroes and heroines of this tittle-tattle from the cocktail parties and night clubs are all second-rate people.'[41] Meanwhile, Earl Winterton was noting how 'All the Yankee peeresses are made to get Ramsay MacDonald and his daughter as novelties . . . Miss MacDonald is said to be horrified at their low dresses and low demeanour.'[42] Occasionally, a surviving grandee from the Edwardian age, such as Daisy, Countess of Warwick, might attempt an apologia for the new times – but only on limited terms.

> In those days [she wrote, harking back to the late nineteenth century] there were London houses where it was possible to get

the best dinners in the world, and every good house in London had a French chef. At that time there was probably not a single hotel or restaurant where a tolerable meal could be had. To-day there are women cooks in the best houses, and there are now a dozen restaurants where one can dine as well as in most private houses. The change is due to the coming of the Americans.[43]

This was fine, except that the Americans hadn't stopped at food or cookery. 'It does seem that London Society is being run by an American syndicate', admitted Patrick Balfour, while Edith Londonderry, on behalf of the dispossessed, went further. 'England', she cried, 'has become Americanized.' How did she know?

It used to be the aim of every foreigner to buy his clothes in London, and his aim was to look like an English gentleman. London was the Mecca of the male sex all over the world, as Paris was for women. Now, however, the young English gentleman, or man about town, more frequently than not tries to appear in his dress and manners as an American tourist – not a really effective imitation.[44]

These cries of distress pointed up the helplessness felt at large by people who weren't Americans, and who, for one reason or another, felt unable to make themselves at home among the new American arrivals. A different kind of society figure was needed, to penetrate their number. This person was Lady Sibyl Colefax: born in 1874, into a family of unhappy, *haut-bourgeois* Anglo-Indians. Her father had toiled as a Commissioner of Excise and Stamps in the North-West Province, and her mother drifted back and forth from England to India, frequently leaving young Sibyl in the hands of her pretentious and embittered London-based aunts. Having struggled through a childhood filled with loneliness and all the compromises of late-Victorian shabby gentility, she made good her escape by marrying the awesomely dull Arthur Colefax in 1901. Arthur became her rock: an expert patent lawyer, he made a handsome income and was knighted in 1920, thus sealing her destiny as a titled lady of sufficient means.

And what she spent Sir Arthur's money on was entertaining. If Lady Londonderry entertained to preserve the family tradition and assist the political career of her husband; and Emerald Cunard entertained because she enjoyed the intellectual stimulation and the emotional *va et vient*, then Sibyl Colefax entertained because she was pathologically unable not to. Like Emerald Cunard, Sibyl Colefax mainly exists now as an aggregate of other people's footnotes, a figure cross-hatched by references and anecdotes, but with no purposive legacy of her own. Unlike Emerald, Sibyl comes across as something of an idiot, helplessly driven on by a compulsion to add to the great laundry-list of her friends and acquaintances, no matter what indignities stood in her way. Her square jaw, willed half-smile, staring eyes, determinedly cheerful and obtuse expression all characterise a person determined to smother unhappinesses in a blizzard of activity. 'I love the things that race through my head', she once blurted out. 'I could write them down hot and strong they would be all right. But I hate doing it – lazy!'[45] Instead, she wrote invitation after invitation after invitation to her various dinner parties, teas and *soirées*, bombarding her victims with summonses and unintelligible protestations of friendship. Lord Berners got so sick of her importunings that he had a model of a laughing blackamoor's head converted to fire Sibyl Colefax's invitation cards out of its open mouth and across the room. 'When I die', he said, 'scatter my ashes over Sibyl Colefax.'[46] Her eighteenth-century home in the King's Road – Argyll House, bought in 1920 – became a kind of Clapham Junction for, mainly, artists, musicians, writers, the well-connected and the socially useful.

> What differentiates me from most people [she wrote to her husband] is that I enjoy *liking* more than disliking – I enjoy *love* more than hate – I enjoy praising far more than decrying and abusing. Now nine out of ten of the people I see are the contrary and I often feel that acutely. Not being spiteful doesn't make one popular, I've long learnt with some surprise and not a little sorrow.[47]

The reason she wrote this, of course, was because society – reduced in size as well as fortune – was ready to exploit someone as desperate as Sibyl Colefax, merely so that they could get out in the evenings, meet people who weren't Sibyl Colefax and get a good meal. Laura Corrigan could afford, financially, to put up with this callous treatment; and besides, had such a curious, dislocated relationship with the *ton* that it was sometimes hard to know what her ambitions really were. Sibyl was not rich or indifferent enough to float above the cynicism and mean-mindedness of her supposed friends. She had to put up with their detractions – which arrived, behind her back, in great quantities. Peter Quennell saw her as 'a professional dealer in what she considered to be human masterpieces, and ranged them, so to speak, on her shelves with a sharp eye for their respective values',[48] which was about as good as it got. Violet Trefusis, Mrs Keppel's daughter, heaped scorn on people with 'bad figures, baddish legs, and quite deplorable hands – rather like Sibyl Colefax'.[49] Sibyl once ingenuously gushed to Virginia Woolf, 'Your words . . . sweep one off one's feet and they throw one on one's knees – and they express all the ineffable, indescribable, thronging, surging emotions, which to the dumb like me are as all things unattainable, beyond hope';[50] while at the same time Virginia Woolf was writing to Vita Sackville-West that Sibyl was 'like a signboard that has hung in the rain and sun since the King [George III] was on the throne'; that 'The reason Colefax is so dull is that she never thinks or feels for herself'; and that she collected 'all the intellectuals around her as a parrot picks up beads'.[51]

Kenneth Clark, sagaciously enough, reckoned that 'The need to collect celebrities was for her an addiction as strong as alcohol or drugs . . . The trouble is that there is something dehumanising about any sort of addiction. One cannot help thinking about people in terms of their obsessions, and until the last few weeks of her life one could not quite believe Lady Colefax was a reasonable person.'[52]

The diplomat Sir Ronald Storrs would observe that at one event there was, typically, 'a perfect collection of guests, ill-managed by Sibyl'; while at another 'She was fussing about, breaking you up just as soon as you were beginning to get on.' Her guilelessly tedious husband occasionally acted as a lightning-rod for the malice of the smart set, among them Lord Berners, who claimed that Sir Arthur had been offered £30,000 by the British government to bore the Channel Tunnel; while Maurice Bowra used to draw up speculative

First Elevens of Bores, all of which were captained by Sir Arthur Colefax. And then the contumely would head back towards Sibyl. Ettie Desborough complained of Sibyl's Argyll House get-togethers, 'She knows how to get us here . . . but she does not know what to do with us when she has got us.' Ronald Storrs detested Sibyl's conversational habits of 'capping everything with a more celebrated but less well-fitting cap' and of 'peering round fearing she might be missing somebody or something else'[53] – a compulsion that would lead her to betray herself whenever a real celebrity came within striking range. Harold Nicolson described to Vita Sackville-West how Sibyl pounced on one of her victims, 'with sharp eyes and almost whimpered with exultation . . . it was more than interest she displayed. It was lust.'[54] As a corollary to this, the word 'Colefaxismus' was coined in order to describe her compulsive boasts of acquaintanceship with the famous or powerful – as Margot Asquith growled in her complaint that 'It is so tiresome that Sibyl is always on the spot. One can't talk about the birth of Christ without that Astrakhan Ass saying she was there in the manger.'[55] Even the benign Stuart Preston complained that much of her conversation 'would be the repetition of the remarks of others, the recommendations of others'.[56]

A generation earlier, all this – Sibyl's moderately undistinguished parentage; her lack of real wealth; her – to say the least – erratic hold on the admiration and affections of those she cultivated – would have left her washed up as a bourgeois nonentity. Yet the world had now changed so much that, apparently, anyone with sufficient entrepreneurial zest could make a substantial impact on the once-hermetically closed existence of the social élite: even Wallis Simpson; even Sibyl Colefax. Brave, highly motivated, as indefatigable as Emerald Cunard, Sibyl Colefax succeeded despite herself. Drawn by the excellence of her cook, Mrs Gray, and by Sibyl's pleasing decorative skills (as in James's *The Spoils of Poynton*, 'In all the great wainscotted house there was not an inch of pasted paper'), the sort of people who attended Emerald Cunard's gatherings likewise turned up as conquests at the Colefaxes' home, although skewed slightly away from politics and slightly more towards arty celebrity: Kenneth Clark, Diana Cooper, H.G. Wells, the Duchess of Buccleuch, Winston and Clementine Churchill, the

unavoidable George Moore (still yearning for Emerald); Arnold
Bennett; Vita Sackville-West (with whom Sibyl enjoyed an unlikely
friendship); Artur Rubinstein. Emerald Cunard, naturally, liked to
sneer: 'Oh dear, I simply must stop. I'm becoming a bore, like Lady
Colefax.' The fact that Sibyl was her profound opposite, and yet
worryingly like her, may have added to her sleepless nights.

By 1935, after some twenty years of hard toil, Sibyl knew more
or less everyone she wanted to know. And this now included – as
for Emerald Cunard, so for Sibyl Colefax – the Prince of Wales and
Wallis. She was part of the inner circle, those who understood what
was really going on. She also had a healthy working realtionship
with America, having been there in the 1920s, met William
Randolph Hearst, Charlie Chaplin and Paul Mellon, and seen her
son Peter emigrate there. She found that rich Americans were full of
'intense thoughtful hospitable kindness' intermixed with 'intense
egotism of the most childish sort'.[57] She also found Elsie de Wolfe,
who had started her successful interior design and decoration
business. This impressed Lady Colefax, who was not only blessed
with good taste, but was finding it increasingly difficult to make
ends meet, once Arthur's legal practice hit problems in the late
1920s. Thus, in 1933, she started 'Sibyl Colefax Limited',
eventually to become 'Colefax & Fowler'. Comfortably transatlantic, immensely hard-working (business during the day, social
industry first thing in the morning and then again at night),
shameless, broadly unaffiliated to the old school of society
hostesses, she was perfectly adapted to the new conditions
surrounding the Prince. Shortly after the the court ball to celebrate
the Jubilee celebrations in May 1935 (to which the Simpsons were
actually invited, arousing horror in the King and Queen), there was
another ball at the Palace which both Lady Colefax and Lady
Cunard attended; confirming their symmetry. Chips Channon was
there too: 'The ball may have been a respectable function but it was
dam' dull', he chided. It was so hot that Emerald Cunard nearly
fainted, while 'The Coalbox' – Lady Colefax – 'chattered and
chirped to everyone. But it was not a fashionable function, though,
of course, a magnificent sight to the uninitiated.'[58] If Lady Colefax
was meant somehow to carry the old stately English verities of, say,
Lady Londonderry, to the heart of the Wallis Simpson/Prince of

Wales *clique*, then she was quite spectacularly the wrong person for the job.

It was noted at this same ball that the Prince was bad-temperedly complaining to anyone who would listen about the reception given to his recent speech on Anglo-German relations. At the Annual Conference of the British Legion on 11 June, he had dared to suggest that Britain should extend the hand of friendship to Nazi Germany. What added to the controversy – for those in the know – was the commonplace that Lady Cunard had worked on the Prince's mind to make him more receptive to German propaganda.

Without a doubt, Emerald's politics – if she could be said to have any politics – were capriciously and cartoonishly right-wing (although when she berated Harold Nicolson for joining the Labour Party, a rebuke from Anthony Eden set her straight). She hated Ramsay MacDonald, toiled on behalf of the Conservative Duff Cooper, made friends with Grandi the Italian ambassador, and took a pro-Hitler, pro-Mussolini line which was born as much from a desire to pique her friends' liberal sensibilities as it was from a larger neurosis that the civilised world was under threat and that the only protection would be found in an authoritarian, far-right government.

Harold Nicolson noted a Cunard luncheon at which Anthony Eden and Walter Elliot (both of whom were charged with League of Nations responsibilities at the time) were present, just as the Abyssinian crisis was starting to boil up:

Emerald is at her best. She well knows that Anthony Eden and Elliot are not able to disclose what happened at the Cabinet this morning. Yet she also knows that by flagrant indiscretion she may get them to say something. 'Anthony,' she says, 'you are all wrong about Italy. Why should she not have Abyssinia? You must tell me that.' As the only guest whom I have not mentioned was de Castellane of the French Embassy, Eden's style was cramped. He just reacted flippantly.[59]

Or again, according to Robert Bruce Lockhart: 'Lunched at Lady Cunard's . . . Sat next Mrs Ronnie Greville who talked pro-Hitler stuff with great vigour. She is a convinced pro-German and is very angry that no one from the British Embassy went to the *Partei-Tag* at Nuremburg.'[60] This was followed by an even more seething luncheon at Sibyl Colefax's. Present at this event were Emerald Cunard, Wallis Simpson, Mrs Vanderbilt, Mrs Otto Kahn, the French painter and author Paul Maze. Bruce Lockhart sat between Wallis Simpson and Emerald, finding the conversation

> Very stupid. Emerald trying to tease the Foreign Office boys by being violently pro-Mussolini. Afterwards had a long talk with Maze who is intelligent and a great admirer of Conrad. He stormed against the stupidity of Englishwomen like Emerald (who is American!) and Maggie Greville, and asked if it were possible that they could have any influence. Said that when French women interfered in politics they were at least intelligent, had read books and had slept with the diplomats.[61]

This was a theme echoed with variations some years later by Harold Nicolson in his complaint (mainly directed against Mrs Greville) that 'The harm which these silly selfish hostesses do is really immense. They convey to foreign envoys the impression that policy is decided in their own drawing-rooms.'[62]

But the worst was Emerald's infatuation with smooth-talking ex-*Sekt* salesman, Joachim von Ribbentrop, who had come to London in 1935 to negotiate the Anglo-German Naval Agreement. Chips daintily described Emerald as 'rather *éprise* with Herr Ribbentrop', which was hardly surprising given that he was highly sociable, cultured, powerful, glowing with the sick phosphorescence of a resurgent Germany and twenty years her junior. 'Much gossip about the Prince of Wales' alleged Nazi leanings; he is alleged to have been influenced by Emerald Cunard', wrote Chips at the time of the Prince's speech, 'through Mrs. Simpson . . . If only the Chancelleries of Europe knew that his speech was the result of Emerald Cunard's intrigues, themselves inspired by Herr Ribbentrop's dimple!'[63]

There was a horrible playfulness in Chips's and Emerald's take on the new world of right-wing extremism. The vindictive Mrs Greville may well have been serious in her approval of Nazi politics; Diana Mosley was, naturally, a cheerful pro-Fascist; Harmsworth's *Daily*

Mail was friendly to both Mussolini and Hitler; the Channons would visit Germany in 1936 and have a wonderful time. Emerald was a natural extreme Tory; but also a games-playing social entrepreneur whose pleasure was all to do with creating narratives out of real life, amusing herself with the possibilities of a theatre of politics. And underlying it all was a growing sense of personal threat – her relationship with Sir Thomas Beecham was rocky; her personal fortune had been badly hit by the Depression; her daughter Nancy was publicly consorting with a black American musician – leading her towards the Third Reich, which, intriguingly, managed to be both highly structured and vengefully destructive. When Chips called round one June evening in 1935, he found her 'in bed looking very seductive as she reclined in blue and lace'. Chit-chat about the Prince of Wales then followed, before

> In the midst of our talk Von Ribbentrop rang up, the arch-Hitler spy of Europe. Emerald flattered him for a few minutes and then asked him to join her at the Opera tomorrow. She then suddenly said: 'Corbin, the French Ambassador, says that you are perfectly charming.' I could hear the German's voice drop with surprise and when, a minute later, I asked Emerald whether Corbin had ever said such a thing, she laughingly admitted that she'd invented it, on the spur of the moment.[64]

As Wallis Simpson would write to Aunt Bessie, a few months later, 'Have just got over a rather political week-end here [Fort Belvedere] – Duff Coopers, Philip Sassoon, Ewan Wallace – all cabinet [Wallace was actually Secretary for Overseas Trade and not in the Cabinet] and Emerald Cunard who thinks she is the Prime Minister.'[65] Emerald, incidentally, reckoned that Mrs Baldwin was the 'Dictator of England'.

In a sense, it hardly mattered what the Prince's political leanings were, or even if they could be said to be strictly political. His intellect, his interests and his emotions were labile and unpredictable at the best of times. More significantly, he never managed to discriminate between them, to put them into discrete mental compartments. He wanted to enjoy his privileges as the second most important member of the royal family – and at the same time, behave just like any other upper-class wastrel. He took the concerns of war veterans and the unemployed deeply to heart, and yet sacked employees, friends and lovers with autocratic cruelty. He was drawn to the manly dynamism, hysterical subservience and fresh-paint smartness of Nazi Germany, but in private acted as an unnervingly solicitous butler to his friends, relations and Wallis Simpson. Everything about him suggested disjunction and discontinuity, apart from his feelings for Wallis. Not that this mattered to the Court now ranged against him, who absolutely failed to see why he could not manage his emotions and his duties with the same bone-headed tidiness as his father.

Tommy Lascelles had actually quit his job as Assistant Private Secretary to the Prince in 1928, on account of irreconcilable personal differences – 'His personal charm has vanished irretrievably so far as I am concerned, and I always feel as if I were working, not for the next King of England, but for the son of the latest American millionaire'[66] – but would soon, uneasily, be obliged to return. Alec Hardinge, however, loomed larger and more severe than the stuffy but decent Lascelles. A fine administrator and completely galvanised with court protocols, Hardinge epitomised everything that the old regime stood for. Sixteen years as George V's Assistant Private Secretary had left him moustachioed, upright, hidebound and obviously in line to take over as the new King's Private Secretary when he assumed the throne. He detested the people now circulating around the Prince; they detested him. 'I think the Court is dead and out-of-date', fulminated Chips at the end of 1935. 'Emerald told us how she had lunched today with Alec Hardinge who, though quite young, has already taken in the Court "colour". He very much criticised the Prince of Wales and his entourage. It is high time such dreary narrow-minded fogies were sacked, as, indeed, they will be, in the next reign.'[67] Hardinge's only ambition, in reality, was to see that the routines of Court life continued in the proper way, purged of ungovernable flirtations with Nazism, society hostesses and Americans.

But the Prince did not stop. In December 1935, Harold Nicolson found himself dining at Lady Colefax's place in the King's Road:

Diana Cooper, Mr and Mrs Simpson, Bruce Lockhart and the Prince of Wales there. The latter is very thin; his complexion has

gone and he is brick-coloured, against which background his fair
eyelashes rise and fall. He talks a great deal about America and
diplomacy. He resents the fact that we do not send our best men
there. He knows an astonishing amount about it all. 'What can I
do?' he says. 'They will only say, "Here's that bloody Prince of
Wales butting in"'.[68]

Lady Colefax, having scored this nice local victory over Emerald
Cunard in enticing Diana Cooper, the Simpsons and the Prince to
her home, followed it up on 13 January with an even grander
moment at the theatre, for the first night of Noël Coward's *Tonight
at Eight-Thirty*. On the way to the Phoenix Theatre, 'Sibyl breaks to
me the fact that the other members of our party are the Prince of
Wales and Mrs Simpson', wrote Nicolson. Things went well at first:

Mrs Simpson is bejewelled, eyebrow-plucked, virtuous and wise. I
was impressed by the fact that she forbade the Prince to smoke
during the *entr'acte* in the theatre itself. She is clearly out to help
him. Our supper-party at the Savoy Grill afterwards goes right
enough, but I find the Prince gazing at my tie and collar [both
chosen by Nicolson with a lusty desire to break the mould] in a
mood of critical abstraction – the eye of Windsor blue surrounded
by jaundice.

Otherwise, the atmosphere surrounding the Prince was relaxed,
relatively undemonstrative, the waiters as well as the guests at the
table appearing resolutely unfussed. 'The Prince is extremely
talkative and charming. I have a sense that he prefers our sort of
society either to the aristocrats or to the professed highbrows or
politicians. Sibyl imagines that she is getting him into touch with
Young England.' And yet Nicolson was gradually overwhelmed by
'an uneasy feeling that Mrs Simpson, in spite of her good intentions,
is getting him out of touch with the type of person with whom he
ought to associate'.[69]

Chips Channon knew and liked Harold Nicolson, claiming that
'He is really affectionate, domestic and simple, but his brain has an
exotic bent, and he is ever striving for the unusual'[70] – which, in this
case, meant riddling through his experience to discover what was

bothering him. 'Go home pondering on all these things and a trifle sad', Nicolson concluded: 'Why am I sad? Because I think Sibyl is a clever old bean who ought to concentrate upon intellectual and not social guests. Because I think Mrs Simpson is a nice woman who has flaunted suddenly into this absurd position. Because I think the P. of W. is in a mess. And because I do not feel at ease in such company.'[71]

FOURTEEN

Endgame

George V died a week later, on 20 January 1936, not before Chips 'Rang up Diana Cooper and Emerald Cunard rang me; both had talked to Mrs. Simpson whom the poor Prince loves so desperately. They were gloomy.'[1]

Chips, on the other hand, was increasingly pleased with the way things were going. In October of the previous year, Honor Channon had given birth to a son, Paul, on the same day that the Duchess of Kent had also given birth to her son. Mrs Corrigan was one of the first to trip round and fondle the new Channon baby, one deracinated American paying tribute to another. The next thing was for the Channons to move house, to their palatial new home in Belgrave Square. Once there, Chips installed Stéphane Boudin to design his startling Amalienburg dining room, as splendid and phoney a piece of artistry as anything attempted by W.W. Astor or W.R. Hearst. Some called it 'London's loveliest room'; while Harold Nicolson was moved to blurt out, 'Oh my God how rich and powerful Lord Channon has become!' at the sight of the Regency drawing room, the orange lobby to the 'Amalienburg', the blue and silver dining room itself, and the proximity of the whole establishment to the chic Kents.

The more fiercely heterosexual members of society had long been troubled by the clever, cultured, handsome Duke of Kent, whose sex life was incredibly busy and incredibly various, taking in lovers as diverse as Margaret Wigham, later Duchess of Argyll; the black American cabaret singer Florence Mills; and Noël Coward. 'I often dined at the Duke and Duchess of Kent's house in Belgrave Square', wrote the Countess of Airlie, 'and I was always impressed not so much by the externals of happiness – the brilliance of the conversation, the beautifully arranged rooms and the perfectly chosen meal – as by the deeper harmony of two temperaments.' This would have been quite enough, but for Lady Airlie's apparently uninflected continuation, to the effect that

> Once when I complimented the Duchess on the dinner she laughed. 'I am really a very bad hostess. I must confess that I didn't know what we were going to eat tonight until the food appeared. My husband chose the dinner and the wine – and the flowers and everything else. He enjoys doing it, and so I always leave the household affairs to him. I let him make all the decisions over furniture and decorations. He has a wonderful sense of colour and design.' She had recognized the artist in him, and the need for expression . . .[2]

The Duke of Kent was close to Chips in temperament as well as postal address. Both had an enjoyment of the sensual and the illicit (Chips being both bisexual *and* keen on putting Benzedrine in the cocktails); both had a well-developed sense of taste and refinement; both were good friends with the Prince of Wales – now King Edward VIII. Chips's centrality was increasing, and increasingly delicious. On 12 February, he and Honor went to tea with the Brownlows – that is, with Perry Lord Brownlow, Personal Lord-in-Waiting to the King – where they found the 'New Court' convivially assembled. Wallis was on her best form – 'charming and gay and vivacious' – and cracking the pleasantry that she hadn't worn black stockings since she gave up the cancan. Chips indulgently saw this as a remark 'typical of her breezy humour, quick and American, but not profound'. The talk was general, involving everything except the elephant in the room, the King himself.[3] At the same time, Emerald Cunard was staging part of *A Storm in a Teacup* for the two lovers, privately at her Grosvenor Square house. *A Storm in a Teacup* was one of the hits of the mid-1930s – 'The Funniest Play London Has Seen for Months', according to the *Daily Herald*; the 'Most Amusing Play of 1936' said the *Daily Telegraph* – and was reviewed by *The Times* as a 'discursive satire which plays about on the surface of character'. More importantly, the plot was built around a pair of irresistible love-triangles, the significance of which would not have been lost on any audience in which sat the Prince and Mrs Simpson. To spare the couple's blushes, and to allow them to see what all the fuss was about, Emerald had the key scenes of the drama staged in her front room. And where was the harm in that?

The harm was everywhere. Not only was Wallis still prominent; she was now close to a King Emperor rather than a Prince. The Court and the society traditionalists had kept her at arm's length for two years, willing the problem to go away. But this not only left them with no purchase on Wallis and the new King; it left plenty of space for the Americans Diana Cooper and Lady Colefax to exercise whatever influence they felt like exercising. It was as if the threat of corruption that everyone so feared from the original transatlantic heiresses had finally realised itself, two generations later: disguised as a varnished, divorced, *Hausfrau*.

For the Americans and the new Court, the question was how to stabilise Edward and Wallis sufficiently so that they could be seen to have gathered a Court around them, rather than a loose aggregate of hangers-on. For the old Court, the question was how to detach Wallis from the increasingly obsessional King. Wallis's hold over him had lost none of its power to surprise; Diana Cooper wrote to Duff from Fort Belvedere in February 1936: 'The King unchanged in manners and love. Wallis tore her nail and said "Oh!" and forgot about it, but he needs must disappear and arrive back in two minutes, panting, with two little emery-boards for her to file the offending nail.'[4]

At the same time, Wallis may well have been dripping with jewellery and absolutely central to the King's view of the world, but she was still full of a sense of her own vulnerability.

> The difference in thought between the 2 countries [she wrote about Britain and the United States] is colossal. I feel unfortunately that I am out of tune and step with my own countrymen. I simply don't react the way they do to things, nor do I in the pure English way either. I seem torn between the 2 nationalities. I prefer the English mode of life, the dignity and the wide outlook – but I prefer the US pep and sense of humour and detest their bourgeois morals.[5]

This was in February, in a letter filled with mild gloom, to Aunt Bessie. Two months later, she appeared to be even more ambivalent about the whole thing, readying herself to play the part (yet again) of a woman abandoned on the ocean of life, compelled to struggle towards whatever haven presented itself.

> Should HM fall in love with someone else [she wrote] I would cease to be as powerful or have all I have today. Perhaps I have made a few new friends and kept some old ones that would always be nice to me – but I expect nothing. I should be comfortably off and have had a most interesting experience, one that does not fall to everyone's lot and the times are exciting now and countries and politics madly thrilling. I have always had the courage for the new things that life sometimes offers.[6]

The phrase 'I should be comfortably off' inevitably has the chilly ring of the mercenary about it: is it a sorrowing admission that the world is, in essence, a purely material place; or a pat on the back for having duped the monarch?

The secrecy that shrouded the whole affair added to its sense of contingency, of mutability, of unreality. It was scintillating to be in on the secret; but it also made it impossible to get any proper perspective on the affair, to reason out a way forward. Almost no one outside the increasingly excited inner circle could be sensibly canvassed. Chips Channon and Lady Cunard, far from seeing a potential catastrophe unfolding before them, were relishing the drama as if it were a piece of Ruritanian fantasy given an extra, thrilling, resonance. Sibyl Colefax was just as light-headed. Ardently trying to fix her own place in Wallis's heart, she wrote to her,

> I've been thinking so very much of you and feel I want to send you this little line – It's not only that you are a great joy and delight as a friend, your wit and fun and *joie de vivre* have been a joy to me ever since we met. And I've grown every month more and more full of delightful admiration for not only your immense wisdom and lovely common (so miscalled!) *sense*, but for your unfailing touch of being exactly right in all judgements and in all kinds of moments in life at every angle.

Her garrulity was boundless. Having staked her claim to Wallis's friendship, she then tried to ensure her own place in the larger structure, by reminding Wallis how indispensable *she* was to the King:

> And you've done something more which I think you must profoundly feel and I hope rejoice in, you have made someone very happy – With everything else in life, happiness had not been much there – and it seems to me that in that happiness a part of history lies and something will be easier in that immense burden – That he is going to be a great King, with an immense heart for his people, the real people, the working and struggling, I have always believed as part of my faith – That he is happier is all due to you – and that will make the immense business, the immense weight, all that is before him, an easier thing.[7]

To her friend Thornton Wilder, meanwhile, she wrote 'This is Ultra Private and for you alone!' before going on to thrill him with gossip: 'Wallis Simpson is gay and very intelligent. She has never tried to use her position for any sort of advancement socially and has only been pulled into the life by Emerald Cunard.' Wilder liked Sibyl, but was known to complain about the 'intermittent rapid attention' she normally paid to any subject or event. On this occasion, though, her focus was sharpened by the matter in hand. 'As far as London life is concerned she is certainly good for him. She is cosy and likes to help him with domestic things, curtains, covers, food . . . She is funny, natural and spontaneous. He used to be very capricious, probably will be so again. His first great love was always hard and in love with someone else.' This last was a scolding reference to Freda Dudley Ward; but not as bad her dismissal of Thelma Furness, who was 'awful'. Wallis, conversely, 'is tactful, helpful and wise and I've seen her at it'.[8]

These pieties were only effective up to a point. On 2 April, Wallis gave a dinner party at her little flat in Bryanston Court. To her joy, Sibyl was invited. So was Harold Nicolson. So, to Sibyl's horror, was Emerald Cunard, who still had her hands firmly attached to the reins of destiny. So, even, was Margot Asquith, Countess of Oxford. Nicolson put on his black tie and black waistcoat before climbing into a taxi and heading off to Bryanston Court. There he found waiting for him, in order, a lift, a butler and a maid at the door,

followed by the drawing room, filled with orchids and white arum
lilies. The guests were Ladies Oxford, Cunard and Colefax; plus
Kenneth Lindsay – Counsellor of the US Embassy at Buenos Aires –
with his wife, and Alexander Woollcott, the American critic,
commentator and former member of the Algonquin Round Table.
The King was then led in by the endlessly patient Ernest Simpson,
occasioning an outbreak of bows and curtseys. The King,
apparently, looked 'very well and gay'. The air around him,
however, was richly poisonous. 'It is evident that Lady Cunard is
incensed by the presence of Lady Colefax, and that Lady Colefax is
furious that Lady Cunard should also have been asked. Lady
Oxford appears astonished to find either of them at what was to
have been a quite intimate party. The King passes brightly from
group to group.' Some cocktail talk ensued. Dinner was announced,
Nicolson taking his place

> between an indignant Emerald and the wife of the U.S. Counsellor
> at B.A. Opposite is Woollcott, and both ends of the table go gaily
> enough but for continued fury on Emerald's part. The King talked
> to Mrs S. and Lady O. all the time. Emerald cannot bear it, and
> begins shouting 'Your Majesty' aloud. That doesn't go at all. Sibyl
> then starts telling a funny story which goes even less well. Then
> the women go and we sit on for hours talking to our Sovereign
> over the port. I must say, he is very alert and delightful. Then back
> to the drawing-room where Margot Oxford gets more and more
> sleepy, and at last at 1 a.m. the King retires.

His verdict? 'Something snobbish in me is rather saddened by all this.
Mrs Simpson is a perfectly harmless type of American, but the whole
setting is slightly second-rate. I do not wonder that the Sutherlands
and the Stanleys are sniffy about it all.'⁹ Did he wonder what Wallis's
purpose was in bringing the two rivals – Colefax and Cunard – so
provocatively together? Was she even aware that they were rivals?
And was he in the least surprised that the King should have been
completely undisturbed by their presence, caring only for Wallis?

The end was measured out in tête-à-têtes, dinner parties, exchanges
of correspondence and increasingly jittery diary enteries. It took on

the form of a hysterical fugue. Shortly after the Simpsons' dinner, Sibyl Colefax retaliated with her own luncheon at Argyll House, supported by Wallis, Harold Nicolson, Winston Churchill and others. Emerald Cunard hit back a few weeks after that, with a grand dinner at which the Simpsons and the King were present, as well as the Channons, Lord Rosebery and Winston Churchill, who was now clearly one of the Simpson faction. The King, in his public manifestations, lacked the punctilio of his father – trying to avoid committing himself to a trip to India; reducing the rights of access enjoyed by privileged bodies such as Oxford University and the Bank of England – but could still impress hugely. He won hearts when he attended the distribution of the Maundy Money; he charmed the Argentine Foreign Minister with his command of Spanish; he expertly hosted a dinner for those who had attended his father's funeral, and so on.

In comparison with these larger events, it hardly mattered who he had dinner with – except for the fact that if she married him, Mrs Simpson would become an American, twice-divorced queen, and thus hated by most of the Empire. She would probably not bring forth an heir to the throne. And, it was generally held, she would consolidate his worst tendencies towards waywardness, selfishness and the company of low-lifers. Nevertheless, the King held a dinner at York House in May, at which he returned Emerald's hospitality by inviting her, along with the Simpsons (the last time the unhappy, conflicted Ernest accompanied his wife on an outing). Lady Astor, according to Harold Nicolson, complained that only well-born Virginian families should appear at such court functions, considering Lady Cunard and Chips Channon as 'disintegrating influences'. Nicolson punctiliously stuck up for both Emerald Cunard and Wallis Simpson, as well as preventing himself from pointing out that 'After all, every American is more or less as vulgar as any other American. Nancy Astor herself, by her vain and self-conscious behaviour in the House, cannot claim to be a model of propriety.'[10] Lord Reith, on discovering that the Simpsons and Lady Cunard had been at the dinner, fell into despair: 'It is too horrible and it is serious and sad beyond calculation.'[11] When the King opened the Royal Victorian Order to women, Reith then added, tragic with fury, 'Will the first GCVOs (female) be Lady Cunard and Mrs. Simpson?'[12]

This, despite the fact that even Queen Mary was supposed to have shifted her attitude towards Mrs Simpson from one of loathing to one of squirming toleration. At the time of the Duke of Kent's wedding, the Queen had wrung her hands over the way the Prince of Wales 'gives Mrs Simpson the most beautiful jewels', before adding, 'I am so afraid that he may ask me to receive her.'[13] Two years later, however, she was able to allow that 'I don't like it, but the one thing that I have always feared for David is drink. I was afraid it would ruin him or make him a laughing-stock. And she [Mrs Simpson] has been a sane influence in that respect. And this is important.'[14] Chips Channon, of course, saw Wallis as a powerfully virtuous force by this time. For him, she was 'clever', and 'behaving well'. Her sense of chic, her drollery, her awareness of the King's obligation to make an effort with the dull and the important – 'to be polite' – confirmed her essential worth. 'Above all', he decided, 'she makes him happy. The Empire ought to be grateful.' Emerald Cunard, equally predictably, and with a corresponding absence of complacency, saw her as an ambivalent, even demonic, force out of Grand Opera, declaring that 'The King is Mrs. Simpson's absolute slave, and will go nowhere where she is not invited.'[15] Robert Bruce Lockhart, meanwhile, sneered that Bridget Paget (wife of Lord Victor Paget) 'who of course does not like Mrs. Simpson, says the King is getting tired of Emerald Cunard, that he always hated her before, and that he will hate her again'.[16] But there was wishful thinking in this. Bruce Lockhart found Emerald hard to tolerate, too. But Chips loved her, Wallis had no choice but to stay in with her and the King went wherever Wallis went.

So when Chips Channon had his great dinner party on 11 June 1936, it was a triumph for him and his set; and a terrible confirmation to the rest of the Court that the King had fallen irretrievably into the hands of the second-rate, the superficial, the unreliable. Yes, the King was there, as was his brother George and George's clothes-horse wife, Marina. Chips and Honor Channon in all their pomp were the hosts; Emerald Cunard was there as a kind of roving ringmistress. Wallis Simpson was there. But who were the others? Leslie Hore-Belisha was present: a minister of transport who had given Britain the Belisha beacon, the Highway Code and proper driving tests. He would later become Minister of War and, being

Jewish, suffer from the murky anti-Semitism practised by the British establishment. Harold Nicolson would contemptuously bracket him with other 'middle-class individuals flattered by the adulation of what they suppose – with extreme incorrectitude – to be the aristocracy'.[17] Harold Balfour, likewise present, was a Conservative MP with an interest in aviation and a seat on the Isle of Thanet. Barbie Wallace was the daughter of Sir Edwin Lutyens, wife to the Conservative MP Euan Wallace, and a minor, all-purpose socialite. Lord Beaverbrook politely declined an invitation; Philip Sassoon accepted. Laura Corrigan was invited to the after-dinner entertainment but, outraged at not being invited to the dinner itself, 'rudely' refused to turn up. Lady Colefax gratefully accepted an invitation to the same after-dinner events. But where were the key political or cultural figures? Where were the outstanding representatives of the British aristocracy?

As it happened, the most interesting figure among these second-rankers round the dining table was the enigmatic baronet, Philip Sassoon. His enterprising enjoyment of the Sassoon family fortune (made from trade in opium, gold and silks) had long made him an object of nervy fascination in society. His Jewishness, his personal flair – occasionally tumbling over into epicene vulgarity – his political ambition (MP for Hythe, PPS to Lloyd George, Under-Secretary of State for Air), his gregariousness and his contrasting air of personal mystery all rendered him centrally important – yet detached, unknowable and so, despite his vast circle of friends, oddly friendless.

The architect Philip Tilden had been one of these quasi-intimates. Despite an evident affection for Sassoon, he none the less wrote, 'He liked at times to give way to artificial tempers tempered with a smile that banished all the clouds in an instant . . . "I do it to protect myself, Philip", he once said to me. Nevertheless, he frightened the life out of me at times, and scared his servants into dumbness in spite of treating them well.'[18] The Earl of Crawford, with whom Sassoon worked on the board of the National Gallery, found himself torn between admiration and fierce disapproval, again flavoured with anti-Semitism. On the one hand, 'How does this extraordinary young man manage to attract people to his side?' he asked himself after a visit to Sassoon's opulent suburban-country seat at Trent Park, in Hertfordshire. 'Partly finance no doubt', was the answer, qualified with the reflection that 'Personally I try and keep aloof from the rich Jew or American and I don't much want to be mixed up with Asiatics – but Sassoon is a keen and loyal colleague on the National Gallery Board, and I wish to see him often; and I confess a peculiar charm in his cool friendliness, or is it a friendly coolness? What fantastic sums that young man must spend on his entertainments.'[19]

On the other hand, a few years after the encounter at Trent Park,

The Prince of Wales turned up at the National Gallery board meeting today. He fairly amazed us. About halfway through our proceedings, which happened to be extremely important, he got bored and started to smoke . . . The cigarette however enlivened the Prince and he began to talk to his neighbours, Sassoon and D'Abernon . . . Sassoon . . . with his raucous Syrian voice and his acute desire to 'honour the King' chattered away – and between them the two made business practically impossible. We were quite bewildered by the time our meeting ended. So far as I could make out, the chatter was chiefly about racing and society.[20]

Chips Channon, who, in his way, was scarcely less foreign or exotic than Philip Sassoon, nevertheless took it upon himself to wear the mantle of plain-dealing English xenophobe on a visit to Sassoon's other great country retreat, at Port Lympne, Kent (which once caused Lady Desborough to write to A.J. Balfour, 'You *must* go to Philip's Futurist house at Lympne. I spent my last Sunday in England there, and my eyes are still agog.'[21]). According to Chips,

We left with Norah Lindsay [the society figure and renowned gardener] for Lympne to stay with Philip Sassoon, whom, as we arrived, we met in the road. He waved us a welcome and went on, 'Very Jewish of him,' Norah remarked. We were received at his fantastic villa by armies of obsequious white-coated servants who seemed willing enough, but second rate. I whispered this to Duff Cooper, who was busy with a jigsaw puzzle, 'Yes, one sees who has the upper hand here,' he laughed.[22]

Channon's unease reflected a guilty sense of kinship with Sassoon. Both were rich, alien, whimsical. Sassoon was an excellent administrator; and prodigiously wealthy – his wealth allowing him to keep up vast establishments at Trent Park, Park Lane and Lympne as well as a succession of light aeroplanes and some of the finest food and drink in the Home Counties. The Channon fortune was smaller, but had he not just transformed part of his house in Belgravia into an off-cut from a miniature rococo palace – a gesture as unfettered by notions of good taste as Sassoon's iteration of Port Lympne as a Moorish–Levantine–Fine Arts country hotel? Did he not collect influential friends as assiduously, using his wealth to beguile them? Was he not as flattered by the attentions of the King? 'Philip and I mistrust each other', Chips wrote. 'We know too much about each other, and I can peer into his Oriental mind with all its vanities.'[23] Sassoon used the occasion of Chips's dinner to try to boost himself for the job of Commissioner of Works by getting Emerald Cunard to put in a good word with the King, who was seated next to her. Channon used the occasion to affirm to himself, finally, that he had become so wonderfully integrated into society that all his dreams and inner fictions concerning the British aristocracy were coming true. As he triumphally put it, a few months after the great event, 'We were invited to eleven dinner parties tonight. The Iveaghs, while amused by our royal activities, are nevertheless impressed. Their gangster son-in-law from Chicago has put their daughter into the most exclusive set in Europe!'[24] He even lost his head to the extent of assuring Emerald Cunard that, according to his information, she had been chosen to succeed the saintly Lady Airlie as Mistress of the Bedchamber, once Wallis was made Queen.

But Chips's excitement was predicated on the idea that people like himself and Emerald Cunard were people the King was especially attracted to: he was there because the King wanted freebooting Americans to help run his kingdom. But the King was there because that was where Wallis was, and Wallis was there not least because she didn't have that many other places to go. Few traditional grandees wanted to go out of their way to befriend her. Many houses were simply closed to her. The Court was out of bounds. By ostracising her, of course, the traditional aristocracy, so far from willing her into disappearance, pushed her closer to the King. So she made the best of the people who wanted her company – which found her making polite conversation with the King and the Channons and the Kents at 5 Belgrave Square. Was Wallis really minded to take Emerald Cunard – 'aged, wrinkled, vivacious and glittering' – as her Mistress of the Bedchamber? If so, it would have been the triumph of the outsiders; a seduction of the King of England by a penniless American; the assumption of a prime court position by an ageing foreign mischief-maker; an inversion of the social order which would have been appalling thirty years earlier; and was still appalling, even now.

The sense of privileged certainty that hung over Chips's great meal lasted for a few more weeks. The dinners and social convocations carried on. Sibyl Colefax threw her last big party, before moving out of Argyll House. An impressive affair, it boasted the King, Mrs Simpson, Noël Coward, Lord Berners and many others. Harold Nicolson applauded her, noting that 'She only made one mistake, and that was to sit on the floor with Diana Cooper to give a sense of informality and youth to the occasion. But Sibyl, poor sweet, is not good at young *abandon*. She looked incongruous on the floor, as if someone had laid an inkstand there.'[25] The King replied with dinner at St James's Palace. At the start of July, Emerald gave a dinner which was a near re-run of Chips's – the King, Wallis, Chips, Philip Sassoon, all in attendance – plus Grandi, the Italian ambassador, and Portia Stanley, the King's old girlfriend. In an access of *noblesse oblige*, Emerald Cunard even invited Laura Corrigan. As a consequence, according to Chips, 'Laura Corrigan was in the seventh heaven of bliss, though I gather the King never spoke to her. There can be no doubt Royalty casts a strange atmosphere.'[26]

Chips was still talking about 'the new Court' a fortnight later, as well as describing Wallis ('the semi-queen') as being 'smothered in rubies' at another of Emerald's meals, then 'dripping with emeralds' in Emerald's box at Covent Garden. Sibyl Colefax harassed Wallis for her company, forcing her to put a stop to Sibyl's endless importunings:

Sibyl dear – I am going to say no to your sweet and kind invitations – because I am in a rather confused and upset state of mind this moment due to the fact that Ernest and myself are going to live apart this winter . . . I know you will understand and will let me see you when I can break the shell I have temporarily gone into. I do hope you are feeling stronger and that the shop is filled with autumn orders.

Sibyl also tried to hustle for some paying work out of the royal family. This was not unreasonable, given that Elsie de Wolfe – Lady Mendl – had done some designs for Fort Belvedere and was being tipped to redecorate Buckingham Palace. But Wallis was again firm: 'As far as I know', she explained, 'neither Buckingham Palace or the Fort are having anything done in the way of "face-lifting" etc to them.'[27] Emerald Cunard, still living as grandly as she could on the residue of her investments, had no such need to prostitute herself. Instead, she went around trying out her position as fully formed constituent of the New Court, by goosing her rivals. According to Daphne Weymouth, 'At one of Laura Corrigan's supper-dances, noticing that cold salmon was on the menu, she raised her eyebrows, pursed her lips and remarked "Our King says that cold salmon is vulgar".'[28]

But Chips had had a presentiment of disaster that night at the opera with Lady Cunard, when Wallis was 'dripping with emeralds'. There he watched 'Poor Wallis, the cynosure of all eyes', and mused that 'She can do no right. All her tact, sweetness and charm – are they enough?'[29] It was November by this time. A good part of the summer had been spent by Wallis and the King aboard the yacht *Nahlin*, cruising the eastern Mediterranean and exciting the comments of the foreign press. Abroad, it was now open season on the King: 'Mayfair hostesses [claimed the *New York Times*] are dropping the drawing room for the kitchen – all because Mrs. Wallis Simpson prepared tasty dinners with her own hands "fit for a king" and the King ate them. The rush for the kitchen began when London's élite learned the American friend of King Edward was an excellent cook and the monarch smilingly sampled her efforts.'[30] 'World Waits With Wally', announced American newsreels. A trip to Balmoral in the early autumn with Mrs Simpson in tow had been managed fairly blatantly and fairly incompetently. When he opened Parliament at the start of the month, the King sounded unnervingly American to most listeners. It was now clear to the informed that

Mrs Simpson was indeed the King's mistress and that she was the lodestar of the New Court.

Much too late in the process, Edith Londonderry awoke to the imminent danger and tried to get involved one evening at Lady Cunard's. She had no real relationship with Wallis Simpson – indeed, was barely on nodding terms, on account of her starchy allegiance to the royal family – but still took it upon herself to browbeat Wallis over her obligations to the Empire, to the Throne, to the British people. Mildly stunned by this intervention, Wallis wrote to Edith the following day, 'I am going to tell him [the King] all the things you told me . . . I am *afraid* I am the innocent victim – put "on the spot" by my own country.'[31]

Nothing, of course, changed, because the King didn't want anything to change. A few days later, Emerald Cunard gave another dinner, in the course of which she tremblingly took Chips to one side and presented him with an anonymous note she had just been sent: 'It began, "You old bitch, trying to make up to Mrs Simpson, in order to curry favour with the King." Emerald was frightened and yet rather flattered. It was in an educated handwriting.'[32] Sibyl Colefax, meanwhile, found *herself* delectably at the centre of events, spending a Sunday down at Fort Belvedere in the company solely of Mrs Simpson and a naval equerry. Wallis, profoundly miserable and anxious, bewailed her position and the counsel that people like Edith Londonderry had been thrusting on her – especially the idea that she should throw off the King and leave the country. 'They do not understand', she told Sibyl – who told Harold Nicolson two days later – 'that if I did so, the King would come after me regardless of anything. They would then get their scandal in a far worse form than they are getting it now.' Both Harold and Sibyl agreed that 'Mrs Simpson is perfectly straightforward and well-intentioned'; and that a constitutional crisis was indeed upon them all.[33] Heedlessly, Chips gave another dinner on 19 November, much like his earlier one – with the King, Wallis and Emerald in attendance – only this time, graced by the presence of his lover, Prince Paul of Yugoslavia, and *his* wife, Princess Olga. They all watched a Mickey Mouse film after the meal.

And then it was, indeed, the end. Late in November, Emerald Cunard plied Leslie Hore-Belisha with drink. Hore-Belisha, grateful to be made a fuss of, told Emerald, who then told Chips, that Baldwin 'had given the King three weeks to make up his mind about Wallis; if he didn't give her up, he, Baldwin, would resign . . . the King would marry, the Conservatives would reign, Churchill would lead the country . . .' Channon, for once, tried to calm Emerald down, 'telling her that Leslie Belisha is an imaginative Jew'.[34] On 2 December, the much more phlegmatic Duff Cooper 'lunched with Emerald [Cunard] who was in a very excited state. She hasn't, of course, the faintest idea of what the British constitution is all about. I forget who was there but I remember that Ivor Churchill and I were the only ones with moderate views. Everyone else was violently on the side of the King.'[35] A few days later, Chips was indulging his fondness for charged grandiloquence when he wrote that

> The Country and the Empire now know that their Monarch, their young King–Emperor, their adored Apollo, is in love with an American twice divorced, whom they believe to be an adventuress. The whole world recoils from the shock; but very few know that she is a woman of infinite charm, gentleness, courage and loyalty, whose influence upon the King, until now, has been highly salutary.[36]

This became even more stagey on 5 December, when he cried, 'If only I had power – My God, I'd do something! Anything! Nothing matters now, no details, they are forgotten. We can only combine to try to save the Sovereign. All day there were telephone messages and plots.'[37] But Chips had no power, any more than Emerald Cunard, Laura Corrigan or Sibyl Colefax. He only had celebrity. His rhetoric was like something out of Franz Lehar: impassioned; essentially decorative.

As it turned out, Baldwin did not resign. In fact, the sudden resourceful elasticity shown by the Establishment abruptly threw the dreams and delusions of the Americans into harsh relief. *The Times*, under Geoffrey Dawson's stiffly pro-Baldwin editorship, sneered at 'American' fantasies of a morganatic relationship between the King and Mrs Simpson (fantasies that had 'gone to the length of predicting a marriage incompatible with the THRONE and of announcing QUEEN MARY's approval of it') and noted that 'The wave of gossip and rumour from across the Atlantic has spread in ever-widening circles throughout this country. It is no longer restricted to a little circle with American connexions.'[38] The secret was out; and without the chimerical power of secrecy, the New Court found itself abruptly reduced in significance. Baldwin moved with some adroitness to canvass the Empire – which broadly objected to Wallis's being a divorcée – and isolate those, like Winston Churchill, who held out the hope of keeping Edward on the throne with Wallis confined to a morganatic relationship which Baldwin had declared constitutionally impossible. 'There are', said *The Times* sorrowingly, 'many daughters of America whom he [the King] might have married with . . . approval and rejoicing . . .'[39]

Whoever the King married *had* to become Queen; the King could not marry Mrs Simpson and (necessarily) make her Queen because she already had two ex-husbands wandering the globe and was thus wholly unsuitable. Impasse: the King was left to agonise over this impossibility for a week, until at last he snapped. Alec Hardinge called in Duff Cooper to negotiate the endgame with the King: Duff, who had been on the *Nahlin* with Diana, the King and Wallis during the summer, was, unlike Diana Cooper, less interested in flirting with the idea of a fresh-looking Anglo-American new Court, and more concerned with making sure the Establishment got its way. His job was to sharpen the King's mind as to the exact modalities of his exit, not to keep him in place. The Duke of York was already being lined up to take Edward's place, and the delightful and approachable Duchess of York, Elizabeth Bowes-Lyon, revealed the splinter of ice at the centre of her heart by steadying her husband for his new role and by making it clear that her interests were exactly congruent with those of Queen Mary and the old Court.

At this moment, all the energies were reversed. Wallis fled into exile. On 8 December, Emerald held the last of her Edward VIII dinners, at which the King, nominally the guest of honour, was unable to be present, on account of being about to abdicate. The Londonderrys were there, as were the Coopers, Ribbentrops, Marlboroughs and Channons. Mary Marlborough asked Chips, 'in her frank breezy way', 'did I not think that all the while Wallis had been playing a double game? She herself had not yet made up her mind, but she added that it enraged her when people attacked

Emerald for entertaining her, as Emerald was only one of many. "We had her to stay at Blenheim, I liked her", was Mary's summing up.'[40]

The stodgy ruthlessness of the British Establishment had won – or, as *The Times* put it, 'A sudden emergency has enabled the British people to prove its nation's greatness.'[41] Disbelieving party-goers at the Café de Paris sat openly reading the early editions round starched white tablecloths. On 10 December, the King signed the Abdication papers in the library of his beloved Fort Belvedere, surrounded by his weeping brothers. And then the ex-King was on the wireless, not sounding in the least American, but patrician, slightly elderly, a hint of Churchill in the resoluteness of his delivery. Such was the sonorous conviction with which he spoke, it was hard not to imagine that all along he had wanted to shed the Crown – a job for which he always held feelings of the greatest mistrust – and that his obsessional cleaving to Wallis Simpson was the act of a drowning man: she was the only person who could save him. And she could save him, because she was an American.

Epilogue

The aftermath found society re-forming itself with surprising fluency. The Duke of Windsor went abroad, where he married Wallis and made her a duchess.

Not very long before, he had sent her some flowers and a note: 'These three gardenias are eanum but they say enormous ooh and that a boy loves a girl more and more and is holding her so tight these trying days of waiting.'[1] Now he had her, permanently, and he had to work out how to spend the rest of his life. 'I'm always busy. I shall find plenty to do', he had told Duff Cooper at the time of the abdication.[2] But what was he to do? He wanted to live in America. Wallis didn't. He would have liked to live in England, but he was scared of the taxes; while Wallis was scared of England. Germany was out of the question, as was Italy. France was the only possibility. Years later, Noël Coward (about whom the Duke had been 'beastly' in earlier years) found himself at the British Embassy in Paris, dining with the Windsors. Wallis was 'very charming and rather touching. He loves her so much, and at long last I am beginning to believe that she loves him.'[3] At around the same time – spring 1948 – the sainted Lady Airlie found herself lunching with Winston Churchill. Winston confided in Lady Airlie that he had always liked Wallis, and that 'The Duke's love for her is one of the great loves of history.' He then went on, 'I saw him when she had gone away for a fortnight. He was miserable – haggard, dejected, not knowing what to do. Then I saw him when she had been back for a day or two, and he was a different man – gay, debonair, self-confident. Make no mistake, he can't live without her.'[4]

Before long, the Windsors would feel so much *chez eux* in France that they would call upon M. Boudin – architect of Chips's dining room in Belgravia – to help redesign their house. And the Duke, unsurprisingly, found that so far from finding plenty to do, he had time on his hands. 'The Duke of Windsor came to see me this morning at his own request', Duff Cooper wrote, during his time as British ambassador in Paris. 'I thought he wanted to consult me about something – but not at all. He sat here for nearly an hour chattering about one thing and another. I expect the truth is that he is so *désoeuvré* that Wallis, to get him out of the house, said "why don't you go round to see Duff one morning and have an interesting talk about politics?"'[5] And so the erstwhile King Edward VIII whiled away his days: a kind of mirror-image of Consuelo Marlborough, that other great abdicant, married for love, lazily spending her fortune in the warm French sunshine.

Those left behind began the task of expunging the traces of Edward VIII and coalescing around George VI and Queen Elizabeth. For the diehards, the 'dreary, narrow-minded fogies', there was a sense of grim and somewhat arbitrary vengeance in the air. The Earl of Crawford, for instance, aggressively minuted that 'There is much to do. The American gang has got to be dispersed', in particular, 'Mendl, Corrigan, Lady Astor, Lady Cunard, Lady Furness – all the touts and toadies who revolved around Mrs Simpson, and whose influence upon society was so corrupting.' The fact that Lady Astor had always been anti-Wallis clearly meant less than the simple truth that she was an American. On top of this 'There were lots of weak and complacent English people who were all too ready to bask in the sunshine of royal favour – what one might call the cabaret set – Dudleys, Marlboroughs, Sutherlands, and others who were glad to entertain the King at the price of entertaining his mistress.'[6] Harold Nicolson wrote, decently enough, to Vita Sackville-West, that 'The main feeling is one of fury that this empty-headed American who has twice been divorced should bring this great Empire to the brink of a very grave crisis', but that, in his view, 'I am sorry for her and blame him. How can one expect a Baltimore girl to appreciate the implications of her action?'[7] Evelyn Waugh noted with malicious satisfaction that

> The Simpson crisis has been a great delight to everyone. At Maidie's nursing home [Maidie Hollis, wife of Christopher Hollis, was recovering from an illness] they report a pronounced turn for the better in all adult patients. There can seldom have been an

event that caused so much general delight and so little pain. Reading the papers and even listening to announcements that there was no news on the wireless took up most of the week.[8]

The Sitwell family had long detested Lady Cunard (Edith was once going to 'wipe the floor with that old woman, and throw the remains on the dust-heap'[9]) and Osbert Sitwell, who had been in a mild fury ever since Mrs Simpson arrived on the scene, at last found release in his satirical poem 'Rat Week', notable for its couplet:

> The Ladies Colefax and Cunard
> Took it very, very hard.

As indeed they did. Sibyl Colefax wrote keeningly to her friend Bernard Berenson, 'There was but one person who was determined on the irrevocable deed, H.M. himself – she didn't want marriage and no-one else did and now to think that the future can't be anything but a terrible and tragic, a sordid and cheap disappointment and all those high hopes shattered . . . and the future effect, which the short-sighted are so glib about – cannot be foretold.'[10]

She also gave Virginia Woolf 'a verbatim, hot from the Kings mouth, account of the Abdication: swore that he and Wally had never been to bed; says Wally is a simple good devoted soul, who implored the King to keep her as his mistress or let her go. "If you do," he said "I shall dog you to the ends of the earth in an aeroplane."' Miss Woolf then went on, unexpectedly, 'I gathered that Sibyl is going to act as liaison officer between them and the implacable Queen Mary.'[11]

Emerald Cunard, on the other hand, came straight to the point and cried aloud, 'How *could* he do this to me?'[12] According to Harold Nicolson, she then tried to rat on Wallis. Writing to Vita, he claimed that Emerald 'came to Maggie Greville and said, "Maggie darling, do tell me about this Mrs Simpson – I have only just met her." That has torn Emerald for me. I would not believe the story if I had not heard it at first hand.'[13] This sounds much more like a piece of malicious stirring on the part of Mrs Greville than a genuine attempt at evidence-burying on the part of Lady Cunard – whose relationship with Wallis was, anyway, common knowledge.

So close was Emerald's identification with the Simpson faction that it fatally compromised her place in society. Several months after the Abdication, the Duke and Duchess of Sutherland held a ball at Hampden House in London. The newly crowned King and Queen were there. Emerald, too, was invited, but had to wait pathetically by the telephone at home for the call that would tell her that the royals had come and gone and that it was safe for her to show her face. When she finally arrived, she was tremulously dressed in white, a diminutive, fragile creature, her vanities and ambitions spent. 'Emerald', wrote Robert Bruce Lockhart at the time, was 'very bitter about Mrs Simpson whom she blames for the abdication. She, Emerald, is sure that the Duke of Windsor has not yet lived with Mrs Simpson, and that he worships her as a virginal saint. I doubt this.'[14]

Elsewhere, a sobered Chips Channon walked through the House of Commons after the Abdication, with Nancy Astor calling after him, 'People who have been licking Mrs Simpson's boots ought to be shot.' Chips's response? 'I was too tired to retort and pretended I did not hear.'[15] Shortly after that, he wrote, 'People are beginning to rat. They "never really liked Mrs Simpson," always disapproved of the King and thought him obstinate and insane; already . . .'[16] Chips had reached his high point, too. He still had his house, his position in the House of Commons, his address book. When the war began, he stayed put, still entertaining in the Amalienburg dining room. One night a bomb blew off the portico and balcony at the front of his house. Chips, rich in sang-froid, sat amid the dust and smoke, rang for his butler, and asked for more drinks. But there was no glory in it, now. His neighbour, the Duke of Kent, died in an aeroplane crash in 1943. His son, Paul, was packed off to America to wait out the conflict. 'All day there were telephone messages and plots', he had written in December 1936. Now, all that high drama had gone.

Mrs Corrigan, to everyone's surprise, drifted across the Channel to Paris, where she did valuable war work, before returning to London in 1942. Emerald was in New York when war broke out, fruitlessly trying to extract some value from a defunct portfolio of tin-mine shares. She also made some final, pathetic advances to Sir Thomas Beecham, who was touring the States at the time. On discovering that he was due to marry Betty Humby, Emerald confessed that she now wanted only to die. Then she crawled back to London, via Lisbon, moved as many of her possessions as she could into a seventh-floor suite in the supposedly bomb-proof Dorchester Hotel, and proceeded to play out the war. Into a handful of rooms she crammed her bibelots, her Buhl cabinets, a bronze statue by Rodin, a selection of 'Louis' chairs and a table round which eight guests could just dine. It 'made the eyes boggle', according to Diana Cooper. The ageing Italian and Swiss waiters who staffed the hotel found it almost impossible to work their way round the seated guests without tipping food and drink into their laps.

But at least the entertainment was free. Sibyl Colefax had retreated to a tiny house in Lord North Street, which got progressively more battered as the Blitz rained around it. Like Emerald, she could not give up her position as a society hostess, even amid the terror and anarchy of the war. Like Emerald, she took refuge in the safety of the Dorchester. Unlike Emerald, she went through the pretence of inviting her guests over to Lord North Street, then abruptly changing the venue at the last minute, moving them all into the concrete security of the hotel. Being even poorer than Emerald, she also charged her guests for what they consumed. These events, known as 'Ordinaries', excited great scorn and detestation, not least because her guests loathed themselves for accepting her hospitality almost as much as they loathed the hospitality itself. 'I used to lunch at Sibyl's awful canteen for 1/- & I can still remember the pain I used to have after it', wrote Nancy Mitford,[17] gracelessly going on to quote Gladwyn Jebb, the diplomat, in *his* strictures concerning the Colefax service: 'He says the Colefax guests leave their money on the mantlepiece having filled in a card to say how many liqueurs etc they have had. The squalor!'[18] Harold Nicolson wrote in 1943 that 'Everybody loathes [the Ordinaries], and one feels a sort of community of dislike binding together what would otherwise be a most uncongenial company. Sibyl knows in a way that people hate these ghastly functions. She adopts a mood of will-power. She manages us firmly as if we had all come to the Dorchester to give a blood-transfusion.'[19]

Still, it may be that the war brought these two increasingly forlorn creatures together. The only time John Lehmann saw Ladies Colefax and Cunard in a matched pair was in the spring of 1943. In the company of Duff Cooper and Leslie Hore-Belisha, they had all been to a poetry reading. 'I saw Emerald and Sybil come together and talk animatedly for a few moments. But Emerald was in one of her most ebullient moods, and as we emerged into Bond Street she pranced away from Sybil and up to Hore-Belisha, crying: "Leslie! Recite me some Ronsard! – You do it so beautifully!"'[20] The former War Minister refused to oblige, and the two once-great hostesses parted. Later, Emerald went with Nancy Mitford to a farce, so 'Roaringly funny', according to Nancy, 'I laughed till I choked.' Emerald, contrastingly, 'sat very seriously as tho' at Shakespeare or Ibsen, looking at the actors through opera glasses'.[21]

Finally exhausted, Emerald Cunard died in July 1948, 'unrivalled in the period between the wars as a patron of music and the arts and as a gracious and enterprising hostess'.[22] Laura Corrigan had died in New York, in January of the same year. The memorial service held for her in London drew the Duchess of Kent, the French ambassador, the Dukes and Duchesses of Buccleuch, Marlborough and Devonshire, as well as Viscount Castlereagh, the Begum Aly Khan and a great turnout of what remained of society. Sibyl Colefax (her 'reluctance to suffer the smallest twinge of boredom might momentarily occlude a great natural kindliness'[23]) hung on until the summer of 1950. In 1955, the Earl Winterton published a volume of reminiscences containing the following bodeful observation:

During the '20's and '30's, both when he was Prince of Wales and King, the Duke of Windsor had an inner circle of intimate friends bearing some similarity to that of King Edward VII. It would be disloyal, impertinent and ungenerous to criticize any Heir Apparent or occupant of the Throne for thus forming a circle around him of those whom he likes. But I think that the choice in this field of Queen Victoria, King George V, King George VI and Her present Majesty is greatly to be preferred.[24]

Chips Channon – such a central figure in the Prince-King's clique – died in October 1958, a mere 61 years old. Thelma Furness held on until 1970; the Duke of Windsor, until 1972. Wallis, redoubtable as ever, kept body and soul together until 1986.

And presiding over the darkest moments of the war, leading the country through the very worst days? That Anglo-American prodigy, product of one of the *great* marriages of the late nineteenth century, Winston Churchill. His father's wild genius; his mother's sense of drama, allied to her obstinacy and tenacity: these made Winston Churchill prevail. After all the vanities and follies of the 1890s; the corruption of society in the 1920s and the Abdication of 1936 – in which Churchill, notional head of the King's Party, had embarrassed himself again – this was the point at which the differences, incomprehensions and frictions ceased to matter. The greatest Englishman of the twentieth century was the embodiment of international unity: the point at which there was no difference between Them and Us.

But afterwards? The centre of gravity had shifted for good – across to New York, and even to Los Angeles, that unconsidered nowhere of a hundred years before. Up to 1939, London and Paris between them commanded enough respect, retained sufficient charisma, to keep themselves as indispensable stopping-off points for the cultured American. After 1945, Europe was in turmoil and London was in ruins. The process of dissolution that hung over the nation's great country houses went on, accelerating in pace and intensity. The primal austerities affecting food, heating, transport, clothing, were more than enough reason to stay away. As the 1950s wore on, one or two old stagers such as Elsa Maxwell or Barbara Hutton (now on to her fifth husband) passed through. In 1959 it was announced that Paul Getty – the latest World's Richest Man – had bought Sutton Place in Surrey, former home of the Duke of Sutherland, and, in an echo of the pre-war days, had decided to put in proper central heating. Fifty years before, such a piece of news would have added to the worrying sense of the ubiquity of the Americans; now it was strange, exceedingly rare. No one looked from west to east any more. The traffic was all the other way. John F. Kennedy became President, combining the demotic glamour of a Hollywood star with the magisterial political presence of F.D. Roosevelt – a perfect, modern, American figurehead. Did the American invasion of British society prefigure a personality like

Kennedy's? Certainly, the heiresses, the millionaires, the hostesses all epitomised the larger forces that were working on Britain: the transfer of power across the Atlantic; the breakdown of the old aristocratic areas of influence; the loosening of social rigidities and personal conduct; the unravelling of stuffiness. Were they the history of Britain's place in the twentieth century, compressed into a few brazen archetypes?

Either way, in 1962, Londonderry House finally left the hands of the Londonderry family, going to a Mr Isaac Klug, who promptly knocked it down. And with that, it might fairly be said that the great days of the heiresses, of high society in torment, of panic-inducing *belles Américaines*, of nightmarish Yankee landowners, of Chips Channon and Lady Cunard, of awful divorcees, of noble titles slavering after American wealth and the faltering defiance of the old aristocracy, had at last come to an end.

Notes

1: Young America

1. Edith Wharton, *The Age of Innocence*, England, Wordsworth Editions, 1993, p. 32.
2. *Ibid.*, p. 151.
3. Matthew Arnold, 'American Civilization in 1883–4', in Allan Nevins (ed.), *America through British Eyes*, New York, Oxford University Press, 1948, p. 372.
4. The Earl of Rosebery, *Lord Rosebery's North American Journal, 1873*, ed. A.R.C. Grant, London, Sidgwick & Jackson, 1967, p. 37.
5. The Earl of Warwick, *Memories of Sixty Years*, London, Cassell, 1917, p. 149.
6. The Earl of Desart, *A Page from the Past: Memoirs of the Earl of Desart*, London, Jonathan Cape, 1936, p. 217.
7. Elizabeth Drexel Lehr, *King Lehr and the Gilded Age*, London, Constable, 1935, p. 45.
8. Ruth Brandon, *The Dollar Princesses*, London, Weidenfeld & Nicolson, 1980, p. 15.
9. Earl of Rosebery, *North American Journal*, p. 125.
10. William Drogo Montague, Duke of Manchester, *My Candid Recollections*, London, Grayson & Grayson, 1932, p. 90

2: The Old World

1. Ralph Waldo Emerson, *English Traits*, Boston, Phillips, Samson & Co., 1857, p. 187.
2. *Ibid.*, p. 188.
3. Wharton, *Age of Innocence*, p. 58.
4. Henry James, *Selected Letters of Henry James*, ed. Leon Edel, London, Rupert Hart-Davis, 1956, p. 74.
5. Paul Johnson, *A History of the Modern World*, London, Weidenfeld & Nicolson, 1984, p. 207.
6. Edmund Ions, *James Bryce and American Democracy 1870–1922*, London, Macmillan, 1968, p. 67.
7. Earl of Rosebery, *North American Journal*, p. 138.
8. *Ibid.*, p. 13.
9. *Ibid.*, p. 40.
10. *Ibid.*, p. 63.

11. *Ibid.*, p. 43.
12. *Ibid.*, p. 140.
13. Algernon Bertram, *Memories*, Vol. II, London, Hutchinson & Co., 1915, p. 589.
14. Earl of Rosebery, *North American Journal*, p. 31.
15. Lady Dorothy Nevill, *The Life and Letters of Lady Dorothy Nevill*, ed. Ralph Nevill, London, Methuen, 1919, p. 277.
16. Ions, *James Bryce and American Democracy*, p. 75.
17. Eric Homberger, *Mrs. Astor's New York: Money and Social Power in a Gilded Age*, London and New Haven, Yale University Press, 2002, p. 5.
18. Lady Dorothy Nevill, *Life and Letters*, p. 277.
19. Oscar Wilde, *The Letters of Oscar Wilde*, ed. Rupert Hart-Davis, London, Rupert Hart-Davis, 1962, p. 86.
20. Richard Ellman, *Oscar Wilde*, London, Penguin, 1988, p. 170.
21. Earl of Rosebery, *North American Journal*, p. 142.
22. Anita Leslie, *Jennie: The Mother of Winston Churchill*, Maidstone, George Mann, 1969, p. 192.
23. Lady Dorothy Nevill, *The Reminiscences of Lady Dorothy Nevill*, ed. Ralph Nevill, London, Edward Arnold, 1906, p. 134.
24. Virginia Cowles, *Edward VII and his Circle*, London, Hamish Hamilton, 1956, p. 78.
25. Lady Dorothy Nevill, *Reminiscences*, p. 162.
26. Price Collier, *England and the English from an American Point of View*, London, Cuckworth, 1911, p. 30.
27. *New York Times*, 18 November 1878.
28. Robert Rhodes James, *Rosebery: A Biography*, London, Weidenfeld & Nicolson, 1963, p. 70.
29. A.N. Wilson, *The Victorians*, London, Hutchinson, 2002, p. 382.
30. F.M.L. Thompson, *English Landed Society in the Nineteenth Century*, London, Routledge & Kegan Paul, 1963, p. 290.
31. Denis Stuart, *Dear Duchess: Millicent, Duchess of Sutherland 1867–1955*, London, Gollancz, 1982, p. 118.
32. Duke of Manchester, *My Candid Recollections*, p. 47.
33. *Ibid.*, p. 69.
34. Churchill Archives: CHAR 28/5/18–21.
35. Thompson, *English Landed Society*, p. 291.
36. *Ibid.*, p. 19.
37. *Ibid.*, p. 20.

3: The First Marriages

1. Earl of Rosebery, *North American Journal*, p. 145.
2. Churchill Archives, CHAR 28/2/16–19.
3. *Ibid.*, CHAR 28/2/26–29.
4. *Ibid.*, CHAR 28/ 2/99–100.

5. *Ibid.*, CHAR 28/2/101–102.
6. *Ibid.*, CHAR 28/2/104–105.
7. Elisabeth Kehoe, *Fortune's Daughters*, London, Atlantic, 2005, p. 52.
8. *Ibid.*, p. 54.
9. Leslie, *Jennie*, p. 32.
10. *Ibid.*, p. 42.
11. *Ibid.*, p. 77.
12. Churchill Archives: CHAR 28/4/54–57.
13. Lady Randolph Churchill, *The Reminiscences of Lady Randolph Churchill*, ed. Mrs George Cornwallis-West, London, Edward Arnold, 1908, p. 38 *et seq.*
14. Maureen E. Montgomery, *Gilded Prostitution: Status, money and transatlantic marriages 1870–1914*, London, Routledge, 1989, p. 51.
15. George Cornwallis-West, *Edwardian Hey-Days*, Wakefield, E.P. Publishing, 1975, p. 118.
16. Richard Henry Dana, *Hospitable England in the Seventies: The Diary of a Young American 1875–1876*, London, John Murray, 1921, p. 55.
17. Margaret Halsey, *With Malice Toward Some*, London, Hamish Hamilton, 1938, p. 155.
18. Earl of Rosebery, *North American Journal*, p. 140.
19. Ralph Nevill, *English Country House Life*, London, Methuen, 1925, p. 92.
20. King Edward VII, *Personal Letters*, ed. Lt-Col. J.P.C. Sewell CMG DSO, London, Hutchinson, 1931, pp. 63, 71.
21. Nevill, *English Country House Life*, p. 94.
22. Stanley Weintraub, *The Importance of Being Edward*, London, John Murray, 2000, p. 276.
23. British Library: Paget Papers: Add.51248/62.
24. King Edward VII, *Personal Letters*, p. 57.
25. *New York Times*, 30 July 1878.
26. Harold Acton, *Memoirs of an Aesthete*, London, Methuen, 1948, p. 220.
27. Vita Sackville-West and Harold Nicolson, *Vita and Harold: The Letters of Vita Sackville-West and Harold Nicolson*, ed. Nigel Nicolson, London, Weidenfeld & Nicolson, 1992, p. 260.
28. British Library: Paget Papers: Add.51248/15.

4: Behaving Badly

1. Duke of Manchester, *My Candid Recollections*, p. 28.
2. *New York Times*, 23 May 1876.
3. *Ibid.*
4. Elizabeth Eliot, *They All Married Well*, London, Cassell, 1960, p. 90.
5. The Duke of Portland, *Men, Women and Things*, London, Faber & Faber, 1937, p. 68.
6. Huntingdon County Record Office: Montagu Family Records, MII/box 114.
7. Duke of Manchester, *My Candid Recollections*, p. 67.

8. Hertford Records Office: Grenfell Archives, D/ERv C1881/3.
9. Huntingdon County Record Office: Montagu Family Records, MII/box 114.
10. *Ibid.*
11. Duke of Manchester, *My Candid Recollections*, p. 25.
12. Hugh Montgomery-Massingberd, *Blenheim and the Churchills*, London, Jarrold, 2004, p. 86.
13. *Ibid.*, p. 95.
14. Marian Fowler, *Blenheim: Biography of a Palace*, London, Viking, 1989, p. 190.
15. Leslie, *Jennie*, p. 137.
16. *Ibid.*, p. 138.
17. Fowler, *Blenheim*, p. 190.
18. Leslie, *Jennie*, p. 66.
19. *Ibid.*, p. 78.
20. *Ibid.*, p. 81.
21. *Ibid.*, p. 121.
22. Sotheby's sale catalogue for Easton Neston, 2005, p. 24 *et seq.*
23. Consuelo Vanderbilt Balsan, *The Glitter and the Gold*, London, Heinemann, 1953, p. 137.
24. Angela Lambert, *Unquiet Souls: The Indian Summer of the British Aristocracy 1880–1918*, London, Macmillan, 1984, p. 228.
25. G.H. Bennett and Marion Gibson, *The Later Life of Lord Curzon of Kedleston*, Lewiston, The Edwin Mellen Press, 2000, p. 47.

5: The Americans Settle In

1. Evelyn Waugh, *A Handful of Dust*, London, Penguin, 1951, p. 14.
2. *Ibid.*, p. 218.
3. P.H. Ditchfield, *Vanishing England*, London, Methuen, 1910, p. 7.
4. Lesley Lewis, *The Private Life of a Country House (1912–1939)*, Newton Abbot, David & Charles, 1980, p. 91.
5. Merlin Waterson (ed.), *The Country House Remembered*, London, Routledge & Kegan Paul, 1985, p. 131.
6. Diana Mosley, *A Life of Contrasts*, London, Gibson Square Books, 2003, p. 30.
7. Waugh, *A Handful of Dust*, p. 149.
8. Peter Mandler, *The Fall and Rise of the Stately Home*, London, Yale University Press, 1997, p. 241.
9. *The Times*, 22 March 1912.
10. Nevill, *English Country House Life*, p. 17.
11. Clive Aslet, *The Last Country Houses*, London, Yale University Press, 1982, p. 19.
12. T.H.S. Escott, *Personal Forces of the Period*, London, Hurst & Blackett, 1898, p. 318.
13. David Sinclair, *Dynasty: The Astors and Their Times*, London, J.M. Dent & Sons, 1983, p. 249.
14. T.H.S. Escott, *Society in the Country House*, London, Fisher Unwin, 1907, p. 417.
15. T.H.S. Escott, *King Edward and his Court*, London, Fisher Unwin, 1903, p. 194.

16. Sinclair, *Dynasty*, p. 257.

17. Frances, Countess of Warwick, *Afterthoughts*, London, Cassell, 1931, p. 113.

18. *Ibid.*

19. Sinclair, *Dynasty*, p. 267.

20. Derek Wilson, *The Astors 1763–1992: Landscape with Millionaires*, London, Weidenfeld & Nicolson, 1993, p. 133.

21. Countess of Warwick, *Afterthoughts*, p. 111.

22. Nevill, *English Country House Life*, p. 18.

23. *Ibid.*, p. 42.

24. Michael Astor, *Tribal Feeling*, London, John Murray, 1963, p. 17.

25. *Ibid.*, p. 94.

26. Nevill, *English Country House Life*, p. 92.

27. Madeleine Bingham, *Earls and Girls: Dramas in High Society*, London, Hamish Hamilton, 1980, p. 83.

28. Susan Tweedsmuir, *The Lilac and the Rose*, London, Duckworth, 1952, p. 82.

29. Lady Violet Greville, *The Gentlewoman in Society*, London, Henry & Co., 1892, p. 134.

30. Hertford Records Office: Grenfell Archives, D/Erv C1981/69.

31. Lady Randolph Churchill, *Reminiscences*, p. 47.

32. Frances, Countess of Warwick, *Life's Ebb and Flow*, London, Hutchinson, 1929, p. 37.

33. Blanchard Jerrold, *London*, London, Grant & Co., 1872, p. 81.

34. King Edward VII, *Personal Letters*, p. 57.

35. Lady Dorothy Nevill, *Leaves from the Notebooks of Lady Dorothy Nevill*, ed. Ralph Nevill, London, Macmillan, 1907, p. 30 *et seq.*

36. *New York American*, 1 October 1909.

37. *New York Times*, 10 February 1896.

38. *The Times*, 29 November 1895.

39. Escott, *King Edward and his Court*, p. 194.

40. Marie Corelli, *Free Opinions Freely Expressed on Certain Phases of Modern Social Life and Conduct*, London, Constable, 1905, p. 119.

41. Lady Dorothy Nevill, *Under Five Reigns*, London, Methuen & Co., 1912, p. 116 *et seq.*

42. Lady Violet Greville, *The Gentlewoman in Society*, p. 112.

43. Arthur Ponsonby, 1st Baron Ponsonby of Shulbrede, *The Decline of Aristocracy*, London, Fisher Unwin, 1912, p. 137 *et seq.*

6: High Water

1. Anthony Trollope, *An Autobiography*, Oxford, Oxford University Press, 1999, p. 314.

2. Anthony Trollope, *He Knew He Was Right, Vol. II*, London, Strahan & Co., 1869, p. 41.

3. Anthony Trollope, *The Way We Live Now*, Oxford, Oxford University Press, p. 391 *et seq.*

4. Anthony Trollope, *The Duke's Children*, Oxford, Oxford University Press, 1999, p. 218 *et seq.*

5. *Ibid.*, Introduction, p. xv.

6. Oscar Wilde, *A Woman of No Importance* in *The Complete Works of Oscar Wilde*, London, HarperCollins, 1994, p. 483 ff.

7. Edith Wharton, *The Buccaneers*, London, Penguin Books, 1994, p. 304.

8. Huntingdon County Record Office: Montagu Family Records, MII/box 114.

9. *Ibid.*

10. Hertford Records Office: Grenfell Archives, D/ERv C507/3.

11. Montgomery-Massingberd, *Blenheim and the Churchills*, p. 95.

12. Churchill Archives, CHAR 28/12/30–32.

13. *Ibid.*

14. Leslie, *Jennie*, p. 165.

15. Duke of Manchester, *My Candid Recollections*, p. 85.

16. Anthony Trollope, *Phineas Redux*, Oxford, Oxford University Press, 2000, p. 215 *et seq.*

17. Balsan, *The Glitter and the Gold*, p. 5.

18. Elisabeth Kehoe, *Fortune's Daughters*, London, Atlantic, 2005, p. 175.

19. Nigel Nicolson, *Mary Curzon*, London, Weidenfeld & Nicolson, 1977, p. 97.

20. Duke of Manchester, *My Candid Recollections*, p. 49.

21. Eliot, *They All Married Well*, p. 181.

22. Duke of Manchester, *My Candid Recollections*, p. 85.

23. *New York Times*, 10, 11, and 13 July 1897.

24. *Ibid.*, 11 May 1898.

25. *Ibid.*, 7 March 1901.

26. Duke of Manchester, *My Candid Recollections*, p. 114.

27. The Earl of Rosslyn, *My Gamble With Life*, London, Cassell & Co., 1928, p. 228.

28. *New York Times*, 7 March 1901.

29. *Ibid.*, 13 February 1881.

30. Leslie, *Jennie*, p. 252.

31. Brandon, *Dollar Princesses*, p. 70.

32. Seymour Leslie, *The Jerome Connexion*, London, John Murray, 1964, p. 54.

33. Churchill Archives, CHAR 28/36/6.

34. *Ibid.*, CHAR 28/36/23.

35. Lady Randolph Churchill, *Reminiscences*, p. 47.

36. Leslie, *Jennie*, p. 254.

37. Countess of Warwick, *Life's Ebb and Flow*, p. 138.

38. Brandon, *Dollar Princesses*, p. 70.

7: Astor

1. Aslet, *Last Country Houses*, p. 194.

2. *Ibid.*, p. 196.

3. Countess of Warwick, *Afterthoughts*, p. 111.

4. Philip Tilden, *True Remembrances: The Memoirs of an Architect*, London, Country Life Limited, 1954, p. 114.

5. Patrick Balfour, *Society Racket*, London, John Long, 1933, p. 215.

6. Andrew Carnegie, *Triumphant Democracy*, New York, Kennikat Press, 1971, p. 491.

7. William Calder, *The Estate and Castle of Skibo*, Edinburgh, The Albyn Press, 1949, p. 33.

8. Joseph Frazier Wall, *Skibo*, Oxford, Oxford University Press, 1984, p. 59.

9. George Bernard Shaw, *Man and Superman* in *The Complete Plays of Bernard Shaw*, London, Hamlyn, 1965, p. 394.

10. Peter Krass, *Carnegie*, New Jersey, John Wiley, 2002, p. 436.

11. Merlin Waterson (ed.), *The Country House Remembered*, London, Routledge & Kegan Paul, 1985, p. 15.

12. J. Mordaunt Crook, *The Rise of the Nouveaux Riches*, London, John Murray, 1999, p. 260.

13. Krass, *Carnegie*, p. 436.

14. Frazier Wall, *Skibo*, p. 83.

15. Calder, *The Estate and Castle of Skibo*, p. 79.

16. Nevill, *English Country House Life*, p. 17.

17. Wilson, *The Astors 1763–1992*, p. 145.

18. *Ibid.*, p. 168.

19. Hugo Vickers, *Gladys, Duchess of Marlborough*, London, Weidenfeld & Nicolson, 1979, p. 68.

20. 'Absence weakens lesser passions and increases great ones, just as the wind blows out candles but fans a fire.' *Ibid.*

21. *Ibid.*, p. 111.

22. Anne de Courcy, *Circe: The Life of Edith, Marchioness of Londonderry*, London, Sinclair-Stevenson, 1992, p. 202.

23. *Ibid.*, p. 94.

24. *Ibid.*, p. 73.

25. Wilson, *The Victorians*, p. 483.

26. Churchill Archives, CHAR 28/27/63.

27. *Ibid.*, CHAR 1/57/57.

28. *Ibid.*, CHAR 1/57/32.

29. *Ibid.*, CHAR 1/65/8–10.

30. Vickers, *Gladys, Duchess of Marlborough*, p. 107.

31. Montgomery, *Gilded Prostitution*, p. 178.

32. Leslie, *Jennie*, p. 275.

33. Hertford Records Office: Grenfell Archives, D/ERv C1085/68.

34. Churchill Archives, CHAR 28/78/44.

35. *Ibid.*, CHAR 28/78/45.

36. Herbert Asquith, *Letters to Venetia Stanley*, eds Michael and Eleanor Brock, Oxford, Oxford University Press, 1982, p. 510.

37. Vickers, *Gladys, Duchess of Marlborough*, p. 143.

38. Balsan, *The Glitter and the Gold*, p. 206.

39. *Ibid.*

40. Winston and Clementine Churchill, *Speaking for Themselves: The Personal Letters of Winston and Clementine Churchill*, ed. Mary Soames, London, Doubleday, 1998, p. 289.

8: The War

1. Madeleine Beard, *English Landed Society in the Twentieth Century*, London, Routledge, 1989, p. 12.

2. Kenneth Rose, *King George V*, London, Weidenfeld & Nicolson, 1983, p. 344.

3. Lady Randolph Churchill, *Reminiscences*, p. 47.

4. Dana, *Hospitable England in the Seventies*, p. 183.

5. Lady Randolph Churchill, *Reminiscences*, p. 47.

6. *Ibid.*

7. *The Times*, 7 July 1909.

8. Cornwallis-West, *Edwardian Hey-Days*, p. 264.

9. Leslie, *Jerome Connexion*, p. 56.

10. Countess of Warwick, *Life's Ebb and Flow*, p. 122.

11. Amanda Foreman, *Georgiana, Duchess of Devonshire*, London, HarperCollins, 1999, p. 65.

12. British Library: Paget Papers, Add.51248/71.

13. Lady Randolph Churchill, *Reminiscences*, p. 320.

14. *Ibid.*, p. 309.

15. *New York Times*, 9 April 1916.

16. *Ibid.*, 12 February 1916.

17. *Ibid.*, 24 March 1916.

18. Churchill Archives, CHAR 28/122/67.

19. *The Times*, 23 March 1915.

20. *Ibid.*, 25 June 1915.

21. Andrew Barrow, *Gossip: A History of High Society*, London, Pan, 1978, p. 3.

22. *Ibid.*, p. 8.

23. *Ibid.*, p. 10.

24. Nevill, *English Country House Life*, p. 42.

25. Evelyn Waugh, *Mr Wu & Mrs Stitch: The Letters of Evelyn Waugh & Diana Cooper*, ed. Artemis Cooper, London, Sceptre, 1992, p. 35.

26. Nevill, *English Country House Life*, p. 18.

27. Henry James, *Selected Letters of Henry James*, ed. Leon Edel, London, Rupert Hart-Davis, 1956, p. 260.

28. *The Times*, 20 October 1919.

29. *Ibid.*, 22 May 1919.

30. Leslie, *Jerome Connexion*, p. 87.

31. *The Times*, 30 June 1921.

32. Winston and Clementine Churchill, *Speaking for Themselves*, p. 12.

33. Vickers, *Gladys, Duchess of Marlborough*, p. 175.

34. Montgomery-Massingberd, *Blenheim and the Churchills*, p. 127.
35. Vickers, *Gladys, Duchess of Marlborough*, p. 220.
36. Fowler, *Blenheim: Biography of a Palace*, p. 224.
37. Evelyn Waugh, *The Diaries of Evelyn Waugh*, London, Weidenfeld & Nicolson, 1976, p. 318.
38. David Lindsay, Earl of Crawford, *The Crawford Papers: The Journals of David Lindsay, Twenty-seventh Earl of Crawford and Tenth Earl of Balcarres, 1871–1940, during the Years 1892–1940*, Manchester, Manchester University Press, 1984, p. 384.
39. Earl Winterton, *Pre-War*, London, Macmillan, 1932, p. 119.
40. Duff Cooper, *A Durable Fire: The Letters of Duff and Diana Cooper 1913–1950*, ed. Artemis Cooper, London, Collins, 1983, p. 202.
41. *Ibid.*, p. 228.
42. Duke of Portland, *Men, Women and Things*, p. 158.

9: Castles and More

1. Nevill, *English Country House Life*, p. 20.
2. Roy Denning, *The Story of St Donat's Castle and Atlantic College*, Cowbridge, South Wales, D. Brown & Sons, 1983, p. 69.
3. Aslet, *Last Country Houses*, p. 199.
4. *The Times*, 3 May 1921.
5. Denning, *Story of St Donat's Castle*, p. 72.
6. *Ibid.*, p. 75.
7. *Ibid.*
8. Countess of Warwick, *Afterthoughts*, p. 250.
9. Waterson, *Country House Remembered*, p. 41.
10. Tilden, *True Remembrances*, p. 51.
11. *Ibid.*, p. 53.
12. Aslet, *Last Country Houses*, p. 215.
13. Tilden, *True Remembrances*, p. 55.
14. *Ibid.*, p. 59.
15. Denning, *Story of St Donat's Castle*, p. 73.
16. Enfys McMurry, *Hearst's Other Castle*, Bridgend, Seren Books, 1999, p. 28.
17. Denning, *Story of St Donat's Castle*, p. 72.
18. Nevill, *English Country House Life*, p. 201.
19. Dana, *Hospitable England in the Seventies*, p. 77.
20. Halsey, *With Malice Toward Some*, p. 78.
21. Johnson, *History of the Modern World*, p. 215.
22. Halsey, *With Malice Toward Some*, p. 69.
23. Sackville-West and Nicolson, *Letters*, p. 239.
24. Robin Fedden, *Anglesey Abbey*, The National Trust, 1980, p. 5.
25. Katharine, Duchess of Atholl, *Working Partnership*, London, Arthur Barker, 1958, p. 171.

10: Changes

1. *New York Times*, 11 November 1926.
2. *Ibid.*, 25 November 1926.
3. *Ibid.*, 26 November 1926.
4. *Ibid.*
5. Balsan, *The Glitter and the Gold*, Foreword.
6. John Lehmann, *I Am My Brother*, London, Longmans, 1960, p. 186.
7. Balsan, *The Glitter and the Gold*, p. 5 et seq.
8. *New York Times*, 26 November 1926, p. 1.
9. Daphne Fielding, *Emerald and Nancy*, London, Eyre & Spottiswoode, 1968, p. 4.
10. Peter Quennell, *The Sign of the Fish*, London, Collins, 1960, p. 129.
11. Anne Chisholm, *Nancy Cunard*, London, Sidgwick & Jackson, 1979, p. 6.
12. Fielding, *Emerald and Nancy*, p. 6.
13. Quennell, *Sign of the Fish*, p. 129.
14. Fielding, *Emerald and Nancy*, p. 24.
15. Asquith, *Letters to Venetia Stanley*, p. 337.
16. *Ibid.*, p. 544.
17. Cooper, *A Durable Fire*, p. 195.
18. Evelyn Waugh, *The Letters of Evelyn Waugh*, ed. Mark Amory, London, Penguin Books, 1982, p. 61.
19. Mosley, *A Life of Contrasts*, p. 104.
20. *Ibid.*, p. 101.
21. Asquith, *Letters to Venetia Stanley*, p. 337.
22. Kenneth Clark, *Another Part of the Wood*, London, John Murray, 1974, p. 218.
23. Lehmann, *I Am My Brother*, p. 182.
24. Quennell, *Sign of the Fish*, p. 137.
25. Acton, *Memoirs of an Aesthete*, p. 213.
26. Fielding, *Emerald and Nancy*, p. 26 et seq.
27. Balsan, *The Glitter and the Gold*, p. 159.
28. Leslie, *Jerome Connexion*, p. 95.
29. Lehmann, *I Am My Brother*, p. 182.
30. *Ibid.*
31. Quennell, *Sign of the Fish*, p. 139.
32. *Ibid.*, p. 83.

11: The New Wave

1. Balfour, *Society Racket*, p. 103.
2. *Ibid.*
3. Cooper, *A Durable Fire*, p. 270.
4. *Ibid.*, p. 271.
5. Winston and Clementine Churchill, *Speaking for Themselves*, p. 324.
6. Hertford Records Office: Grenfell Archives, D/ERv C2482/89.

7. Balfour, *Society Racket*, p. 134.
8. Cecil Beaton, *The Wandering Years: Diaries 1922–1939*, London, Weidenfeld & Nicolson, 1961, p. 131.
9. Cooper, *A Durable Fire*, p. 269.
10. *Retrospect*, p. 244.
11. *Ibid.*, p. 247.
12. *Ibid.*, p. 147.
13. Balfour, *Society Racket*, p. 134.
14. *Ibid.*, p. 126.
15. Leslie, *Jerome Connexion*, p. 109.
16. Fielding, *Emerald and Nancy*, p. 99.
17. Barrow, *Gossip*, p. 12.
18. *Ibid.*, p. 23.
19. Lord and Lady Aberdeen and Temair, *More Cracks With 'We Twa'*, London, Methuen & Co., 1929, p. 5.
20. Duke of Manchester, *My Candid Recollections*, p. 75.
21. Edith Marchioness of Londonderry, *Retrospect*, London, Frederick Muller, 1938, p. 251.
22. Mabell Countess of Airlie, *Thatched with Gold*, Bath, Cedric Chivers, 1972, p. 191.
23. Balfour, *Society Racket*, p. 44.
24. *Ibid.*, p. 56.
25. Duke of Portland, *Men, Women and Things*, p. 151.
26. Lee Israel, *Miss Tallulah Bankhead*, London, W.H. Allen, 1972, p. 83.
27. *Ibid.*, p. 25.
28. Beaton, *Wandering Years*, p. 314.

12: The Prince

1. Gloria Vanderbilt and Thelma Lady Furness, *Double Exposure: A Twin Autobiography*, London, Frederick Muller, 1959, p. 3.
2. *Ibid.*, p. 185.
3. *Ibid.*, p. 126.
4. Barrow, *Gossip*, p. 29.
5. Duff Cooper, *The Duff Cooper Diaries*, ed. John Julius Norwich, London, Weidenfeld & Nicolson, 2005, p. 119.
6. Vanderbilt and Lady Furness, *Double Exposure*, p. 177.
7. *Ibid.*, p. 226.
8. Edward, Duke of Windsor, *Letters from a Prince*, ed. Rupert Godfrey, London, Little Brown, 1998, p. 169.
9. *Ibid.*, p. 177.
10. Philip Ziegler, *King Edward VIII: The Official Biography*, London, Collins, 1990, p. 119.
11. *Ibid.*, p. 120.
12. Duke of Windsor, *Letters from a Prince*, p. 124.

13. *Ibid.*, p. 140.
14. Ibid., p. 218.
15. Ziegler, *King Edward VIII*, p. 120.
16. Duke of Windsor, *Letters from a Prince*, p. 151.
17. Earl Winterton, *Fifty Tumultuous Years*, London, Hutchinson, 1955, p. 304.
18. Ziegler, *King Edward VIII*, p. 121.
19. *New York Times*, 31 August 1924.
20. Ziegler, *King Edward VIII*, p. 152.
21. *New York Times*, 31 August 1924.
22. *Ibid.*, 17 September 1924.
23. Ziegler, *King Edward VIII*, p. 153.
24. Duke of Manchester, *My Candid Recollections*, p. 116.
25. Ziegler, *King Edward VIII*, p. 121.
26. Vanderbilt and Lady Furness, *Double Exposure*, p. 269.
27. Robert Bruce Lockhart, *The Diaries of Sir Robert Bruce Lockhart: 1915–1938*, London, Macmillan, 1973, p. 190.
28. Sir Henry Channon, *Chips: The Diaries of Sir Henry Channon*, ed. Robert Rhodes James, London, Phoenix, 1996, p. 50.
29. *Ibid.*
30. Nicolson, *Diaries and Letters 1930–1939*, London, Collins, 1966, p. 74.
31. Earl of Crawford, *Crawford Papers*, p. 572.
32. Vanderbilt and Lady Furness, *Double Exposure*, p. 282.
33. The Duchess of Windsor, *The Heart Has Its Reasons*, London, Landsborough Publications, 1959, p. 124.
34. *Ibid.*, p. 137.
35. Fielding, *Emerald and Nancy*, p. 118.
36. Duke of Windsor, *Letters from a Prince*, p. 196.
37. Ziegler, *King Edward VIII*, p. 225.
38. Vanderbilt and Lady Furness, *Double Exposure*, p. 274.
39. Duchess of Windsor, *The Heart Has Its Reasons*, p. 142.
40. *Ibid.*, p. 163.
41. Vanderbilt and Lady Furness, *Double Exposure*, p. 274.
42. Duke and Duchess of Windsor, *Wallis & Edward: Letters 1931–1937*, ed. Michael Bloch, London, Weidenfeld & Nicolson, 1986, p. 22.
43. Duchess of Windsor, *The Heart Has Its Reasons*, p. 145.
44. Duke and Duchess of Windsor, *Wallis & Edward*, p. 22.
45. Duchess of Windsor, *The Heart Has Its Reasons*, p. 149.
46. Vanderbilt and Lady Furness, *Double Exposure*, p. 275.
47. Duke and Duchess of Windsor, *Wallis & Edward*, p. 36.
48. Duke of Windsor, *Letters from a Prince*, p. 117.
49. Vanderbilt and Lady Furness, *Double Exposure*, p. 291.
50. Duchess of Windsor, *The Heart Has Its Reasons*, p. 163.
51. Vanderbilt and Lady Furness, *Double Exposure*, p. 297.
52. Duchess of Windsor, *The Heart Has Its Reasons*, p. 164.

53. *Ibid.*, p. 165.
54. Duke and Duchess of Windsor, *Wallis & Edward*, p. 93.
55. Ziegler, *King Edward VIII*, p. 229.
56. *Ibid.*, p. 230.
57. Rebecca West, *Selected Letters of Rebecca West*, ed. Bonnie Kime Scott, New Haven and London, Yale University Press, 2000, p. 139.

13: The American Set

1. Beaton, *Wandering Years*, p. 299.
2. Acton, *Memoirs of an Aesthete*, p. 212.
3. Lehmann, *I Am My Brother*, p. 182.
4. Quennell, *Sign of the Fish*, p. 133.
5. *Ibid.*, p. 139.
6. Clark, *Another Part of the Wood*, p. 217.
7. Balfour, *Society Racket*, p. 134.
8. Fielding, *Emerald and Nancy*, p. 52.
9. Duke of Windsor, *Letters from a Prince*, p. 203.
10. Fielding, *Emerald and Nancy*, p. 67.
11. *Ibid.*, p. 118.
12. Channon, *Chips*, p 22.
13. *Ibid.*, p. 23.
14. *Ibid.*, p. 31.
15. *Ibid.*, p. 33.
16. *Ibid.*
17. *Ibid.*, p. 34.
18. *Ibid.*, p. 15.
19. *Ibid.*, p. 6.
20. *Ibid.*, p. 2.
21. *Ibid.*, p. 3.
22. *Ibid.*, p. 8.
23. West, *Selected Letters*, p. 65.
24. Sackville-West and Nicolson, *Letters*, p. 242.
25. Hertford Records Office: Grenfell Archives, D/ERv C71/69.
26. Channon, *Chips*, p. 3.
27. *Ibid.*, p. 9.
28. *Ibid.*, p. 6.
29. *Ibid.*, p. 11.
30. Nancy Mitford, *The Letters of Nancy Mitford: Love From Nancy*, ed. Charlotte Mosley, London, Hodder & Stoughton, 1993, p. 465.
31. Montgomery-Massingberd, *Blenheim and the Churchills*, p. 142.
32. Channon, *Chips*, p. 22.
33. *Ibid.*, p. 69.
34. Churchill Archives, CHAR 28/2/16-19.

35. Duke and Duchess of Windsor, *Wallis & Edward*, p. 202.
36. Waugh, *Mr Wu & Mrs Stitch*, p. 90.
37. Diana Cooper, *The Light of Common Day*, London, Rupert Hart-Davis, 1959, p. 162.
38. Channon, *Chips*, p. 36.
39. *Ibid.*, p. 29.
40. Marchioness of Londonderry, *Retrospect*, p. 253.
41. Earl of Crawford, *Crawford Papers*, p. 544.
42. Earl Winterton, *Fifty Tumultuous Years*, p. 332.
43. Countess of Warwick, *Life's Ebb and Flow*, p. 77.
44. Marchioness of Londonderry, *Retrospect*, p. 251.
45. Kirsty McLeod, *A Passion for Friendship*, London, Michael Joseph, 1991, p. 59.
46. *Ibid.*, p. 92.
47. *Ibid.*, p. 53.
48. Quennell, *Sign of the Fish*, p. 134.
49. McLeod, *Passion for Friendship*, p. 3.
50. *Ibid.*, p. 107.
51. *Ibid.*, p. 82.
52. Clark, *Another Part of the Wood*, p. 212.
53. McLeod, *Passion for Friendship*, p. 93.
54. *Ibid.*, p. 110.
55. *Ibid.*, p. 94.
56. *Ibid.*, p. 93.
57. *Ibid.*, p. 75.
58. Channon, *Chips*, p. 36.
59. Nicolson, *Diaries and Letters*, p. 211.
60. Lockhart, *Diaries*, p. 309.
61. *Ibid.*, p. 332.
62. Nicolson, *Diaries and Letters*, p. 396.
63. Channon, *Chips*, p. 35.
64. *Ibid.*, p. 36.
65. Duke and Duchess of Windsor, *Wallis & Edward*, p. 162.
66. P. Magnus, *King Edward VIII*, London, John Murray, p. 193.
67. Channon, *Chips*, p. 45.
68. Nicolson, *Diaries and Letters*, p. 232.
69. *Ibid.*, p. 238.
70. Channon, *Chips*, p. 8.
71. Nicolson, *Diaries and Letters*, p. 238.

14: Endgame

1. Channon, *Chips*, p. 53.
2. Countess of Airlie, *Thatched with Gold*, p. 195.

3. Channon, *Chips*, p. 58.

4. Cooper, *Light of Common Day*, p. 163.

5. Duke and Duchess of Windsor, *Wallis & Edward*, p. 163.

6. *Ibid.*, p. 173.

7. McLeod, *Passion for Friendship*, p. 144.

8. *Ibid.*, p. 145.

9. Nicolson, *Diaries and Letters*, p. 255.

10. *Ibid.*, p. 261.

11. Magnus, *King Edward VIII*, p. 281.

12. *Ibid.*

13. Countess of Airlie, *Thatched with Gold*, p. 198.

14. Lockhart, *Diaries*, p. 357.

15. Channon, *Chips*, p. 60.

16. Lockhart, *Diaries*, p. 349.

17. Nicolson, *Diaries and Letters*, p. 396.

18. Tilden, *True Remembrances*, p. 40.

19. Earl of Crawford, *Crawford Papers*, p. 519.

20. *Ibid.*, p. 535.

21. Hertford Records Office: Grenfell Archives, D/ERv C1085/109.

22. Channon, *Chips*, p. 73.

23. *Ibid.*, p. 24.

24. *Ibid.*, p. 81.

25. Nicolson, *Diaries and Letters*, p. 263.

26. *Ibid.*, p. 88.

27. McLeod, *Passion for Friendship*, p. 144.

28. Fielding, *Emerald and Nancy*, p. 120.

29. *Ibid.*, p. 99.

30. *New York Times*, 23 November 1936.

31. de Courcy, *Circe*, p. 265.

32. Channon, *Chips*, p. 80.

33. Nicolson, *Diaries and Letters*, p. 279.

34. Channon, *Chips*, p. 83.

35. Cooper, *Diaries*, p. 236.

36. Channon, *Chips*, p. 89.

37. *Ibid.*, p. 92.

38. *The Times*, 3 December 1936.

39. *Ibid.*, 4 December 1936.

40. Channon, *Chips*, p. 97.

41. *The Times*, 12 December 1936.

Epilogue

1. Duke and Duchess of Windsor, *Wallis & Edward*, p. 203.

2. Cooper, *Diaries*, p. 230.

3. Noël Coward, *The Noël Coward Diaries*, ed. Graham Payn and Sheridan Morley, London, Phoenix Press, 2000, p. 54.

4. Countess of Airlie, *Thatched with Gold*, p. 201.

5. Cooper, *Diaries*, p. 403.

6. *Crawford Papers*, p. 575.

7. Sackville-West and Nicolson, *Vita and Harold*, p. 289.

8. Evelyn Waugh, *The Diaries of Evelyn Waugh*, ed. Michael Davie, London, Weidenfeld & Nicolson, 1976, p. 415.

9. Geoffrey Elborn, *Edith Sitwell*, London, Sheldon Press, 1981, p. 64.

10. McLeod, *Passion for Friendship*, p. 148.

11. Virginia Woolf, *Congenial Spirits: The Selected Letters of Virginia Woolf*, ed. Joanne Trautmann Banks, London, Pimlico, 2003, p. 395.

12. Fielding, *Emerald and Nancy*, p. 120.

13. Nicolson, *Diaries and Letters*, p. 283.

14. Lockhart, *Diaries*, p. 372.

15. Channon, *Chips*, p. 99.

16. *Ibid.*, p. 100.

17. Mitford, *Letters*, p. 299.

18. *Ibid.*, p. 454.

19. Nicolson, *Diaries and Letters*, London, Collins, 1967, p. 335.

20. Lehmann, *I Am My Brother*, p. 190.

21. Mitford, *Letters*, p. 136.

22. *The Times*, 12 July 1948.

23. *Ibid.*, September 26 1950.

24. Earl Winterton, *Fifty Tumultuous Years*, p. 77.

Bibliography

Primary sources

Churchill Archives, Churchill College, Cambridge
Grenfell – Desborough Archives, County Hall, Hertford
Manchester Archives, County Record Office, Huntingdon
Paget Papers, British Library

Printed works

Aberdeen and Temair, Lord and Lady, *More Cracks with 'We Twa'*, London, Methuen, 1929
Acton, Harold, *Memoirs of an Aesthete*, London, Methuen, 1948
Airlie, Mabell, Countess of, *Thatched with Gold*, Bath, Cedric Chivers, 1972
Aslet, Clive, *The Last Country Houses*, London, Yale University Press, 1982
Asquith, Lady Cynthia, *Diaries, 1915–1918*, London, Century, 1987
Asquith, Herbert, *Letters to Venetia Stanley*, Oxford, Oxford University Press, 1982
Asquith, Margot, *Myself when Young: By Famous Women of Today*, London, Frederick Muller, 1938
Astor, Michael, *Tribal Feeling*, London, John Murray, 1963
Atholl, Katharine, Duchess of, *Working Partnership*, London, Arthur Barker, 1958
Balfour, Arthur, *The Letters of Arthur Balfour and Lady Elcho 1885–1917*, London, Hamish Hamilton, 1992
Balfour, Patrick, Lord Kinross, *Society Racket*, London, John Long, 1933
Balsan, Consuelo Vanderbilt, *The Glitter and the Gold*, London, Heinemann, 1953
Barrington, Charlotte, Viscountess, *Through Eighty Years (1855–1935)*, London, John Murray, 1936
Barrow, Andrew, *Gossip: A History of High Society*, London, Pan, 1978
Beard, Madeleine, *English Landed Society in the Twentieth Century*, London, Routledge, 1989
Beaton, Cecil, *The Wandering Years: Diaries 1922–1939*, London, Weidenfeld & Nicolson, 1961
Becker, Robert, *Nancy Lancaster: Her Life, Her World, Her Art*, New York, Alfred A. Knopf, 1996
Bennett, G.H. and Gibson, Marion, *The Later Life of Lord Curzon of Kedleston*, Lewiston, The Edwin Mellen Press, 2000

298 *Bibliography*

Bertie, Lord, *The Diary of Lord Bertie of Thame, 1914–1918*, ed. Lady Algernon Gordon-Lennox, London, Hodder & Stoughton, 1924

Bignell, Alan, *Lady Baillie at Leeds Castle*, Leeds Castle Enterprises, 2002

Bingham, Madeleine, *Earls and Girls: Dramas in High Society*, London, Hamish Hamilton, 1980

Bloch, Michael, *The Duchess of Windsor*, London, Weidenfeld & Nicolson, 1996

Boxer, Arabella, *Book of English Food*, London, Penguin, 1991

Brandon, Ruth, *The Dollar Princesses*, London, Weidenfeld & Nicolson, 1980

Brendon, Piers, *The Dark Valley: A Panorama of the 1930s*, London, Jonathan Cape, 2000

Brough, James, *Consuelo: Portrait of an American Heiress*, New York, Coward, McCann & Geoghegan, 1979

Calder, William, *The Estate and Castle of Skibo*, Edinburgh, Albyn Press, 1949

Cannadine, David, *Aspects of Aristocracy*, London, Penguin, 1994

——, *The Decline and Fall of the British Aristocracy*, London, Papermac, 1996

Carnegie, Andrew, *Triumphant Democracy*, New York, Kennikat Press, 1971

Carpenter, Humphrey, *The Brideshead Generation*, London, Weidenfeld & Nicolson, 1989

Channon, Sir Henry, *Chips: The Diary of Sir Henry Channon*, ed. Robert Rhodes James, London, Phoenix, 1996

Chisholm, Anne, *Nancy Cunard*, London, Sidgwick & Jackson, 1979

Churchill, Lady Randolph, *The Reminiscences of Lady Randolph Churchill*, ed. Mrs George Cornwallis-West, London, Edward Arnold, 1908

Churchill, Winston and Clementine, *Speaking for Themselves: The Personal Letters of Winston and Clementine Churchill*, ed. Mary Soames, London, Doubleday, 1998

Clark, Kenneth, *Another Part of the Wood*, London, John Murray, 1974

Clifford, Colin, *The Asquiths*, London, John Murray, 2002

Collier, Price, *England and the English from an American Point of View*, London, Cuckworth, 1911

Cooke, Alistair, *The American in England*, Cambridge, Cambridge University Press, 1975

Cooper, Diana, *The Light of Common Day*, London, Rupert Hart-Davis, 1959

Cooper, Duff, *Diaries*, ed. John Julius Norwich, London, Weidenfeld & Nicolson, 2005

——, *A Durable Fire: The Letters of Duff and Diana Cooper 1913–1950*, London, Collins, 1983

Corelli, Marie, *Free Opinions Freely Expressed on Certain Phases of Modern Social Life and Conduct*, London, Constable, 1905

Cornwallis-West, George, *Edwardian Hey-Days*, Wakefield, EP Publishing, 1975

Cottenham, Mark Everard Pepys, Earl of, *Mine Host America*, London, Collins, 1937

de Courcy, Anne, *1939: The Last Season*, London, Phoenix, 1989

——, *Circe: The Life of Edith, Marchioness of Londonderry*, London, Sinclair-Stevenson, 1992

——, *The Viceroy's Daughters*, London, Weidenfeld & Nicolson, 2000

Courtney, Nicholas, *In Society*, London, Pavilion, 1986

Coward, Noël, *The Noël Coward Diaries*, ed. Graham Payn and Sheridan Morley, London, Phoenix Press, 2000

Cowles, Virginia, *The Astors*, London, Weidenfeld & Nicolson, 1979

——, *Edward VII and his Circle*, London, Hamish Hamilton, 1956

Crapol, E.P., *America for Americans: Economic Nationalism and Anglophobia in the Late Nineteenth Century*, London, Greenwood Press, 1973

Crawford, David Lindsay, Earl of, *The Crawford Papers: The Journals of David Lindsay, Twenty-seventh Earl of Crawford and Tenth Earl of Balcarres, 1871–1940, during the Years 1892–1940*, Manchester, Manchester University Press, 1984

Crewe, Quentin, *The Frontiers of Privilege*, London, Collins, 1961

Crook, J. Mordaunt, *The Rise of the Nouveaux Riches*, London, John Murray, 1999

Dana, Richard Henry, *Hospitable England in the Seventies: The Diary of a Young American 1875–1876*, London, John Murray, 1921

Denning, Roy, *The Story of St Donat's Castle and Atlantic College*, Cowbridge, South Wales, D. Brown & Sons, 1983

Desart, Earl of, *A Page from the Past: Memoirs of the Earl of Desart*, ed. Lady Sybil Lubbock, London, Jonathan Cape, 1936

Ditchfield, P.H., *Vanishing England*, London, Methuen, 1910

Donaldson, Frances, *Edward VIII*, London, Weidenfeld & Nicolson, 1974

Duff, David, *Queen Mary*, London, Collins, 1985

Dunraven, Earl of, *Past Times and Pastimes*, London, Hodder & Stoughton, 1922

Edward VII, King, *Personal Letters*, ed. Lt-Col. J.P.C. Sewell, London, Hutchinson, 1931

Elborn, Geoffrey, *Edith Sitwell*, London, Sheldon Press, 1981

Eliot, Elizabeth, *They All Married Well*, London, Cassell, 1960

Ellman, Richard, *Oscar Wilde*, London, Penguin, 1988

Emerson, Ralph Waldo, *English Traits*, Boston, Phillips, Samson, 1857

Escott, T.H.S., *King Edward and his Court*, London, Fisher Unwin, 1903

——, *Personal Forces of the Period*, London, Hurst & Blackett, 1898

——, *Society in the Country House*, London, Fisher Unwin, 1907

Fedden, Robin, *Anglesey Abbey*, The National Trust, 1980

Fielding, Daphne, *Emerald and Nancy*, London, Eyre & Spottiswoode, 1968

Fitzgerald, F. Scott, *The Beautiful and the Damned*, London, Garland, 1990

Foreman, Amanda, *Georgiana, Duchess of Devonshire*, London, HarperCollins, 1999

Fowler, Marian, *Blenheim: Biography of a Palace*, London, Viking, 1989

——, *In a Gilded Cage*, Toronto, Random House of Canada, 1993

Franklin, Jill, *The Gentleman's Country House and its Plan, 1835–1914*, London, Routledge & Kegan Paul, 1981

Friedman, Dennis, *Darling Georgie: The Enigma of King George V*, London, Peter Owen, 1998

Gifford, John, *The Buildings of Scotland; Highlands and Islands*, London, Penguin, 1992

Girouard, Mark, *Life in the English Country House*, London, Yale University Press, 1978

Gordon, Lyndall, *A Private Life of Henry James: Two Women and his Art*, London, Vintage, 1998

Greville, Lady Violet, *The Gentlewoman in Society*, London, Henry & Co., 1892

Halsey, Margaret, *With Malice Toward Some*, London, Hamish Hamilton, 1938

Hobsbawm, E.J., *The Age of Empire*, London, Abacus, 1994

Homberger, Eric, *Mrs. Astor's New York: Money and Social Power in a Gilded Age*, London and New Haven, Yale University Press, 2002

Hynes, Samuel, *The Edwardian Turn of Mind*, London, Oxford University Press, 1968

Ions, Edmund, *James Bryce and American Democracy 1870–1922*, London, Macmillan, 1968

Israel, Lee, *Miss Tallulah Bankhead*, London, W.H. Allen, 1972

Jackson, Stanley, *The Sassoons*, London, Heinemann, 1968

James, Henry, *Selected Letters of Henry James*, ed. Leon Edel, London, Rupert Hart-Davis, 1956

James, Robert Rhodes, *Rosebery: A Biography*, London, Weidenfeld & Nicolson, 1963

Jerrold, Blanchard, *London*, London, Grant & Co., 1872

Johnson, Paul, *A History of the Modern World*, London, Weidenfeld & Nicolson, 1984

Judd, Denis, *The Life and Times of George V*, London, Weidenfeld & Nicolson, 1973

Kehoe, Elisabeth, *Fortune's Daughters*, London, Atlantic, 2005

King, Greg, *The Duchess of Windsor: The Uncommon Life of Wallis Simpson*, London, Aurum Press, 1999

Krass, Peter, *Carnegie*, New Jersey, John Wiley, 2002

Lambert, Angela, *Unquiet Souls: The Indian Summer of the British Aristocracy 1880–1918*, London, Macmillan, 1984

Lehmann, John, *I Am My Brother*, London, Longman, 1960

Lehr, Elizabeth Drexel, *King Lehr and the Gilded Age*, London, Constable, 1935

Leslie, Anita, *Jennie: The Mother of Winston Churchill*, Maidstone, George Mann, 1969

Leslie, Seymour, *The Jerome Connexion*, London, John Murray, 1964

Lewis, Lesley, *The Private Life of a Country House (1912–1939)*, Newton Abbot, David & Charles, 1980

Lockhart, Robert Bruce, *The Diaries of Sir Robert Bruce Lockhart: 1915–1938*, London, Macmillan, 1973

Londonderry, Edith, Marchioness of, *Retrospect*, London, Frederick Muller, 1938

McKibbin, Ross, *Classes and Cultures: England, 1918–1951*, Oxford, Oxford University Press, 1998

McLeod, Kirsty, *A Passion for Friendship*, London, Michael Joseph, 1991

——, *Battle Royal*, London, Constable, 1999

McMurry, Enfys, *Hearst's Other Castle*, Bridgend, Seren Books, 1999

Magnus, P., *King Edward VII*, London, John Murray, 1964

Montague, William Drogo, Duke of Manchester, *My Candid Recollections*, London, Grayson & Grayson, 1932

Mandler, Peter, *The Fall and Rise of the Stately Home*, London, Yale University Press, 1997

Margetson, Stella, *The Long Party: High Society in the Twenties and Thirties*, Farnborough, Saxon House, 1974

Masters, Brian, *Great Hostesses*, London, Constable, 1982

Middlemas, Keith, *Pursuit of Pleasure: High Society in the 1900s*, London, Gordon & Cremonesi, 1977

Mitford, Nancy, *The Letters of Nancy Mitford: Love from Nancy*, ed. Charlotte Mosley, London, Hodder & Stoughton, 1993

Montgomery, Maureen E., *Gilded Prostitution: Status, Money and Transatlantic Marriages 1870–1914*, London, Routledge, 1989

Montgomery-Massingberd, Hugh, *Blenheim and the Churchills*, London, Jarrold, 2004

Mosley, Diana, *A Life of Contrasts*, London, Gibson Square Books, 2003

Mosley, Nicholas, *Julian Grenfell: His Life and the Times of his Death 1885–1915*, London, Weidenfeld & Nicolson, 1976

Nevill, Lady Dorothy, *Under Five Reigns*, London, Methuen, 1912

——, *Leaves From the Notebooks of Lady Dorothy Nevill*, ed. Ralph Nevill, London, Macmillan, 1907

——, *The Life and Letters of Lady Dorothy Nevill*, ed. Ralph Nevill, London, Methuen, 1919

——, *The Reminiscences of Lady Dorothy Nevill*, ed. Ralph Nevill, London, E. Arnold, 1906

Nevill, Ralph, *English Country House Life*, London, Methuen, 1925

Nevins, Allan, *America through British Eyes*, New York, Oxford University Press, 1948

Nicholson, Virginia, *Among the Bohemians*, London, Viking 2002

Nicolson, Harold, *Diaries and Letters 1930–1939*, ed. Nigel Nicolson, London, Collins, 1966

——, *Diaries and Letters 1939–1945*, ed. Nigel Nicolson, London, Collins, 1967

——, *Diaries and Letters 1945–1962*, ed. Nigel Nicolson, London, Collins, 1968

Nicolson, Nigel, *Mary Curzon*, London, Weidenfeld & Nicolson, 1977

——, *Portrait of a Marriage*, London, Futura, 1976

Ponsonby, Arthur, *The Decline of Aristocracy*, London, Fisher Unwin, 1912

Portland, Duke of, *Men, Women and Things*, London, Faber & Faber, 1937

Priestley, J.B., *The Edwardians*, London, Heinemann, 1970

Quelch, Eileen, *Perfect Darling – The Life and Times of George Cornwallis-West*, London, Cecil & Amelia Woolf, 1972

Quennell, Peter, *The Sign of the Fish*, London, Collins, 1960

Redesdale, Algernon Bertram Mitford, Lord, *Memories*, Vol. II, London, Hutchinson, 1915

Rose, Norman, *The Cliveden Set*, London, Jonathan Cape, 2000

Rose, Kenneth, *King George V*, London, Weidenfeld & Nicolson, 1983

Rosebery, Earl of, *Lord Rosebery's North America Journal, 1873*, ed. A.R.C. Grant, London, Sidgwick & Jackson, 1967

Rosslyn, Earl of, *My Gamble with Life*, London, Cassell, 1928

Sackville-West, Vita and Nicolson, Harold, *Vita and Harold: the Letters of Vita Sackville-West and Harold Nicolson*, ed. Nigel Nicolson, London, Weidenfeld & Nicolson, 1992

Salisbury, Marquess of, *Salisbury–Balfour Correspondence 1869–1892*, Hertfordshire Record Society, 1988

Shaw, George Bernard, *Complete Plays*, London, Hamlyn, 1965

Sinclair, David, *Dynasty: The Astors and Their Times*, London, J.M. Dent & Sons, 1983

Sitwell, Edith, *Selected Letters*, London, Virago, 1997

Sutherland, Stella, *American Public Opinion and the Windsors*, Montpelier, Vt, Driftwind Press, 1938

Simon Sykes, Christopher, *The Big House: The Story of a Country House and its Family*, London, HarperCollins, 2004

Souhami, Diana, *Mrs Keppel and Her Daughter*, London, HarperCollins, 1996

Spencer, Fifth Earl, *The Red Earl: The Papers of the Fifth Earl Spencer, 1835–1910*, ed. Peter Gordon, Northamptonshire Record Society, 1981

Stansky, Peter, *Sassoon: The Worlds of Philip and Sybil*, London, Yale University Press, 2003

Stuart, Denis, *Dear Duchess: Millicent, Duchess of Sutherland 1867–1955*, London, Gollancz, 1982

Symons, Julian, *The Thirties: A Dream Revolved*, London, Faber, 1975

Thompson, F.M.L., *English Landed Society in the Nineteenth Century*, London, Routledge & Kegan Paul, 1963

Thorold, Peter, *The London Rich*, London, Viking, 1999

Tilden, Philip, *True Remembrances: The Memoirs of an Architect*, Country Life Limited, London, 1954

Trollope, Anthony, *An Autobiography*, Oxford, Oxford University Press, 1999

——, *The Way We Live Now*, Oxford, Oxford University Press, 1999

——, *He Knew He Was Right*, London, Strahan & Co., 1869

——, *The Duke's Children*, Oxford, Oxford University Press, 1999

——, *Phineas Redux*, Oxford, Oxford University Press, 2000

Troubridge, Lady Laura, *The Book of Etiquette*, London, Associated Bookbuyers' Co., 1931

Twain, Mark, *The Gilded Age*, London, Chatto & Windus, 1885

Tweedsmuir, Susan, *The Lilac and the Rose*, London, Duckworth, 1952

Vanderbilt, Gloria and Furness, Thelma, *Double Exposure: A Twin Autobiography*, London, Frederick Muller, 1959

Vickers, Hugo, *Cocktails and Laughter: The Albums of Loelia Lindsay*, London, Hamish Hamilton, 1983

——, *Gladys, Duchess of Marlborough*, London, Weidenfeld & Nicolson, 1979

Wall, Joseph Frazier, *Skibo*, Oxford, Oxford University Press, 1984

Warwick, Christopher, *George and Marina, Duke and Duchess of Kent*, London, Weidenfeld & Nicolson, 1988

Warwick, Frances, Countess of, *Afterthoughts*, London, Cassell, 1931

——, *Life's Ebb and Flow*, London, Hutchinson, 1929

Warwick, Earl of, *Memories of Sixty Years*, London, Cassell, 1917

Waterson, Merlin (ed.), *The Country House Remembered*, London, Routledge & Kegan Paul, 1985

Waugh, Evelyn, *The Diaries of Evelyn Waugh*, ed. Michael Davie, London, Weidenfeld & Nicolson, 1976

——, *The Letters of Evelyn Waugh*, ed. Mark Amory, London, Penguin Books, 1982

——, *Mr Wu and Mrs Stitch: The Letters of Evelyn Waugh and Diana Cooper*, ed. Artemis Cooper, London, Sceptre, 1991

——, *A Handful of Dust*, London, Penguin, 1951

Weintraub, Stanley, *The Importance of Being Edward*, London, John Murray, 2000

West, Rebecca, *Selected Letters*, New Haven and London, Yale University Press, 2000

Westminster, Loelia, Duchess of, *Grace and Favour*, London, Weidenfeld & Nicolson, 1962

Wharton, Edith, *The Age of Innocence*, London, Wordsworth Editions, 1993

——, *The Buccaneers*, London, Penguin, 1994

Wilde, Oscar, *The Letters of Oscar Wilde*, ed. Rupert Hart-Davis, London, Rupert Hart-Davis, 1962

——, *The Complete Works*, London, HarperCollins, 1994

Williams, Susan, *Ladies of Influence: Women of the Elite in Inter-war Britain*, London, Allen Lane, 2000

——, *The People's King*, London, Allen Lane, 2003

Willoughby de Broke, Baron, *The Passing Years*, London, Constable, 1924

Wilson, A.N., *The Victorians*, London, Hutchinson, 2002

Wilson, Derek, *The Astors 1763–1992: Landscape with Millionaires*, London, Weidenfeld & Nicolson, 1993

Windsor, Duke and Duchess of, *Wallis and Edward: Letters 1931–1937*, ed. Michael Bloch, London, Weidenfeld & Nicolson, 1986

Windsor, Edward, Duke of, *Letters from a Prince*, ed. Rupert Godfrey, London, Little, Brown, 1998

Windsor, Duchess of, *The Heart Has Its Reasons*, London, Landsborough Publications, 1959

Winterton, Earl, *Fifty Tumultuous Years*, London, Hutchinson, 1955

——, *Pre-War*, London, Macmillan, 1932

Woolf, Virginia, *Congenial Spirits: The Selected Letters of Virginia Woolf*, ed. Joanne Trautmann Banks, London, Hogarth, 2003

Ziegler, Philip, *King Edward VIII: The Official Biography*, London, Collins, 1990

Journals

Time

The Times

The New York Times

Index